Mastering Large Language Models with Python

Unleash the Power of Advanced Natural Language Processing for Enterprise Innovation and Efficiency Using Large Language Models (LLMs) with Python

Raj Arun R

www.orangeava.com

First published: April 2024

Published by: Orange Education Pvt Ltd, AVA™

Address: 9, Daryaganj, Delhi, 110002, India

275 New North Road Islington Suite 1314 London,
N1 7AA, United Kingdom

ISBN: 978-81-97081-82-8

www.orangeava.com

Dedicated To

My Parents:

R. Sundar Ramalingam
Samundeeswary

and

My Beloved Wife, Kavitha M.R., and My Kids, Shivayu R.K. and Vishvayu R.K.

Blessed to be with you

About the Author

Raj Arun is a distinguished expert in Artificial Intelligence and Data Science, with over fifteen years of industry experience. He holds an MBA from the Indian Institute of Management, Trichirapalli, and specialized diplomas in blockchain technology from Indian Institute of Technology in Madras and Guwahati. Raj is also certified as a quantum Qiskit developer from IBM, marking him as a versatile professional who bridges the gap between traditional computing and quantum advancements.

Throughout his career, Raj has worked in software engineering and development to big data, DevOps, and, more recently, the nuanced field of Generative AI. He believes in using technology as a powerful tool for the greater good, aiming at benefiting humanity through creativity and innovation.

Raj's expertise is not confined to a single industry; he has made significant contributions across both B2B and B2C verticals, demonstrating a unique blend of thought leadership and hands-on skills and delivering scalable and innovative solutions. His approach to AI, viewing it as a semantic layer that seamlessly connects the physical with the virtual, has the potential to create profound societal impacts.

In addition to his professional pursuits, Raj is an ardent supporter of open-source initiatives, contributing his knowledge and expertise to foster a collaborative environment. He is deeply invested in mentoring, guiding both students and professionals alike, sharing his insights while also learning from the community in return.

His dedication to Responsible AI is evident in his work, ensuring that AI-augmented products and services are ethical, fair, and unbiased.

Raj Arun envisions a future where Generative AI acts as a great equalizer, providing universal access to resources and opportunities- and advocates for inclusiveness, empathy, and compassion. Through his work and vision, Raj continues to push the boundaries of possibility, leveraging technology to create a more inclusive, resourceful, and connected world.

About the Technical Reviewers

Dr. Deborah Dahl is an expert in Conversational AI and related standards, with over 30 years of experience in the major technical approaches to natural language processing, including Large Language Models. Dr. Dahl focuses on innovative, practical, and scalable conversational AI applications that push the boundary between theory and practice. Her customers range from small start-ups to large government agencies, seeking out her expertise in applying conversational AI technologies in novel and pioneering applications. Reflecting her interest in standards and interoperability of conversational systems, she currently serves as the Senior Advisor for the Open Voice Interoperability Initiative of the Linux Foundation AI and Data Foundation. In this role, she leads efforts to develop standards for interoperable messaging between conversational AI systems. Dr. Dahl is also a Co-chair of the World Wide Web Consortium Voice Interaction Community Group. She has written many technical papers and four books, including Multimodal Interaction with W3C Standards: Toward Natural User Interfaces to Everything, published in 2016, and Natural Language Understanding with Python, published in 2023.

Rohan Chikorde, a seasoned Data Science expert with a decade of experience, specializes in Machine Learning, Large Language Models, and AI. Currently, he serves as an AI Architect at Zensar Technologies, fostering innovation through his technical and leadership skills. His career spans multinational corporations and startups, enhancing his understanding of diverse business applications and honing his skills in advanced machine learning models. A post-graduate in Machine Learning and AI, Rohan is proficient in R, Python, Azure, AWS, GCP, Machine Learning, Deep Learning, AI, DevOps pipelines, LLMs, SQL, Spark, and more. He excels in communicating complex concepts effectively, transforming technical insights into strategic decisions, and mentoring. His expertise spans various domains, and he has a natural flair for leadership. Rohan is recognized as a rising star in the Data Science industry by Digital Vidya. He is open to AI and Data Science management opportunities and can be reached at rohan.chikorde@gmail.com.

Pratik Kotian is an accomplished professional with 8 years of extensive expertise in Natural Language Processing (NLP), Machine Learning (ML), Generative AI, and Python programming. Hailing from Mumbai, India, Pratik has dedicated his career to advancing the frontiers of AI technology and its applications. Pratik's delved into the realm of AI during his academic years, focusing on neural networks. Since then, he has designed and implemented cutting-edge solutions for data-intensive enterprise applications, both on-premises and in the cloud. His passion for integrating AI and ML into these applications has been a driving force throughout his career. With experience across various sectors, including technology, telecommunications, finance, retail, and more, Pratik has honed his skills in leadership roles in research and development, technical consultancy, and team management. Currently, Pratik serves as a Manager at Deloitte, where he leads the Generative AI Team with a focus on pioneering innovative solutions for clients. He drives transformative initiatives, enabling businesses to unlock value through AI-driven strategies. Pratik is dedicated to building and nurturing high-performing teams of experts to support organizational goals. In his spare time, Pratik remains actively engaged in the AI community, sharing knowledge and contributing to advancements in the field. His passion for AI's potential makes him a valued leader in the domain.

Acknowledgements

Embarking on the journey of writing *Mastering Large Language Models with Python* has been an enriching experience, for which I am profoundly grateful to all those who played pivotal roles in its creation. This project would not have reached its potential without the unwavering support, insightful guidance, and shared expertise of countless individuals.

I extend my deepest appreciation to the open-source community, whose innovative spirit and collaborative efforts have propelled this technology to remarkable heights. It is both an honor and a privilege to contribute to and benefit from this vibrant ecosystem. My gratitude also goes to the technical reviewers, whose diligent scrutiny and valuable feedback have significantly elevated the quality of this book. Their expertise and commitment have been instrumental in ensuring the precision and clarity of its content.

To my family, your unconditional support, love, and patience have been my pillars of strength. Navigating the complexities of this endeavor would have been insurmountable without your understanding and encouragement. Special thanks to my partner, Kavitha M.R., whose boundless enthusiasm, insightful advice, and unwavering belief in my capabilities have been my guiding light through challenging times.

I also wish to acknowledge the dedication and hard work of everyone at the publishing house. Your collective efforts have immensely contributed to the fruition of this project. The spirit of cooperation and your willingness to accommodate my vision has been truly remarkable.

Lastly, to you, the readers, who have chosen this book to enrich your understanding of Large Language Models within the enterprise domain – I hope it serves as a valuable resource on your journey to mastery. May it guide you through the evolving landscape of artificial intelligence and technology with confidence and insight.

Thank you all for being part of this remarkable journey.

Preface

In the landscape of artificial intelligence, the emergence of Generative AI, spearheaded by Large Language Models (LLMs) such as GPT-3 and BERT, represents a paradigm shift in how we interact with, process, and leverage language data. *Mastering Large Language Models with Python* embarks on a mission to demystify these technological marvels, offering a deep dive into their architecture, functionalities, and the expansive horizon of their applications across various sectors.

The book is structured to provide a comprehensive journey through the intricate world of LLMs, segmented into focused sections that evolve from foundational theories to tangible, real-world applications. It starts with an exploration of the basics of LLMs, shedding light on their architectural nuances and the principles guiding their operation. This foundation paves the way for subsequent chapters that delve into both the open-source realm and the proprietary technologies behind enterprise LLMs, exploring their potential to revolutionize industries.

Chapter 1 offers an introduction to the world of LLMs, presenting their architecture and a wide array of applications, thereby establishing the significance of these models in AI's evolution.

Chapter 2 takes a closer look at open-source LLMs, their advantages, challenges, and the pivotal role they play in advancing AI technology, enriched with practical examples and code snippets.

Chapter 3 transitions into the domain of closed-source LLMs, exploring their diverse applications from natural language understanding to AI-generated media, providing insights into models developed by leading organizations.

Chapter 4 focuses on the practicalities of LLM APIs, specifically within the Hugging Face ecosystem, detailing their use in various tasks across NLP, audio processing, and computer vision.

Chapter 5 uniquely addresses integrating the Cohere API in Google Sheets, showcasing the application of LLMs in code generation, supported by real-world examples and exercises.

Chapter 6 introduces the synergistic use of transformers and vector databases for creating dynamic movie recommendation systems, highlighting the technological fusion's potential beyond entertainment.

Chapter 7 explores AI-powered QA bots, detailing their implementation and the transformative impact they have on customer service, education, and research.

Chapter 8 discusses the quantization of LLMs, offering insights into making these models more accessible and efficient for broader use.

Chapters 9 and **10** dive into fine-tuning and evaluating LLMs, presenting methodologies and practical applications to enhance model performance.

Chapter 11 outlines the operational landscape with LLMOps, providing a blueprint for deploying and managing LLMs at scale, addressing data management, model training, and security.

Chapter 12 details implementing LLMOps in practice using tools such as MLFlow on Databricks, emphasizing model lifecycle management and real-time inference.

Chapters 13 and **14** concentrate on prompt engineering, from basic techniques to advanced design patterns, illustrating how to craft effective prompts for optimized AI interactions.

Chapter 15 addresses the ethical considerations and regulatory frameworks surrounding LLMs, advocating for responsible AI development.

Chapter 16 looks towards the future, exploring emerging trends, use cases, and the societal impact of LLMs, particularly through the lens of Trust-Interpretable Generative AI.

By the conclusion of this book, readers are not just familiarized with the theoretical underpinnings of LLMs but are also equipped with the hands-on experience necessary to implement these models in practical scenarios. Tailored for AI researchers, industry professionals, and academic students, this book serves as a comprehensive guide to navigating the promising yet complex world of Large Language Models, paving the way for innovative applications and ethical practices in the AI domain.

Get a Free eBook

We hope you are enjoying your recently purchased book! Your feedback is incredibly valuable to us, and to all other readers looking for great books.

If you found this book helpful or enjoyable, we would truly appreciate it, if you could take a moment to leave a short review with a 5 star rating on Amazon. It helps us grow, and lets other readers discover our books.

As a thank you, we would love to send you a free digital copy of this book, and a **30%** discount code on your next cart value on our official websites:

www.orangeava.com

www.orangeava.in (For Indian Subcontinent)

☑ **Here's how:**

Leave a review for the book on Amazon.

Take a screenshot of your review, and send an email to **info@orangeava.com** (it can be just the confirmation screen).

Once, we receive your screenshot, we will send you the digital file, within 24 hours.

Thank you so much for your support – it means a lot to us!

Downloading the code bundles and colored images

Please follow the links or scan the QR codes to download the ***Code Bundles and Images*** of the book:

https://github.com/ava-orange-education/Mastering-Large-Language-Models-with-Python

The code bundles and images of the book are also hosted on ***https://rebrand.ly/mbw75vd***

In case there's an update to the code, it will be updated on the existing GitHub repository.

Errata

We take immense pride in our work at **Orange Education Pvt Ltd,** and follow best practices to ensure the accuracy of our content to provide an indulging reading experience to our subscribers. Our readers are our mirrors, and we use their inputs to reflect and improve upon human errors, if any, that may have occurred during the publishing processes involved. To let us maintain the quality and help us reach out to any readers who might be having difficulties due to any unforeseen errors, please write to us at :

errata@orangeava.com

Your support, suggestions, and feedback are highly appreciated.

DID YOU KNOW

Did you know that Orange Education Pvt Ltd offers eBook versions of every book published, with PDF and ePub files available? You can upgrade to the eBook version at **www.orangeava.com** and as a print book customer, you are entitled to a discount on the eBook copy. Get in touch with us at: **info@orangeava.com** for more details.

At **www.orangeava.com**, you can also read a collection of free technical articles, sign up for a range of free newsletters, and receive exclusive discounts and offers on AVA™ Books and eBooks.

PIRACY

If you come across any illegal copies of our works in any form on the internet, we would be grateful if you would provide us with the location address or website name. Please contact us at **info@orangeava.com** with a link to the material.

ARE YOU INTERESTED IN AUTHORING WITH US?

If there is a topic that you have expertise in, and you are interested in either writing or contributing to a book, please write to us at **business@orangeava.com**. We are on a journey to help developers and tech professionals to gain insights on the present technological advancements and innovations happening across the globe and build a community that believes Knowledge is best acquired by sharing and learning with others. Please reach out to us to learn what our audience demands and how you can be part of this educational reform. We also welcome ideas from tech experts and help them build learning and development content for their domains.

REVIEWS

Please leave a review. Once you have read and used this book, why not leave a review on the site that you purchased it from? Potential readers can then see and use your unbiased opinion to make purchase decisions. We at Orange Education would love to know what you think about our products, and our authors can learn from your feedback. Thank you!

For more information about Orange Education, please visit **www.orangeava.com**.

Table of Contents

CHAPTER 1

The Basics of Large Language Models and Their Applications

Introduction

Large language models (LLMs) continue to evolve and become more sophisticated. They are poised to revolutionize how we interact with language and data, impacting industries such as healthcare, finance, government, and education. By understanding the basics of large language models and their applications, we can better harness their potential to drive innovation and improve our lives.

Structure

In this chapter, the following topics will be covered:

- Introduction to Large Language Models
- Transformer and Large Language Models
- Scaling Laws and Key Techniques
- Resources and Configuration of LLMs
- Chain-Of-Thought Prompting and Evaluation Benchmarks

Introduction to Large Language Models

Large Language Models are an advanced form of artificial intelligence (AI) algorithms that leverage deep learning techniques and vast datasets to interpret, synthesize, generate, and foresee textual content. Rooted in transformer architecture, these models operate by taking input, processing it through an intricate encoding mechanism, and then decoding it to yield predictive outputs.

The hallmark of LLMs lies in their capacity for broad-spectrum language comprehension and production. This capability is cultivated through the assimilation of extensive data, allowing them to learn and integrate billions of parameters. Such a learning process, alongside their operational demands, necessitates substantial computational power.

The practical applications of LLMs are diverse and far-reaching. They play a pivotal role in natural language processing tasks, evident in dynamic chatbots, AI-driven assistants, and other interactive platforms. Search engines leverage LLMs to deliver nuanced, conversational responses, while in the realm of life sciences, these models assist in deciphering complex biological entities such as protein, DNA, and RNA. Beyond these, LLMs aid in software development, robotics training, and in the business sphere, they streamline customer feedback analysis and enhance product categorization through sophisticated language understanding.

Large language models are a crucial breakthrough in the artificial intelligence arena, with their roots firmly planted in the field of natural language processing (NLP). These models build upon language modeling, a key methodology in language comprehension and generation, that has undergone evolution over the past couple of decades. The evolution of language models has seen them transform from statistical language models into neural language models, and lately, into pre-trained language models (PLMs).

'Large Language Model' is a term used to depict PLMs of considerable size, often involving tens or hundreds of billions of parameters. Within the context of LLMs, a parameter is a model component that is honed using historical training data. Parameters in LLMs are the adjustable elements that are refined through training, allowing the model to learn from data, and effectively perform language-related tasks. The sheer number and complexity of these parameters are what make LLMs remarkably capable in processing and generating human language. LLMs have demonstrated distinctive abilities such as in-context learning, which is the model's proficiency to generate responses based on the input's context, once their parameter scale surpasses a particular threshold. This is a noteworthy enhancement over their smaller counterparts, which lack these abilities.

Large language models have made a significant impact in the domain of artificial intelligence. Their ability to comprehend and generate human-like text holds the promise of transforming industries such as healthcare, finance, and customer service. For example, in the healthcare industry, LLMs can interpret medical literature, offering physicians with the latest information. In the financial sector, they can scrutinize financial documents to provide valuable insights. However, these models also introduce challenges such as ethical dilemmas and computational demands.

In this section, we will explore the fundamentals of large language models and their potential applications in depth. We will start with an exploration of the evolution of language models, then transition into the architecture and operation of LLMs. We will also take a look at how these models are being implemented in the real world, their influence on various sectors, and the difficulties they pose. At the end of this section, you will have a firm understanding of large language models and their importance in the current world in which artificial intelligence reigns.

Unfolding the Journey of Language Models

Language models have undergone significant evolution, moving through four primary stages: statistical language models (SLMs), neural language models (NLMs), pre-trained language models (PLMs), and large language models (LLMs). Each step indicates a notable breakthrough, paving the path for the next advancement in language comprehension capabilities.

The journey begins with Statistical Language Models. A well-known instance of these models is phrase-based statistical machine translation (SMT). This technique divides sentences into fragments or clusters of words, translating each segment independently. Statistical methods are then leveraged to pick the most likely translation given the context. However, these models often face difficulties with longer sentences and struggle to sustain contextual coherence over long spans of text.

Next come Neural Language Models , which utilize neural networks to ascertain the likelihood of specific word sequences. A significant development introduced by NLMs was the distributed representation of words. Instead of representing each word as a distinct entity, words are denoted as a composite of features, allowing the model to grasp the semantic essence of words. Word2Vec, a model that employs a shallow neural network to extract word embeddings from a text corpus, is a prime example of this phase.

Subsequently, the PLMs era arose, which incorporated models such as ELMo and BERT. ELMo, which stands for embeddings from language models, takes into account both the distinct characteristics of words and their context-dependent meanings. In contrast, BERT (bidirectional encoder representations from transformers) can be considered a direct descendant of GPT, but with a significant enhancement – it trains bidirectionally, learning to anticipate the context from both left and right.

GPT represents a sophisticated class within large language models, pioneered by OpenAI. These models, a subset of artificial intelligence, are trained on extensive text datasets, enabling them to respond to natural language inputs in a remarkably human-like manner.

Models like GPT-3 and GPT-3.5, notable examples of GPT LLMs, are distinguished by their proficiency in crafting high-quality, coherent text that frequently mirrors human writing. Their training involves the analysis of colossal text corpora, often encompassing several billion words. This extensive training empowers them to grasp the subtle complexities and nuances of human language.

However, it is crucial to recognize that despite their advanced capabilities, GPT LLMs are not infallible. There are instances where they might produce responses that are either incorrect or lack contextual relevance, underscoring the need for continuous refinement and oversight in their application.

The latest development in this field is the evolution of large language models (as shown in *Figure 1.1*). Exemplified by OpenAI's GPT-3, these models are essentially scaled versions of PLMs. They often lead to augmented model performance in downstream tasks. LLMs distinguish themselves from smaller PLMs in their behavior, exhibiting an impressive capacity to handle a wide array of complex tasks. The evolution of these models demonstrates the rapid progress made in language understanding and offers a promising glimpse into future possibilities.

Each stage in the evolution of language models has brought significant improvements over the previous one, overcoming limitations and expanding the capabilities of these models. This progression has had a profound impact on the field of natural language processing, leading to the development of models that can understand and generate human-like text.

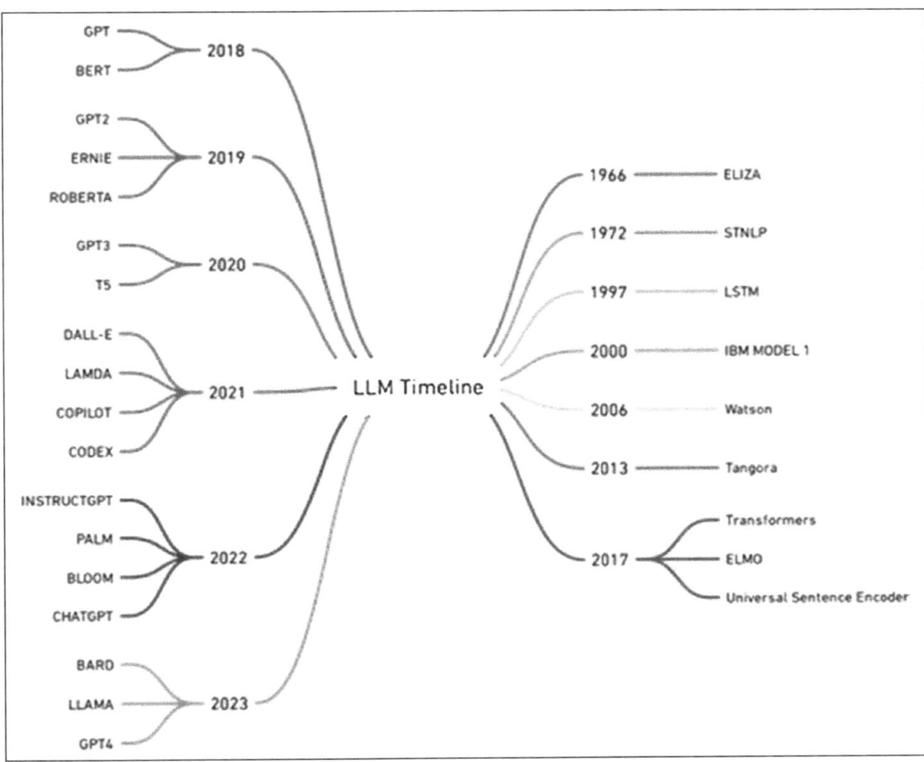

Figure 1.1: *Evolution of Large Language Model*

In summary, the evolution of language models has seen a progression from statistical methods to neural networks, and then to pre-training models on large-scale unlabeled corpora. The latest stage in this evolution is the development of large language models, which are scaled versions of pre-trained models and have shown impressive performance in a variety of complex tasks.

Influence of Large Language Models

Large language models are transforming the AI landscape, introducing a new era of advanced AI algorithms. These models have captivated the AI world, with applications such as ChatGPT, an AI-driven chatbot chiefly engineered on LLMs, that has gained widespread recognition. The creation of LLMs integrates vast practical experience in handling large-scale data and conducting parallel distributed training, thereby melding research and engineering.

Nevertheless, implementing LLMs is not without obstacles. Their computational demands are substantial, necessitating robust hardware and proficient algorithms. Ethical issues also come into play, as the potential misuse of these models could result in harmful or biased outcomes.

Despite these hurdles, the promise held by LLMs is immense. As we refine these models and discover innovative applications, their impact on AI and other sectors is poised to expand even further.

Introducing Transformers and Their Importance

Transformers represent a key construct in understanding large language models. They are the foundation of many cutting-edge LLMs, such as BERT, GPT-3, and others. Presented in the ground-breaking paper "*Attention is All You Need*" by Vaswani and colleagues, transformers reshaped the natural language processing domain and are fundamental to many modern LLMs.

Understanding Transformers

Transformers are a unique form of neural network architecture crafted to manage sequential data. Unlike earlier models like recurrent neural networks (RNNs) and long short-term memory (LSTM) networks, transformers do not process sequential data linearly. Instead, they leverage a mechanism called '**attention**' to assign significance to different words in a sentence, thereby efficiently capturing the context of each word (as shown in *Figure 1.2*).

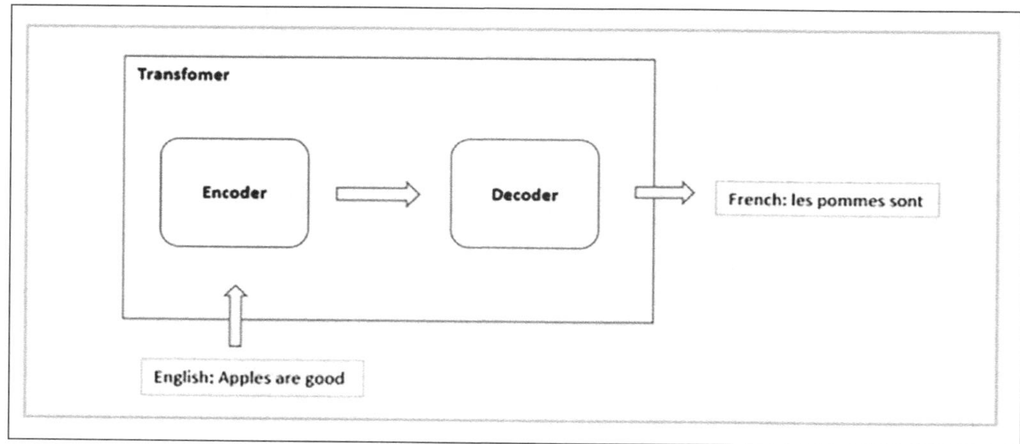

Figure 1.2: *Transformers Simplified View*

Transformers have significantly improved upon previous models in several ways:

- **Computational Efficiency**: Transformers facilitate parallel computation across all sequence elements, thereby enhancing computational efficiency.
- **Modeling Long-Range Dependencies**: Transformers can form direct connections between words far apart in a sentence – a vital aspect for tasks such as translation.
- **Interpretability**: The attention weights in transformers can be interpreted as the model's perception of the relationships among different words, granting some understanding of the model's workings.
- **Impact on NLP**: Transformers have triggered a revolution in the NLP field, resulting in substantial progress in tasks like machine translation, text summarization, and speech recognition.

Transformers in Large Language Models

Transformers play a vital role in large language models. They empower these models to process substantial amounts of text data concurrently, boosting their efficiency and effectiveness. The attention mechanism in transformers helps LLMs to comprehend the context of words in a sentence, even when those words are significantly distanced. This has resulted in notable enhancements in the performance of LLMs on various NLP tasks.

Model Architecture

The transformer model comprises two primary components: an encoder and a decoder. Each of these components includes multiple identical layers stacked on top of each other.

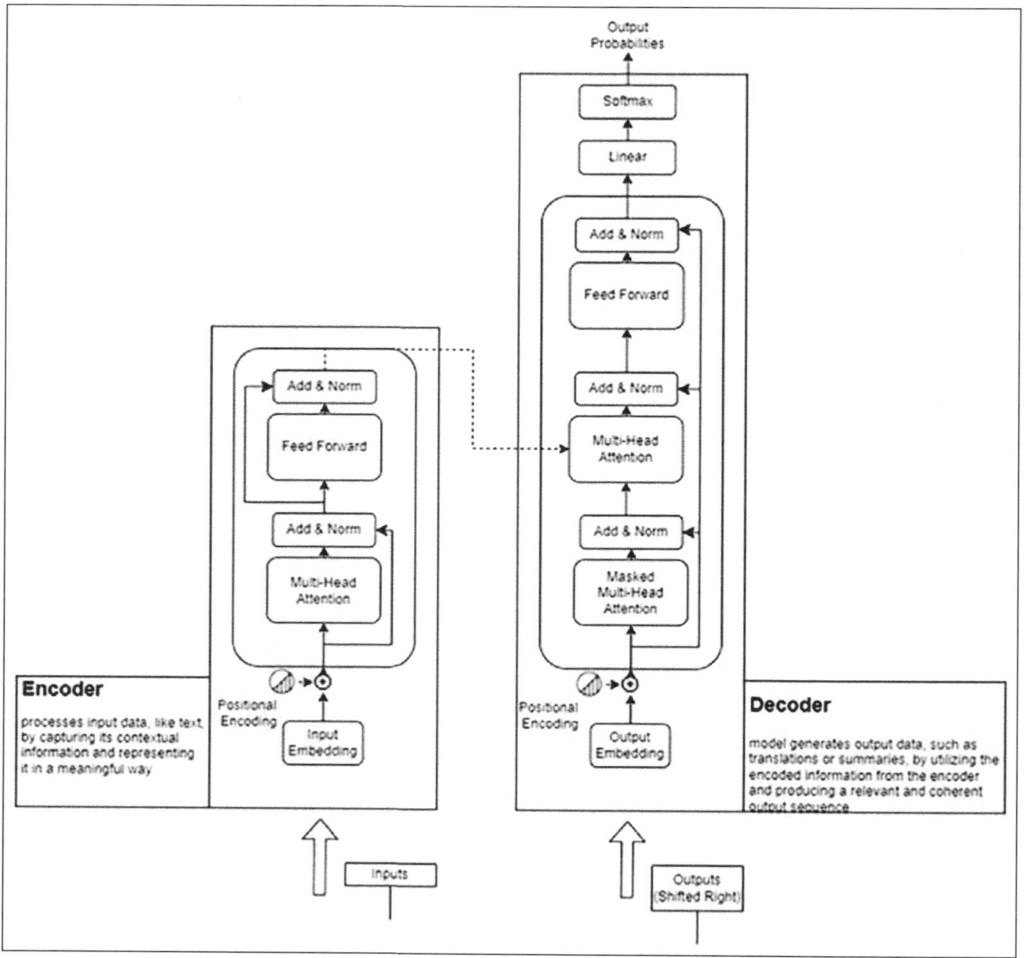

Figure 1.3: *Transformer Architecture*

Encoder

The encoder's primary function is to meticulously analyze and process the input data, which could be a sentence in a source language such as English. It meticulously examines this input, breaking it down and comprehending its various elements, from individual words to overall structure and contextual nuances. This analysis results in the creation of a comprehensive, continuous representation of the input sequence. Imagine this as a high-dimensional vector that encapsulates the core meaning and subtleties of the entire input sentence. This vector acts as a condensed, encoded version of the original input, ready to be passed on for further processing.

Decoder

The decoder takes on from the encoder. It uses the rich, continuous representation provided by the encoder as a foundation with which to construct the output sequence. If we continue with the translation example, the decoder works on translating the sentence into a target language, such as French. This process is sequential and cumulative, where each element (or word) in the output is generated inconsideration with the preceding elements. The decoder, therefore, builds the sentence in the target language, step by step, ensuring that each word aligns with the overall meaning conveyed by the encoded vector, while maintaining the coherence and grammatical integrity of the entire sentence.

Sub-layers

In the structure of both the encoder and decoder, there exist two underlying components. The initial component is a mechanism known as multi-head self-attention. This mechanism enables the model to evaluate and assign significance to varying portions of the input sequence, while formulating each part of the resulting sequence. The secondary component is a position-wise fully interconnected feed-forward network. This network performs the function of transforming the data received from the attention mechanism, ensuring an organized flow of information.

Example

For instance, when translating the English sentence "*She enjoys reading books*" to Spanish, the attention mechanism might concentrate more on the word "*enjoys*" when generating the Spanish word "*disfruta*". This is because "*disfruta*" is the direct translation of "*enjoys*". Similarly, when translating "*reading books*", the attention mechanism might distribute its focus between both words to generate "*leyendo libros*", accurately capturing the meaning of the entire phrase. This dynamic ability to shift focus simultaneously on different parts of the input sentence as required is a fundamental strength of transformer architecture, and a crucial component of what makes large language models so powerful.

Attention Mechanisms

The crux of the transformer model lies in its attention mechanism. Picture it as the spotlight of the model, highlighting various parts of the input sequence as it decodes the output sequence. It is pivotal in understanding the context and meaning of words in a sentence.

Within the transformer model is a distinct attention mechanism called the 'Scaled Dot-Product Attention'. It discerns the significance of different parts of the input sequence to each part of the output sequence. It does so by correlating the output element being processed (the query) with all input elements (the keys), scaling each by the square root of the key dimension and applying a **`softmax`** function to determine the values (input element weights).

Mathematically, scaled dot-product attention can be represented as follows:

```
Attention(Q, K, V) = softmax((QK^T)/sqrt(d_k))V
```

where **`Q`** is the query, **`K`** is the keys, **`V`** is the values, and **`d_k`** is the dimension of the keys.

Let us take a simple example of translating "*She loves to play soccer*" from English to Spanish. The attention mechanism might pay more heed to "*loves*" while generating the Spanish counterpart "*ama*". Similarly, for translating "*play soccer*", the mechanism could distribute its attention between both English words to generate "*jugar al fútbol*", effectively preserving the meaning of the entire phrase. This adaptability in focusing on varying parts of the input sentence as needed is a key strength of transformer architecture, making large language models (LLMs) highly effective.

Multi-Head Attention

Transformers take the attention concept a notch higher with "*Multi-Head Attention*". This method allows the model to focus on diverse information types in the input sequence. For example, during sentence translation, one attention head might concentrate on syntactic information (sentence grammatical structure), while another might target semantic information (meaning of words and sentences). This results in capturing a richer set of information than a single attention mechanism.

In the multi-head attention mechanism, the input first undergoes a linear transformation into multiple sets of Queries, Keys, and Values (**Q**, **K**, **V**). Each set is then channeled into a separate scaled dot-product attention mechanism, producing multiple output vectors. These vectors are then concatenated and linearly transformed to produce the final output.

Mathematically, multi-head attention can be represented as follows:

```
MultiHead(Q, K, V ) = Concat(head_1, ..., head_h)W_O
```

where each `head_i = Attention(QW_{Qi}, KW_{Ki}, VW_{Vi})`

Here, `W_{Qi}`, `W_{Ki}`, `W_{Vi}`, and `W_O` are parameter matrices, `h` is the number of heads, and `Attention` is the scaled dot-product attention. The inclusion of multi-head attention enhances the model's versatility and effectiveness by allowing it to capture different information types from varying positions in the input sequence.

Importance of Attention

Self-attention mechanism forms a cornerstone of the transformer model. It empowers the model to gauge the importance of various parts of the input sequence while generating each output sequence element, which is fundamental for understanding sentence context and word meanings.

The paper "*Attention is All You Need*" presents four reasons why self-attention is a good choice for the transformer model:

- **Computational Efficiency**

  Self-attention is computationally efficient because it allows for parallel computation across all elements in the sequence. This is in contrast to RNNs, which require sequential computation. For instance, if we have a sentence with 10 words, an RNN would need to process these words one by one. However, a transformer model can process all 10 words at the same time, leading to faster computation.

- **Ability to Model Long-Range Dependencies**

  In many tasks, such as translation, understanding a word can depend on far-away words. Self-attention allows for direct dependencies between distant words, whereas RNNs require many steps of computation to establish such a dependency. For example, in the sentence "The man, who was from Spain and loved football, decided to visit the stadium", understanding the word "stadium" might require understanding the distant word "football". Self-attention allows the model to directly relate these two words without needing to process all the intermediate words.

- **Interpretability**

  The attention weights in self-attention can be interpreted as the model's understanding of how different words relate to each other, providing some insight into the model's operation. For instance, in the sentence "*The cat sat on the mat*", the model might assign high attention weights between "*cat*" and "*sat*", and between "*sat*" and "*mat*", indicating that these pairs of words are closely related in the meaning of the sentence.

- **Positional Encoding**

  Positional encoding is critical for sequence data, as the position or sequence of words is key to understanding the meaning of a sentence. For example, "The cat chased the dog" and "The dog chased the cat" have different meanings, although they have the same words. Traditional models like RNNs inherently understand word order because they process words sequentially. However, since the transformer model processes all words simultaneously, it needs a mechanism to consider word positions in a sentence.

  To tackle this, the transformer model uses a technique called positional encoding. It adds a specific vector to each input embedding to indicate the word's position in the sentence. The design of positional encodings enables the model to easily learn to pay attention to relative positions. This means that if a word at position 4 relates to a word at position 7 in the input sequence, the model should also learn that the word at position 5 relates to the word at position 8, thereby understanding the underlying relationship and patterns of words appearing in a sentence or a text corpus.

  The specific positional encoding employed uses sine and cosine functions of varying frequencies. This choice allows the model to potentially learn to pay attention to relative positions and generalize to sequence lengths longer than those encountered during training.

Add and Norm (Residual Connection and Layer Normalization)

In the transformer model, after the self-attention layer, there is an operation called '`Add and Norm`'. This is a combination of a residual connection (the '`Add`') and layer normalization (the '`Norm`').

The residual connection is a shortcut connection that skips one or more layers. The input to the self-attention layer is added to its output, which helps in preventing the vanishing gradient problem during training.

The Vanishing Gradient Problem is a significant challenge encountered in training deep neural networks. It occurs during backpropagation, the process used for updating network weights via gradient descent. As gradients, calculated using the chain rule, are propagated backwards from the output to the input layer, they can become exceedingly small. This diminishing effect results in negligible or no updates to the weights of the early layers, a phenomenon termed as the vanishing gradient problem.

Think of the '`Add`' part as a shortcut. Suppose you are in a maze, trying to find your way out. You could go through every twist and turn, or you could take a shortcut that gets you to the end faster. That is what the residual connection does. It provides a shortcut for the information, allowing it to bypass one or more layers. This helps the model learn faster and reduces the risk of gradient vanishing during training, which can be a problem in deep networks.

Layer normalization is a technique used to standardize the inputs to a layer, that is, it normalizes the values across each feature, making the model more stable, allowing it to learn effectively.

The '`Norm`' part is like a standardization process. Imagine you are a teacher grading a set of assignments. To be fair, you decide to grade on a curve, meaning that you adjust the grades based on the overall performance of the class. Layer normalization works in a similar way. It adjusts the values in a layer to make sure they have a mean of 0 and a standard deviation of 1. This makes the training process more stable and efficient.

Feed Forward

The feed-forward network in the transformer model is like a mini neural network applied to each word separately. It consists of two layers. The first layer transforms the word into a higher dimensional space, and the second layer brings it back to the original space. In between, there is a ReLU (rectified linear unit) activation function, which essentially helps the network learn complex patterns by introducing non-linearity to the model.

Masked Multi-Head Attention

Masked multi-head attention is a variant of multi-head attention in which certain values are masked to prevent them from attending to future positions in the sequence. This is used in the decoder part of the transformer model to ensure that the prediction for a certain position is only dependent on known words or positions.

Masked multi-head attention is like a privacy filter. Suppose you are reading a mystery novel, and you do not want to spoil the ending. You cover up the upcoming pages to prevent your eyes from wandering ahead. That is what masked multi-head attention does. It prevents the model from seeing future words in the sentence, ensuring that the prediction for a certain word is based only on the words that came before it.

Linear and Softmax Layers

The linear layer, also known as a fully connected layer, is a basic layer in neural networks that applies a linear transformation to the incoming data. It is used in the transformer model to transform the output of the self-attention and feed-forward layers. It takes the input, performs a specific calculation on it, and produces an output. In the case of the linear layer, this calculation involves multiplying the input by a set of weights (which the model learns during training), and adding a bias term.

The softmax layer is typically used in the final part of the model. It takes the output of the linear layer and converts it into probability scores for each possible output, making it suitable for tasks such as classification or language modeling. In the context of transformers, it is used in the output layer to generate the probability distribution of vocabulary for next word prediction.

The softmax layer is like a voting system. Suppose you have a group of people voting on multiple options. Each person gives a score to each option, and in the end, you want to know the probability of each option being chosen. The softmax layer takes the scores (which can be any real numbers) and converts them into probabilities (which are between 0 and 1), so that they can be interpreted as the model's confidence in each possible output. In the context of transformers, it is used in the output layer to generate the probability distribution of vocabulary for next word prediction.

Transformers and Large Language Models

Transformer models have become the key driving force behind many large language models. Think about well-known models like BERT, GPT-3, and their variants. These models go through a two-part training process: first is the pre-training, followed by the fine-tuning stage.

In the pre-training phase, these models learn from a large collection of text data. The main goal is to guess a word by looking at the surrounding words in a sentence. This step enables the models to pick up on the structure and nuances of language.

Next, during the fine-tuning phase, the model is given a specific job, such as classifying sentiments in the text or answering questions. This part of the training helps the model to hone its abilities and apply the learnt language skills to particular tasks.

Take GPT-3 as an example. This model, which is based on transformer architecture, is one of the biggest and most sophisticated LLMs in use today. With its 175 billion parameters, GPT-3 was trained on a wide array of internet text. But there is a twist – unlike most of its predecessors, GPT-3 does not undergo fine-tuning for specific tasks. Instead, it creates text by predicting the next word in a given sequence.

In summary, getting to grips with transformers is a crucial step in understanding the world of LLMs. Due to its ability to deal with long-distance dependencies in text, scalable design, and data insights, transformer architecture has become an essential tool in natural language processing. As we keep pushing the boundaries of what is possible with more advanced and capable LLMs, the principles and workings of the transformer model will undoubtedly remain at the heart of these innovations.

Scaling Laws for Large Language Models

Scaling laws give us a clear picture of the 'scaling effect', enabling us to foresee how large language models might perform during their training phase. Let us take a look at two significant scaling laws associated with transformer language models.

KM Scaling Law

Introduced by Kaplan and colleagues, this law outlines the correlation between the performance of a model and three key aspects: the size of the model, the volume of the dataset, and the computing power used in training. In simple terms, it states that bigger models, when trained on more extensive data using more powerful computers, are likely to deliver better results.

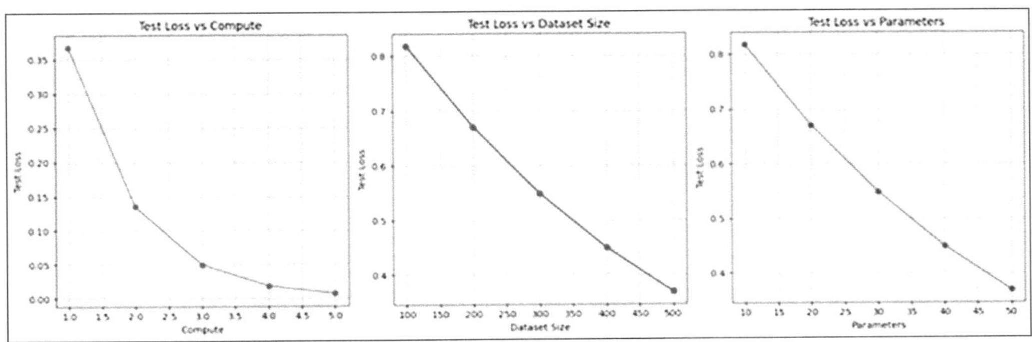

Figure 1.4: *KM Scaling Law*

Chinchilla Scaling Law

This law, put forward by Hoffmann and others, offers a different perspective on scaling laws, focusing on the most effective use of computing resources during the training of LLMs. It indicates that the best way to allocate computing resources is to simultaneously increase the size of both the model and the dataset. This implies that just increasing the model size or the dataset is not enough; both should be scaled up together for optimal outcomes.

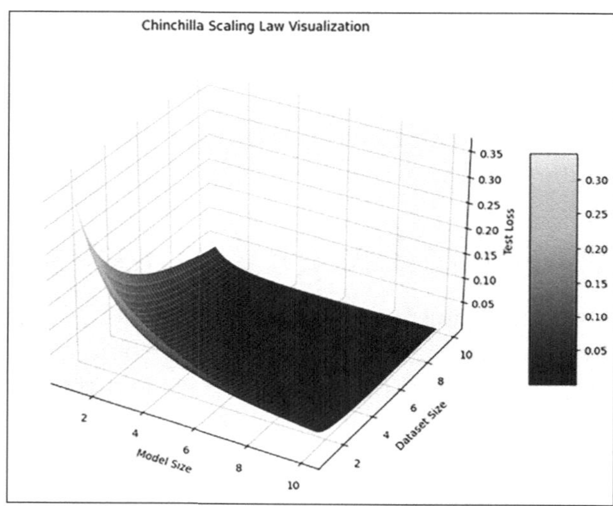

***Figure 1.5**: Chinchilla Scaling Law*

These scaling laws are quite handy as they offer a method to anticipate the performance of a model before the training process begins. This ability to predict can aid in making informed decisions about how to set up and train our models, ensuring we use our resources efficiently.

Key Techniques for Large Language Models

The development of LLMs has been facilitated by several pivotal techniques, which have significantly enhanced their capabilities. These techniques include:

Scaling

The performance of LLMs is often directly proportional to their size, the volume of data they are trained on, and the computational power used in their training. Larger models trained on more extensive datasets with more robust computational resources tend to exhibit superior performance.

Training

Distributed training algorithms are crucial for learning the network parameters of LLMs. Additionally, optimization strategies play a significant role in ensuring training stability and enhancing model performance.

Ability Eliciting

Designing suitable task instructions or specific in-context learning strategies can help highlight the abilities of LLMs. For instance, the technique of reinforcement learning with human feedback can be used to align LLMs with human values.

Despite significant progress and impact of these techniques, the underlying principles of LLMs remain a mystery. Questions such as why emergent abilities occur in LLMs instead of smaller PLMs, and how to align LLMs with human values or preferences, are still to be answered.

Alignment Tuning and Tools Manipulation

In the context of large language models, the terms '*Alignment Tuning*' and '*Tools Manipulation*' refer to specific methods that help in improving the performance of the model.

'*Alignment Tuning*' is like fine-tuning the focus of the model. Imagine you are trying to take a picture, but the image is blurry. What do you do? You adjust the focus, right? Similarly, 'Alignment Tuning' is the process of adjusting or 'focusing' the model to better understand and respond to specific tasks or questions. It helps the model to align more closely with the kind of responses we want it to generate.

On the other hand, '*Tools Manipulation*' is about the methods or techniques that are used to change or improve how the model works. Just like a mechanic might use different tools to fix a car, in the context of LLMs, '*tools*' are different strategies or techniques that developers use to enhance the performance of the model. This could be anything from tweaking the architecture of the model, changing the way it is trained, or even adjusting how it handles data.

Simply put, '*Alignment Tuning*' is like adjusting the focus of a camera to get a better picture, and '*Tools Manipulation*' is like using different tools to fix or improve that camera. Both of these methods are important in making sure that the language models work as well as possible.

Large language models are designed to understand and mirror the patterns in the data they have been trained on. This sometimes results in content that can be deemed as offensive, prejudiced, or even damaging. As such, there is a need to attune these LLMs with human values such as being of assistance, being trustworthy, and causing no harm.

The InstructGPT model offers an efficient approach to fine-tune these LLMs so they can adhere to specified instructions. It employs the principles of reinforcement learning and integrates human feedback into the training process through carefully planned labeling strategies. A perfect example of this is ChatGPT, which is built using a technique similar to InstructGPT. It exhibits the capacity to generate high-quality, non-harmful responses, such as declining to answer disrespectful queries.

Regulating Model Behavior

The focus on developing a diverse range of standards to control the actions of LLMs is growing. For our discussion, we will focus on three key alignment standards – being helpful, honest, and harmless. These have been extensively applied in the field. Other criteria such as behavior, intent, incentive, and internal aspects can also be adopted. These are somewhat similar to the primary three. Furthermore, these criteria can be adapted to specific needs, such as replacing honesty with accuracy or concentrating on certain specific standards.

Helpful Behavior

A helpful LLM should strive to assist users in resolving their issues or answering their queries in a direct and efficient way. When more information is required, the LLM should be capable of extracting the necessary details through appropriate questions, displaying a high level of sensitivity, insight, and discretion. However, achieving this alignment is a challenge due to the complexity of accurately defining and understanding the user's intent.

Honest Behavior

At a fundamental level, an honest LLM should provide truthful information to users without making up data. It should also express appropriate levels of uncertainty in its responses to prevent the misinterpretation or distortion of information. This demands that the model be aware of its abilities and limitations (that is, 'known unknowns'). Based on this explanation, honesty is a more objective standard than helpfulness and harmlessness, making the alignment process potentially less dependent on human involvement.

Harmless Behavior

For an LLM to be considered harmless, it should not produce content that is offensive or biased. It should be able to identify and prevent attempts to extract harmful information. For instance, if asked to perform a dangerous task, such as committing a crime, the LLM should courteously decline. The definition of what constitutes harmful behavior, however, can vary greatly based on the user, the nature of the question, and the context in which the LLM is being used.

These standards are heavily influenced by human cognition, making them subjective and challenging to incorporate directly as optimization goals for LLMs. Current research provides various methods to achieve these standards when aligning LLMs. One promising method is '*red teaming*', in which e manual or automated methods are used to pressure LLMs into generating harmful outputs. These outputs are then used to update and improve the LLMs, preventing such harmful outputs in the future.

Tools Manipulation

Language learning models primarily serve as text generators and are trained on vast amounts of text data. However, they often fall short when it comes to tasks not naturally expressed in text form, such as mathematical calculations. Also, their knowledge is restricted to their training data, which means that they struggle with information that has emerged after their training period.

To counter these shortcomings, recent strategies include the use of external tools to supplement LLM capabilities. For instance, to make accurate computations, an LLM can use a calculator. To retrieve information unknown to it, a search engine can come in handy. Taking this concept further, ChatGPT has introduced a feature that allows it to use external plugins, which can be existing apps or newly created ones. These plugins act like the "*eyes and ears*" of LLMs, significantly widening their range of capabilities.

In this way, these language models can overcome their inherent limitations and expand their abilities, making them more effective and versatile in responding to a wider array of user queries and tasks.

Creating and Nurturing Large Language Models

Producing or replicating large language models is not an easy task. It involves a handful of technical obstacles and requires a substantial amount of computational resources. A practical solution is to learn from pre-existing LLMs and reuse the resources publicly available for their ongoing development or study. In this piece, we will briefly outline the publicly accessible resources essential for developing LLMs, which include model checkpoints (or APIs), datasets, and libraries.

Publicly Available Model Checkpoints or APIs

Because of the high cost associated with training models, pre-trained models or checkpoints are crucial for researchers working on LLMs. Considering the scale of parameters is an essential factor while using LLMs, we divide these public models into two categories based on their scale (tens of billions of parameters and hundreds of billions of parameters). This categorization helps users find suitable resources as per their budget. Moreover, for model inference, we can utilize public APIs directly to perform tasks, avoiding the need to run the model locally.

Publicly Available Corpora

The quality and diversity of pre-training datasets play a crucial role in the performance of LLMs. Here, we introduce some commonly used datasets for training LLMs.

CommonCrawl

CommonCrawl is a large-scale dataset comprising extensive webpage data. It has been employed for training various LLMs, such as T5, LaMDA, Gopher, and UL2. Its multilingual version, known as mC4, is used in mT5. Other subsets of CommonCrawl, such as CC-Stories, REALNEWS, and CC-News, are also frequently used for pre-training.

Reddit Links

Reddit is a social media platform where users can post links and texts, which are then voted on by others. Posts with a high number of upvotes are considered valuable and can be used to create high-quality datasets. While the well-known WebText corpus made up of highly upvoted Reddit links is not publicly accessible, there is an open-source alternative called OpenWebText available.

Another dataset extracted from Reddit is PushShift.io. It is a constantly updated dataset containing historical data from the inception of Reddit. Pushshift provides not only monthly data dumps but also handy tools to help users search, summarize, and conduct initial investigations on the entire dataset.

Wikipedia

Wikipedia is an online encyclopedia with numerous high-quality articles on a wide range of topics and languages. It is often used for training LLMs, including GPT-3, LaMDA, and LLaMA.

Pile

Pile is a large-scale, diverse, and open-source text dataset that includes over 800GB of data from various sources. It is widely used in models with different parameter scales, such as GPT-J, CodeGen, and Megatron-Turing NLG. Besides this, ROOTS is composed of various smaller datasets (totally 1.61 TB of text) and covers 59 different languages, which have been used for training BLOOM.

Training LLMs usually requires a blend of different data sources, not just a single corpus. Therefore, existing studies often mix several ready-made datasets such as C4, OpenWebText, and Pile, and then conduct further processing to obtain the pre-training corpus. Furthermore, to train LLMs that are adaptive to specific applications, it is crucial to extract data from relevant sources, like Wikipedia and BigQuery, to enrich the corresponding information in pre-training data.

Collecting Data

In contrast to smaller-scale language models, LLMs necessitate a larger pool of high-quality data for pre-training, and their capabilities largely hinge on the nature of the pre-training corpus and the methods used to process it. In this segment, we will delve into how pre-training data is gathered and processed, touching on data sources, pre-processing techniques, and an in-depth analysis of how pre-training data impacts LLM performance.

Data Source

To develop an adept LLM, it is crucial to gather a broad natural language corpus from various sources. Current LLMs primarily use a blend of public textual datasets for the pre-training corpus.

Pre-training corpus sources can generally be divided into two categories: general data and specialized data.

General Text Data

A large proportion of LLMs use general-purpose pre-training data, such as web pages, books, and conversation text, providing a wide array of topics in rich textual formats.

Specialized Text Data

Specialized datasets can enhance specific abilities of LLMs on downstream tasks. For instance, models such as BLOOM and PaLM show impressive performance in multilingual tasks like translation, summarization, and multilingual question answering, often outperforming or matching the state-of-the-art models that are fine-tuned.

Formatting Existing Datasets

Before the introduction of instruction tuning, several early studies used instances from a diverse range of tasks (such as text summarization, classification, and translation) to create multi-task training datasets. Existing multi-task training datasets, paired with natural language task descriptions, serve as a prime source for instruction tuning instances.

Recent works augment labeled datasets with human-written task descriptions to instruct LLMs to understand the tasks by explaining the task goals. For example, a task description such as "Please answer this question" is added to each example in a question- answering task. After instruction tuning, LLMs are able to generalize well to other unseen tasks by following their task descriptions.

It has been demonstrated that instructions play a vital role in task generalization abilities for LLMs. When a model is fine-tuned on labeled datasets with task descriptions removed, it results in a significant drop in performance. To effectively generate labeled instances for instruction tuning, a crowd-sourcing platform, PromptSource, has been proposed. This platform facilitates the creation, sharing, and verification of task descriptions for different datasets.

To increase the number of training instances, several studies attempt to invert the input-output pairs of existing instances with specifically designed task descriptions for instruction tuning. For example, given a question-answer pair, a new instance can be created by predicting the question conditioned on the answer (for example, "Please generate a question based on the answer"). Additionally, some studies use heuristic task templates to convert large amounts of unlabeled text into labeled instances.

Formatting Human Needs

Despite the fact that a large number of training instances have been formatted with instructions, they mainly come from public NLP datasets and may lack instruction diversity or fail to align with real human needs. To address this,

InstructGPT uses the queries real users have submitted to the OpenAI API as task descriptions. These queries, expressed in natural language, are particularly suited for improving the instruction following ability of LLMs.

In addition, to increase task diversity, human labelers are asked to compose instructions for real-life tasks, including open-ended generation, open question answering, brainstorming, and chatting. Another group of labelers then directly answers these instructions as the output. The instruction (the collected user query) and the expected output (the human-written answer) are paired as a training instance.

Notably, Instruct-GPT also uses these real-world tasks formatted in natural language for alignment tuning. GPT-4, for example, has developed instructions for high-risk scenarios and has trained the model to reject these instructions through supervised fine-tuning to ensure safety. Furthermore, to alleviate the demands on human annotators, a few semi-automated methods have been proposed for creating instances. These methods involve feeding existing instances into LLMs to generate a diverse range of task descriptions and instances.

Publicly Accessible Libraries

Libraries are crucial resources for developers and researchers who aim to experiment with or improve upon LLMs. These libraries typically provide tools for processing and generating text, as well as for training and fine-tuning models. Hugging Face's Transformers, PyTorch, and TensorFlow are examples of widely-used libraries in this field.

Hugging Face's Transformers is a highly popular library that provides APIs for state-of-the-art machine learning models like BERT, GPT, T5, and more. It simplifies the process of using these models and makes them more accessible to a wider audience.

PyTorch and TensorFlow are open-source machine learning libraries that provide the necessary tools for creating, training, and using machine learning models. They are extensively used in the research and development of LLMs due to their flexibility, efficiency, and large community support.

In conclusion, creating and working with LLMs requires a combination of high-quality datasets, efficient libraries, and robust pre-processing techniques. Publicly available resources such as model checkpoints, APIs, and libraries significantly aid in the process. For successful deployment and development, understanding how these resources interact and complement each other is essential.

Configuring LLMs in Detail

The comprehensive setup of LLMs involves facets such as the method of normalization, activation function, position embedding, attention, and bias handling.

Normalization

Layer normalization (LN) is commonly used in transformer designs to mitigate issues with training instability. The placement of LN plays a crucial role in the performance of LLMs. While the original transformer employed post-LN, most LLMs use pre-LN for more stable training, even though this might slightly reduce performance. Recently, various advanced normalization strategies have been introduced as alternatives to LN.

Activation Functions

Properly defining activation functions in feed-forward networks is essential for achieving optimal performance. Current LLMs frequently use Gaussian Error Linear Unit (GeLU) activations. Recent models, such as PaLM and LaMDA, have also started to use GLU activation variants, notably SwiGLU and GeGLU, which often deliver superior results. However, they require about 50% more parameters in the feed-forward networks compared to GeLU.

Position Embeddings

Position embeddings are used to provide absolute or relative position information for modeling sequences. The vanilla transformer offers two variants of absolute position embeddings: sinusoids and learned position embeddings, with the latter being more common in LLMs.

Attention and Bias

Aside from the complete self-attention mechanism used in the original transformer, GPT-3 has adopted a sparse attention mechanism with lower computational complexity, known as Factorized Attention. Efforts to effectively and efficiently model longer sequences have led to the development of unique attention patterns and considerations for GPU memory access, such as FlashAttention.

Optimizer for LLMs

The optimizer selected for training LLMs is vital. Optimizers such as Adam and AdamW are widely used in LLM training, for example, in GPT-3. These optimizers work based on adaptive estimates of lower-order moments for first-order gradient-based optimization. Another option used in training LLMs like PaLM and T5 is the Adafactor optimizer. Adafactor is a variant of the Adam optimizer, designed to conserve GPU memory during training.

Stabilizing the Training

Training LLMs can be characterized by instability, which may lead to model collapse. To counter this, weight decay and gradient clipping are often employed. Typical settings for gradient clipping threshold and weight decay rate are 1.0 and 0.1, respectively. However, with larger LLMs, training loss spikes can occur, leading to further instability. To alleviate this, some models like PaLM and OPT use a simple tactic of restarting the training process from an earlier checkpoint.

Pre-Training

Pre-training sets the foundation for LLM capabilities. Through pre-training on large-scale datasets, LLMs can acquire vital language comprehension and generation skills. During this process, the size and quality of the pre-training corpus are critical for LLMs to gain powerful abilities. Furthermore, to efficiently pre-train LLMs, model architectures, acceleration methods, and optimization techniques need to be carefully designed.

Emergent Abilities of Large Language Models

Emergent abilities refer to the capabilities that are not explicitly programmed but arise as the model size increases. These abilities are not present in smaller models, but they become apparent in larger models, hence the use of the term 'emergent'. In the context of LLMs, there are three primary emergent abilities:

In-Context Learning

This ability allows LLMs to adapt to new information presented in the input prompt, without requiring additional training or gradient updates. The model generates the expected output for test instances by completing the word sequence of the input text. This ability is akin to learning on the fly, and the model adjusts its responses based on the context provided in the input.

Instruction Following

Large language models can be carefully adjusted using different types of datasets that are arranged in a way that is easy to understand, similar to everyday language. This way of training helps these models do a good job at handling new tasks they have not seen before, especially if these tasks are described as step-by-step instructions. In simple words, the model is taught to understand the guidelines given in a question or prompt, and then come up with the right answers or responses.

Step-by-Step Reasoning

With a strategy known as 'chain-of-thought' prompting, LLMs can solve complex tasks that involve multiple reasoning steps. The model is prompted to think through a problem step-by-step, allowing it to handle tasks that require a sequence of interrelated decisions or actions.

These emergent abilities make LLMs incredibly versatile and powerful tools for a wide range of applications. They allow the models to adapt to new information, follow instructions, and reason through complex problems, all of which are capabilities critical for advanced natural language understanding and generation.

Exploring the Inner Workings of LLMs

The underlying principles of large language models is a captivating field to delve into, especially in understanding the influence of pre-training on In-Context Learning (ICL) and the way LLMs handle ICL during inference.

Understanding Pre-training and ICL

ICL is an ability that becomes more pronounced in larger models. However, research has shown that even smaller models can exhibit robust ICL capabilities when provided with specially crafted training tasks. This indicates that the design of the training tasks plays a vital role in enhancing the ICL proficiency of LLMs. Furthermore, the origin of pre-training data significantly impacts the performance of ICL, suggesting the importance of quality and variety in the pre-training dataset. Certain studies propose that ICL begins to manifest when the training data can be grouped into several rare categories, as opposed to a uniform distribution. This perspective has brought forth the theoretical explanation that ICL results from pre-training on documents demonstrating long-range coherence.

Performing ICL

During the inference phase, LLMs generate meta-gradients concerning demonstrations and perform implicit gradient descent through the attention mechanism. This process is typically examined through the lens of gradient descent and is viewed as implicit fine-tuning. Certain attention heads in LLMs are equipped to perform task-agnostic atomic operations such as copying and prefix matching, operations that are integral to the ICL capability. Some research interprets ICL as a process of learning algorithms, where LLMs embed implicit models into their parameters during pre-training. Given the examples in ICL, LLMs are capable of implementing learning algorithms such as gradient descent or directly calculating the closed-form solution to update these models during forward computation.

Chain-of-Thought Prompting in Large Language Models

The strategy of Chain-of-Thought (CoT) prompting is an innovative technique to enhance the proficiency of large language models in handling complex reasoning tasks. Contrary to traditional In-Context Learning that leverages input-output pairs, CoT incorporates steps of intermediate reasoning into prompts, directing the model towards the final solution.

Confluence of ICL and CoT

CoT can be done with ICL in two main scenarios: few-shot and zero-shot.

Few-shot CoT

This method is employed when LLMs are tasked with completing a task that has a limited set of examples. The model receives a handful of examples to learn from and uses these examples to grasp the expected task outcome. For instance, if the task is translating English sentences into French, the model might be fed a few examples of English sentences and their French counterparts. It would then use these examples to guide its translation of more English sentences. Nonetheless, few-shot CoT is not always consistent. The performance can fluctuate depending on the nature of the task, the provided examples, and the employed prompts.

Zero-shot CoT

This scenario does not necessitate any demonstrations. It directly provides the task description and the reasoning steps to LLMs to generate the ultimate answer. Similar to few-shot CoT, the design of reasoning steps is vital for the performance of zero-shot CoT. Research suggests using the task description as the prompt to guide LLMs to generate high-quality reasoning steps.

CoT Prompt Design

The crafting of CoT prompts is critical for the successful performance of few-shot CoT. To generate top-notch CoT prompts, human experts are typically enlisted. However, the manual creation of CoT prompts is labor-intensive and time-consuming. To lessen this burden, studies suggest automatically generating CoT prompts with the help of LLMs. For this, the task description is initially fed into LLMs to generate the reasoning steps, then these steps are used to construct the CoT prompts.

When and Why CoT Works

CoT is a skill that emerges only in sufficiently large models (typically containing 10B or more parameters), and not in smaller models. Also, as CoT supplements standard prompting with intermediate reasoning steps, it is primarily effective in improving tasks that require sequential reasoning, such as arithmetic reasoning, commonsense reasoning, and symbolic reasoning. Conversely, for other tasks that do not rely on intricate reasoning, it might perform worse than standard prompting.

The source of CoT capability is widely hypothesized to be due to training on code, since models trained on it demonstrate strong reasoning ability. However, this hypothesis still lacks publicly reported evidence of ablation experiments (with and without training on code). Additionally, instruction tuning does not appear to be the key reason for obtaining the CoT ability, as it has been empirically shown that instruction tuning on non-CoT data does not enhance performance on held-out CoT benchmarks.

The performance of CoT can differ depending on the specifics of the task, the examples given, and the prompts used. While the model can generate plausible responses, it does not truly understand the task in the way a human would. It is simply predicting what text is likely to come next, based on its training.

Several studies have aimed to unravel the underlying mechanism of CoT. For example, the study "*Chain-of-Thought Prompting Elicits Reasoning in Large*

Language Models" by Wei et al. found that LLMs essentially encode implicit models through their parameters during pre-training. With the examples provided in ICL, LLMs can implement learning algorithms such as gradient descent or directly compute the closed-form solution to update these models during the process of computation. This framework suggests that LLMs can effectively learn simple linear functions and even some complex functions such as decision trees through ICL.

A separate study, "*Towards Understanding Chain-of-Thought Prompting: An Empirical Study of What Matters*" by Wang et al., explores the factors that influence the effectiveness of CoT. The study discovered that the performance of ICL is largely influenced by the source of the pre-training corpora rather than its scale.

Practically, CoT is a hopeful strategy to enhance the reasoning ability of LLMs. However, to completely comprehend its mechanism and to optimize its performance across various tasks, further research is required.

In summary, the application of Chain-of-Thought prompting to LLMs is a remarkable breakthrough. The strategy of intertwining CoT and ICL is transforming how these models handle complex reasoning tasks. However, the understanding and application of CoT in real-world scenarios is still in its infancy. As researchers continue to dig deeper into this approach, we anticipate the discovery of more insights that could further improve and optimize the performance of large language models.

Assessment Yardsticks for Large Language Models

Recent times have seen the launch of several extensive benchmarks aimed at evaluating large language models. Following are some of the most representative and frequently applied benchmarks:

Massive Multitask Language Understanding (MMLU)

This multipurpose benchmark is ideal for conducting a large-scale evaluation of multi-task knowledge comprehension. It encompasses a broad array of knowledge domains, from Mathematics and Computer Science to the Humanities and Social Sciences. The complexity of these tasks ranges from basic to advanced. In this benchmark, LLMs typically outpace smaller models by a significant margin.

GPT-4, the latest model, has even set a remarkable record in MMLU, performing substantially better than its predecessor models.

BIG-bench

This is a collective benchmark designed to scrutinize LLMs from various perspectives. It includes 204 tasks covering a wide range of subjects such as Linguistics, Childhood Development, Mathematics, Common Sense Reasoning, Biology, Physics, Social Bias, and Software Development, among others. With the increase in model size, LLMs can surpass average human performance in the few-shot setting on 65% of tasks in BIG-bench. Given the extensive evaluation cost of the entire benchmark, a streamlined version called BIG-bench-Lite has been proposed, which includes 24 small yet diverse and challenging tasks from BIG-bench. Additionally, the BIG-bench hard (BBH) benchmark has been created to focus on currently unsolvable tasks for LLMs, selecting tasks where LLMs perform less efficiently than humans.

HELM

This is a comprehensive benchmark that currently consists of 16 core scenarios and 7 metric categories. It builds on many previous studies, offering a holistic evaluation of language models. As demonstrated by the HELM experimental results, instruction tuning consistently enhances the performance of LLMs in terms of accuracy, robustness, and fairness. Furthermore, for reasoning tasks, LLMs that have been pre-trained on a code corpus demonstrate superior performance.

In-depth Analysis of the Capabilities of LLMs

Besides constructing large-scale evaluation benchmarks, there has been an influx of studies conducting in-depth analyses to investigate the strengths and weaknesses of LLMs. Here are some of the primary aspects.

Generalist

The exceptional performance of LLMs has led to systematic evaluations of their general capabilities, exploring their competence across a variety of different tasks or applications. These studies mainly focus on recently emerged LLMs, such as ChatGPT and GPT-4, which have not been thoroughly explored earlier. It has been found that LLMs are more robust than smaller language models in a variety of tasks, but may face new challenges, such as robustness instability and prompt sensitivity.

Specialist

As LLMs have been pre-trained on large-scale corpora from a variety of sources, they can grasp rich knowledge from the pre-training data. Thus, LLMs are also employed as domain experts or specialists for specific areas. Therefore, recent studies have explored the use of LLMs for solving domain-specific tasks and evaluated the adaptation capacity of LLMs. Typically, these studies collect or construct domain-specific datasets to evaluate the performance of LLMs using in-context learning. Three domains that have received significant attention from the research community are healthcare, education, and law.

Conclusion

Large language models represent a significant milestone in the field of artificial intelligence. Their ability to understand and generate human-like text has opened up a plethora of applications across various industries. Transformer architecture, with its attention mechanisms and positional encoding, forms the backbone of these powerful models.

However, as we have seen, working with LLMs is not without its challenges. From the careful crafting of prompts, to guiding model behavior, and the need for vigilance against biases in the output of the model, the use of LLMs requires a nuanced understanding of their strengths and limitations.

Furthermore, as LLMs continue to evolve and improve, new challenges and risks are likely to emerge. Ensuring the safety, security, and ethical use of these models is of paramount importance. Despite these challenges, the potential of LLMs to revolutionize industries and contribute to societal advancement is immense.

As we move forward to subsequent chapters, we will delve deeper into the intricacies of LLMs, exploring more advanced topics and applications. The foundational understanding of LLMs gained in this chapter will serve as a stepping stone towards fully harnessing the power of these models. Whether you are a graduate, a professional, or a technical or non-technical person, the journey into the world of LLMs promises to be an exciting and enlightening one.

References

- BERT: Pre-training of Deep Bidirectional Transformers for Language Understanding
- Deep contextualized word representations
- Scaling Laws for Neural Language Models
- Training Compute-Optimal Large Language Models
- Towards Understanding Chain-of-Thought Prompting: An Empirical Study of What Matters

CHAPTER 2
Demystifying Open-Source Large Language Models

Introduction

The field of natural language processing (NLP) has seen a significant surge in the development of large language models (LLMs) in recent years. These models, capable of understanding and generating text that closely resembles human language, have demonstrated remarkable capabilities across various NLP tasks. Open-source LLMs, in particular, have garnered significant attention due to their potential to democratize access to cutting-edge AI technologies and foster collaborative research.

Structure

In this chapter, the following topics will be covered:

- Introduction to Open-Source Models
- Detailed Overview of Bloom, Replit, and Dolly
- Unique Features and Uses of Each Model
- Practical Use Cases and Examples

Overview

This chapter provides a comprehensive overview of several popular and trending open-source large language models. We will delve into the details of each model, exploring their history, data sources, training processes, accuracy, and more.

We will start our journey with StableLM by Stability AI, a model designed for stability and consistency. We will then explore Google's BERT, a revolutionary model that introduced the concept of bidirectional training to the world. Our exploration will also include BLOOM, a multilingual model by BigScience, as well as RedPajama and Falcon by OpenAI, among others.

Each of these models comes with its unique set of features, strengths, and limitations. We will provide Python code snippets for each model, serving as a practical guide for those interested in implementing these models in their projects.

By the end of this chapter, you will have a comprehensive understanding of the open-source large language model ecosystem, equipping you with the knowledge to leverage these models in your projects and research.

Open-Source versus Proprietary Large Language Models

Companies are often faced with the task of deciding whether to use open-source or proprietary large language models. This decision is influenced by several factors, including accessibility, cost, customization, community involvement, support, and licensing.

- **Accessibility**: Open-source LLMs are publicly accessible, enabling developers to access, modify, and distribute the code. On the other hand, proprietary LLMs have limited access, and users may need to purchase a license to use the software.
- **Cost**: Open-source LLMs are typically free to use, making them a more cost-effective choice for developers and organizations. Proprietary LLMs, on the other hand, often require users to pay for licenses and maintenance fees, which can add up. For a more detailed understanding of the cost implications, you can refer to the article, "*The Economics of Large Language Models*".
- **Customization**: Open-source LLMs provide more flexibility and customization options, as developers can alter the source code to meet

their specific requirements. Proprietary LLMs, in contrast, offer limited customization options, as users cannot access or modify the source code.

- **Community involvement**: Open-source LLMs benefit from a large community of developers who contribute to the development and maintenance of the models. This collaborative approach can lead to faster innovation and improvements. Proprietary LLMs are developed and maintained by a closed team of individuals or groups, which may limit the scope of innovation and improvement.
- **Support**: Proprietary LLMs often come with dedicated support from the company that has developed them, while open-source LLMs rely on community support. However, this does not necessarily mean that proprietary LLMs have better support, as the open-source community can be highly responsive and helpful.
- **Licensing**: Open-source LLMs typically have more permissive licenses, allowing users to freely use, modify, and distribute the software. Proprietary LLMs have more restrictive licenses, which may limit how the software can be used and distributed.
- **Data privacy and security**: Healthcare organizations handle sensitive patient data, which requires strict adherence to data privacy and security regulations. Open-source LLMs allow organizations to review and modify the source code, ensuring that the model meets their specific data privacy and security requirements. Proprietary LLMs may not offer the same level of transparency and control. For a deeper understanding of data privacy and security concerns in healthcare with the use of large language models, you can refer to the article titled, "*Attention is not all you need: the complicated case of ethically using large language models in healthcare and medicine*".

Risks and Drawbacks of Open-Source LLMs

Despite their numerous benefits, open-source large language models come with potential risks and drawbacks. These include data privacy and security concerns, model reliability issues, biases, environmental impact, intellectual property and licensing issues, and support and maintenance challenges.

- **Data privacy and security**: Open-source LLMs may inadvertently expose sensitive information or intellectual property, as their source code and training data are publicly available. This can be a concern for industries that handle sensitive data, such as healthcare, finance, and government.

- **Model reliability**: Open-source LLMs may not have the same level of quality control and support as proprietary models, which could lead to less reliable performance in certain tasks. This can be a concern for industries that require high levels of accuracy and reliability, such as healthcare and finance.
- **Bias and ethical concerns**: Open-source LLMs, like proprietary models, can exhibit biases and generate harmful content due to the data they are trained on. This can be a concern for industries that prioritize fairness, accountability, and transparency, such as human resources, education, and social services.
- **Intellectual property and licensing**: Open-source LLMs typically have more permissive licenses, which can lead to potential intellectual property issues and conflicts with proprietary software.
- **Support and maintenance**: Open-source LLMs rely on community support, which may not be as responsive or specialized as dedicated support from a proprietary LLM provider. This can be a concern for industries that require prompt assistance with technical issues.

Companies should carefully weigh the benefits and drawbacks of using open-source LLMs in their specific industries or use cases, considering factors such as cost, customization, support, licensing, data privacy, and security.

Security Vulnerabilities in Open-Source LLMs

Large language models, despite their impressive capabilities, are not without risks and vulnerabilities. Some of the security vulnerabilities or bugs found in LLMs include prompt injections, data leakage, inadequate sandboxing, overfitting risks, poisoning attacks, and regression bugs.

- **Prompt injections**: Attackers can manipulate the input prompts to generate malicious or harmful content from the LLM.
- **Data leakage**: LLMs may inadvertently expose sensitive information or intellectual property due to their training data being publicly available.
- **Inadequate sandboxing**: Insufficient isolation between different user sessions may lead to unauthorized access to sensitive data or code execution.
- **Overfitting risks**: Overfitting in LLMs can lead to model memorizing and reproducing copyrighted content or sensitive information from its training dataset.

- **Model reliability**: Open-source LLMs may not have the same level of quality control and support as proprietary models, which could lead to less reliable performance in certain tasks.
- **Bias and ethical concerns**: LLMs can exhibit biases and generate harmful content due to the data they are trained on. This is a concern for industries that prioritize fairness, accountability, and transparency. For a deeper understanding of the ethical concerns and biases in large language models, you can refer to the article titled, "*Ethical and Social Risks of Harm from Language Models*".
- **Poisoning attacks**: Attackers can manipulate the training data or fine-tuning process of LLMs to introduce malicious behavior or biases in the model.
- **Regression bugs**: LLMs may exhibit inconsistent behavior between different versions, and model updates can introduce new errors or regressions.

These vulnerabilities highlight the importance of understanding the risks associated with using open-source LLMs in various industries and use cases. Companies should carefully weigh the benefits and drawbacks of using open-source LLMs in their specific industries or use cases, considering factors such as cost, customization, support, licensing, data privacy, and security.

Introducing the Models

As we analyze open-source large language models, we will be exploring a variety of popular and trending models. Each of these models has its unique features, strengths, and limitations. In the following sections, we will present a detailed analysis of each model, discussing their history, data sources, training processes, accuracy, pros, cons, and example code snippets for using them in Python.

StableLM: Empowering Language Generation with Stability AI

StableLM represents a remarkable suite of open-source large language models developed by Stability AI, offering enhanced capabilities for text and code generation. The Alpha version of the model is currently available in 3 billion and 7 billion parameters, with plans to release models ranging from 15 billion to 65 billion parameters in the future.

Overview

StableLM is an auto-regressive language model built upon the GPT architecture, designed to overcome the context window limitations of existing open-source language models. It achieves this by pre-training on an expanded version of the Pile dataset, a comprehensive open-source dataset encompassing a vast array of information from diverse sources such as Wikipedia, Stack Exchange, and PubMed.

History

Stability AI, renowned for its AI-powered stable diffusion image generator, spearheads the development of StableLM. The company's mission revolves around democratizing AI tools and collaborating with the non-profit organization EleutherAI to contribute to the development of open-source language models.

Data Source and Training Data Curation

StableLM draws its training from an enlarged version of the Pile dataset, ensuring the incorporation of information from various reliable sources. This includes a wealth of data from platforms such as Wikipedia, Stack Exchange, and PubMed, contributing to the rich and diverse knowledge base of the model.

Model Training Process

StableLM models are built upon the GPT architecture, harnessing the power of auto-regressive language modeling. The models undergo pre-training on a diverse collection of English datasets, with a specific focus on sequences with a length of 4096, thereby enabling an expanded context for improved language generation.

Accuracy

While the provided sources do not explicitly mention the accuracy of StableLM, its primary objective lies in efficiently generating text and code. This strongly suggests that the model performs effectively in its designated tasks, attaining a high level of accuracy.

Pros

- StableLM is an open-source solution, offering developers the opportunity to freely utilize and adapt the models according to their requirements.
- The models are trained on a wide range of diverse English datasets, ensuring a comprehensive understanding of the language and its nuances.

- StableLM effectively addresses the context window limitations encountered in existing open-source language models, providing expanded capabilities for language generation.

Cons

- The accuracy of the model has not been explicitly stated in the available sources.

BERT: Advancing Language Representations with Bidirectional Encoder Representations from Transformers

BERT (Bidirectional Encoder Representations from Transformers) is a significant language model developed by Google, showcasing its prowess in pre-training methods for language representations. BERT can be fine-tuned for a wide range of natural language processing (NLP) tasks, including question-answering and sentiment analysis.

Overview

BERT adopts a transformer-based model architecture that leverages bidirectional training, enabling it to grasp contextual relations between words in a text. Pre-training on a vast corpus of texts, such as Wikipedia, equips BERT with a strong foundation. It can then be further fine-tuned for specific tasks using smaller, task-specific datasets.

History

Google introduced BERT in 2018 as a groundbreaking pre-training approach for natural language processing tasks. Since its inception, BERT has gained immense popularity across various NLP applications, owing to its exceptional performance and ease of fine-tuning.

Data Source and Training Data Curation

BERT undergoes pre-training on a large corpus of texts, commonly derived from sources like Wikipedia. This extensive pre-training phase allows BERT to capture a broad range of language patterns. Subsequently, the model can be fine-tuned on smaller datasets that are specific to particular tasks.

Model Training Process

BERT's transformer-based model architecture capitalizes on bidirectional training, enabling it to grasp the intricate contextual relations between words.

The model undergoes pre-training on a substantial corpus of texts, equipping it with comprehensive language understanding. The subsequent fine-tuning process further optimizes the model for specific tasks, utilizing smaller, task-specific datasets.

Accuracy

The accuracy of BERT is task-dependent and relies on specific fine-tuning for each target task. Generally, BERT has demonstrated state-of-the-art performance across a wide range of NLP tasks, affirming its reputation as a highly accurate model.

Pros

- BERT exhibits state-of-the-art performance across diverse NLP tasks, reflecting its versatility and efficacy.
- The ability of the model to be fine-tuned using smaller, task-specific datasets allows for efficient customization, enhancing its applicability.
- The transformer-based architecture of BERT, coupled with bidirectional training, enables it to capture complex contextual relationships within the text.

Cons

- The large model size of BERT can pose resource-intensive challenges during both training and inference processes, potentially impacting computational requirements and scalability.

BLOOM: Empowering Open Science with the Largest Multilingual Language Model

BLOOM, the BigScience Large Open-science Open-access Multilingual Language Model, stands as the world's most extensive open-science, open-access multilingual large language model (LLM). Created through the collective efforts of over 1000 AI researchers, BLOOM boasts an impressive parameter count of 176 billion.

Overview

BLOOM serves as a freely available large language model, catering to individuals eager to explore its capabilities. Leveraging a transformer-based model architecture, BLOOM possesses the ability to generate text in 46 natural languages and 13 programming languages. This inclusivity makes it a versatile tool for a diverse range of linguistic tasks.

History

BLOOM stems from a collaboration between various renowned teams, including Hugging Face's BigScience team, Microsoft's DeepSpeed team, NVIDIA Megatron-LM team, IDRIS/GENCI team, PyTorch team, and volunteers within the BigScience Engineering workgroup. This collective effort signifies the commitment to advancing open science through collaborative endeavors.

Data Source and Training Data Curation

BLOOM's training data originates from a comprehensive selection of 46 natural languages and 13 programming languages. This expansive dataset amounts to approximately 1.6 terabytes of pre-processed text, which translates to 350 billion unique tokens. Such extensive coverage facilitates BLOOM's ability to handle diverse language-related tasks.

Model Training Process

BLOOM adopts a decoder-only transformer model architecture, deriving inspiration from the Megatron-LM GPT-2. This modified architecture enables BLOOM to excel in language generation tasks while ensuring efficient training and inference processes.

Accuracy

The accuracy of BLOOM is reliant upon the specific task that it is fine-tuned for. In general, BLOOM has demonstrated state-of-the-art performance across various NLP tasks, affirming its reputation as a highly accurate language model.

Pros

- BLOOM embraces an open-science and open-access paradigm, ensuring that the model is available to all individuals.
- The extensive training of the model on a vast number of tokens and its support for multiple languages contribute to its versatility and applicability.
- The development of BLOOM is the result of a collaborative effort involving a large community of AI researchers, fostering innovation and collective knowledge.

Cons

- The significant size of BLOOM poses resource-intensive demands, potentially affecting computational resources required for training and inference processes.

RedPajama: Advancing Open-Source Language Models

RedPajama is an innovative project focused on the development of cutting-edge, fully open-source models. It aims to bridge the quality gap between open and closed models by demonstrating that open-source solutions not only rival commercial offerings but also foster incredible creativity through broad community participation.

Overview

RedPajama brings together reputed organizations including Together, Ontocord.ai, ETH DS3Lab, Stanford CRFM, Hazy Research, and MILA Québec AI Institute. This collaborative effort aims to create comprehensive open-source models that can be utilized across various tasks and applications.

History

Launched as a pioneering initiative, RedPajama seeks to deliver a reproducible, fully open, and leading language model. Although the project is still in its early stages, further details about the models and their capabilities will be unveiled as the project progresses.

Data Source and Training Data Curation

RedPajama has successfully reproduced the extensive LLaMA training dataset, consisting of over 1.2 trillion tokens. This dataset encompasses data from diverse sources such as Commoncrawl, C4, GitHub, Books, ArXiv, Wikipedia, and StackExchange, ensuring a comprehensive and representative training corpus.

Model Training Process

While the specific details of the model training process for RedPajama have not been fully disclosed, it is expected to adhere to standard practices employed for training large-scale language models. This includes techniques such as pre-training on extensive datasets and fine-tuning for specific tasks.

Accuracy

The accuracy of RedPajama models will vary based on the specific tasks they are fine-tuned for. As the project is still in its early stages, additional insights regarding the model's performance will be disclosed as the project advances.

Pros

- Fully open-source models, encouraging transparency, collaboration, and community engagement.
- Collaboration between multiple renowned organizations and research groups, fostering diverse expertise and insights.
- Successful reproduction of the LLaMA training dataset, ensuring comprehensive and representative training data.

Cons

- The project is currently in its early stages, and additional information regarding the models and their capabilities will be disclosed progressively as the project unfolds.

Falcon-40B: Empowering Open-Source Language Models

Falcon-40B, a groundbreaking 40-billion-parameter causal decoder-only model, is the result of extensive efforts by the Technology Innovation Institute (TII). Trained on an impressive corpus of 1000 billion tokens derived from RefinedWeb and curated corpora, Falcon-40B has emerged as the leading open-source model, surpassing its counterparts such as LLaMA, StableLM, RedPajama, MPT, and others.

Overview

Falcon-40B boasts of an architecture meticulously optimized for inference, featuring FlashAttention and multi-query capabilities. This powerful model is made accessible under the TII Falcon LLM License, enabling its utilization for commercial purposes.

History

TII spearheaded the development of Falcon-40B, leveraging its expertise to train the model on a substantial corpus of 1000 billion tokens sourced from RefinedWeb, further enhanced with curated corpora.

Data Source and Training Data Curation

Falcon-40B is meticulously trained on the RefinedWeb corpus, which is enriched with carefully curated corpora. This meticulous curation ensures a comprehensive and representative training dataset.

Model Training Process

Falcon-40B is a specialized causal decoder-only model exclusively crafted by TII. Its training process involves extensive training on the RefinedWeb corpus, incorporating the carefully curated corpora to enhance its language generation capabilities.

Accuracy

Falcon-40B surpasses other open-source models, including LLaMA, StableLM, RedPajama, MPT, and others. Its superior performance is demonstrated on the esteemed OpenLLM Leaderboard.

Pros

- Currently recognized as the best open-source language model available, setting a new standard of excellence.
- Delivers an optimized architecture designed specifically for efficient inference, incorporating FlashAttention and multi-query functionalities.
- Facilitates commercial use under the TII Falcon LLM License, fostering practical applications and innovation.

Cons

- As a raw, pre-trained model, fine-tuning is recommended to tailor it to specific use cases. This process optimizes the model's performance for targeted applications, ensuring optimal results.

StarCoder: Empowering Developers with Code Generation

StarCoder is a sophisticated language model trained on an extensive corpus of 15.5 billion parameters. Its training dataset, sourced from The Stack (v1.2), encompasses over 80 programming languages while excluding opt-out requests. StarCoder is purpose-built to generate code and provide invaluable assistance across a wide range of programming tasks.

Overview

StarCoder stands as a powerful language model explicitly designed to comprehend and generate code in multiple programming languages. Its capabilities extend to aiding developers with code completion, bug fixing, and code generation, streamlining the development process.

History

BigCode, a prominent organization specializing in AI models for programming tasks, spearheaded the development of StarCoder. The model draws from a diverse dataset known as The Stack (v1.2), a vast compilation of code snippets originating from over 80 programming languages.

Data Source and Training Data Curation

StarCoder's training draws extensively from The Stack (v1.2), a meticulously curated dataset of code samples from over 80 programming languages. The dataset is thoughtfully curated, excluding opt-out requests, to ensure that the model respects the preferences of developers who do not wish their code to be utilized for training purposes.

Model Training Process

StarCoder leverages a transformer-based architecture and undergoes rigorous training on a comprehensive dataset containing codes from diverse programming languages. Although explicit details regarding the model training process are not available, it adheres to established practices commonly employed in training transformer-based language models.

Accuracy

The accuracy of StarCoder is contingent upon the specific programming task at hand. It is purposefully engineered to excel in various programming tasks, ranging from code completion to bug fixing and code generation, empowering developers throughout the software development lifecycle.

Pros

- Trained on an extensive and diverse dataset of code from over 80 programming languages.
- Designed to provide substantial assistance to developers across a wide spectrum of programming tasks.
- Respect opt-out requests, ensuring compliance with the preferences of developers regarding the usage of their code.

Cons

- The specific details of the model training process are not explicitly provided in the available sources.

Replit-Code: Empowering Developers with Intelligent Code Completion

Replit-Code represents a powerful causal language model, boasting 2.7 billion parameters, with a primary focus on code completion. This model has been meticulously trained on a subset of the Stack Dedup v1.2 dataset, encompassing a diverse range of programming languages, including Markdown, Java, JavaScript, Python, TypeScript, PHP, SQL, and more.

Overview

Replit-Code is purpose-built to offer comprehensive code completion suggestions for developers working across various programming languages. Leveraging its training on a diverse dataset of code snippets, it excels in assisting developers with a myriad of code-related tasks.

History

Replit, a leading online integrated development environment (IDE), spearheaded the development of Replit-Code. The platform allows users to write, run, and collaborate on the code seamlessly within a web browser, fostering a vibrant developer community.

Data Source and Training Data Curation

Replit-Code derives its training from a carefully curated subset of the Stack Dedup v1.2 dataset, encompassing 20 distinct programming languages. This subset provides a representative sample of code from diverse language ecosystems. The training dataset contains 175 billion tokens, which were repeated over three epochs, resulting in a total of 525 billion tokens.

Model Training Process

Replit-Code undergoes meticulous training on a rich dataset comprising code snippets from multiple programming languages. The training process leverages the MosaicML platform and makes use of 256 x A100-40GB GPUs. Notably, the latest LLM examples repo is utilized during training.

Accuracy

The accuracy of Replit-Code is contingent upon the specific programming task at hand. As a versatile language model, it excels in various programming tasks, including code completion, bug fixing, and code generation, empowering developers throughout their workflow.

Pros

- Trained on a diverse dataset encompassing codes from 20 different programming languages, providing broad language support.
- Designed to assist developers with diverse programming tasks, enhancing productivity and code quality.
- Developed by Replit, a popular and trusted online IDE, ensuring a robust and reliable coding environment.

Cons

- While Replit-Code boasts of a substantial number of parameters, it is relatively smaller compared to some other large language models. This size difference may impact its performance in specific tasks.

GPT-Neo: Empowering Open and Collaborative Research in Language Models

GPT-Neo represents a remarkable series of large-scale generative language models developed by EleutherAI, an independent research organization committed to fostering open and collaborative research in the field of artificial intelligence. Available in 1.3-billion and 2.7-billion parameter versions, GPT-Neo models are meticulously trained on the expansive Pile dataset, a comprehensive collection of diverse text sources.

Overview

GPT-Neo models serve as an open-source alternative to GPT-3, delivering comparable capabilities in natural language understanding and generation tasks. These transformer-based models possess the flexibility to be fine-tuned for a wide array of natural language processing (NLP) tasks, including text classification, question answering, and text generation.

History

Developed by EleutherAI, GPT-Neo models exemplify the organization's mission to promote open and collaborative research in artificial intelligence. The models have been extensively trained on the Pile dataset, which is also an EleutherAI creation.

Data Source and Training Data Curation

GPT-Neo models draw from the rich and varied Pile dataset, a vast collection encompassing diverse text sources such as scientific articles, books, and web pages. This dataset is thoughtfully curated to provide a broad and representative sample of human knowledge

Model Training Process

GPT-Neo models are transformer-based architectures trained on the Pile dataset. While explicit details of the training process are not provided in the available sources, it is reasonable to assume that standard practices employed in training large language models have been followed.

Accuracy

The accuracy of GPT-Neo models is contingent upon the specific task they are fine-tuned for. Generally, these models have demonstrated competitive performance across a range of NLP tasks when compared to other large language models.

Pros

- Offers an open-source alternative to GPT-3, promoting transparency and collaboration in the field of language models.
- Trained on the comprehensive Pile dataset, encompassing a broad and representative sample of human knowledge.
- Developed by EleutherAI, an independent research organization dedicated to fostering open and collaborative research initiatives.

Cons

- In comparison to GPT-3, GPT-Neo models are relatively smaller in size. Consequently, their performance in certain tasks may be impacted to some extent.

Galactica: Revolutionizing Scientific Knowledge with Meta AI

Galactica stands as an extraordinary large language model developed by Meta AI, purpose-built to store, combine, and reason about scientific knowledge. This impressive model undergoes training on a vast corpus of 48 million examples, including scientific articles, websites, textbooks, lecture notes, and encyclopedias.

Overview

Galactica emerges as a formidable 120-billion-parameter scientific language model, enabling powerful functionalities such as academic literature search and summarization, math problem-solving, and scientific code generation. Its architecture, based on the transformer framework, leverages attention mechanisms to establish global dependencies between input and output.

History

Galactica was introduced by Meta AI in collaboration with Papers with Code, marking a significant milestone in streamlining scientific research discovery and facilitating scientific text generation.

Data Source and Training Data Curation

Galactica's training is grounded in a comprehensive dataset consisting of 48 million diverse sources, including scientific papers, textbooks, lecture notes, millions of compounds and proteins, scientific websites, and encyclopedias. This broad range of data ensures the incorporation of extensive human knowledge.

Model Training Process

Galactica's architecture is built on the transformer framework, incorporating attention mechanisms that foster global dependencies between input and output. The model is structured as a decode-only setup, featuring modifications such as GeLU activation function usage, learned position embedding, vocabulary employing byte pair encoding, and absence of bias parameters in dense-kernel or layer-norms.

Accuracy

Galactica has shown remarkable performance, surpassing existing language models in benchmarks such as MMLU and MATH. This demonstrates its prowess in effectively addressing scientific tasks and challenges.

Pros

- Designed to offer invaluable assistance to scientists, facilitating the creation of relevant scientific compositions.
- Trained on a diverse dataset encompassing an extensive range of human knowledge, ensuring comprehensive coverage.
- Empowers users with the ability to search and summarize academic literature, solve mathematical problems, and generate scientific codes.

Cons

- Certain criticisms have emerged, highlighting instances where Galactica generates non-sensical output and may struggle with accurately solving rudimentary mathematical questions. These limitations are areas for potential improvement and refinement.

Segment Anything Model (SAM): Advancing Image Segmentation with Meta AI

Segment Anything Model (SAM) stands as a cutting-edge image segmentation model developed by Meta AI, representing a significant milestone in the field. Trained on a dataset comprising 11 million images and 1.1 billion masks, SAM exhibits exceptional zero-shot performance across various segmentation tasks.

Overview

SAM is purposefully designed to produce high-quality object masks based on input prompts, such as points or boxes. It possesses the capability to generate masks for all objects within an image, catering to diverse segmentation requirements.

History

Meta AI introduced SAM with the intention of democratizing image segmentation. This endeavor involves the introduction of a new task, dataset, and model, contributing to advancements in the field.

Data Source and Training Data Curation

SAM draws its training from the Segment Anything 1-Billion mask dataset (SA-1B), widely recognized as the most extensive segmentation dataset till date. Comprising over 1 billion masks, meticulously curated from 11 million licensed and privacy-respecting images, SA-1B ensures a robust and representative training environment.

Model Training Process

SAM builds upon foundation models that have played a pivotal role in the realm of natural language processing (NLP). It focuses on promptable segmentation tasks, employing prompt engineering techniques to adapt and address a wide array of downstream segmentation challenges effectively.

Accuracy

SAM's zero-shot performance is highly impressive, frequently comparable to, if not surpassing, the outcomes achieved through previous fully supervised approaches. This showcases the remarkable proficiency of the model across various segmentation tasks.

Pros

- Trained on the most extensive segmentation dataset to date, underscoring the model's comprehensive training environment.
- Demonstrates robust zero-shot performance across diverse segmentation tasks, highlighting its versatility and adaptability.
- Facilitates object segmentation through user-friendly interaction, enabling users to generate masks by simply clicking or interactively selecting points.

Cons

- SAM may exhibit limitations in capturing fine structures, occasionally resulting in the generation of small, disconnected components or less crisp boundaries. These aspects warrant consideration, particularly when more computationally expensive models are required for specific use cases.

Dolly: Empowering Natural Language Processing with Databricks

Dolly emerges as an open-source large language model developed by Databricks, offering text generation capabilities and comprehensive assistance across various natural language processing tasks. Designed as an alternative to ChatGPT by OpenAI, Dolly 2.0 represents the next-generation model, available for both research and commercial use.

Overview

Dolly boasts of a remarkable 12-billion-parameter architecture, based on the EleutherAI Pythia model family. The model is meticulously fine-tuned using a high-quality human-generated instruction-following dataset, collaboratively crowdsourced among Databricks employees. Dolly is purpose-built to exhibit ChatGPT-like human interactivity, enabling seamless instruction-following capabilities.

History

Databricks introduced Dolly with the primary objective of democratizing AI for the enterprise while offering an open-source alternative to ChatGPT. The release of Dolly 2.0 expanded its accessibility, allowing independent developers and companies to utilize the model for commercial purposes.

Data Source and Training Data Curation

Dolly's training draws from the databricks-dolly-15k dataset, comprising 15,000 prompt/response pairs of exceptional quality. This dataset is generated by Databricks employees, ensuring a high standard of human-generated instructions and responses.

Model Training Process

Built upon the EleutherAI Pythia model family, Dolly undergoes fine-tuning utilizing a human-generated instruction-following dataset. While specific details of the training process are not explicitly mentioned, the model leverages the collective intelligence of the dataset to enhance its performance.

Accuracy

The accuracy of Dolly is context-dependent and relies on specific fine-tuning for each task. As a versatile language model, Dolly demonstrates its proficiency across various natural language processing tasks, including text generation and instruction-following.

Pros

- Represents an open-source alternative to ChatGPT, fostering transparency and collaboration within the AI community.
- Licensed for both research and commercial use, promoting its utilization in a broad range of applications.
- Trained on a meticulously curated instruction-following dataset generated by Databricks employees, ensuring the quality and relevance of the training data.

Cons

- Dolly's parameter size is relatively smaller compared to certain large language models. Consequently, its performance in specific tasks may be affected to some extent.

Model	Overview	History	Data Source and Training	Training Process	Accuracy	Pros	Cons
StableLM	Auto-regressive LM with 3-65B parameters, overcomes context window limitations	Developed by Stability AI, collaborated with EleutherAI	Expanded Pile dataset including sources like Wikipedia, and Stack Exchange	GPT architecture, pre-trained on diverse English datasets	Not explicitly mentioned	Open-source, diverse training data, addresses context limitations	Accuracy not explicitly stated
BERT	Transformer-based, bidirectional training for various NLP tasks	Introduced by Google in 2018	Large corpus, primarily Wikipedia	Bidirectional training, fine-tuned on specific datasets	Task-dependent, generally high	State-of-the-art performance, bidirectional training, customizable	Large model size, resource-intensive
BLOOM	176B parameters, text generation in 46 languages and 13 programming languages	Collaboration of various teams like Hugging Face and Microsoft	1.6TB dataset, 350B unique tokens in multiple languages	Decoder-only transformer model inspired by Megatron-LM GPT-2	Task-dependent, generally high	Open-science, multilingual, collaborative development	Large size, high resource demand
RedPajama	Open-source models for various tasks and applications	Early-stage project by organizations like Ontocord.ai and Stanford CRFM	Reproduced LLaMA dataset with 1.2 trillion tokens	Standard large-scale LM training practices	Varies, project in early stages	Fully open-source, diverse training data, collaborative effort	Early-stage project, limited information
Falcon-40B	40B-parameter model, optimized for inference	Developed by Technology Innovation Institute (TII)	RefinedWeb corpus, 1,000B tokens from curated corpora	Causal decoder-only model, extensive training on RefinedWeb	Surpasses other open-source models	Best open-source LM, optimized architecture, commercial use license	Requires fine-tuning for specific use cases
StarCoder	15.5B parameters, trained for code generation in 80+ languages	Developed by BigCode	The Stack (v1.2) dataset, 80+ programming languages	Transformer-based, rigorous training on diverse code datasets	Contingent on programming tasks	Extensive dataset, aids in various programming tasks, respects opt-out requests	Training process details not fully disclosed

Replit-Code	2.7B parameters, focused on code completion	Developed by Replit, an online IDE platform	Subset of Stack Dedup v1.2, 20 programming languages	Trained using MosaicML platform, 256 x A100-40GB GPUs	Task-dependent, versatile	Broad language support, enhances productivity, developed by a trusted IDE	Smaller model size compared to others
GPT-Neo	Open-source alternative to GPT-3, 1.3B and 2.7B parameter versions	Developed by EleutherAI	Pile dataset, diverse text sources	Transformer-based, standard LM training practices	Competitive performance across NLP tasks	Open-source GPT-3 alternative, comprehensive training dataset, fosters collaborative research	Smaller size, may impact performance
Galactica	120B parameters, focuses on scientific knowledge	Developed by Meta AI in collaboration with Papers with Code	48 million examples from scientific texts, websites, and more	Transformer-based with attention mechanisms, decode-only setup	High performance in benchmarks like MMLU and MATH	Assists in scientific tasks, trained on diverse knowledge, powerful functionalities	Generates non-sensical output at times, struggles with some mathematical tasks
SAM (Segment Anything Model)	Image segmentation model by Meta AI	Introduced by Meta AI to democratize image segmentation	SA-1B dataset with 1.1B masks from 11M images	Based on foundation models from NLP, promptable segmentation tasks	Robust zero-shot performance	Extensive dataset, versatile and adaptable, user-friendly interaction	Limitations in capturing fine structures, computational demands
Dolly	12B parameters, alternative to ChatGPT, text generation and NLP tasks	Developed by Databricks, Dolly 2.0 for wider use	databricks-dolly-15k dataset, human-generated prompt/response pairs	Fine-tuned on a human-generated instruction-following dataset	Context-dependent, task-specific fine-tuning	Open-source ChatGPT alternative, commercial and research license, high-quality training data	Smaller parameter size, may affect performance

Table 2.1: *Open-Source Models Summary*

Conclusion

In this chapter, we embarked on a journey into the world of open-source large language models (LLMs), investigating their attributes, uses, and the distinctive traits that differentiate them. We scrutinized models such as Stability AI's StableLM, Google's BERT, BigScience's BLOOM, RedPajama, Falcon, and others. Each of these models, with their individual strengths and weaknesses, contributes to the varied ecosystem of open-source LLMs.

We discussed the elements that sway the choices made by companies between open-source or proprietary LLMs, such as accessibility, cost, adaptability, community participation, support, and licensing. We also analyzed how these elements might fluctuate across different sectors and applications, using the healthcare sector as an illustrative example.

We understood some of the potential risks and disadvantages of using open-source LLMs, including data privacy and security issues, model dependability problems, bias and ethical concerns, environmental impact, intellectual property and licensing issues, and support and maintenance hurdles.

We also touched upon some of the security vulnerabilities and bugs that have been discovered in LLMs, such as prompt injections, data leakage, inadequate sandboxing, overfitting risks, bias and ethical concerns, poisoning attacks, and regression bugs.

In conclusion, open-source large language models present a plethora of opportunities for advancing natural language processing tasks. They democratize access to cutting-edge AI technologies and encourage collaborative research. However, they also come with their own set of challenges and risks that need to be carefully managed. As we continue to push the boundaries of what these models can achieve, it is crucial to foster a culture of responsible and ethical AI development and use. In the next chapter, we will look into the other side of closed-source LLMs, which are proprietary yet widely used and well adopted.

References

- StableLM: https://github.com/Stability-AI/StableLM
- BERT: https://github.com/google-research/bert
- BLOOM: https://github.com/dptrsa-300/start_with_bloom
- RedPajama: https://github.com/togethercomputer/RedPajama-Data
- Falcon-40B: https://github.com/Decentralised-AI/falcon-40b

- StarCoder: https://github.com/bigcode-project/starcoder
- Replit-Code: https://github.com/replit/ReplitLM
- GPT-Neo: https://github.com/EleutherAI/gpt-neo
- Galactica: https://github.com/paperswithcode/galai
- Segment Anything Model (SAM): https://github.com/facebookresearch/segment-anything
- Dolly: https://github.com/databrickslabs/dolly

Chapter 3
Closed-Source Large Language Models

Introduction

In this chapter, we will delve into the world of closed-source LLMs, exploring their intricacies, capabilities, and the myriad ways they are being utilized in today's digital age.

While OpenAI's GPT-3 has been a trailblazer in this field, it is by no means the only player in the game. A host of other organizations have developed their own LLMs, each with its own unique features and applications. From Cohere's natural language understanding models to Google's Bard, the landscape is rich with innovation and diversity.

We will also explore alternatives to OpenAI's models, such as Claude, Bing AI Chat, Chatsonic, and Jasper, each offering unique functionalities and use cases. The world of code generation and assistance is another area in which LLMs have made a significant impact. Tools such as GitHub Copilot, Amazon's Code Whisperer, and DeepCode are revolutionizing the way in which we write and understand code.

In the realm of personalized AI, models such as Poe by Quora and Perplexity AI are pushing the boundaries of possibilities , offering personalized responses and interactions. Lastly, we will touch upon the fascinating world of AI-generated media with tools such as Synthesia and Midjourney.

This chapter aims to provide a comprehensive overview of closed-source LLMs, offering insights into their workings, strengths, and potential applications. As we delve into this exciting world, we hope to demystify these complex models and highlight their transformative potential in various fields. So, let us embark on this journey together, exploring the fascinating world of closed-source large language models.

Structure

In this chapter, the following topics will be covered:

- Detailed Overview of OpenAI and Its Language Understanding Models
- Detailed Overview of Cohere and Its Language Understanding Models
- Alternatives to OpenAI's Models: An In-depth Look at Claude, Bing AI Chat, Chatsonic, and Jasper
- The Role of LLMs in Code Generation and Assistance: A Study of GitHub Copilot, Amazon's Code Whisperer, and DeepCode
- Personalized AI: Understanding Poe by Quora and Perplexity AI
- AI-Generated Media: A dive into Synthesia and Midjourney

OpenAI

OpenAI, a leading entity in the realm of artificial intelligence, is dedicated to the creation and deployment of Artificial General Intelligence (AGI), with the goal of serving humanity at large. Established in 2015 by a group of visionaries, including Elon Musk, Sam Altman, Greg Brockman, Wojciech Zaremba, Ilya Sutskever, and John Schulman, OpenAI's mission is to develop AI systems that are not only technologically advanced but also ethically sound and universally beneficial.

Operating from its base in San Francisco, OpenAI has been instrumental in a multitude of AI research initiatives, with particular focus on generative models and the alignment of AI with human values. The organization's mission is centered around the development of AGI, a form of AI that exhibits human-like capabilities across a wide range of tasks, to ensure its benefits are accessible to all.

OpenAI's approach to AI research sets it apart from its counterparts in several ways:

- **Mission and Focus**: OpenAI's commitment to the development of AGI, as opposed to more narrow AI applications, is a defining aspect of its mission.
- **Iterative and Empirical Approach**: OpenAI employs a hands-on, iterative approach to alignment research, striving to align AI systems with human values and intentions.

- **Collaboration and Openness**: OpenAI fosters a collaborative ecosystem, sharing its principles and models with other research organizations.
- **Safety and Ethics**: OpenAI places a high emphasis on the safety and ethical use of AI, pioneering trust and safety in the AI domain.
- **Broad Research Areas**: OpenAI's research encompasses a wide array of areas, including deep learning, in-context learning, alignment, summarization, and image generation.

However, OpenAI's journey is not without its challenges. The development of resource-intensive models, ensuring safety and ethics, navigating a competitive landscape, dealing with regulatory and governance issues, ensuring data privacy and security, addressing model limitations, and encouraging adoption and integration of its technologies are all part of the complex puzzle that OpenAI seeks to solve. Balancing the need for openness with the protection of proprietary interests adds another layer of complexity to their mission.

Despite these challenges, OpenAI continues to innovate and push the boundaries of what is possible in the domain of AI. With projects such as GPT-3, DALL·E, and ChatGPT under its belt, OpenAI is not only shaping the future of AI but also redefining how we interact with technology.

Let us explore some of OpenAI's most influential models. Each of these models represents a significant milestone in the journey toward artificial general intelligence, a type of AI that is as capable as a human across a broad range of tasks. We will delve into the capabilities, applications, and unique features of each model, providing a comprehensive overview of the groundbreaking work being done at OpenAI.

GPT-4 Limited Beta

GPT-4, currently in a limited beta phase, is OpenAI's latest and most advanced model. It is a large multimodal model that accepts text inputs and emits text outputs, with future plans to accept image inputs. GPT-4 is optimized for chat but also performs well for traditional completion tasks. It is more capable than GPT-3.5 models and able to handle more complex tasks due to its broader general knowledge and advanced reasoning capabilities. However, access to GPT-4 is currently limited and requires joining a waitlist.

GPT-3

GPT-3 models can understand and generate natural language. These models were superseded by the more powerful GPT-3.5 generation models. However, the original GPT-3 base models (Davinci, Curie, Ada, and Babbage) are currently the only models that are available to fine-tune.

GPT-3.5

GPT-3.5 models are designed to understand and generate both natural language and code. The most capable and cost-effective model in this family is GPT-3.5-turbo, which has been optimized for chat, but also works well for traditional completion tasks. Despite the introduction of GPT-4, GPT-3.5 models continue to be recommended due to their lower cost and improved performance.

DALL·E Beta

DALL·E is an AI system that can create realistic images and art from a description in natural language. The current version of DALL·E available through the API is the second iteration, which generates more realistic, accurate, and higher-resolution images than the original model.

Whisper Beta

Whisper is a general-purpose speech recognition model. It is trained on a large dataset of diverse audio and can perform multilingual speech recognition, as well as speech translation and language identification. The Whisper v2-large model is currently available through API.

Embeddings

OpenAI offers text and code embeddings, which are numerical representations of concepts that can be easily utilized by machine learning models and algorithms. The second-generation embedding model, text-embedding-ada-002, is designed to replace the previous 16 first-generation embedding models at a fraction of the cost.

Moderation

Moderation models are designed to check whether content complies with OpenAI's usage policies. The models provide classification capabilities that look for content in various categories, including hate, self-harm, sexual content, violence, and more.

Each of these models and endpoints represents a significant milestone in OpenAI's journey towards developing artificial general intelligence. They offer a wide range of capabilities, from understanding and generating natural language to creating realistic images from text descriptions, transcribing speech, and moderating content. As OpenAI continues to innovate and push the boundaries of AI, we can expect to see even more advanced models and capabilities in the future.

Codex

The Codex model series, an offshoot of the GPT-3 series, was trained on a combination of natural language and billions of lines of code. It demonstrated proficiency in Python and a variety of other languages, including JavaScript, Go, Perl, PHP, Ruby, Swift, TypeScript, SQL, and Shell. During its initial limited beta period, usage of Codex was free of charge.

Applications of Codex

Codex was designed to assist with a range of tasks, such as:

- Converting comments into executable code
- Providing context-aware suggestions for the next line or function in a code
- Recommending useful libraries or API calls for applications
- Adding comments to existing code
- Refactoring code for improved efficiency

Note: *Please note that while Codex has been deprecated, these functionalities can be achieved with newer Chat models.*

Accessing GPT Models via OpenAI API

To harness the power of a GPT model, you can send a request containing the inputs and your API key to the OpenAI API. In return, you will receive a response containing the model's output. The latest models, GPT-4 and GPT-3.5-turbo, can be accessed through the chat completions API endpoint, while the older legacy models are available via the completions API endpoint.

Experimenting with GPT Models via Playground

OpenAI provides a playground where you can experiment with GPT models. If you are unsure about which model to use, GPT-3.5-turbo or GPT-4 are generally recommended.

In this chapter, we will dive into the playground to experiment with these models to gain a hands-on understanding of their functionality. As we progress through the following chapters, we will harness the power of OpenAI's APIs to programmatically interact with these models, laying the foundation for project development centered around them.

Understanding Chat Completions API

Chat Completions API is a feature provided by OpenAI that allows developers to create interactive and dynamic conversations with AI models. It is designed to handle both single-turn tasks and multi-turn conversations. The Chat Completions API works by taking a list of messages as input and returning a model-generated message as output. Each message in the list is an object that has a role (either "*system*", "*user*", *or* "*assistant*") and content.

OpenAI provides APIs that empower developers to engage with their AI models and tailor the outputs to their specific needs. There are several adjustable parameters, including temperature, maximum length, top_p, frequency penalty, and presence penalty. Let us delve into each of these parameters:

- `Temperature`: This parameter is a key determinant of the randomness and creativity in the text generated by the model. A lower temperature yields more deterministic and focused outputs, while a higher temperature encourages more creative and diverse results. For creative tasks, a temperature setting between 0.70 and 0.90 is often used.
- `Maximum Length`: Also known as 'max tokens', this parameter sets a limit on the number of tokens that can be generated in the output. It is a useful tool for controlling the length of the generated text and ensuring it does not exceed the model's token limit.
- `Top_p`: Also referred to as 'nucleus sampling', top_p offers an alternative method for controlling the randomness and creativity of the generated text. It sets a cumulative probability threshold and only selects tokens from the smallest set of words that exceed this threshold. This allows the model to dynamically adjust the number of words it considers during text generation.
- `Frequency Penalty`: This parameter influences how the model penalizes new tokens based on their frequency in the text. Positive values decrease the likelihood of the model repeating the same line verbatim by penalizing tokens that have already been used frequently.
- `Presence Penalty`: This parameter allows you to encourage or discourage the model from using specific words or phrases in its response. By increasing the presence penalty (that is, setting it to a positive value), you

can make the model avoid certain words or topics. Conversely, setting a negative value can encourage the model to include specific words or phrases.

By fine-tuning these parameters, developers can optimize the outputs from OpenAI models, harnessing the power of AI for a variety of applications such as content generation, text summarization, search, and more.

Here are the steps:

1. Create an account and log in to https://openai.com/.
2. Click **`Playground`** and it will take you to the following page:

Figure 3.1: *OpenAI Playground*

3. On the right-hand side, select mode as **`Chat`** and **`Model`** as **`gpt-3.5-turbo`**.
4. Play around with the values of **`Temperature`**, **`Maximum length`**, **`Top_p`**, **`Frequency penalty`**, and **`Presence penalty`**.
5. Provide an awareness statement for the AI. This will help the AI agent to be characterized. This can be given under **`SYSTEM`**.
6. In the User chat box, type the query for which you wish to get the answer, and click **`Submit`**.
7. The **`ASSISTANT`** will respond based on the information it has been trained with.
8. You can keep adding the messages to continue the chat by clicking the **`Add message`**.

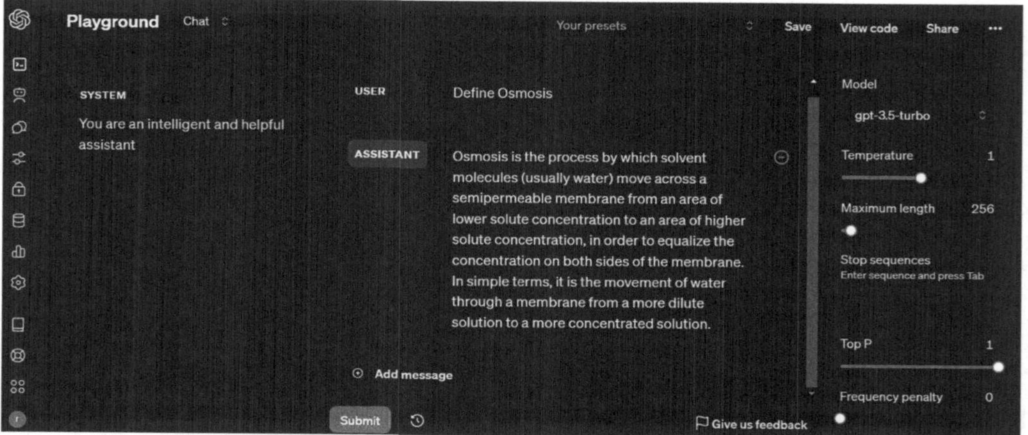

Figure 3.2: *OpenAI Playground Chat API*

9. There is a clock dial-like icon next to the **`Submit`** button. Clicking that will show the history of conversations in the current session.

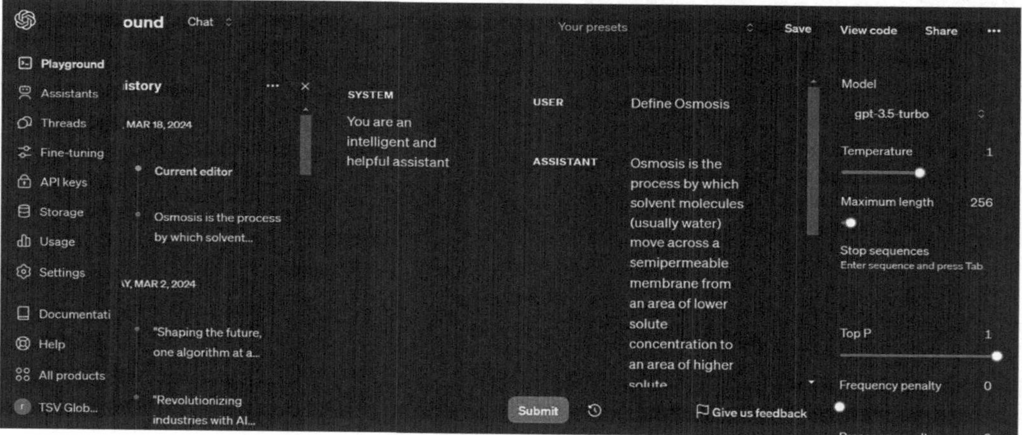

Figure 3.3: *OpenAI Playground Show History*

Function Calling with OpenAI

One of the powerful features of OpenAI's models is its ability to understand and respond to function calls. This feature allows developers to create more dynamic and interactive applications, where the AI model can generate structured data that can be used to call functions in a code.

What is Function Calling?

In the context of OpenAI, function calling refers to the ability of the AI model to generate a JSON object that adheres to a custom schema based on the user's input. This JSON object can then be used to call a function in the code. It is important to note that the AI model does not execute the function, it merely generates the JSON object that you can use to call the function.

How Does Function Calling Work?

The process of function calling involves a series of steps:

1. **Defining the Function**: First, you need to define the function in your code. This function should take certain parameters and return a result. The function can do anything you want, such as fetching data from an API, performing a calculation, or interacting with a database.
2. **Sending the Function to the AI Model**: Next, you send the user's input along with the function definition to the AI model. The function definition should be in a format that the AI model can understand. This typically involves specifying the function name, description, and parameters.
3. **Generating the Function Call**: The AI model processes the user's input and decides whether a function needs to be called. If it decides that a function should be called, it generates a JSON object that adheres to the function's schema.
4. **Calling the Function in Your Code**: You can then parse the JSON object and use it to call the function in your code. The function executes and returns a result.
5. **Sending the Function Response to the AI Model**: Finally, you send the function response back to the AI model. The model can then generate a user-friendly message based on the function response.

Since OpenAI does not provide a playground for testing this feature, we will delve into a detailed programmatic example in the subsequent chapters.

Completions API

The Completions API endpoint differs from the chat completions endpoint in that the input is a freeform text string called a prompt, rather than a list of messages. This API can provide log probabilities associated with the most likely tokens for each output token, which can be useful in assessing the confidence of the model in its output.

Here are the steps:

1. Change the mode on the playground to **`Complete`**.
2. Choose **`text-davinci-003`** under **`Model`**.
3. On the drop-down, select the task as **`Classification`**.
4. Provide a classification task in the text editor.

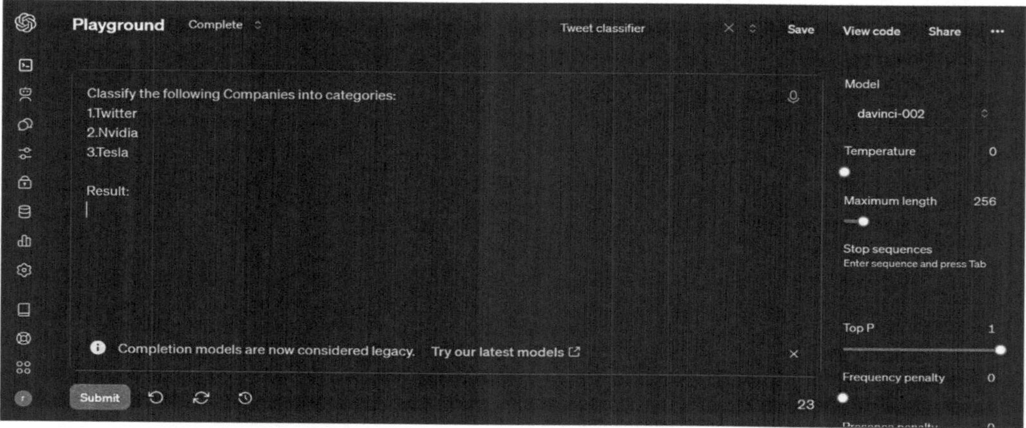

Figure 3.4: *OpenAI Playground Completion API*

5. Once done, click **`Submit`**.
6. The model then classifies the task based on its understanding.

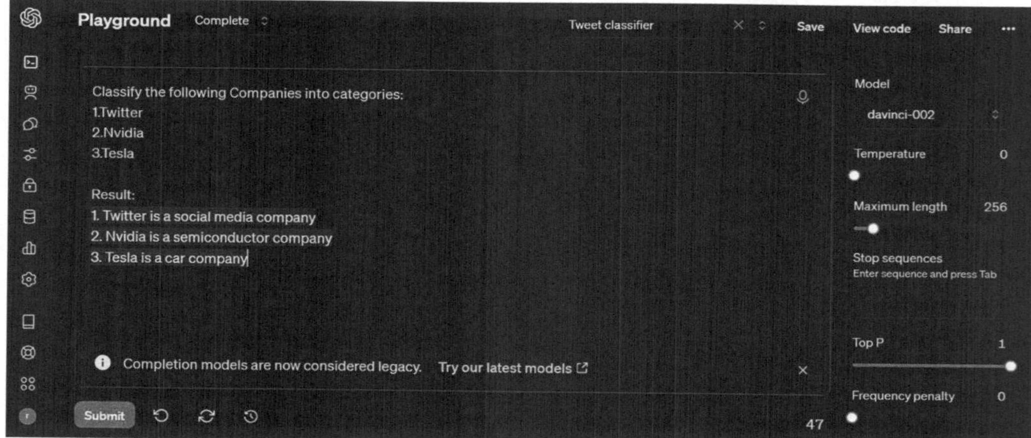

Figure 3.5: *OpenAI Playground Completion API Result*

7. When you hover over a model from the **`Model`** dropdown, it provides useful information about the model for users to make an informed decision.

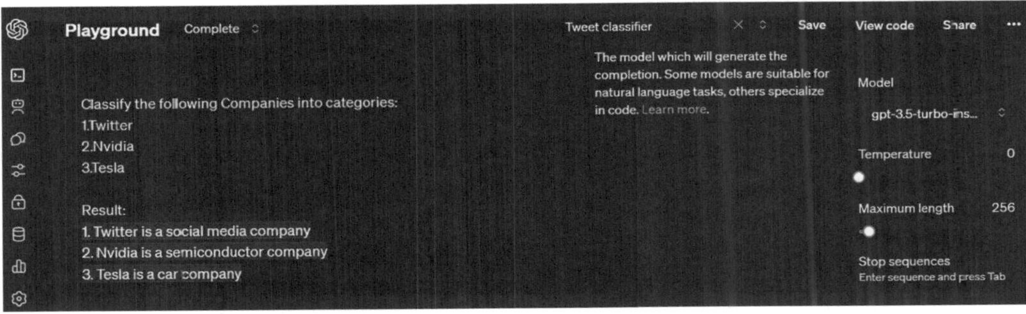

Figure 3.6: *OpenAI Playground Model Information*

8. Click **`View Code`** button. This will give you the code template that can be used to replicate this example.

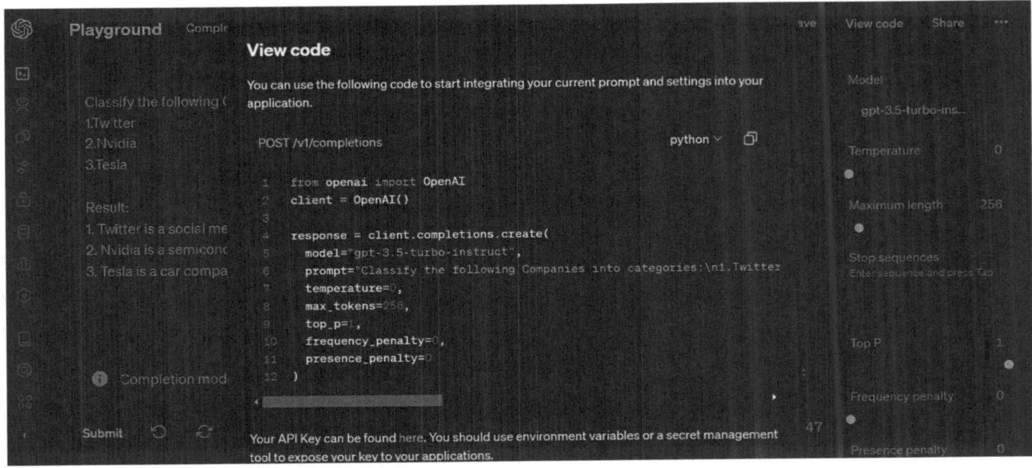

Figure 3.7: *OpenAI Playground Model API Code*

Working with GPT models involves a learning curve, and understanding the best practices can significantly enhance application performance. It is also important to understand the limitations and potential issues, such as model outputs being inconsistent, the impact of the temperature parameter on output, data storage policies, and the need for a moderation layer to prevent content that violates OpenAI's usage policies from being shown.

In conclusion, OpenAI's GPT models offer a powerful tool for a wide range of applications, from drafting documents to creating conversational agents. By understanding how to access and use these models effectively, you can unlock their full potential and transform the way you interact with technology.

DALL·E Image Generation Models

DALL·E models, currently in their beta phase, offer a unique approach to image generation and manipulation. These models interact with images in three distinct ways:

- **Image Creation**: This involves generating images from scratch using a text prompt.
- **Image Editing**: This involves modifying an existing image based on a new text prompt.
- **Image Variation**: This involves creating different versions of an existing image.

These three methods are facilitated through the Images API, which is designed to be user-friendly and efficient. To see these methods in action, you can explore the DALL·E preview app.

Image Generation

The image generation endpoint of Images API allows you to create an original image using a text prompt. The size of the generated images can range from 256x256 to 1024x1024 pixels, with smaller sizes being quicker to generate. You can request between 1 and 10 images at a time using the 'n' parameter.

The more detailed your description, the more likely you are to get the result that you or your end user want. For example, a prompt such as "*a close up, studio photographic portrait of a white Siamese cat that looks curious, backlit ears*" will yield a more specific result than a simple "*a white Siamese cat*".

Let us try out an example using the lab environment provided by OpenAI.

Here are the steps:

1. Go to https://labs.openai.com/.
2. You will get a screen like this:

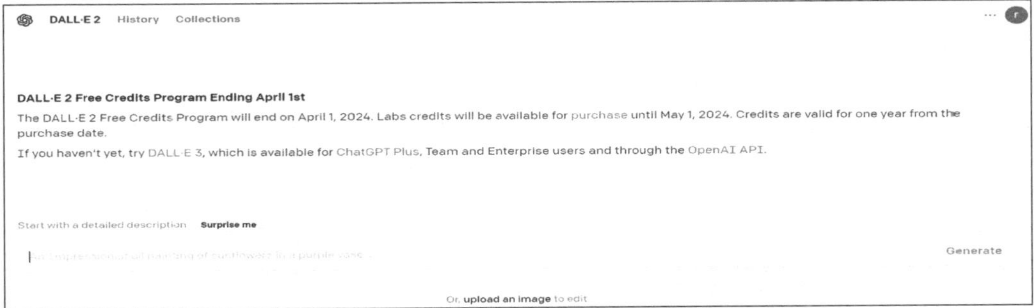

Figure 3.8: *Image Generation Lab*

3. Click the **`Surprise me`** button to get an intuition behind generating a prompt:

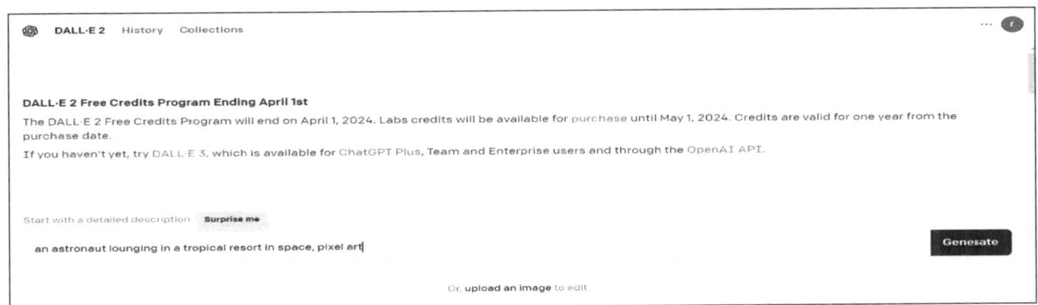

Figure 3.9: *Image Generation Lab - Surprise Feature*

4. Click **`Generate`** and wait for the image to be created based on the natural language prompt:

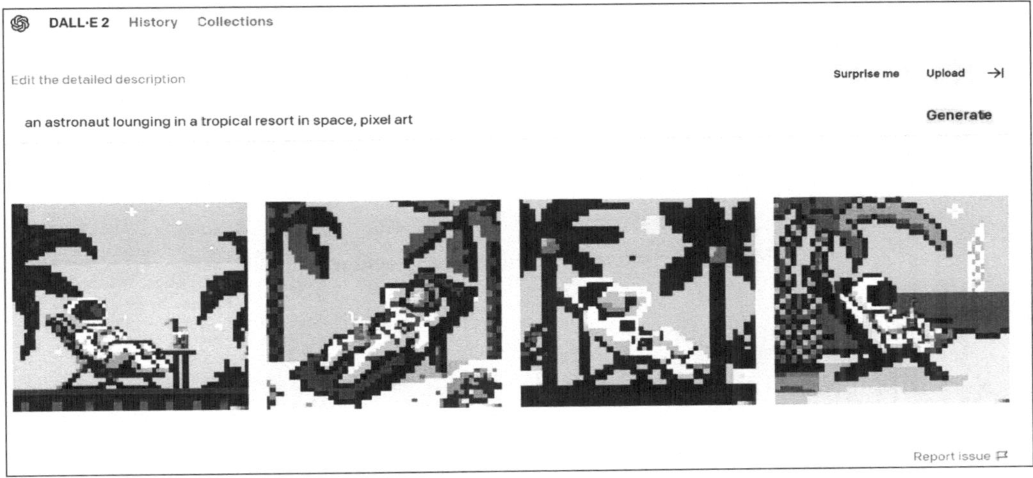

Figure 3.10: *Image Generation Lab - Image Prompt and Generate*

Image Editing

The image editing endpoint allows you to modify and extend an image by uploading a mask. The transparent areas of the mask indicate where the image should be edited, and the prompt should describe the full new image, not just the erased area. This feature can enable experiences like the editor in the DALL·E preview app.

The uploaded image and mask must both be square PNG images, less than 4MB in size, and must also have the same dimensions as each other. The non-transparent areas of the mask are not used when generating the output, so they do not necessarily need to match the original image.

Image Variation

The image variations endpoint allows you to generate a variation of a given image. Similar to the edits endpoint, the input image must be a square PNG image, less than 4MB in size.

Now let us use the lab again to edit images.

Here are the steps:

1. Click **Or**, upload an image to edit.

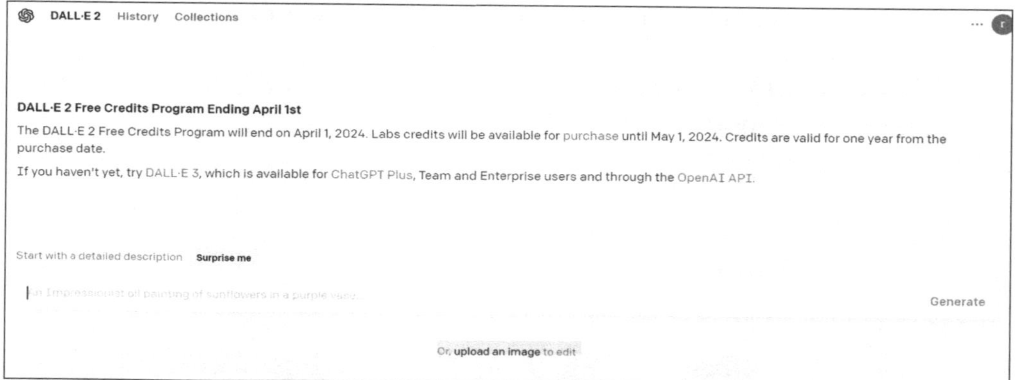

Figure 3.11: *Image Generation Lab - Image Upload*

2. Select a picture to upload.
3. Crop, if required, or skip it.

Figure 3.12: *Image Generation Lab - Image Crop*

4. You can then select between editing the image or generating variations.

Figure 3.13: *Image Generation Lab - Edit versus Generate*

5. As part of this example, **`Generate variations`** has been selected, and the output display is shown as follows:

Figure 3.14: *Image Generation Lab - Results*

Content Moderation

Prompts and images are filtered based on our content policy, returning an error when a prompt or image is flagged. If you have any feedback on false positives or related issues, these can be addressed through the help center.

Language-specific tips

For developers using Node.js or Python, there are specific tips and examples available for using in-memory image data and working with TypeScript. Error handling is also an important aspect to consider, as API requests can potentially return errors due to invalid inputs, rate limits, or other issues.

In conclusion, the DALL·E models and Images API provide a powerful and flexible toolset for image generation and manipulation. Whether you are creating images from scratch, editing existing images, or generating variations, these models offer a wide range of possibilities.

Embedding Model - Understanding Embeddings

OpenAI's text embeddings are a powerful tool for measuring the relatedness of text strings. These embeddings are vectors or lists of floating point numbers, where the distance between two vectors indicates their relatedness. The smaller the distance, the higher the relatedness, and vice versa.

Embeddings are versatile and can be used for a variety of applications, including:

- **Search**: Ranking results based on relevance to a query string.
- **Clustering**: Grouping text strings by similarity.
- **Recommendations**: Recommending items with related text strings.
- **Anomaly detection**: Identifying outliers with little relatedness.
- **Diversity measurement**: Analyzing similarity distributions.
- **Classification**: Classifying text strings by their most similar label.

Accessing Embeddings

To access an embedding, you can send your text string to the embeddings API endpoint along with the choice of an embedding model ID. The response will contain an embedding, which you can extract, save, and use for your specific application.

Embedding Models

OpenAI offers a variety of embedding models, including one second-generation model and 16 first-generation models. The second-generation model, text-embedding-ada-002, is recommended for most use cases due to its superior performance, cost-effectiveness, and simplicity.

Limitations and Risks

While OpenAI's embeddings are powerful, they do have certain limitations and risks. For instance, they may encode social biases, such as stereotypes or negative sentiments toward certain groups. Additionally, the models lack knowledge of events that occurred after April 2023, which may affect their performance in certain use cases.

In conclusion, OpenAI's embeddings provide a powerful and flexible tool for measuring the relatedness of text strings. Whether you are using them for search, clustering, recommendations, anomaly detection, diversity measurement, or classification, these embeddings offer a wide range of possibilities.

Whisper: OpenAI's Speech-to-Text Model

Whisper, OpenAI's speech-to-text model, provides two key endpoints: transcriptions and translations. These endpoints are built on the state-of-the-art open-source large-v2 Whisper model. They can be used to transcribe audio into the language it is spoken in or to translate and transcribe audio into English. The model currently supports audio files up to 25 MB in size and accepts various file types, including mp3, mp4, mpeg, mpga, m4a, wav, and webm.

Transcriptions with Whisper

The transcriptions API allows you to transcribe an audio file into the language it is spoken in. You can specify the desired output file format for the transcription. The API supports multiple input and output file formats. By default, the response type will be JSON with the raw text included. However, you can set additional parameters in a request to customize the output format.

Translations with Whisper

The translations API allows you to translate and transcribe audio into English. This differs from the transcriptions endpoint as the output is not in the original input language, but it is translated to English. Currently, translation into English is the only supported option.

Supported Languages

Whisper currently supports a wide range of languages through both the transcriptions and translations endpoint. These include Afrikaans, Arabic, Armenian, Azerbaijani, Belarusian, Bosnian, Bulgarian, Catalan, Chinese, Croatian, Czech, Danish, Dutch, English, Estonian, Finnish, French, Galician, German, Greek, Hebrew, Hindi, Hungarian, Icelandic, Indonesian, Italian, Japanese, Kannada, Kazakh, Korean, Latvian, Lithuanian, Macedonian, Malay, Marathi, Maori, Nepali, Norwegian, Persian, Polish, Portuguese, Romanian, Russian, Serbian, Slovak, Slovenian, Spanish, Swahili, Swedish, Tagalog, Tamil, Thai, Turkish, Ukrainian, Urdu, Vietnamese, and Welsh.

Handling Longer Inputs

The default functionality of the Whisper API is designed to handle files with a size limit of 25 MB. In case you have an audio file exceeding this limit, it is necessary to divide it into smaller chunks of 25 MB or less. Alternatively, you can utilize a compressed audio format. To ensure optimal performance, it is advisable to avoid splitting the audio in the middle of a sentence, as this may result in the loss of contextual information.

Prompting

Prompts can be employed to enhance the quality of transcripts generated by the Whisper API. The model attempts to match the style of the provided prompt, making it more inclined to incorporate capitalization and punctuation accordingly. However, it is important to note that the current prompting system in OpenAI's Whisper model offers limited control over the generated audio.

To summarize, OpenAI's Whisper model offers a versatile and robust solution for converting speech into text. Whether you require transcription or translation services, Whisper provides a wide range of possibilities to cater to your needs.

Moderation Model: Ensuring Content Compliance

OpenAI's Moderation API is a powerful tool designed to ensure that content aligns with OpenAI's usage policies. This API endpoint can be used to identify content that violates OpenAI's policies, allowing developers to take necessary actions such as filtering out non-compliant content.

The Moderation API classifies content into several categories, including:

- **Hate**: This category includes content that promotes or incites hate based on race, gender, ethnicity, religion, nationality, sexual orientation, disability status, or caste. It does not cover hateful content aimed at non-protected groups, such as chess players.
- **Hate/Threatening**: This category covers hateful content that also includes violence or serious harm towards targeted groups.
- **Self-Harm**: This category includes content that promotes, encourages, or depicts acts of self-harm, such as suicide, cutting, and eating disorders.
- **Sexual**: This category includes content meant to arouse sexual excitement, such as the description of sexual activity, or that promotes sexual services. It excludes sex education and wellness content.
- **Sexual/Minors**: This category includes sexual content that involves an individual who is under 18 years of age.
- **Violence**: This category includes content that promotes or glorifies violence or celebrates the suffering or humiliation of others.
- **Violence/Graphic**: This category includes violent content that depicts death, violence, or serious physical injury in extreme graphic detail.

The Moderation API is free to use when monitoring the inputs and outputs of OpenAI APIs. Other use cases are currently disallowed.

Using the Moderation API

To use the Moderation API, you can make a request to the moderation endpoint. This request will return a classification for the input text. The response will include several fields:

- **Flagged**: This field will be set to true if the model classifies the content as violating OpenAI's usage policies, and false otherwise.
- **Categories**: This field contains a dictionary of per-category binary usage policy violation flags. For each category, the value is true if the model flags the corresponding category as violated, and false otherwise.
- **Category Scores**: This field contains a dictionary of per-category raw scores output by the model, denoting the model's confidence that the input violates OpenAI's policy for the category. The value is between 0 and 1, with higher values denoting higher confidence. These scores should not be interpreted as probabilities.

In conclusion, OpenAI's Moderation API provides a robust tool for ensuring that content aligns with OpenAI's usage policies. By classifying content into various categories, it allows developers to easily identify and filter out non-compliant content.

Cohere

In the rapidly evolving landscape of artificial intelligence, Cohere, a Canadian AI firm, is making a name for itself by providing developers and businesses with access to cutting-edge natural language processing tools. Founded in 2019 by Aidan Gomez, Ivan Zhang, and Nick Frosst, Cohere is driven by the ambition to create AI systems that not only understand the world but also make it safely accessible to everyone.

Cohere's platform is a treasure trove of models, including Generate, Embed, Semantic Search, and Classify. These models cater to a broad spectrum of applications, ranging from content generation to text summarization and search. Cohere's mission is to empower businesses to harness the power of AI to streamline their operations. It offers a suite of AI-powered tools that can automate tasks, enhance customer service, and drive sales.

One of the defining features of Cohere is the simplicity of use and integration of its products. This user-friendly approach allows developers to effortlessly incorporate NLP models into applications. It also enables businesses to infuse NLP capabilities into their operations using tools like chatbots, without the need for in-house AI expertise.

Cohere's approach to AI research and development distinguishes it from OpenAI in several key ways:

- **Mission and Focus**: While OpenAI is committed to the development of artificial general intelligence (AGI) for the benefit of all, Cohere zeroes in on specific areas of NLP and language understanding.
- **Customer-Centric Approach**: Cohere is dedicated to meeting its customers' technological needs by providing accessible and deployable large language models for enterprises.
- **Multicloud Strategy**: Cohere has embraced a multicloud strategy from the get-go, offering customers a choice of cloud hosting options.
- **Collaboration**: Cohere emphasizes providing easy-to-use APIs and tools for developers and businesses to integrate their AI models into applications.
- **Scale**: Although smaller in scale than OpenAI, Cohere has made significant strides in the realm of large language models and NLP.

Like any other player in the AI development arena, Cohere faces its fair share of challenges. From developing data and computation-intensive models to standing up to competition from both established tech giants and emerging startups, the challenges are numerous. Overcoming the limitations of their models, promoting wider adoption and integration of their technologies, and striking a balance between maintaining openness and protecting proprietary interests further add to the complexity of their mission. However, undeterred by these hurdles, Cohere remains unwavering in its commitment to innovation, continually pushing the boundaries in the field of NLP and large language models to deliver value to businesses and developers.

As we delve deeper into subsequent sections, we will explore Cohere's documentation to gain a better understanding of their models, their applications, and how they can be integrated into various business operations. This exploration will provide a comprehensive view of Cohere's contribution to the AI landscape and its potential to revolutionize enterprise operations.

Models

Cohere's platform is a rich repository of models that cater to a wide range of use cases. For those seeking more customization, Cohere offers the option to train a model, tuning it to your specific needs.

Command

Command is Cohere's flagship generation model. It takes a user's instruction (or command) and generates text in accordance with the instruction. The Command models also possess conversational capabilities, making them ideal for chat applications.

Generation

The Generation model produces natural language that can be used for interactive autocomplete, augmenting human writing processes, summarization, text rephrasing, and other text-to-text tasks in non-sensitive domains.

Representation

Representation models have the ability to create embeddings from text or classify it using different criteria. These embeddings serve multiple purposes, such as estimating the semantic similarity between two sentences, predicting the most probable sentence to follow another, or categorizing user feedback.

The results obtained from the Classify endpoint are applicable for any classification or analysis task. Moreover, the Representation model offers a range of auxiliary functions, including language detection for input and tokenization/detokenization capabilities.

Rerank (Beta)

The Rerank model can enhance created models by re-organizing their results based on certain parameters. This can be used to improve search algorithms.

Please note that Rerank accepts full strings rather than tokens, so the token limit does not apply. For more information about formatting documents for the Rerank endpoint, please refer to Cohere's best practice guide (https://docs.cohere.com/docs/reranking-best-practices).

Summarize (Beta)

The Summarize model generates a concise version of a provided text. This summary conveys the most important messages of the text, and a user can configure the results with a variety of parameters to support unique use cases.

Exploring Cohere Playground

Cohere Playground is a user-friendly, visual interface that allows users to experiment with Cohere's large language models without the need for coding. It serves as an excellent starting point for users to familiarize themselves with Cohere's endpoints. By clicking the Generate or Calculate button on each endpoint page, users can observe the outputs and test their use cases. Once users are ready to incorporate Cohere's functionality into their applications, they can simply click Export Code.

Using Playground

- **Generate**

The Generate function produces natural language text in response to an input prompt. For instance, if you provide a prompt related to product descriptions and keywords, the model generates text based on these inputs.

To optimize the results for your use case, Cohere provides a Prompt Engineering guide. Users can also experiment with different temperature and token-picking settings to modify the model's output behavior. For more focused text generation on a specific topic, users can upload a sample text to train the model.

We will be discussing prompt engineering in later chapters.

The Show Likelihood button within Advanced Parameters outputs the likelihood of each token being generated by the model in the given sequence, as well as the average log-likelihood of each token in the input. This is useful for evaluating model performance, especially when testing user-trained models.

- **Embed**

The Embed function in Playground allows users to assign numerical representations to strings and visualize comparative meaning on a two-dimensional plane. Similar phrases should ideally be closer together on this visualization. Cohere's embeddings can be used to train a semantic classifier, saving users countless hours of data gathering to train a model themselves.

- **Classify**

The Classify endpoint enables users to create a classifier from a few labeled examples. This can be a powerful tool for categorizing and analyzing data.

Let us try an example using the playground:

- **Steps:**

  1. **`Sign up/Login`** to Cohere.
  2. Click **`Playground`** on the top-right corner of the webpage.

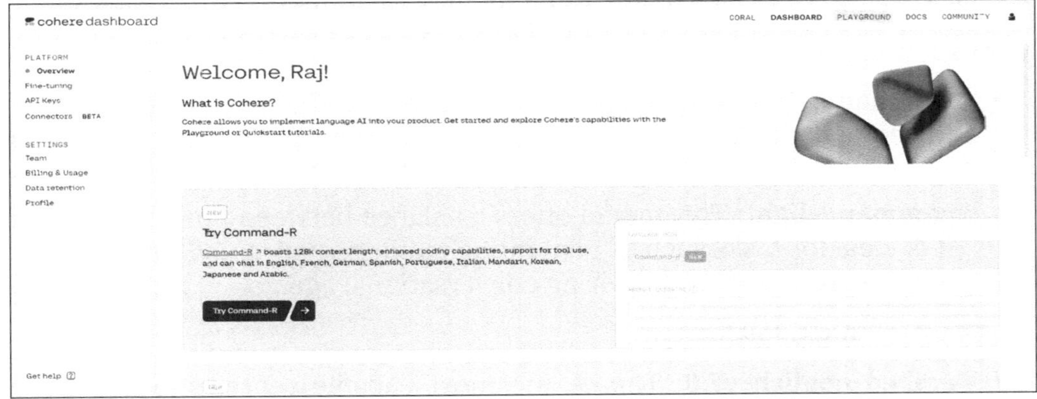

Figure 3.15: *Cohere - Playground*

  3. We have selected the **`Generate`** option and asked the LLM to write a poem as prompted.
  4. Click **`RUN`** in the bottom right corner to execute the command.
  5. The Generate API seamlessly creates a poem based on the prompt.

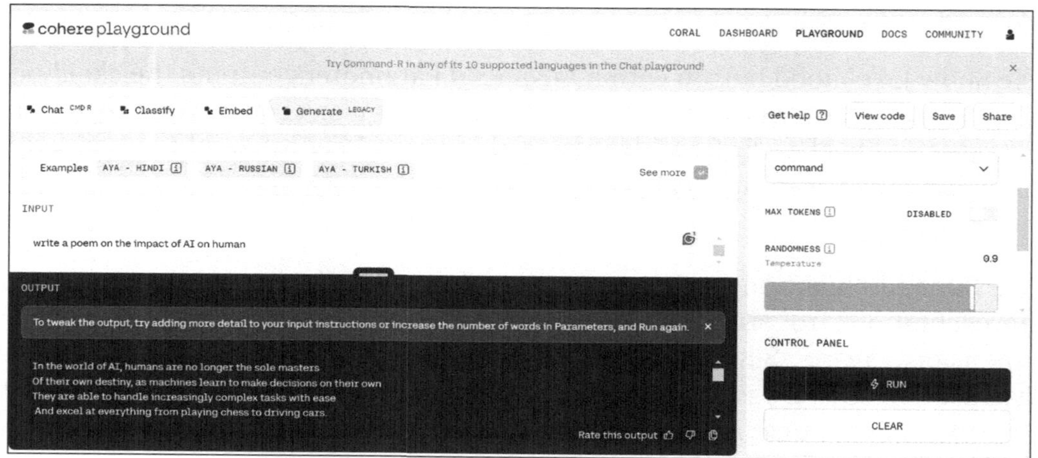

Figure 3.16: *Playground - Generate Example*

Please feel free to use Playground to explore the options and capabilities of Cohere models, and pick the one that best suits your use case.

Selecting the Right Model Size

Choosing the right model size is crucial, as larger models are more capable of complex tasks but smaller models offer faster response times and are less expensive. Here is a guideline for which model size to use for various tasks:

Generation models

- **command**: This is the most capable generative model and is well suited for complex tasks including extraction, rewriting, question-answering, summarization, conversation, and brainstorming.
- **command-light**: This model offers a balance between power and speed. It is ideal for tasks such as generating marketing ad-copy, extracting key entities from text, or powering conversational agents.

Representation models

- **embed-english-v2.0**: This is the most capable representation model. The large model performs better at few-shot classification tasks in both single-label and multi-label scenarios.
- **embed-english-light-v2.0**: This is the fastest model and has the lightest storage requirements.
- **embed-multilingual-v2.0**: This is the only multilingual representation model available on the platform.

Other AI-Powered Tools

This section provides an overview of some AI-powered tools that can be used for various purposes.

AI for Search Purposes

- **Perplexity AI:** Perplexity AI is an artificial intelligence-powered chat tool that serves as an efficient search engine. When users pose a question, the AI model searches the web to deliver an answer, while also displaying the source of the information. The Perplexity AI website resembles Google, featuring a central search bar where users can ask the AI any question.

AI for Code Review and Assistance

- **DeepCode**: An AI-powered code review tool that automates the process using machine learning techniques. It learns from billions of lines of code and code fixes, providing insightful suggestions to developers. DeepCode supports multiple programming languages and is free for open-source software and commercial teams of up to 30 developers.
- **GitHub Copilot**: An AI pair programmer that offers autocomplete-style suggestions as users code. Powered by OpenAI Codex, it generates suggestions based on the context of the file being edited and related files. GitHub Copilot supports various programming languages and is available through a subscription plan.
- **Amazon CodeWhisperer**: An AI coding companion that generates whole-line and full-function code suggestions in IDEs to help developers work more efficiently. Trained on billions of lines of code, CodeWhisperer can generate code suggestions ranging from snippets to full functions in real time based on comments and existing code. It also offers code security features, scanning code to detect vulnerabilities and providing suggestions to remediate them.

AI for Content Generation and Assistance

- **Synthesia**: An AI video generation platform that allows users to create realistic videos with virtual avatars by simply typing text. The software offers various tools, including custom avatars, video templates, and support for multiple languages.
- **Jasper AI**: An AI-powered writing tool that leverages advanced artificial intelligence technology to generate content up to five times faster than an average human copywriter. It is designed to assist with various writing tasks, including blog posts, social media content, and more.

- **Google Bard**: An experimental, conversational AI chat service developed by Google. It is designed to function similarly to ChatGPT, with the primary difference being that Bard is grounded in Google's understanding of quality information and is trained to generate responses relevant to the context.
- **Claude**: A next-generation AI assistant developed by Anthropic, a company backed by Google. It is based on Anthropic's research into training helpful, honest, and harmless AI systems. Claude can assist with summarization, search, creative and collaborative writing, questions and answers, coding, and more.

AI for Conversational Purposes

- **Poe by Quora**: A chatbot service that enables users to interact with various chatbots developed by different companies. It includes well-known chatbots such as ChatGPT and Quora's own general knowledge bot, Sage.
- **Bing AI Chat**: An AI chatbot experience developed by Microsoft, based on the popular ChatGPT (version 4) LLM from OpenAI. It offers human-like responses to questions and is designed to provide complete answers instead of a list of links that traditional search engines generate.
- **Ernie**: A natural language processing deep-learning model developed by Baidu, containing 10 billion parameters. It is trained on both unstructured text and structured knowledge graph data, which helps the model output coherent responses.
- **Chatsonic**: A conversational AI tool powered by GPT-3.5 and GPT-4. It offers features such as text creation, image creation, voice command, and questions and answers.

AI for Creative Purposes

- **Midjourney**: A generative artificial intelligence program and service created by San Francisco-based independent research lab Midjourney, Inc. The program generates images from natural language descriptions, called "prompts," similar to OpenAI's DALL-E and Stable Diffusion.

Conclusion

This chapter provided a comprehensive overview of various topics related to OpenAI and its models. It starts with an introduction that outlines the structure of the content. The discussion covers OpenAI as a company, specifically focusing on GPT-3, GPT-3.5, DALL·E Beta, and Whisper Beta. The concept of embeddings and their applications is explored, along with moderation and Codex. The chapter also delves into accessing GPT models via the OpenAI API, experimenting with GPT models through Playground, and understanding the Chat Completions API.

Furthermore, the chapter discusses function calling with OpenAI, the Completions API, and DALL·E image generation models, including image editing and variation. Topics including content moderation, language-specific tips, and embedding models are covered as well. The document presents use cases, limitations, and risks associated with these models.

Specifically focusing on Whisper, OpenAI's speech-to-text model, the content covers transcriptions and translations, supported languages, handling longer inputs, and prompting. The moderation model and its implementation through the Moderation API are also discussed. The chapter briefly discusses Cohere, its models, commands, generation, representation, and summarize (beta), and also explores Cohere Playground. Additionally, it provides insights into selecting the right model size and mentions other AI-powered tools for search, content generation and assistance, conversational purposes, and creative purposes. Overall, this chapter serves as a comprehensive guide to various AI models and tools offered by OpenAI and Cohere.

In the next chapter, we will comprehensively explore the usage of LLMs as a service for various NLP and computer vision tasks.

References

- https://openai.com/
- https://cohere.com/
- https://www.perplexity.ai/
- https://claude.ai/chats
- https://poe.com/
- https://github.com/features/copilot
- https://www.midjourney.com/

Chapter 4

LLM APIs for Various Large Language Model Tasks

Introduction

This chapter is designed to serve as a comprehensive guide to mastering the use of Hugging Face, along with the Inference APIs for accessing models from Hugging Face, OpenAI, and Cohere. Aimed at equipping readers with a thorough understanding of the expansive applications and potential challenges of these tools, the chapter offers insights into the Hugging Face ecosystem, API inferencing with large language models, and the varied use cases spanning natural language processing (NLP), audio, and computer vision. We delve into the complexities of these models, explore their functionalities, and address important issues such as the advantages, disadvantages, and security concerns when working with sensitive data. This chapter strives to offer a blend of theoretical knowledge and practical application, thereby enabling readers to effectively leverage these technologies in their respective fields.

Note: The code for this entire chapter can be accessed at https://github.com/ava-orange-education/Hands-On-Large-Language-Models-for-Enterprise/blob/main/Chapter_4_LLM_APIs_for_Various_Large_Language_Model_Tasks.ipynb

Structure

In this chapter, the following topics will be covered:

- Introduction to the Hugging Face Ecosystem
- Mastering the Inference API: Accessing Models in Hugging Face
- Advantages and Disadvantages of API Inferencing with Large Language Models
- Expansive Use Cases across Natural Language Processing, Audio, and Computer Vision
- Mastering the Inference API: Accessing Models in OpenAI and Cohere
- Exploration of Different Functionalities Provided by OpenAI and Cohere

A Tour of the Hugging Face Ecosystem

At its core, the Hugging Face ecosystem comprises several key components:

- **Transformers Library:** A Python-based library featuring a plethora of state-of-the-art, pre-trained models for NLP tasks including, but not limited to, BERT, GPT-2, and RoBERTa.
- **Datasets Library:** A useful tool for loading and pre-processing datasets meant for machine learning tasks.
- **Tokenizers Library:** A library dedicated to text tokenization, a fundamental step in preparing data for NLP models.
- **Hugging Face Hub:** A central repository for hosting and sharing pre-trained models, datasets, and other resources.

Mastering the Inference API: Accessing Models in Hugging Face

Hugging Face's Inference API allows effortless integration of pre-trained models for various tasks such as text classification, named entity recognition, translation, and more. Using the Inference API involves the following process:

1. **Select a Model:** Navigate through the Hugging Face Hub to locate a pre-trained model appropriate for your task. Models can be searched on the basis of tasks, architecture, or other relevant criteria.

2. **Generate an API Token:** Register for a Hugging Face account and generate an API token via your account settings. This token is essential to authenticate your requests to the Inference API.

    a. Steps

        i. Login/signup to hugging face.

        ii. Click the profile icon and select *Settings*.

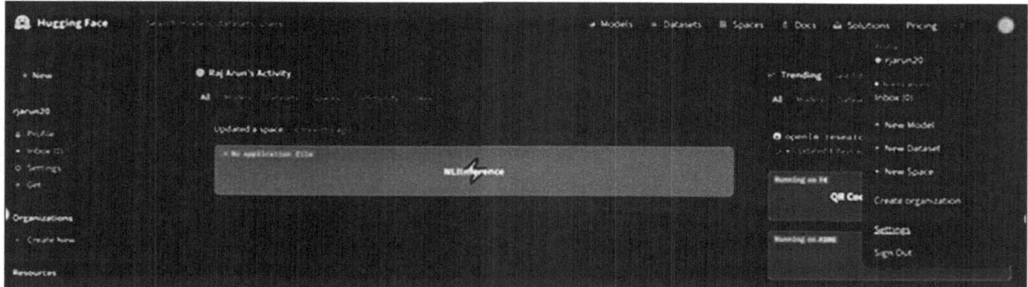

Figure 4.1: *Hugging Face – Settings*

        iii. Select Access Tokens and New token.

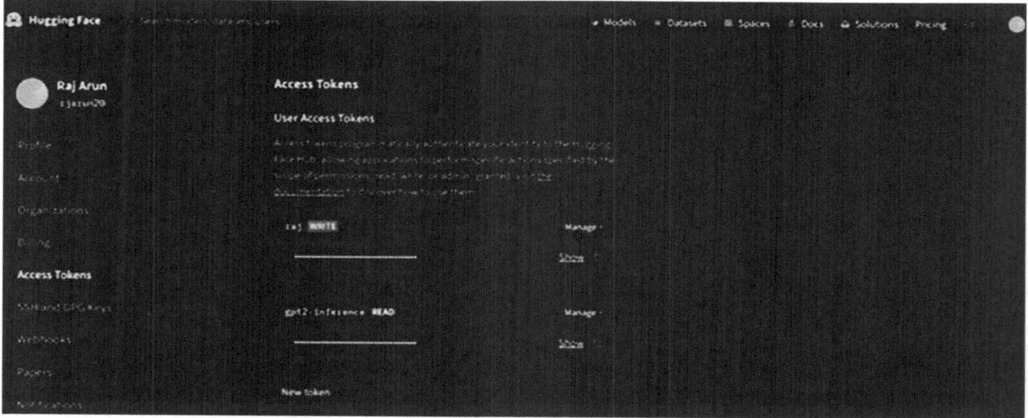

Figure 4.2: *Hugging Face – Access Token*

        iv. Click **`New token`** and provide a Name and give the Role as **`read`**. Then click **`Generate a token`**.

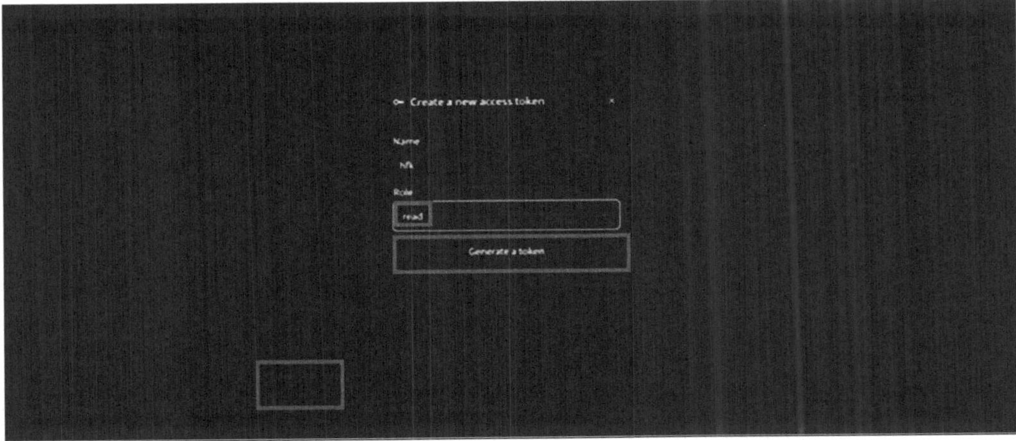

Figure 4.3: *Generate Token*

v. A new access token will be generated. Copy it and we will be using this in our exercises while using hugging face APIs.

Figure 4.4: *Copy Access Token*

3. **Make API Requests:** Deploy the API token to make HTTP requests to the Inference API, specifying the model ID and input data in the request payload. The API will respond with the model's predictions in a JSON format.

Advantages and Disadvantages of API Inferencing with Large Language Models

Using API inferencing for large language models (LLMs) provides several benefits over running the models locally, especially when faced with hardware limitations.

However, while API inferencing offers several advantages, it also comes with some trade-offs when compared to executing large language models locally. These include latency issues, dependency on external services, costs related to the number of requests or resources used, data privacy and security concerns, limited customization options, and possible rate limits or throttling. Each of these considerations needs to be thoroughly assessed based on the specific requirements of your application.

Security Concerns when Using API Inferencing with Sensitive Data

Working with sensitive data using API inferencing introduces several security risks, including data privacy and leakage, dependency on external services, potential security breaches at the API level, and limited customization. To address these concerns, you must deploy stringent data protection measures like encryption, secure protocols, and access controls, along with a thorough review of the API service provider's security practices and privacy regulation compliance.

To maximize data security when using API inferencing, consider implementing strong authentication and authorization mechanisms, use encryption for data in transit, limit the exposure of sensitive data, regularly monitor and audit API usage, and choose a trusted API service provider with a strong security track record.

Security Risks and Concerns:

- **Data Privacy and Leakage**

Sensitive data is at risk of exposure when using APIs for inferencing. This can occur through data breaches, unauthorized access, or accidental leaks. The risk is exacerbated by the dependency on external services, which may not have the same level of security as internal systems.

- **Dependency on External Services**

Using APIs often means relying on third-party services, which can introduce vulnerabilities if these services are compromised. It's crucial to assess the security measures of any external service provider.

- **Potential Security Breaches at the API Level**

APIs themselves can be targets for cyberattacks, as they are the gateways to sensitive data. Breaches can occur if APIs are not properly secured.

- **Limited Customization**

APIs may offer limited options for customization, which can restrict the ability to implement specific security measures tailored to an organization's needs.

Best Practices for Maximizing Data Security

- **Implement Strong Authentication and Authorization**

It is essential to verify the identity of users and ensure they have the appropriate permissions to access sensitive data. This can be achieved through robust authentication and authorization mechanisms.

- **Use Encryption for Data in Transit**

Encrypting data while it is being transferred between systems helps protect it from interception. Secure protocols such as SSL/TLS should be used for all communications.

- **Limit Exposure of Sensitive Data**

Access to sensitive data should be restricted to only those who need it for their job functions. Additionally, measures should be taken to minimize the amount of sensitive data that is exposed during API interactions.

- **Regular Monitoring and Auditing of API Usage**

Keeping track of how APIs are used and by whom can help detect and prevent unauthorized access or abnormal patterns of behavior.

- **Choose a Trusted API Service Provider**

Selecting an API service provider with a strong track record in security is crucial. This includes reviewing their security practices and ensuring they comply with privacy regulations.

Additional Security Measures

- Rate limiting to prevent automated attacks.
- Using API gateways as a protective layer.
- Encrypting locally stored data.
- Implementing Web Application Firewalls (WAFs) to filter malicious traffic.
- Keeping APIs updated with the latest security patches.
- Ensuring security practices are implemented across the entire application stack.
- Conducting security testing to ensure APIs behave as expected and reject invalid requests.
- Using API management platforms to secure APIs across different environments.
- Understanding the unique challenges presented by different API protocols, such as REST and SOAP.

Use Cases across Natural Language Processing, Audio, and Computer Vision

The practical applications of Hugging Face's LLMs span across diverse fields:

Natural Language Processing

Mask Filling Task

In the realm of expansive language models, the mask filling task is about concealing certain words in a sentence and then predicting the most probable replacements based on the surrounding context. The mask filling task can be applied in the following ways:

- **Data expansion:** Creating new training samples by concealing and predicting words in existing sentences.
- **Language comprehension:** Assessing the model's grasp of grammar, syntax, and semantics.
- **Domain customization:** Tailoring models to specific tasks in a particular domain by concealing and predicting words in texts related to that domain.
- **Error rectification:** Spotting and correcting spelling or grammatical mistakes in text.
- **Text completion:** Offering suggestions for incomplete sentences or phrases.

Abstracting Task

The abstracting task is about condensing lengthy text into shorter, succinct summaries while preserving the main points. The abstracting task can be applied in the following ways:

- **News abstraction:** Creating summaries of news articles for quick reading.
- **Meeting notes:** Summarizing the main points discussed in a meeting.
- **Academic paper abstraction:** Creating abstracts or summaries of scholarly papers.
- **Legal document abstraction:** Summarizing extensive legal documents for easier comprehension.
- **Content compilation:** Creating summaries of articles or blog posts for content aggregation platforms.

Query Response Task

The query response task is about finding the most accurate response to a given query from a predefined text. The query response task can be applied in the following ways:

- **Customer service:** Automating responses to frequently asked questions using a knowledge base.
- **Information extraction:** Searching for specific information within a document or dataset.
- **Educational tools:** Providing answers to questions in educational materials or quizzes.
- **Fact verification:** Checking the accuracy of statements or claims in a text.
- **Personal assistants:** Responding to user queries in voice-activated or text-based personal assistant applications.

Table Query Response Task

The table query response task is about extracting responses from tabular data to answer natural language questions. The table query response task can be applied in the following ways:

- **Data examination:** Responding to questions about data in spreadsheets or databases.
- **Business intelligence:** Generating insights from structured data in reports or dashboards.
- **Decision support:** Providing responses to questions based on data for decision-making.
- **Data visualization:** Generating textual descriptions or summaries of data visualizations.
- **Data-driven journalism:** Responding to questions about data in news articles or reports.

Sentence Similarity Task

The sentence similarity task is about determining the degree of semantic similarity between two sentences. The sentence similarity task can be applied in the following ways:

- **Information extraction:** Ranking documents or search results based on their relevance to a query.

- **Text abstraction:** Identifying similar sentences within a text for creating succinct summaries.
- **Text categorization:** Grouping or clustering texts based on their semantic similarity.
- **Plagiarism detection:** Comparing the similarity between sentences in different documents to identify potential plagiarism.
- **Question answering:** Finding the most relevant responses to a given question by comparing the similarity between the question and potential responses.

Text Categorization Task

The text categorization task is about categorizing a given text into one of several predefined classes. The text categorization task can be applied in the following ways:

- **Sentiment analysis:** Determining the sentiment (positive, negative, or neutral) expressed in a piece of text.
- **Topic modeling:** Identifying the main topics or themes in a collection of documents.
- **Spam detection:** Classifying emails or messages as spam or non-spam.
- **Language identification:** Determining the language of a given text.
- **Genre classification:** Categorizing texts, such as books or articles, based on their genre or subject matter.

Text Generation Task

The text generation task is about generating coherent and contextually relevant text based on initial input. The text generation task can be applied in the following ways:

- **Chatbots:** Generating human-like responses in conversational agents.
- **Creative writing:** Generating story ideas, poetry, or other forms of creative text.
- **Paraphrasing:** Rewriting a given text in a different way while preserving its meaning.
- **Data expansion:** Generating new training examples for machine learning models.
- **Content creation:** Creating contextually relevant content for websites, blogs, or social media.

Text2Text Generation Task

The text2text generation task is about transforming a given piece of text into another format, such as translating it into another language. The text2text generation task can be applied in the following ways:

- **Machine translation:** Translating text from one language to another.
- **Text simplification:** Rewriting complex text in a simpler form for easier understanding.
- **Text summarization:** Generating shorter summaries of longer texts while retaining key information.
- **Paraphrasing:** Rewriting text in a different way while preserving its meaning.
- **Text normalization:** Converting non-standard or colloquial language into a more standard form.

Token Categorization Task

The token categorization task is about categorizing individual tokens (words or subwords in a sentence) into predefined classes. The token categorization task can be applied in the following ways:

- **Part-of-speech tagging:** Assigning grammatical categories (such as noun, verb, and adjectives) to individual words in a sentence.
- **Named Entity Recognition (NER):** Identifying proper names (such as person names, organizations, and locations) in the text.
- **Sentiment analysis:** Assigning sentiment labels (positive, negative, or neutral) to individual words or phrases in a text.
- **Semantic role labeling:** Identifying the semantic roles of words in a sentence (such as agent, patient, or action).
- **Chunking:** Grouping words in a sentence based on their syntactic or semantic relationships.

Named Entity Recognition (NER) Task

The named entity recognition (NER) task is a sub-task of token classification that involves identifying proper names (such as person names, organizations, and locations) in the text. The NER task can be applied in the following ways:

- **Information extraction:** Extracting structured information from unstructured text.
- **Question answering:** Identifying relevant entities in a question to retrieve appropriate answers from a knowledge base.

- **Text summarization:** Generating focused and informative summaries by identifying important named entities in a text.
- **Sentiment analysis:** Analyzing the sentiment associated with identified entities in a text.
- **Data integration and disambiguation:** Linking entities mentioned in different texts or data sources for effective data integration and disambiguation.

Translation Task

The translation task is about translating a piece of text from one language to another. The translation task can be applied in the following ways:

- **Machine translation:** Automatically translating text between languages for various purposes, such as communication, content localization, or language learning.
- **Multilingual content creation:** Creating content in multiple languages for websites, blogs, or social media.
- **Cross-lingual information retrieval:** Searching for information in different languages based on a query in one language.
- **Language learning:** Providing translations of texts or phrases to assist language learners.
- **Subtitle creation:** Creating subtitles for movies, videos, or presentations in different languages.

Zero-Shot Classification Task

The zero-shot classification task is about making predictions without any training examples for a specific task, using the model's understanding of related tasks. The zero-shot classification task can be applied in the following ways:

- **Cross-domain adaptation:** Adapting models to new domains or tasks without requiring labeled data for the target domain.
- **Rapid prototyping:** Quickly testing and evaluating models on new tasks without investing time and resources in collecting labeled data.
- **Transfer learning:** Leveraging knowledge learned from one task to improve performance on a related task.
- **Few-shot learning:** Improving model performance on tasks with limited labeled data by leveraging knowledge from related tasks.
- **Multi-task learning:** Training models to perform multiple tasks simultaneously, leveraging shared knowledge between tasks.

Dialogue Task

The dialogue task is about developing models that can engage in meaningful dialogue with humans. The dialogue task can be applied in the following ways:

- **Chatbots:** Developing conversational agents for customer support, sales, or general-purpose interactions.
- **Personal assistants:** Building voice-activated or text-based personal assistants that can answer questions, perform tasks, or provide recommendations.
- **Social robots:** Developing robots with natural language capabilities for social interaction or companionship.
- **Language learning:** Creating conversational agents for practicing and improving language skills.
- **Interactive storytelling:** Developing interactive narratives where users can engage in dialogue with characters or influence the direction of the story.

Feature Extraction Task

The feature extraction task is about extracting meaningful features from text data that can be used for various machine learning tasks. The feature extraction task can be applied in the following ways:

- **Text classification:** Using extracted features to categorize texts into predefined classes.
- **Sentiment analysis:** Analyzing the sentiment of texts based on extracted features.
- **Information retrieval:** Ranking documents or search results based on their relevance to a query using extracted features.
- **Text clustering:** Grouping texts based on their similarity using extracted features.
- **Anomaly detection:** Identifying unusual or suspicious patterns in text data based on extracted features.

Audio

Speech-to-Text Conversion Task

The speech-to-text conversion task is about converting spoken language into written text. The speech-to-text conversion task can be applied in the following ways:

- **Voice user interfaces:** Enabling users to interact with devices and applications using their voice.
- **Transcription services:** Transcribing audio recordings, such as meetings, interviews, or lectures, into text.
- **Voice assistants:** Providing voice-based assistance in various tasks, such as answering questions or performing actions.
- **Language learning:** Helping learners practice their pronunciation and listening skills by transcribing their speech.
- **Accessibility:** Assisting individuals with hearing impairments by providing real-time transcriptions of spoken language.

Audio Categorization Task

The audio categorization task is about assigning a label or class to a given audio. The audio categorization task can be applied in the following ways:

- **Command recognition:** Classifying user commands in voice-controlled systems.
- **Language identification:** Determining the language of a spoken audio clip.
- **Speaker identification:** Recognizing the speaker in an audio recording.
- **Emotion recognition:** Identifying the emotional state of a speaker based on their voice.
- **Environmental sound recognition:** Classifying sounds in the environment, such as animal calls or traffic noise.

Computer Vision

Image Categorization Task

The image categorization task is about classifying images into predefined categories based on their content. The image categorization task can be applied in the following ways:

- **Object recognition:** Identifying objects in images for various purposes, such as surveillance or robotics.
- **Scene recognition:** Understanding the context of a scene in an image, such as indoor or outdoor environments.
- **Facial recognition:** Identifying individuals based on their facial features in images.

- **Medical image analysis:** Diagnosing diseases or abnormalities in medical images, such as X-rays or MRIs.
- **Content-based image retrieval:** Searching for images based on their visual content, rather than textual metadata.

Object Detection Task

The object detection task is about identifying objects within an image and typically providing a bounding box around each detected object. The object detection task can be applied in the following ways:

- **Surveillance**: Detecting and tracking objects of interest in security footage.
- **Autonomous vehicles**: Identifying and tracking objects, such as pedestrians and vehicles, for safe navigation.
- **Robotics**: Enabling robots to interact with their environment by recognizing and locating objects.
- **Augmented reality**: Overlaying digital information on real-world objects in images or video streams.
- **Image editing**: Automatically selecting and manipulating objects in images for editing purposes.

Image Segmentation Task

The image segmentation task is about dividing an image into multiple segments or regions, each corresponding to a specific object or part of the image. The image segmentation task can be applied in the following ways:

- **Medical imaging**: Identifying and delineating specific structures or regions in medical images, such as tumors in an MRI.
- **Autonomous vehicles**: Understanding the environment by segmenting different objects and areas, such as roads, pedestrians, and other vehicles.
- **Computer vision research**: Developing more advanced image analysis techniques based on precise object boundaries.
- **Augmented reality**: Creating more immersive experiences by accurately overlaying digital content on real-world images.
- **Image editing**: Enabling more precise editing and manipulation of specific regions in an image.

In summation, the Hugging Face ecosystem, with its robust collection of pre-trained models and versatile APIs, offers an extensive range of possibilities across various fields. This vast array of use cases enables developers to effectively tackle diverse problems, offering great value in enterprise settings. However, it is essential to carefully consider the security and privacy implications, especially when dealing with sensitive data. With thoughtful application, these tools can become a potent component in any organization's AI toolkit.

Now let us dive into some of these tasks and get to see the APIs in action. This is a great starting point to understand the APIs and holistically understand the business potential of LLMs.

Code Overview – Hugging Face APIs in Action

In this section, we will walk through a Python script that uses Hugging Face's Inference API to perform various LLM tasks. The script is designed to be flexible and easy to extend to new tasks.

Detailed documentation has been provided that can be followed along with the code. We will go through the code construct at a high level.

Function Signature

The script is organized around a single function, **`select_llm_task`**, which takes the name of a task as input and returns the response from the API for that task. The function uses a dictionary to map each task name to its corresponding API URL and payload. This design makes it easy to add new tasks: simply add a new entry to the dictionary.

Here's the function signature:

```
def select_llm_task(task: str) -> dict:
```

The task parameter is a string that specifies the name of the task to be performed. The function returns a dictionary containing the response from the API and the payload used in the request.

Setting Up

Before calling the function, the script retrieves the API token from the environment variables and sets up the authorization header. We have discussed how to create an access token, that is, API token for Hugging Face in the section **Mastering the Inference API: Accessing Models in Hugging Face.**

```
API_TOKEN = os.environ["API_TOKEN"]
headers = {"Authorization": f"Bearer {API_TOKEN}"}
```

Task Selection

The function begins by defining a dictionary that maps each task name to its corresponding API URL and payload:

```
tasks = {
    "Fill Mask": {
        "API_URL": "https://api-inference.huggingface.co/models/
        bert-base-uncased",
        "payload": "The earth is a big [MASK]"
    },
    # ... other tasks are defined here ...
}
The function then checks if the input task is valid:


if task not in tasks:
    raise ValueError("Invalid LLM task selected.")


If the task is valid, the function retrieves the API URL and payload for
that task:


task_info = tasks[task]
API_URL = task_info["API_URL"]
payload = task_info["payload"]
```

Sending the Request

The function defines a nested function, **request**, that sends a request to the API with the specified payload and returns the response. If the payload is a string and the task involves file handling (for example, audio or image tasks), the function reads the file as binary. Otherwise, it converts the payload to JSON:

```
def request(payload):
    if isinstance(payload, str) and task in ["Automatic Speech
Recognition", "Audio Classification", "Image Classification", "Object
Detection"]:
        with open(payload, "rb") as f:
            data = f.read()
```

```
        response = requests.request("POST", API_URL, headers=headers, data=data)
    else:
        data = json.dumps(payload)
        response = requests.request("POST", API_URL, headers=headers, data=data)
    return {"response": json.loads(response.content.decode("utf-8")), "payload": payload}
```

Finally, the function calls a request with the payload for the selected task and returns the result:

```
return request(payload)
```

Example Usage

Here is how you can use the function to perform the "**`Token Classification`**" task:

```
response = select_llm_task(task="Token Classification")
display(response)
```

This will send a request to the API and display the response.

Response

The response is a dictionary with two keys: response and payload.

```
{'response': [{'entity_group': 'PER', 'score': 0.9970178604125977, 'word': 'John Doe', 'start': 11, 'end': 19}, {'entity_group': 'LOC', 'score': 0.9992094039916992, 'word': 'New York City', 'start': 34, 'end': 47}], 'payload': {'inputs': 'My name is John Doe and I live in New York City'}}
```

Payload contains the input data that was sent to the API. In this case, it is a dictionary with a single key-value pair: inputs: 'My name is John Doe and I live in New York City'. This is the sentence that was sent to the API for token classification.

The response contains the output data returned by the API. It is a list of dictionaries, where each dictionary represents an entity that was recognized in the input sentence. Each dictionary has the following keys:

- **`entity_group`**: The type of entity. In this case, 'PER' stands for person and 'LOC' stands for location.
- **`score`**: The confidence score of entity recognition. It is a float between 0 and 1, with 1 indicating the highest confidence.

- `word`: The actual entity that was recognized in the input sentence.
- `start` **and** `end`: The start and end positions of the character corresponding entity in the input sentence. They are zero-based and inclusive at the start and exclusive at the end.

So, in this example, the API recognized two entities in the sentence 'My name is John Doe and I live in New York City': 'John Doe' as a person with a confidence score of approximately 0.997, and 'New York City' as a location with a confidence score of approximately 0.999.

Keep in mind that the response received for each API differs in metadata received and has to be interpreted in accordance with that. Please refer to the Hugging Face documentation for more information.

Mastering the Inference API: Accessing Models in OpenAI

OpenAI provides a powerful API that allows developers to interact with its AI models. This API can be accessed through HTTP requests from any programming language, using OpenAI's official Python bindings, Node.js library, or a community-maintained library.

Installation

To install the official Python bindings, use the following command:

```
pip install openai
```

Authentication

The OpenAI API uses API keys for authentication. You can retrieve your API key from your API Keys page on the OpenAI website. Remember, your API key is a secret and should not be shared or exposed in any client-side code. All API requests should include your API key in an authorization HTTP header.

Let us first get the API keys from OpenAI.

Steps:

1. Login/SignUp to OpenAI.
2. For a new account, OpenAI provides a 20$ credit which can be used for research and experimentation. Else please add payment details and enable billing.

3. Click your profile icon on the top-right corner and select **`View API`** keys.
4. Then click **`Create new secret key`** in the middle open of the page:

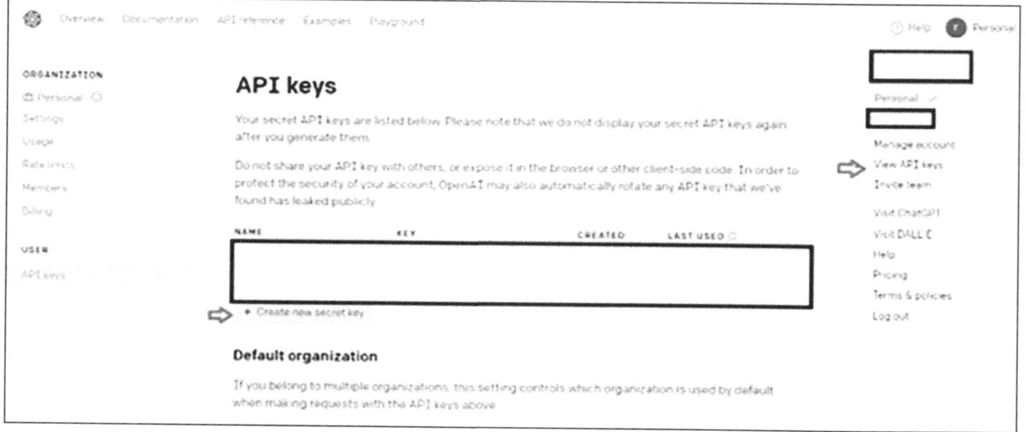

Figure 4.5: *OpenAI API Key*

5. Create your secret key and save it securely. The secret key cannot be retrieved later even from the GUI of OpenAI. The only available option is to create a new key.
6. That's it, now we can use this key to access OpenAI APIs.

Models

The OpenAI API offers a range of models that are available for use. To understand the available models and their differences, you can refer to the comprehensive models documentation provided.

List Models

To obtain a list of currently available models and basic information about each model, such as the owner and availability, you can send a GET request to the endpoint: https://api.openai.com/v1/models.

Here is an example of how you can achieve this using Python:

```
import os  # Importing the os module to access environment variables
import openai  # Importing the OpenAI library


openai.api_key = os.getenv("OPENAI_API_KEY")  # Setting the OpenAI
```

```
API key by accessing the environment variable OPENAI_API_KEY
openai.Model.list()  # Retrieving a list of currently available models using the OpenAI Model API
```

Retrieve Model

To retrieve information about a specific model instance, you can send a GET request to the endpoint: https://api.openai.com/v1/models/{model}, where **`{model}`** represents the ID of the desired model. This request will provide you with essential details about the model, including the owner and permissioning.

Here is an example of how you can accomplish this using Python:

```
import os  # Importing the os module to access environment variables
import openai  # Importing the OpenAI library


openai.api_key = os.getenv("OPENAI_API_KEY")  # Setting the OpenAI API key by accessing the environment variable OPENAI_API_KEY
openai.Model.retrieve("text-davinci-003")  # Retrieving information about a specific model instance with the ID "text-davinci-003"
```

Chat

The model is capable of generating responses based on a given conversation composed of a list of messages. To create a model response for a chat conversation, you can make a POST request to the endpoint: https://api.openai.com/v1/chat/completions.

Here is an example of how you can achieve this using Python:

```
import os  # Importing the os module to access environment variables
import openai  # Importing the OpenAI library


openai.api_key = os.getenv("OPENAI_API_KEY")  # Setting the OpenAI API key by accessing the environment variable OPENAI_API_KEY


completion = openai.ChatCompletion.create(
  model="gpt-3.5-turbo",  # Specifying the model to use as "gpt-3.5-turbo"
  messages=[
    {"role": "system", "content": "You are a friendly assistant."},  #
```

```
System message providing context for the conversation
    {"role": "user", "content": "I am from India."},  # User message as
part of the conversation
    {"role": "assistant", "content": "Wow, great to know! How can I help
you?"},  # Assistant response in the conversation
    {"role": "user", "content": "What is the GMT time zone of my coun-
try?"}  # User query in the conversation
  ]
)


print(completion.choices[0].message)  # Printing the generated response
from the model
```

Output

```
{ "role": "assistant", "content": "India Standard Time (IST) is the time
zone used in India, and it is 5 hours and 30 minutes ahead of
Coordinated Universal Time (UTC+5:30)." }
```

In this example, we are using the gpt-3.5-turbo model and providing a list of messages that comprise the conversation so far. The model then generates a response based on these messages. If you notice, the AI assistant is able to understand the question based on the current and previous conversations. The chat history in the chat API is crucial to maintain the context of the conversation to make the user experience lively.

Completion

OpenAI's text completion API harnesses the power of advanced models such as instruct-based and fine-tuned GPT-3 and GPT-4 models. This API provides an exceptional solution for generating and manipulating text. By supplying a sentence or partial sentence as input, the API leverages its instruction-based approach to predict and generate subsequent text based on the given context. The instruction-based nature of the models allows them to perform a diverse range of tasks, taking into account the provided instructions, prompts, and contextual cues. This adaptability enables the API to deliver impressive results across various applications and scenarios.

Here is an example of how you can achieve this using Python:

```
import os  # Importing the os module to access environment variables
import openai  # Importing the OpenAI library
```

```
openai.api_key = os.getenv("OPENAI_API_KEY")  # Setting the OpenAI API key by accessing the environment variable OPENAI_API_KEY


context = """
Context:
Given a text, I want to identify from destination, to destination, and the estimated departure.


Text: "John is planning to visit New York next week. He is currently staying in Paris."


From:
To:
Estimated Departure:
"""


response = openai.Completion.create(
  model="text-davinci-003",
  prompt=context,
  max_tokens=100,
  temperature=0
)


named_entities = response.choices[0].text.strip().split("\n")  # Splitting the generated text into lines


for entity in named_entities:
    print("- " + entity)  # Printing each named entity with a bullet point prefix
```

Output

```
- From: Paris - To: New York - Estimated Departure: Next Week
```

The API was able to follow the instruction and identify the relevant entities and map with the expected output format.

Edit

OpenAI's Edits API is an advanced and versatile solution for modifying existing text based on user-specified instructions. It operates by taking two inputs: instruction and the prompt text that requires modification. The API is specifically designed to edit the text in accordance with the provided instruction, offering valuable capabilities for a wide range of applications. Whether it is rewriting paragraphs, refactoring code, or performing other text modifications, the Edits API proves to be an indispensable tool. Its adaptability and powerful editing capabilities make it an essential asset in enhancing and transforming textual content.

Here is an example of how you can achieve this using Python:

```
# Import necessary libraries
from os import getenv
import openai


# Set OpenAI API key
openai.api_key = getenv("OPENAI_API_KEY")


# Call the Edit.create() method to correct spelling errors in a given text
openai.Edit.create(
  model="text-davinci-edit-001",  # Using the text-davinci-edit-001 model
  input="The text is expcted to have mistaks which hs tp be corrected", # Text with a spelling mistake
  instruction="Correct any spelling errors"  # Instruction to the model
)
```

Output

```
&lt;OpenAIObject edit at 0x7f74e0d96840&gt; JSON: { "object": "edit", "created": 1687776230, "choices": [ { "text": "The text is expcted to have mistakes which has to be corrected\n", "index": 0 } ], "usage": { "prompt_tokens": 33, "completion_tokens": 42, "total_tokens": 75 } }
```

This API has corrected the text based on the instruction given and can be extended for performing any editorial tasks over a content.

Images

OpenAI offers three APIs for images, and we will discuss them further.

Create Image API

The image generation API offers a powerful solution for generating unique and original images based on text prompts. By providing descriptive text, the API creates visually representative images that align with the given prompt.

Here is an example of how you can achieve this using Python:

```
import os  # Importing the os module to access environment variables
import openai  # Importing the OpenAI library
import requests  # Importing the requests library for making HTTP requests


openai.api_key = os.getenv("OPENAI_API_KEY")  # Setting the OpenAI API key by accessing the environment variable OPENAI_API_KEY


response = openai.Image.create(
  prompt="A beautiful lotus creating ripples in a pond ",
  n=2,
  size="256x256"
)


image_urls = [image["url"] for image in response.data]  # Extracting the image URLs from the response


# Download and save the images
for index, url in enumerate(image_urls):
    response = requests.get(url)  # Sending a GET request to download the image
    if response.status_code == 200:  # Checking if the request was successful
        with open(f"image_{index}.png", "wb") as file:  # Opening a file to save the downloaded image in binary write mode
            file.write(response.content)  # Writing the image content to the file
```

```
            print(f"Image {index} downloaded and saved.")
    else:
        print(f"Failed to download Image {index}.")
```

Output

Figure 4.6: *Create Image API Response*

The functionality of the code revolves around utilizing the image generation capabilities of OpenAI API. It takes a text prompt, in this case, "A *beautiful lotus creating ripples in a pond*", and requests the API to generate a specified number of images based on that prompt. The generated image URLs are then retrieved from the API response. The code uses the requests library to download the images from the obtained URLs and saves them locally as PNG files. This process allows users to programmatically generate and obtain images based on specific prompts, enabling a range of creative applications and possibilities.

Create Image Edit API

The image editing API provides the capability to modify pre-existing images using user-specified instructions. By supplying an original image, a mask, and an instruction, the API performs edits on the image according to the provided instruction, resulting in a modified version of the image.

Here is an example of how you can achieve this using Python:

```
import os
import openai
from PIL import Image
```

```
openai.api_key = os.getenv("OPENAI_API_KEY")

# Create the main image (red image)
image = Image.new("RGBA", (512, 512), (255, 0, 0, 255))
image.save("image.png")

# Create the mask image (fully transparent)
mask = Image.new("RGBA", (512, 512), (0, 0, 0, 0))
mask.save("mask.png")

prompt = """Create an image of a banyan tree"""

response = openai.Image.create_edit(
  image=open("image.png", "rb"),  # Load the main image
  mask=open("mask.png", "rb"),  # Load the mask image
  prompt=prompt,  # Provide the description or prompt for the desired
image
  n=2,  # Generate 2 edited images
  size="256x256"  # Set the size of the generated images
)

print(response)  # Print the response containing the edited images
```

Output

Figure 4.7: Image Edit API Response

The image edit API by OpenAI is not primarily based on the input image and the mask that you provide. The input image and mask act more as a guide or a reference for the AI model to generate a new image based on your textual prompt.

It is important to remember that this API does not edit the provided image directly. Instead, it creates a new image based on the textual instruction that you provide. The text instruction is where the main context is derived from. The API does not necessarily create an image by editing the input picture; rather, it generates a new image from scratch that matches the description in your prompt.

So, even though you have provided a red image and a transparent mask, if your instruction is to create an image of a "*baby sea otter wearing a beret*", the model would try to generate a new image resembling the description in the instruction.

In short, the Image Edit API does not behave like a typical image editing tool, it is more of an image generation tool that creates an image based on the text prompt that you provide.

Please note that the behavior of the model can also vary based on a variety of factors, such as, the complexity of the prompt, the size of the image, the number of outputs requested, and more.

Create Image Variation API

With the image variation API, you can generate diverse variations of an existing image. By inputting an original image along with a text prompt, the API generates new images that exhibit variations based on the original image and the given prompt. This allows for the creation of a range of unique images derived from the original.

Here is an example of how you can achieve this using Python:

```
import os
import openai
import requests
from PIL import Image
import io

openai.api_key = os.getenv("OPENAI_API_KEY")
```

```
# Call the OpenAI Image Variation API to generate variations of the input
image
response = openai.Image.create_variation(
  image=open(“./data/image_0.png”, “rb”),
  n=2,
  size=”256x256”
)

# Iterate through the images in the response and display them
for image_data in response[“data”]:
    image_url = image_data[“url”]

    # Send a HTTP request to the URL of the image
    response = requests.get(image_url)

    # Read the content of the server’s response
    response_content = response.content

    # Use BytesIO to handle the byte data
    byte_stream = io.BytesIO(response_content)

    # Create a PIL.Image object and display the image
    image = Image.open(byte_stream)
    image.show()
```

Output

Figure 4.8: *Image Variation Response*

The code demonstrates the usage of the OpenAI image variation API to generate variations of an input image and display the generated images. It provides a way to obtain multiple versions of the original image, which can be useful for tasks like image synthesis, style transfer, or generating alternative visual representations.

In this code, **`requests.get(image_url)`** is used to send an HTTP request to the server and download the image. The content of the server's response, which is the binary data of the image, is stored in **`response.content`**.

The binary data is then turned into a byte stream using **`io.BytesIO(response_content)`**, and finally a PIL.Image object is created from the byte stream, which can be displayed using the **`show()`** method of the **`PIL.Image`** object. This method opens the image in the default image viewer of your system.

Keep in mind that the images are temporarily available for a limited period as indicated by the URL's expiration time. You might want to consider downloading and storing the images if you need them for a longer period.

Embeddings

OpenAI's embeddings API is an advanced and robust solution for creating numeric representations of text strings. It enables the extraction of contextual information, semantic meaning, and relationships between words or phrases. These embeddings serve as valuable resources that can be seamlessly integrated into various machine learning models and algorithms. By leveraging the power of embeddings, developers can enhance the performance of natural language processing (NLP) tasks and achieve more accurate and efficient results. The flexibility and versatility of the embeddings API make it an indispensable tool for a wide range of applications in the field of NLP.

Here is an example of how you can achieve this using Python:

```
import os
import openai


openai.api_key = os.getenv("OPENAI_API_KEY")  # Setting the OpenAI API
key by accessing the environment variable OPENAI_API_KEY


response = openai.Embedding.create(
  model="text-embedding-ada-002",  # Specifying the model to use as
"text-embedding-ada-002"
  input="The rivers banks was line with beautiful trees and bushes"  #
```

```
Providing the input text for which we want to generate embeddings
)

#sample trimmed output

print(response["data"][0]["embedding"][0:10])

#total length of  the embedding vector
len(response["data"][0]["embedding"])
```

Output

```
[0.0011639235308393836, -0.003664502641186118, 0.012088015675544739,
0.015729917213320732, -0.01202344335615635, 0.022225935012102127,
-0.015277909114956856, -8.687051013112068e-05, 0.0020840850193053484,
-0.03339701890945434 6]
1536
```

Executing this code will send a request to the OpenAI embeddings API with the specified model and input text, and then display the response received from the API. The response will include the generated embeddings for the provided input text.

Audio

OpenAI provides a comprehensive suite of APIs specifically designed for audio processing tasks. These APIs, namely create transcription and create translation, offer robust functionalities for converting spoken language in audio files into written text and translating spoken language into English language in text form. Let us explore each API in detail.

Creating transcription

The create transcription API allows users to effortlessly transcribe spoken language in audio files into written text. This API leverages OpenAI's Whisper, an advanced automatic speech recognition (ASR) system. Whisper is trained on extensive multilingual and multitask supervised datasets, allowing it to accurately recognize and transcribe spoken language with high precision and accuracy.

Here is an example of how you can achieve this using Python:

```
import os

import openai


openai.api_key = os.getenv("OPENAI_API_KEY")  # Setting the OpenAI API key by accessing the environment variable OPENAI_API_KEY

audio_file = open("/data/harvard.wav", "rb")  # Opening the audio file in binary modetranscript = openai.Audio.transcribe("whisper-1", audio_file) # Calling the transcribe method of the Audio class to transcribe the audio file
```

Output

```
<OpenAIObject at 0x7f74e0bc9fd0> JSON: { "text": "The stale smell of old beer lingers. It takes heat to bring out the odor. A cold dip restores health and zest. A salt pickle tastes fine with ham. Tacos al pastor are my favorite. A zestful food is the hot cross bun." }
```

Create translation

The create translation API is specifically designed to facilitate the translation of spoken language in audio files into written text in English language. It combines the powerful capabilities of the Whisper ASR system with OpenAI's ChatGPT, a state-of-the-art language model widely recognized for its proficiency in translation tasks. By leveraging the Whisper ASR system and ChatGPT's translation capabilities, the create translation API enables users to obtain accurate and reliable translations from spoken language to text in English.

Here is an example of how you can achieve this using Python:

```
import os

import openai

openai.api_key = os.getenv("OPENAI_API_KEY")  # Setting the OpenAI API key by accessing the environment variable OPENAI_API_KEY

audio_file = open("german.m4a", "rb")  # Opening the audio file in binary mode

transcript = openai.Audio.translate("whisper-1", audio_file)  # Calling the translate method of the Audio class to translate the audio file
```

Moderation

OpenAI provides a moderation API that serves as a valuable resource for developers to ensure the compliance of their AI model-generated content with

OpenAI's usage policies. The create moderation API is specifically designed to verify whether the input and output content of OpenAI API calls aligns with these policies, effectively identifying any content that may be deemed inappropriate or harmful. This API empowers developers to proactively moderate and filter content to maintain a safe and respectful environment for users. By leveraging the create moderation API, developers can mitigate risks associated with potential policy violations and ensure that the content generated by their AI models meets the desired standards of quality and appropriateness.

Create Moderation

The moderation API offers an extensive range of content detection capabilities, enabling developers to identify and classify content across multiple categories including hate speech, threats, self-harm, sexual content, violence, and graphic violence. By leveraging the create moderation API, developers can integrate a robust moderation layer into their AI implementations. This ensures that the content generated by their applications adheres to safety and appropriateness guidelines, creating a secure and user-friendly environment for their users. The moderation API acts as a valuable tool in maintaining the integrity and responsible usage of AI models, empowering developers to proactively address potential issues and deliver content that aligns with ethical and community standards.

Here is an example of how you can achieve this using Python:

```
import os

import openai

openai.api_key = os.getenv("OPENAI_API_KEY")  # Setting the OpenAI API
key by accessing the environment variable OPENAI_API_KEY

openai.Moderation.create(

  input="I want to knock him down and hurt him badly",  # Specifying the
input content to be checked by the moderation API

)
```

Output


```
"model": "text-moderation-004", "results": [ { "flagged": true, "catego-
ries": { "sexual": false, "hate": false, "violence": true, "self-harm":
false, "sexual/minors": false, "hate/threatening": false, "violence/
graphic": false }, "category_scores": { "sexual": 0.00014459451, "hate":
0.03163073, "violence": 0.9959437, "self-harm": 4.924251e-10, "sexu-
al/minors": 9.606293e-08, "hate/threatening": 0.0014658701, "violence/
graphic": 0.00018577298 }
```

Based on the response, we were able to flag the content as '`violent`'. Such tags can act as effective content filters and autonomously monitor any content that gets published.

Mastering the Inference API: Accessing Models in Cohere

Cohere is an innovative AI platform that specializes in the development and utilization of large language models (LLMs) with a strong focus on providing natural language processing (NLP) services. Through a user-friendly API, Cohere enables seamless integration of their advanced LLMs into diverse systems, empowering developers to harness their capabilities for a multitude of text-based tasks. These tasks include, but are not limited to, summarization, content generation, semantic search, and classification.

One of the key strengths of Cohere's models lies in their exceptional ability to comprehend the meaning, sentiment, and intent behind words. This proficiency makes them highly suitable for a broad range of applications such as chatbots, content creation, and automation of customer support services. By leveraging Cohere's platform, developers gain access to cutting-edge AI research and a comprehensive suite of tools. This enables them to construct intelligent applications that possess the capacity to efficiently process and comprehend human language, thereby enhancing the overall user experience and functionality of their systems.

Installation

The Python SDK can be installed via the following command:

```
pip install cohere
```

Authentication

The Cohere API uses API keys for authentication. You can retrieve your API key from your API Keys page on the Cohere website. Remember, your API key is secret and should not be shared or exposed in any client-side code. All API requests should include your API key in an authorization HTTP header.

Let us first get the API keys from Cohere.

Steps:

1. Start by logging in or signing up to Cohere's platform.
2. Visit the website at https://dashboard.cohere.ai/.

3. Navigate to the settings section and click **`API Keys`**.
4. Cohere offers two types of API keys: trial and production keys. The production keys are intended for production-grade implementations and applications, requiring billing setup. On the other hand, trial keys are designed for exploration purposes and are subject to rate limitations.
5. By default, a trial key is generated for you. It is important to note that, unlike OpenAI, Cohere allows users to retrieve lost keys.

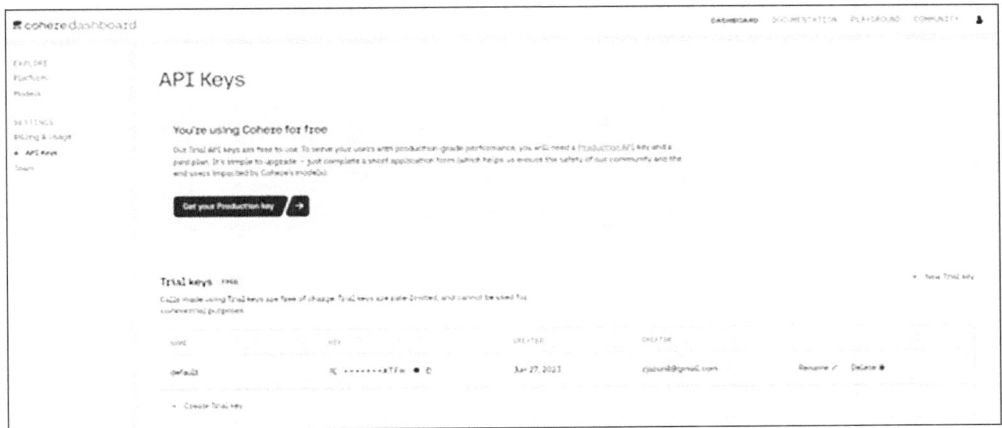

Figure 4.9*: Cohere API Keys*

7. That's it! Now you can utilize the generated API key to access the diverse range of Cohere APIs and leverage their functionality.

`Co.Generate`

Cohere offers **`Co.Generate`**, an API endpoint that enables developers to generate authentic text based on a provided input. By utilizing a POST request to the following URL: https://api.cohere.ai/v1/generate, developers can harness the power of Cohere's expansive language models to produce text completions that are contextually relevant and logically coherent.

The **`Co.Generate`** API endpoint proves beneficial across a diverse range of applications, including content generation, chatbot development, and creative writing assistance. To leverage this functionality, developers simply need to supply a prompt or text input as the basis, and in return, the API will generate a text completion that seamlessly aligns with the context and style of the original input.

Here's an example of how you can achieve this using Python:

```
import cohere  # Import the "cohere" module to interact with Cohere's API

    co = cohere.Client(os.getenv("<<apiKey>>"))  # Create a client
    object by initializing a Cohere client using the API key stored
    in the environment variable

    response = co.generate(
      prompt='Explain future of LLM like i am 5',  # Set the prompt
    for generating text: "Explain future of LLM like I am 5"
      max_tokens=200  # Set the maximum length of the generated text
    to 200 tokens
    )

    print(response)  # Print the generated text response
```

Output

```
    [cohere.Generation {      id: 72c2a9ca-29c4-4984-960d-96fd268b-
f7ea  prompt: Explain future of LLM like i am 5     text: The future
of LLM is difficult to predict, as the field is constantly evolving and
developing new technologies. However, some possible future directions
for LLM include: 1. continued development of large language models that
can generate increasingly complex and sophisticated text 2. development
of language models that can be customized for specific tasks or domains
3. use of language models in applications such as language translation,
text summarization, and text classification 4. continued research into
the use of language models for artificial intelligence and machine learn-
ing applications Overall, the future of LLM is likely to be shaped by
the development of new technologies and the use of language models in
a variety of applications.      likelihood: None   finish_reason: None
token_likelihoods: None }]
```

The code snippet utilizes the Cohere API to generate text based on a prompt. After importing the "`Cohere`" module, a client object is created using the Cohere API key stored in an environment variable. The **`co.generate()`** function is then called with a prompt that asks to explain the future of LLM as if explaining to a 5-year-old. The maximum length of the generated text is set to 200 tokens. The response from the API call is printed, which provides insights into the possible future directions of LLM, including the development of more sophisticated language models, customization for specific tasks, and utilization in various applications such as translation and summarization. The future of LLM is expected to be shaped by advancements in technology and the wide-ranging applications of language models.

Co.Embed

Cohere provides **Co.Embed**, an API endpoint that facilitates the retrieval of text embeddings. By sending a POST request to https://api.cohere.ai/v1/embed, developers gain access to a collection of floating-point numbers that encapsulate semantic information pertaining to the given text.

Text embeddings have diverse applications, including the creation of text classifiers and the enhancement of semantic search capabilities. An embedding represents textual data as numerical values, enabling tasks such as measuring similarity, clustering documents, and training machine learning models.

To utilize the **Co.Embed** API, developers must provide the text input, and in return, the API will furnish the corresponding text embeddings. For comprehensive guidance on embeddings and their effective utilization, developers can consult the Cohere documentation, specifically the Semantic Search Guide, which delves deeper into the topic.

Here is an example of how you can achieve this using Python:

```
import cohere  # Import the "cohere" module to interact with Co-
here's API


co = cohere.Client(os.getenv("<<apiKey>>"))  # Create a client
object by initializing a Cohere client using the API key stored
in the environment variable


response = co.embed(
texts=['hello', 'goodbye'],  # Provide a list of texts to be
embedded: ['hello', 'goodbye']
model='embed-english-light-v2.0',  # Specify the model to be used
for embedding: 'embed-english-light-v2.0')


print(response)  # Print the response, which includes the embed-
dings


print("embeddings length:", len(response.embeddings[0]))  # Print
the length of the embeddings
```

Output

```
cohere.Embeddings {embeddings: [[-0.16711426, -1.2080078, ....., 0.15039062, 1.8398438, -1.1650391, 1.4277344, -0.30151367, -0.45239258, -0.020019531, -0.1640625, 0.77734375, -1.578125]]
compressed_embeddings: [],meta: {'api_version': {'version': '1'}}}
embeddings length : 1024
```

The code uses the Cohere library to interact with Cohere's API and perform text embedding. It initializes a client object using the API key stored in the environment variable **`<<apiKey>>`**. Then, it calls the embed method to embed a list of texts, in this case, [**`'hello', 'goodbye'`**], using the 'embed-english-light-v2.0' model. The response object contains the embeddings, which are printed. Finally, the code prints the length of the embeddings.

Co.Classify

Cohere offers **`Co.Classify`**, an API endpoint designed to facilitate accurate predictions for text classification tasks. By utilizing a POST request to the URL https://api.cohere.ai/v1/classify, developers can leverage the provided examples of text-label pairs as reference to classify their own text inputs.

The **`Co.Classify`** API endpoint proves invaluable for a wide range of applications, including sentiment analysis, topic classification, and intent recognition. To utilize the **`Co.Classify`** API, developers are required to provide the text inputs along with their corresponding labels. In return, the API will generate predicted labels for each input, providing valuable insights into the classification of the provided texts.

Here is an example of how you can achieve this using Python:

```
import cohere
from cohere.responses.classify import Example

# Create a client object to interact with the Cohere API
co = cohere.Client(os.getenv("<<apiKey>>"))

# Generated examples
novel_examples = [
  Example("Limited time offer: 50% off on all products!", "Spam"),
  Example("Congratulations! You've won a free vacation package!",
```

```
    "Spam"),
    Example("URGENT: Your account security has been compromised!",
    "Spam"),
    Example("Invitation to an exclusive VIP event", "Not spam"),
    Example("Thank you for your purchase. Here's your order confir-
    mation.", "Not spam"),
]

# Replace the examples with the novel examples
examples = novel_examples

# Define the inputs that need to be classified
inputs = [
    "Confirm your email address",
    "hey i need u to send some $",
]

# Use the co.classify() method to classify the inputs based on
the examples
response = co.classify(
    inputs=inputs,
    examples=examples,
)

# Print the response, which contains the classification results
for each input
print(response)
```

Output

```
[Classification<prediction: "Not spam", confidence: 0.804226,
labels: {'Not spam': LabelPrediction(confidence=0.804226), 'Spam': La-
belPrediction(confidence=0.195774)}>, Classification<prediction: "Spam",
confidence: 0.80892587, labels: {'Not spam': LabelPrediction(confi-
dence=0.19107413), 'Spam': LabelPrediction(confidence=0.80892587)}>]
```

The provided code utilizes the " **`Cohere`**" library to interact with the Cohere API and classify inputs as either "**`spam`**" or "**`not spam`**" based on predefined examples.

It begins by importing the necessary modules and creating a client object using the Cohere API key. A set of novel examples is generated, with each example consisting of a text input and its corresponding label. These novel examples are then used to replace the original examples.

Next, a list of inputs is defined, representing the text that needs to be classified. The **`co.classify()`** method is employed to classify the inputs based on the provided examples. The classification results, including the predicted label, confidence score, and label probabilities, are stored in the response variable.

Finally, the classification results for each input are printed. The output includes the predicted label, confidence score, and the probabilities associated with both "**`spam`**" and "**`not spam`**" labels.

This output indicates the classification results for the provided inputs. The first input is classified as "**`not spam`**" with a confidence score of 0.804226, while the second input is classified as "**`spam`**" with a confidence score of 0.80892587. The label probabilities are also provided for each classification.

Co.Tokenize

Cohere offers **`Co.Tokenize`**, an API endpoint specifically designed to divide input text into smaller units known as tokens using byte-pair encoding (BPE). Developers can leverage this functionality by sending a POST request to https://api.cohere.ai/v1/tokenize, enabling them to preprocess text for various NLP.

The **`Co.Tokenize`** API endpoint serves as a valuable tool for applications that require text preprocessing, including text classification, sentiment analysis, and language modeling. To utilize the **`Co.Tokenize`** API, developers simply need to provide the text input, and in response, the API will generate the tokenized version of the text, which is ideal for subsequent NLP tasks.

Here is an example of how you can achieve this using Python:

```
import cohere


#Create a client object to interact with the Cohere API
co = cohere.Client(os.getenv("<<apiKey>>"))


#Define the text to be tokenized
text = 'I love programming! #CodeLife'
```

```
#Tokenize the text using the co.tokenize() method You can optionally
specify the model to use for tokenization
#If not specified, the default model 'command' will be used
response = co.tokenize(
text=text,
model='command' # optional
)

#Print the response, which contains the tokenized version of the
text
print(response)
```

Output

```
cohere.Tokens {     tokens: [48, 3207, 9461, 8, 2817, 6109,
17017]       token_strings: ['I', ' love', ' programming', '!', ' #',
'Code', 'Life']     meta: {'api_version': {'version': '1'}} }
```

The code snippet demonstrates how to use the cohere library to tokenize text.

First, the code imports the necessary cohere module. Then, a client object is created to interact with the Cohere API. The client is initialized with the API key retrieved from the environment **variable.Next**, a text string '**I love programming! #CodeLife**' is defined as the input for tokenization. The **co.tokenize()** method is called to tokenize the text. The method takes the text and an optional parameter model which specifies the tokenization model to be used. If not specified, the default model '**command**' will be used. The tokenization process is performed, and the result is stored in the response variable. Finally, the tokenized version of the text is printed by accessing the response object.

The response object contains the tokenized text represented as a list of tokens. Each token is assigned a numerical ID, and the corresponding token strings are provided in the **token_strings** attribute. Additionally, the meta-attribute contains metadata information about the API version.

Co.Detokenize

Cohere provides **Co.Detokenize**, an API endpoint that facilitates the conversion of tokens back into their original text representation. By sending a POST request to https://api.cohere.ai/v1/detokenize, developers can easily reverse the tokenization process.

The **Co.Detokenize** API endpoint proves to be highly beneficial for applications that necessitate the transformation of tokenized text into a human-readable format. This is particularly useful for tasks such as text generation and summarization. To utilize the Co.Detokenize API, developers are required to provide the tokenized text as input, and in return, the API will generate the detokenized version of the text, enabling seamless integration into subsequent processes.

Here is an example of how you can achieve this using Python:

```
import cohere

co = cohere.Client(os.getenv("<<apiKey>>"))  # Create a client
object to interact with the Cohere API


response = co.detokenize(

  tokens=[48, 3207, 9461, 8, 2817, 6109, 17017],  # List of tokens
to be detokenized

  model="command"  # Optional: Specify the detokenization model
(default: 'command')

)


print(response)  # Print the detokenized text
```

Output

```
I love programming! #CodeLife
```

The given code snippet showcases the use of the cohere library to detokenize a sequence of tokens and obtain the original text. Initially, the code imports the cohere module. Then, an instance of the **cohere.Client()** class is created to establish a connection with the Cohere API. The API key is retrieved from the environment variable **<<apiKey>>**. It is important to replace **<<apiKey>>** with the actual API key for proper authentication.

Subsequently, the **co.detokenize()** method is invoked with the following parameters:

- **tokens**: A list of tokens represented by the sequence [48, 3207, 9461, 8, 2817, 6109, 17017]. These tokens are to be detokenized.
- **model**: An optional parameter allowing the specification of the detokenization model. The default model used is 'command'.

The detokenization process is executed, and the resulting detokenized text is stored in the response variable. Lastly, the detokenized text is printed to the console using the **print()** function.

Co.Detect_language

Cohere offers **Co.Detect_language**, an API endpoint that accurately determines the language of each provided text. Developers can take advantage of this functionality by sending a POST request to https://api.cohere.ai/v1/detect-language, enabling them to effectively handle multilingual content.

The **Co.Detect_language** API endpoint proves to be invaluable for applications that necessitate language identification, such as translation services, content localization, and language-based filtering. To utilize the **Co.Detect_language** API, developers simply need to provide the text input, and in response, the API will provide the detected language for each text, allowing for seamless integration into various language-dependent processes.

Here is an example of how you can achieve this using Python:

```
import cohere


# Create a Cohere client object to interact with the Cohere API
co = cohere.Client(os.getenv("<<apiKey>>"))


# Define a list of texts to detect their language
texts = ['Bonjour le monde', "'भारत से नमस्ते›»]


# Use the co.detect_language() method to detect the language of the
texts
response = co.detect_language(
    texts=texts
)


# Print the response, which contains the detected language for each text
print(response)
```

Output

```
cohere.DetectLanguageResponse {  results: [Language<language_code: «fr», 
language_name: «French»>, Language<language_code: «hi», language_name: 
«Hindi»>]    meta: {‹api_version›: {‹version›: ‹1›}} }
```

The code begins by importing the necessary cohere module. Then, a client object is created using the **cohere.Client** class to establish a connection with the Cohere API, utilizing the provided API key. A list called texts is defined, and it contains two texts: «**Bonjour le monde**» (which is in French) and «›भारत से नमस्ते›» (which is in Hindi). These texts represent the inputs for language detection. The **co.detect_language()** method is called, passing the texts list as input. This method performs language detection on the given texts using the Cohere API. The resulting language detection information is stored in the response variable. It contains an object of type **cohere.DetectLanguageResponse**, which includes the detected language for each input text. Finally, the **print()** function is used to display the contents of the response object. The output shows the detected languages: 'French' for the first text and 'Hindi' for the second text. Overall, the code effectively detects the language of the provided texts using the cohere library and displays the detected languages as the output.

Co.Summarize

Cohere offers **Co.Summarize**, an API endpoint designed to generate concise summaries in English for the text provided. Developers can utilize this functionality by sending a POST request to https://api.cohere.ai/v1/summarize, enabling them to condense lengthy articles or documents into more manageable and succinct summaries.

The **Co.Summarize** API endpoint proves to be highly valuable for applications that require text summarization, including news aggregation, content curation, and note-taking. To use the **Co.Summarize** API, developers are required to provide the text input, and in return, the API will generate a summary that captures the essential points of the original text. This enables efficient handling of large volumes of information and supports streamlined content processing in a variety of contexts.

Here is an example of how you can achieve this using Python:

```
#Create a Cohere client object to interact with the Cohere API
co = cohere.Client(os.getenv("<<apiKey>>"))


text = (
"Ice cream is a sweetened frozen food typically eaten as a snack or dessert. "
"It may be made from milk or cream and is flavored with a sweetener, "
"either sugar or an alternative, and a spice, such as cocoa or vanilla, "
```

```
"or with fruit such as strawberries or peaches. "
"It can also be made by whisking a flavored cream base and liquid nitrogen together. "
"Food coloring is sometimes added, in addition to stabilizers. "
"The mixture is cooled below the freezing point of water and stirred to incorporate air spaces "
"and to prevent detectable ice crystals from forming. The result is a smooth, "
"semi-solid foam that is solid at very low temperatures (below 2 °C or 35 °F). "
"It becomes more malleable as its temperature increases.\n\n"
"The meaning of the name 'ice cream' varies from one country to another. "
"In some countries, such as the United States, 'ice cream' applies only to a specific variety, "
"and most governments regulate the commercial use of the various terms according to the "
"relative quantities of the main ingredients, notably the amount of cream. "
"Products that do not meet the criteria to be called ice cream are sometimes labeled "
"'frozen dairy dessert' instead. In other countries, such as Italy and Argentina, "
"one word is used for all variants. Analogues made from dairy alternatives, "
"such as goat's or sheep's milk, or milk substitutes "
"(e.g., soy, cashew, coconut, almond milk or tofu), are available for those who are "
"lactose intolerant, allergic to dairy protein or vegan."
)

#Use the co.summarize() method to generate a summary of the text
response = co.summarize(
text=text,
)

print(response)
```

Output

```
SummarizeResponse(id='51debf3c-b857-4d13-80d1-34ae0ede0614', summary='Ice
cream is a sweetened frozen food typically eaten as a snack or dessert.
It may be made from milk or cream and is flavored with a sweetener, either
sugar or an alternative, and a spice, such as cocoa or vanilla, or with
fruit such as strawberries or peaches.', meta={'api_version': {'version':
'1'}})
```

The given code snippet utilizes the Cohere API to generate a summary of a text about ice cream. It begins by creating a client object to interact with the Cohere API using the provided API key.

The text is a comprehensive description of ice cream, covering its composition, preparation methods, variations across countries, and options for individuals with specific dietary needs.

To generate the summary, the code employs the **`co.summarize()`** method from the Cohere API. The text variable contains detailed text about ice cream. The method generates a summary based on this text.

The resulting summary is stored in the response variable. Finally, the code prints the generated summary.

The output provides the generated summary of the text, offering a condensed overview of the information provided.

Co.Rerank

Cohere provides **`Co.Rerank`**, an API endpoint that enhances search quality in applications by assigning relevance scores to a list of texts based on a given query. Developers can take advantage of this feature by sending a POST request to https://api.cohere.ai/v1/rerank, leveraging Cohere's extensive language models to rank search results according to their semantic relevance.

The **`Co.Rerank`** API endpoint is versatile and finds applications in various scenarios, including search engines, recommendation systems, and content discovery platforms. By providing both a query and a list of texts, developers can retrieve an ordered array of texts, with each text assigned a relevance score. This allows for the effective organization and prioritization of search results, improving the overall user experience and facilitating accurate information retrieval.

Here is an example of how you can achieve this using Python:

```
import cohere


co = cohere.Client(os.getenv("<<apiKey>>"))  # Create a client object to interact with the Cohere API


docs = [
    'Carson City serves as the administrative capital of Nevada in the United States.',
    'The Commonwealth of the Northern Mariana Islands comprises a cluster of Pacific Ocean islands. Its principal city is Saipan.',
    'Washington, D.C., also known as Washington or D.C., is the designated capital of the United States. It functions as a federal district.',
    'Capital punishment, commonly referred to as the death penalty, has been practiced in the United States since before its formation as a nation. Presently, capital punishment is legally recognized in 30 out of the 50 states.'
]


response = co.rerank(
    model='rerank-english-v2.0',  # Specify the model for reranking
    query='What is the official capital of the United States?',  # Provide the query to be reranked
    documents=docs,  # Pass the list of documents to be reranked
    top_n=3,  # Specify the number of top-ranked documents to return
)


print(response)  # Print the response, which contains the reranked documents
```

Output

```
    [RerankResult<document['text']: Washington, D.C., also known as Washington or D.C., is the designated capital of the United States. It functions as a federal district., index: 2, relevance_score: 0.9716717>, RerankResult<document['text']: Capital punishment, commonly referred to as the death penalty, has been practiced in the United States since before its formation as a nation. Presently, capital punishment is legally recognized in 30 out of the 50 states., index: 3, relevance_score:
```

```
0.098772585>, RerankResult<document['text']: Carson City serves as the administrative capital of Nevada in the United States., index: 0, relevance_score: 0.07329728>]
```

The provided code snippet demonstrates the use of the **`co.rerank()`** method from the Cohere API. It aims to rerank a list of documents based on a given query using the specified reranking model (**rerank-english-v2.0**). The query in this example is, 'What is the official capital of the United States?' and the list of documents contains information about various capital cities and related topics.

Upon execution, the code outputs a response containing the reranked documents. Each reranked document is represented as a **`RerankResult`** object, containing the text of the document, its index within the original document list, and its **`relevance_score`** indicating the degree of relevance to the query.

The output provides the top three reranked documents, with their respective text, index, and **`relevance_score`**. The document at index 2, which describes Washington, D.C. as the designated capital of the United States, has the highest relevance score of 0.9716717. The document at index 3, discussing capital punishment in the United States, has a relevance score of 0.098772585. Finally, the document at index 0, describing Carson City as the administrative capital of Nevada, has a relevance score of 0.07329728.

This output demonstrates the reranked documents in descending order of their relevance scores to the query.

Conclusion

This chapter offered a comprehensive and detailed overview of the Hugging Face ecosystem, highlighting its wide-ranging applications in Natural Language Processing (NLP), audio processing, and computer vision. The utilization of the Inference API for models within Hugging Face, OpenAI, and Cohere has been thoroughly explored.

The chapter provided insights into various tasks that can be accomplished through API inferencing, encompassing mask filling, text categorization, translation, and dialogue tasks for NLP, as well as speech-to-text conversion and audio categorization tasks for audio, and object detection and image segmentation tasks for computer vision.

The reader is also guided through important considerations regarding API inferencing with large language models, including the potential advantages, disadvantages, and critical security concerns associated with handling sensitive data.

Furthermore, a comprehensive code overview is presented, offering practical implementation examples of Hugging Face APIs. Additionally, the chapter delved into the process of accessing models through the Inference API in OpenAI and Cohere. This exploration encompassed installation and authentication procedures, as well as the functionalities available, such as text completion, image editing, translation, moderation, and text summarization.

Overall, this chapter serves as a thorough and valuable guide for individuals seeking to leverage the capabilities of the Hugging Face ecosystem and harness the power of API inferencing with large language models across diverse applications. The practical examples and clear explanations provided throughout equip readers with the necessary knowledge and tools to effectively utilize these technologies in their own projects and endeavors.

In the next chapter, we will work on an application where google sheets can be given the power of LLMs by integrating with LLM service providers.

CHAPTER 5

Integrating Cohere API in Google Sheets

Introduction

In the era of digital transformation, the ability to harness and utilize data has become a critical skill. With the advent of artificial intelligence (AI) and machine learning (ML), we can now automate complex tasks, gain insights from massive datasets, and even generate human-like text. One such AI model that has been making waves in the field of natural language processing (NLP) is Cohere. It can be used for a variety of tasks such as drafting emails, writing code, creating written content, answering questions, tutoring in a variety of subjects, translating languages, simulating characters for video games, and much more. The possibilities are endless, and the applications are only limited by our imagination.

In this chapter, we will explore how to leverage the power of Cohere APIs to perform tasks such as text classification, text generation, and text summarization. We will be integrating these APIs with Google Sheets using Google Apps Script, a rapid application development platform that makes it fast and easy to create business applications that integrate with Google Workspace.

Google Sheets is a web-based spreadsheet program that is part of the Google Workspace suite of tools. It allows users to create, update, and modify spreadsheets and share them with others. Google Apps Script, on the other hand, is a JavaScript-based scripting language that allows you to automate tasks across Google products, including Google Sheets.

The combination of Google Sheets, Google Apps Script, and Cohere APIs provides a powerful toolset for automating tasks, analyzing data, and generating insights. Whether you're a business analyst looking to automate data analysis tasks, a content creator in need of generating text, or a developer looking to build complex applications, this chapter will provide you with the knowledge and skills you need to harness the power of these tools.

In the following sections, we will delve into the specifics of each use case, starting with a brief introduction, followed by a detailed walkthrough of the code, and finally, testing the use cases to ensure they work as expected. We will also cover the prerequisites needed to follow along with this chapter, including setting up Google Sheets and Google Apps Script and obtaining the Cohere API key.

By the end of this chapter, you will have a solid understanding of how to use Cohere APIs with Google Sheets and Google Apps Script, and you will be equipped with the skills to apply these tools to your own projects and use cases. So, let's get started on this exciting journey of exploring the power of AI with Cohere and Google Workspace!

The Google sheet with examples and code can be found here: (https://docs.google.com/spreadsheets/d/1Q7FfwxnerV3oouIfbABZ5TnDX-eegBv27_5Px38rJIg/edit?usp=sharing)

Structure

In this chapter, we will cover the following topics:

- Introduction to Google Sheets and Google Apps Script
- Understanding the Use Cases
- Use Cases Development and Testing
- Best Practices and Tips

Introduction to Google Sheets

Google Sheets is a powerful, web-based spreadsheet program that forms part of the Google Workspace suite of productivity tools. It is designed to enable users to create, format, and work on spreadsheets simultaneously with other collaborators, regardless of their geographical location.

Google Sheets supports a wide range of functionalities that are common in most spreadsheet software, such as creating and editing cells, using formulas to perform calculations, generating graphs and charts for data visualization, and much more. However, what sets Google Sheets apart from traditional spreadsheet software is its cloud-based nature, which allows for real-time collaboration and sharing, automatic saving and versioning, and seamless integration with other Google Workspace applications like Google Docs and Google Slides.

In addition to these features, Google Sheets also supports the use of Google Apps Script, a powerful tool that can be used to automate tasks, customize applications, and interact with other Google Workspace services. This makes Google Sheets not just a spreadsheet program, but a versatile platform for data analysis, project management, and even application development.

Introduction to Google Apps Script

Google Apps Script is a cloud-based scripting language for lightweight application development in the Google Workspace platform. It is based on JavaScript and provides easy ways to automate tasks across Google products and third-party services.

With Google Apps Script, you can create custom functions for Google Sheets, automate repetitive tasks, integrate with external APIs, and create user interfaces for your scripts. You can even build web applications and publish them to the Google Workspace Marketplace.

Google Apps Script has access to built-in libraries for Google Workspace, which means you can easily interact with data in Google Sheets, Google Docs, Gmail, Google Calendar, and more. You can also connect to external APIs, databases, and other services that provide a web-based API.

One of the key advantages of Google Apps Script is that it runs on Google's servers. This means you don't have to worry about setting up any infrastructure or servers to run your scripts. You can write your code directly in the Apps Script Editor, and Google handles the execution, server management, and scaling for you.

In the context of our chapter, we will be using Google Apps Script to interact with the Cohere API and perform tasks such as text classification, text generation, and text summarization directly within Google Sheets. This will allow us to create a powerful tool that leverages the capabilities of AI and machine learning, all within the familiar and accessible interface of Google Sheets.

In the next sections, we will delve deeper into the specifics of setting up Google Sheets and Google Apps Script, obtaining the Cohere API key, and building our custom functions. So, let's move forward and start exploring these exciting possibilities!

Understanding the Use Cases

In this section, we will delve into the specific use cases that will be addressed using Google Sheets, Google Apps Script, and the Cohere API. These use cases revolve around three key functionalities: text classification, text generation, and text summarization. Let's explore each of these in detail.

Text Classification

Text classification is a common task in natural language processing (NLP) that involves categorizing text into predefined classes. This can be useful in a variety of applications, such as spam detection, sentiment analysis, and topic labeling.

In our case, we will be using the Cohere API's text classification functionality to classify a set of input texts based on a set of examples. For instance, we could classify a list of customer reviews into categories like "**Positive**", "**Negative**", and "**Neutral**", or categorize a set of documents into topics like "**Science**", "**Art**", "**Music**", and so on.

Text Generation

Text generation is another important task in NLP, where the goal is to generate human-like text based on a given input. This can be used for a wide range of applications, from generating responses in a chatbot to creating content for articles or social media posts.

With the Cohere API, we can create a custom function in Google Sheets that generates text based on a given prompt. For example, we could generate a paragraph about a specific topic, create a response to a user's question, or even generate a story based on a given starting line.

Text Summarization

Text summarization involves creating a concise summary of a larger text. This can be particularly useful when dealing with large documents or articles, where you want to get a quick understanding of the content without having to read the entire text.

Using the Cohere API, we can create a function in Google Sheets that takes a large text as input and returns a concise summary. This could be used to summarize news articles, research papers, meeting minutes, and more.

In the following sections, we will walk through the process of setting up our Google Sheets environment, obtaining the necessary API key from Cohere, and creating our custom functions for text classification, text generation, and text summarization. By the end of this chapter, you will have a powerful tool at your disposal that can perform these complex NLP tasks right within your Google Sheets.

Prerequisites

Before we dive into the implementation of our use cases, it's important to ensure that we have all the necessary tools and knowledge at our disposal.

Required Knowledge and Tools

To get the most out of this chapter, you should have a basic understanding of the following:

- **Google Sheets**: Google Sheets is a web-based spreadsheet program that is part of the Google Drive office suite. You should be familiar with basic spreadsheet operations like entering data, creating formulas, and using functions.
- **Google Apps Script**: Google Apps Script is a rapid application development platform that makes it fast and easy to create business applications that integrate with Google Workspace. You don't need to be an expert, but familiarity with JavaScript (the language used in Apps Script) will be helpful.
- **Basic understanding of APIs**: We will be interacting with the Cohere API, so understanding what APIs are and how they work will be beneficial.

As for tools, you will need:

- **A Google Account**: This is required to access Google Sheets and Google Apps Script.
- **A web browser**: Google Sheets and Google Apps Script are web-based, so you'll need a modern web browser. Google Chrome is recommended, but most browsers should work.
- **A Cohere account**: You'll need to sign up for a free account with Cohere to get your API key.

Setting up Google Sheets and Google Apps Script

Setting up Google Sheets is as simple as logging into your Google account and navigating to the Google Sheets homepage. From there, you can create a new spreadsheet with a click of a button.

To access Google Apps Script, you can click the "**`Extensions`**" menu in Google Sheets and select "**`Apps Script`**." This will open a new tab with the Apps Script editor, where you can write and run your scripts.

Getting the Cohere API key

To interact with the Cohere API, you'll need an API key. This is a unique identifier that authenticates your requests to the API. You can get your API key by signing up for a free account on the Cohere website. Once you've signed up and logged in, you can find your API key in your account settings. We have discussed this in detail in our previous chapters. Kindly refer to it and ensure the API key is created and saved for your purpose only.

Please note that it's important to keep your API key secure and not share it with anyone. It's also a good practice to limit the use of your API key to specific IP addresses or domains when possible.

With these prerequisites in place, we're ready to start building our custom functions in Google Sheets using Google Apps Script and the Cohere API. Let's get started!

Setup

1. Create a blank Google sheet from the URL https://docs.google.com/spreadsheets/u/0/.

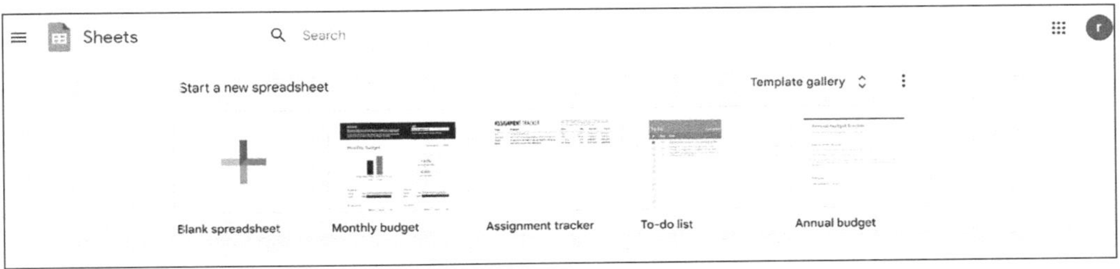

Figure 5.1: *Create a Google sheet*

2. Create a sheet named "**`configurations`**". This sheet will be used to set up the configuration required for developing the use case.
3. In the configurations sheet, the following are the entries that have to be created. Let's get into each of them.

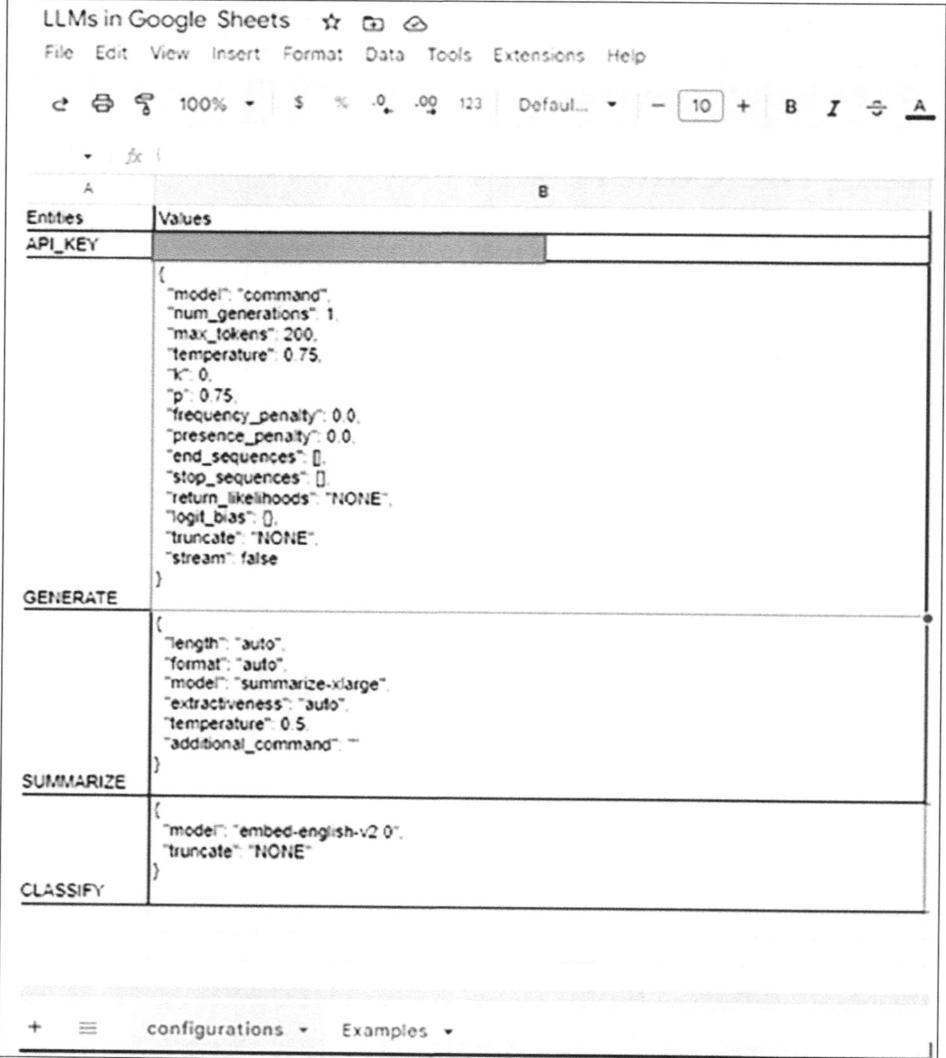

Figure 5.2: *Create configurations sheet*

4. We created two columns "**`Entities`**" and "**`Values`**". The Entities will have the following rows.
    - **`API_KEY`**: This is your Cohere API key.
    - **`GENERATE`**, **`SUMMARIZE`**, and **`CLASSIFY`**: These are the API references which we will be using to perform generation, summarization and classification tasks respectively.

5. The "**`Values`**" column corresponding to the respective entities will have the values.
    - **`API_Key`** entity will have the API Key value from Cohere.
    - The Generate, Summarize and Classify entities will have the respective parameters used by the API. More details on the parameters can be found in the official documentation of Cohere API Docs.
6. Once the configuration sheet is completed, let's now open up the Google Sheets script editor to start with the development.
7. Click "**`Extensions`**" on the toolbar and then select "**`Apps Script`**" from the dropdown options.

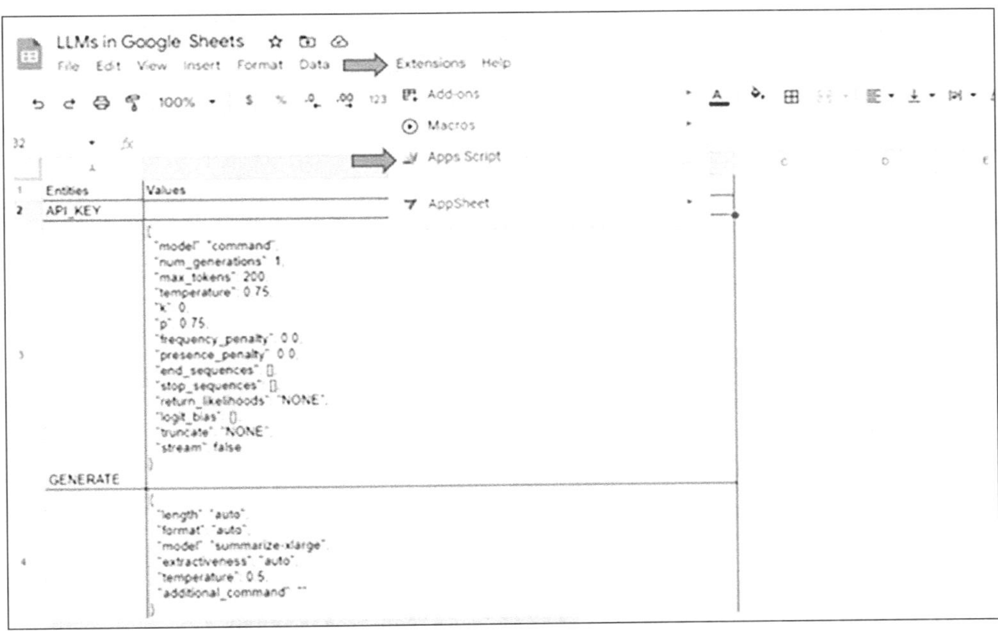

***Figure 5.3**: App script editor navigation*

8. This opens up the editor where we can code. The default file name will be **`code.gs`**.
9. Let's use that and start developing the functionalities according to the use case described earlier.

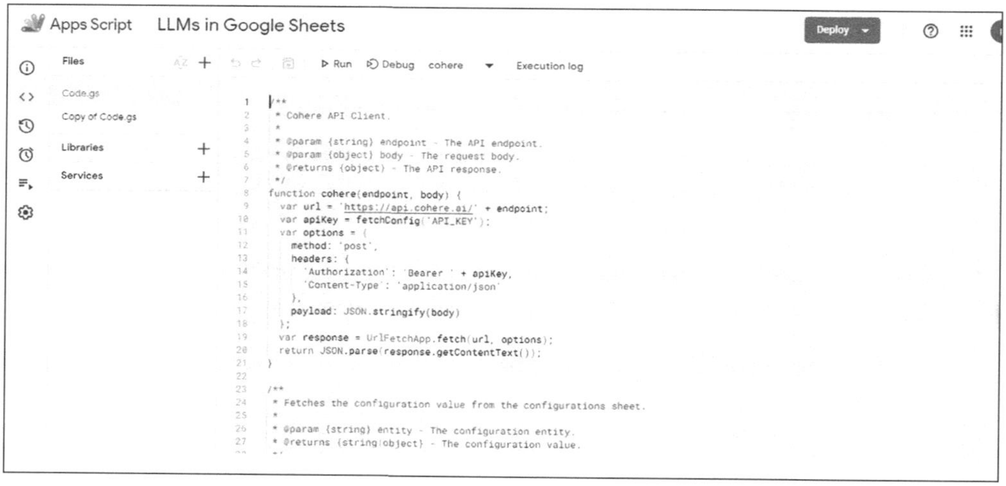

Figure 5.4: App script editor

All the codes and configurations have been developed for your reference. Please refer to the "*LLMs in Google Sheets*" sheet that is provided as part of the repository. The only prerequisite for using the sheet is for you to have the API key and it has to be entered against the **API_KEY** entity under the Value column

Boilerplate code development and walkthrough

In this section, we will be discussing the boilerplate code that forms the foundation of our custom functions in Google Sheets. This code will handle the interaction with the Cohere API and provide a structure for our specific use case implementations.

Explanation of the Boilerplate code

The boilerplate code consists of a few key components:

- **Cohere API Client:** This is a function that handles the interaction with the Cohere API. It takes an endpoint and a request body as parameters, constructs the API request, and sends it to the Cohere API. It then parses the response and returns it.

```
function cohere(endpoint, body) {
  var url = 'https://api.cohere.ai/' + endpoint;
  var apiKey = fetchConfig('API_KEY');
```

```
  var options = {
    method: 'post',
    headers: {
      'Authorization': 'Bearer ' + apiKey,
      'Content-Type': 'application/json'
    },
    payload: JSON.stringify(body)
  };
  var response = UrlFetchApp.fetch(url, options);
  return JSON.parse(response.getContentText());
}
```

- **Fetch Config Function:** This function retrieves the configuration values from a specific Google Sheets tab named **'configurations'**. These configurations include the Cohere API key and the specific parameters for each Cohere API function (**generate**, **classify**, and **summarize**).

```
function fetchConfig(entity) {
  var sheets = SpreadsheetApp.getActiveSpreadsheet().getSheets();
  var sheet = null;

  // Loop through all sheets to find the one that matches case in-
  sensitively
  for (var i = 0; i < sheets.length; i++) {
    if (sheets[i].getName().toLowerCase() === 'configurations') {
      sheet = sheets[i];
      break;
    }
  }

  // If no matching sheet was found, throw an error
  if (sheet === null) {
    throw new Error('No configurations sheet found.');
  }
```

```
    var data = sheet.getDataRange().getValues();
    for (var i = 0; i < data.length; i++) {
      if (data[i][0].toLowerCase() === entity.toLowerCase()) {
        // Return a string if the entity is 'API_KEY', and JSON for
all other entities
        var value = entity === 'API_KEY' ? data[i][1] : isJson-
String(data[i][1]) ? JSON.parse(data[i][1]) : data[i][1];

        // Print the value to the console
        console.log(entity + ':', value);

        return value;
      }
    }

  // If no matching entity was found, throw an error
  throw new Error('No matching entity found in configurations.');
}
```

- **JSON String Validator**: This is a helper function that checks if a string is a valid JSON. It's used in the **fetchConfig** function to parse JSON strings in the configurations.

```
function isJsonString(str) {
  try {
      JSON.parse(str);
  } catch (e) {
      return false;
  }
  return true;
}
```

Walkthrough of the code and its structure

Let's walk through the code to understand how it works:

- **Cohere API Client:** The cohere function begins by constructing the URL for the API request using the provided endpoint. It then retrieves the API key using the **fetchConfig** function. The API key is used to authenticate our requests to the Cohere API.

```
function cohere(endpoint, body) {
  var url = 'https://api.cohere.ai/' + endpoint;
  var apiKey = fetchConfig('API_KEY');
  ...
}
```

The function then sets up the options for the API request, including the HTTP method (POST), the headers (which include the API key), and the payload (which is the **stringified** version of the provided body).

```
var options = {
  method: 'post',
  headers: {
    'Authorization': 'Bearer ' + apiKey,
    'Content-Type': 'application/json'
  },
  payload: JSON.stringify(body)
};
```

The function then sends the API request using the **UrlFetchApp.fetch** method and parses the response using **JSON.parse**. The parsed response is then returned.

```
var response = UrlFetchApp.fetch(url, options);
return JSON.parse(response.getContentText());
```

- **Fetch Config Function:** The **fetchConfig** function starts by getting all the sheets in the active spreadsheet. It then loops through these sheets to find the one named **'configurations'**. If it can't find this sheet, it throws an error.

```
function fetchConfig(entity) {
  var sheets = SpreadsheetApp.getActiveSpreadsheet().getSheets();
  var sheet = null;

  // Loop through all sheets to find the one that matches case
  insensitively
  for (var i = 0; i < sheets.length; i++) {
```

```
        if (sheets[i].getName().toLowerCase() === 'configurations') {
          sheet = sheets[i];
          break;
        }
      }
      ...
    }
```

The function then gets all the values in the configurations sheet and loops through them to find the one that matches the provided entity (case-insensitive). If it can't find a matching entity, it throws an error.

```
    var data = sheet.getDataRange().getValues();
    for (var i = 0; i < data.length; i++) {
      if (data[i][0].toLowerCase() === entity.toLowerCase()) {
        ...
      }
    }
```

If the function finds a matching entity, it checks if the entity is '**`API_KEY`**'. If it is, it returns the corresponding value as a string. If it's not, it checks if the value is a valid JSON string using the **`isJsonString`** function. If it is, it parses the JSON string and returns the resulting object. If it's not, it returns the value as it is.

```
    if (data[i][0].toLowerCase() === entity.toLowerCase()) {
      // Return a string if the entity is 'API_KEY', and JSON for all other entities
      var value = entity === 'API_KEY' ? data[i][1] : isJsonString(data[i][1]) ? JSON.parse(data[i][1]) : data[i][1];

      // Print the value to the console
      console.log(entity + ':', value);

      return value;
    }
```

- **JSON String Validator**: The **`isJsonString`** function tries to parse the provided string as JSON using **`JSON.parse`**. If it succeeds, it returns true. If it fails (because the string is not valid JSON), it catches the error and returns false.

```
function isJsonString(str) {
  try {
      JSON.parse(str);
  } catch (e) {
      return false;
  }
  return true;
}
```

This boilerplate code provides a solid foundation for interacting with the Cohere API. We will build upon this foundation to implement our specific use cases.

Functionality-specific Development and Walkthrough

Let's delve into the specific functionalities of our Google Sheets custom functions: Text Classification, Text Generation, and Text Summarization. The following sections will explain the code for each functionality and walk you through how it works.

Text Classification

Text classification is the task of categorizing text into organized groups. Using the Cohere API, we can classify text based on the examples provided.

Code explanation and walkthrough

The **COHERE_CLASSIFY** function is our custom function for text classification. It accepts two parameters: inputs and examples. inputs are the texts to classify, and examples are the texts that will be classified.

```
function COHERE_CLASSIFY(inputs, examples) {
  var body = fetchConfig('CLASSIFY');
  body.inputs = JSON.parse(inputs.trim());
  body.examples = JSON.parse(examples.trim());
  ...
}
```

The function starts by fetching the configuration for the **'CLASSIFY'** entity using the **fetchConfig** function. It then parses the inputs and examples parameters as

JSON and adds them to the body. The function then calls the cohere function with the '**v1/classify**' endpoint and the body. This sends a request to the Cohere API to classify the inputs based on the examples.

```
var response = cohere('v1/classify', body);
```

The function then checks if the response contains classifications. If it does, it maps over the classifications and returns an array of the predicted labels and their confidence scores. If it doesn't, it throws an error.

```
if (response.classifications && response.classifications.length > 0) {
  return response.classifications.map(classification =>
classification.prediction + ' (' + classification.confidence + ')');
} else {
  throw new Error('No classifications found in the response.');
}
```

Text Generation

Text generation is the task of generating text based on a given prompt. With the Cohere API, we can generate text that follows the style and context of the prompt.

Code explanation and walkthrough

The **COHERE_GENERATE** function is our custom function for text generation. It accepts two parameters: instruction and data. instruction is the prompt for the text generation, and data is additional data to include in the prompt.

```
function COHERE_GENERATE(instruction="about llms", data) {
  var body = fetchConfig('GENERATE');
  body.prompt = instruction + ': \n' + (data || '');
  ...
}
```

The function starts by fetching the configuration for the 'GENERATE' entity using the fetchConfig function. It then constructs the prompt by concatenating the instruction and data parameters and adding them to the body. The function then calls the cohere function with the 'v1/generate' endpoint and the body. This sends a request to the Cohere API to generate text based on the prompt.

```
var response = cohere('v1/generate', body);
```

The function then checks if the response contains generations. If it does, it maps over the generations and returns an array of the generated texts. If it doesn't, it throws an error.

```
if (response.generations && response.generations.length > 0) {
  return response.generations.map(generation => generation.text);
} else {
  throw new Error('No generations found in the response.');
}
```

Text Summarization

Text summarization is the task of creating a concise and coherent summary of a larger text. With the Cohere API, we can generate a summary of a given text.

Code explanation and walkthrough

The `COHERE_SUMMARIZE` function is our custom function for text summarization. It accepts one parameter: text, which is the text to summarize.

```
function COHERE_SUMMARIZE(text) {
  var body = fetchConfig('SUMMARIZE');
  body.text = text;
  ...
}
```

The function starts by fetching the configuration for the '**SUMMARIZE**' entity using the fetchConfig function. It then adds the text parameter to the body.

The function then calls the cohere function with the 'summarize' endpoint and the body. This sends a request to the Cohere API to summarize the text.

```
var response = cohere('v1/summarize', body);
```

The function then checks if the response contains a summary. If it does, it returns the summary. If it doesn't, it throws an error.

```
if (response.summary) {
  return response.summary;
} else {
  throw new Error('No summary found in the response.');
}
```

These custom functions provide a powerful way to leverage the Cohere API directly from Google Sheets. They can be used to classify text, generate text, and summarize text, all based on the data in your spreadsheet.

Testing the Use Cases

After developing the code and understanding its structure and functionalities, it's time to put it to the test. Let's understand the process of testing the use cases we discussed earlier. We will also understand the expected results and how to interpret them.

Step-by-step guide on how to test the use cases:

1. **Text classification:** To test the text classification functionality, you need to provide a list of input texts and a list of example texts with their labels. Enter these values in separate cells in your Google Sheets. For instance, you can enter the input texts in cell B4 and the example texts in cell C4. Then, in another cell, enter the custom function =`COHERE_CLASSIFY(B4, C4)`. The function will classify the input texts based on the example texts and return the predicted labels in the cell.

The inputs and examples have to be in a specific format.

- **Inputs**: Inputs are a list of texts that require to be classified.

  ["Looking for off-the-beaten-path travel destinations. Any hidden gems?", "What's the best spot to capture stunning nature photography?", "In need of a good laugh. Can you recommend a comedy show?"]

- **Examples**: The examples are a list of dictionaries where each dictionary is a key value pair of text and its expected label. This is an example of few-shot learning, wherein API learns the patterns through the examples and is able to extrapolate that knowledge to unclassified sample texts. A high-quality and diverse example set can enable the LLM to make accurate and consistent predictions.

```
        [ { "text": "I just discovered a new hiking trail with
breathtaking views.", "label": "Outdoor" }, { "text": "I love
camping in the wilderness.", "label": "Outdoor" }, { "text":
"This book kept me on the edge of my seat till the very last
page.", "label": "Thriller" }, { "text": "The suspense in the
novel was intense.", "label": "Thriller" },]
```

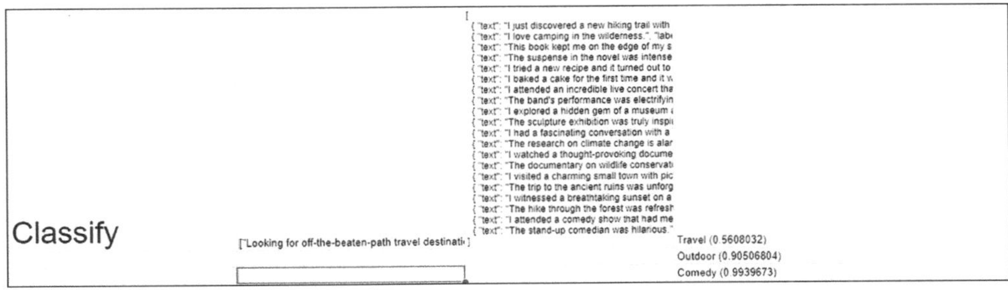

Figure 5.5: *Testing text classification*

2. **Text Generation:** To test the text generation functionality, you need to provide an instruction or prompt and optionally additional data. Enter these values in separate cells in your Google Sheets. For example, you can enter the instructions in cell B3 and the additional data in cell C3. Then, in another cell, enter the custom function **`=COHERE_GENERATE(B3, C3)`**. The function will generate text based on the **`instruction`** and the additional data and return the generated text in the cell.

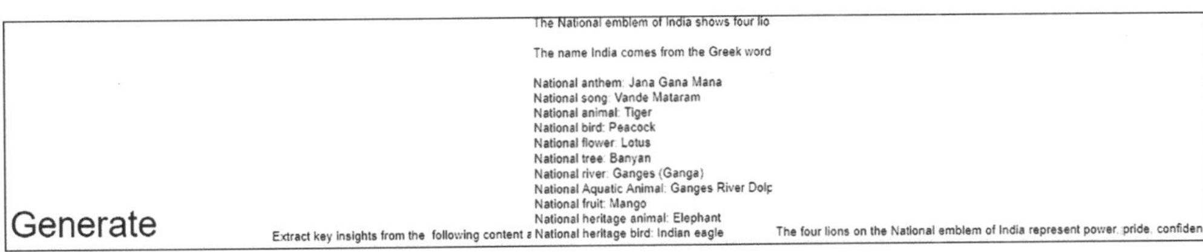

Figure 5.6: *Testing text generation*

In this example, we are providing **`instruction`** in cell B3 to extract key insights from the content in cell C3.

3. **Text summarization:** To test the text summarization functionality, you need to provide a text to summarize. Enter this value in a cell in your Google Sheets. For instance, you can enter the text in cell C2. Then, in another cell, enter the custom function **`=COHERE_SUMMARIZE(C2)`**. The function will summarize the text and return the summary in the cell.

Task	Prompt/Inputs	Data/Examples	API Response
Summarize		The National emblem of India shows four lio The name India comes from the Greek word National anthem: Jana Gana Mana National song: Vande Mataram National animal: Tiger National bird: Peacock National flower: Lotus National tree: Banyan National river: Ganges (Ganga) National Aquatic Animal: Ganges River Dolp National fruit: Mango National heritage animal: Elephant National heritage bird: Indian eagle	The National emblem of India is four lions standing back-to-back representing Peacock is the National bird of India, and the Lotus is the National flower. The Finally, the National anthem of India is 'Jana Gana Mana', and the National so

Figure 5.7: *Testing text summarization*

Expected results and how to interpret them

The results of the custom functions are returned in the cells where you entered the functions. Here's what to expect:

1. For text classification, the function returns the predicted labels for the input texts. Each label is followed by a confidence score in parentheses. The confidence score indicates the model's confidence in the prediction. A higher score means the model is more confident in the prediction.

2. For text generation, the function returns the generated text. The text is generated based on the instructions and the additional data you provided. The generated text can be a continuation of the instruction, a response to it, or a text that includes the additional data in a meaningful way.

3. For text summarization, the function returns the summary of the text. The summary is a shorter version of the text that retains the main points and the overall meaning of the text.

Remember, the results are generated by machine learning models, which means they are probabilistic and can vary slightly each time you run the functions. Also, the quality of the results depends on the quality of the input data. For best results, make sure to provide clear and well-structured input data.

Putting it all Together

After developing the boilerplate code and the specific functionalities for text classification, text generation, and text summarization, we now have a powerful tool that integrates Google Sheets with the Cohere API. This tool allows us to leverage the power of machine learning models for natural language processing tasks directly from our spreadsheet.

The code we developed is organized into several functions, each with a specific role. The cohere function is the core function that interacts with the Cohere API. It sends a POST request to a specified endpoint with a given request body and returns the response.

The **`fetchConfig`** function retrieves configuration values from a Google Sheets tab named **`'configurations'`**. This function is used to fetch the API key and the request bodies for the different API endpoints.

The **`isJsonString`** function checks if a string is a valid JSON. It is used in the **`fetchConfig`** function to parse configuration values that are JSON strings.

The **COHERE_CLASSIFY**, **COHERE_GENERATE**, and **COHERE_SUMMARIZE** functions are custom functions that can be used directly in the spreadsheet. They fetch the appropriate configuration, prepare the request body, call the Cohere function to interact with the Cohere API and process the response to return the results in a format that can be used in the spreadsheet.

To use these custom functions, you can enter them in a cell like any other Google Sheets function. For example, to classify a text, you can enter **=COHERE_CLASSIFY(A2, B2)** where A2 contains the input text and B2 contains the example texts. The function will classify the input text based on the example texts and return the result in the cell.

Error Handling and Debugging

In the process of working with Google Apps Script and Cohere APIs, you may encounter some errors. Understanding these errors and knowing how to handle them is crucial for the smooth execution of your code. In this section, we will discuss some common errors and their solutions. We will also provide some tips for debugging the code.

Common errors and their solutions:

- **SyntaxError**: This error occurs when there's a mistake in the syntax of your code. For instance, you might have forgotten a closing bracket or used the wrong operator. The error message usually points to the line of code where the error occurred. To fix this error, review your code carefully and correct the syntax.
- **TypeError**: This error occurs when an operation is performed on a value of an inappropriate type. For example, you might be trying to call a function on a null or undefined value. To fix this error, make sure that the values you're working with are of the correct type.
- **Error: No matching entity found in configurations**: This error occurs when the fetchConfig function can't find a matching entity in the configurations sheet. To fix this error, check the configurations sheet and make sure that the entity exists and is spelled correctly.
- **Error: No classifications found in the response**: This error occurs when the **COHERE_CLASSIFY** function doesn't find any classifications in the response from the Cohere API. This could be due to an issue with the API or the input data. To fix this error, check the input data and the API response.

Tips for debugging the code:

- Use **`console.log`**: The **`console.log`** function is a powerful tool for debugging. You can use it to print the values of variables at different stages of your code. This can help you track the flow of data and identify where things go wrong.
- Break down complex functions: If a function is complex and causing errors, try breaking it down into smaller, more manageable functions. This can make the code easier to understand and debug.
- Check the API documentation: If you're getting unexpected results from the Cohere API, check the API documentation. It can provide valuable information about the expected input and output formats, error codes, and more.
- Use the Apps Script debugger: Google Apps Script has a built-in debugger that allows you to step through your code one line at a time. You can use it to inspect the values of variables and see exactly what your code is doing.

Remember, debugging is a normal part of coding. Don't be discouraged by errors. Instead, use them as opportunities to learn and improve your code.

Best Practices and Tips

As we wrap up this chapter, let's discuss some best practices and tips for using Cohere APIs and Google Apps Script. Following these chapter lines can help you write cleaner, more efficient code and make the most of these powerful tools.

Best practices for using Cohere APIs and Google Apps Script:

- **Keep your API key secure**: Your Cohere API key is like a password. It gives you access to Cohere's services, and anyone who has it can use it to make requests on your behalf. Therefore, it's crucial to keep it secure. Don't share it with anyone, and don't include it directly in your code. Instead, store it in a secure place, like the configurations sheet we used in this chapter.
- **Handle errors gracefully**: Your code should be able to handle errors without crashing. This includes both errors from the Cohere API (like rate limits or invalid requests) and errors in your own code (like syntax errors or type errors). Use **`try-catch`** blocks to catch errors and provide helpful error messages to the user.

- **Use descriptive variable and function names**: Your variable and function names should clearly describe what they represent or do. This makes your code easier to read and understand.
- **Comment your code**: Comments can help others understand your code, and they can also help you remember what your code does when you come back to it later. Include comments that explain what each part of your code does, why you made certain decisions, and any important details about the code.

Tips for improving the code and extending the functionalities:

- **Refactor your code**: Refactoring is the process of improving your code without changing its functionality. This could involve removing duplicate code, simplifying complex functions, or improving the structure of your code. Regular refactoring can keep your code clean, efficient, and easy to maintain.
- **Extend the functionalities**: The functionalities we covered in this chapter are just the beginning. Cohere offers many other APIs that you can use to add more features to your Google Sheets. For example, you could use the Similarity API to find similar texts, or the Embed API to generate embeddings for texts.
- **Integrate with other services**: You can integrate your Google Sheets with other services to create more complex applications. For example, you could use Google Forms to collect data, Google Sheets to process and analyze the data, and Cohere APIs to generate insights from the data.

Conclusion

We've come a long way in this chapter. We started with an introduction to Google Sheets, Google Apps Script, and Cohere APIs, and then we delved into the specifics of how to use these tools to perform tasks like text classification, text generation, and text summarization. We also covered how to handle errors, debug the code, and follow best practices for using these tools.

The use cases we explored in this chapter are just the tip of the iceberg. With the power of Cohere APIs and Google Apps Script, you can create a wide range of applications. For example, you could build a sentiment analysis tool to analyze customer feedback, a content recommendation system based on text similarity, or a language translation tool using Cohere's translation API.

The future of this field is exciting. As natural language processing technology continues to evolve, we can expect Cohere and similar services to offer even more powerful and easy-to-use APIs. This will open up new possibilities for applications and use cases.

In terms of future work, you could extend the functionalities of the Google Sheets application we built in this chapter. You could add more Cohere APIs, integrate with other services, or improve the user interface. You could also explore other areas of natural language processing and machine learning, and apply what you've learned in this chapter to new projects.

This chapter has provided you with a solid foundation for using Cohere APIs with Google Apps Script in Google Sheets. I hope that you found it informative and inspiring. Remember, the key to mastering these tools is practice and continuous learning. So keep experimenting, keep learning, and most importantly, have fun coding!

In the next chapter, we will explore the intricate synergy between Transformers and Vector Databases, harnessing their combined potential to pave the way for an extraordinary leap in personalized movie recommendations.

CHAPTER 6

Dynamic Movie Recommendation Engine Using LLMs

Introduction

In the digital era, where an abundance of information is available at our fingertips, personalization is key. One powerful way to provide personalization is through recommendation systems. These systems are prevalent in various digital platforms, be it e-commerce, social media, or streaming platforms. They cater to the individual preferences of users, providing suggestions based on their behavior, activity, or likeness. The core of these recommendation engines is often a set of machine learning algorithms. In this chapter, we are going to explore one such powerful and sophisticated approach – a Vector Search-Based Recommendation Engine.

Structure

In this chapter, the following topics will be covered:

- Building a Movie Recommendation engine
- Generating embeddings using transformers
- Exploring vector search using Redis as a vector db store and search service

Introduction to Vector Search-Based Recommendation Engine

A vector search-based recommendation engine leverages the prowess of vector search and embeddings in providing recommendations. Vector search, as the name suggests, is a method of retrieving the most relevant items in response to a query by computing their proximity in a vector space. By representing data items and queries as vectors in a high-dimensional space, we can quantify similarity by calculating the distance between these vectors.

When it comes to text data, like movie descriptions, user reviews, or product details, these vectors can be computed using natural language processing models, one of the types being transformer models. Transformer models are deep learning models used for understanding semantic relationships between words and creating dense vector representations of sentences, paragraphs, or even entire documents.

By pairing a transformer model with a vector search database, we can create a recommendation engine that captures the nuanced semantics of user queries and returns highly relevant recommendations.

Understanding the Use Case: Movie Recommendations

To make the concept of a vector search-based recommendation engine more tangible, let us delve into a practical use case: movie recommendations.

Imagine you are the owner of an online movie streaming platform. You have an extensive catalog of movies, documentaries, short films, and TV-released movies, each with associated data like the title, director, stars, IMDb rating, category, duration, censor-board-rating, and release year. To enhance user experience on your platform, you decide to implement a movie recommendation system that suggests movies based on user queries.

For instance, a user might input a query like, "*I want to watch a comedy movie with an IMDb rating of 8 and above.*" Our goal is to create a recommendation engine that interprets the semantics of this query and returns the most relevant movie suggestions from our catalog.

This chapter will guide you through the step-by-step process of building such a recommendation engine. We will start with installing the necessary tools, setting up the vector database, preparing and indexing our data, and finally, implementing and running our movie recommender. By the end, you will have a fully functioning vector search-based recommendation engine capable of generating accurate and semantic-rich movie recommendations.

Introduction to Essential Components

Transformers are a revolutionary approach in the field of natural language processing (NLP). They fundamentally changed the way we handle text data, bringing significant improvements in language understanding tasks. The key idea behind transformers is the concept of "*attention*," which allows the model to focus on different parts of the input sequence when producing an output, thereby effectively capturing the contextual relationships among words or phrases in a sentence.

In the context of generating vector embeddings, transformers play a vital role. They convert text data into numerical representations (vectors), capturing semantic meaning of words, sentences, or entire documents. These high-dimensional vectors can then be used in various NLP tasks such as information retrieval, text classification, sentiment analysis, or in our use case –powering a recommendation engine.

Background of Sentence Transformers /all-MiniLM-L12-v1

The sentence transformers '`all-MiniLM-L12-v1`' is a model fine-tuned specifically for creating sentence and short paragraph embeddings. The original pre-trained model, '`microsoft/MiniLM-L12-H384-uncased`', is further refined using a contrastive learning objective on a large dataset of over a billion sentence pairs.

The contrastive learning objective is a type of self-supervised learning where the model learns to identify which sentences are paired together in the dataset from a set of randomly sampled sentences. The model was developed during a community week organized by Hugging Face using JAX/Flax for NLP and CV, and Google's Flax, JAX, and Cloud teams provided assistance in creating an efficient deep learning framework.

The resulting model, '`sentence-transformers/all-MiniLM-L12-v1`', is intended to be used as a sentence and short paragraph encoder. Given an input text, it generates a vector that encapsulates the semantic information of the input.

Such sentence vectors can be used for various NLP tasks, including information retrieval, clustering, or sentence similarity tasks.

Vector Databases: An Overview and Importance

Vector databases are essential components in systems dealing with high-dimensional data, such as a recommendation engine. They provide an efficient way to store and search through large amounts of vector data. Specifically, they offer functionalities to perform similarity searches in a vector space, which is key for tasks like nearest neighbor search or recommendation systems.

The importance of vector databases cannot be overstated in our context. It allows us to efficiently store and retrieve movie embeddings, enabling quick and precise movie recommendations based on user queries. By providing fast and scalable solutions, vector databases are instrumental in offering a seamless user experience.

Redis as a Vector Database

Redis is a widely used open-source, in-memory data structure store that is commonly used as a database, cache, and message broker. It provides data structures such as strings, hashes, lists, sets, sorted sets with range queries, and more.

While Redis is often used as a cache due to its speed and in-memory nature, it can also be leveraged as a vector database, capable of handling vector similarity search. This can be achieved through the use of Redis modules, such as RediSearch, which offers functionalities like full-text search and vector similarity search directly on the Redis DB.

One of the standout features of Redis as a vector database is its speed, especially for data loading. Redis is also convenient for teams that do not want the overhead of maintaining a large, self-hosted Redis deployment since high-availability Redis has been made much simpler with services like RedisCloud.

Additionally, Redis's Python SDKs make working with the database a breeze, allowing developers to load, store, and retrieve vectors efficiently and conveniently. The Python library further simplifies the interaction with Redis, especially when it comes to vector similarity search.

In a nutshell, by using Redis as a vector database, we can easily manage our movie embeddings and perform quick and efficient similarity searches to power our recommendation engine.

Installation and Pre-requisites

Throughout this chapter, we will be using Google Colab as our IDE for the ease of development activities as our focus will be on developing the use case and understanding the concepts:

- The GitHub repo can be accessed at https://github.com/ava-orange-education/Hands-On-Large-Language-Models-for-Enterprise/blob/main/Chapter%206%20-%20Movie_Recommendation.ipynb
- The data folder will have the datasets for the exercises.

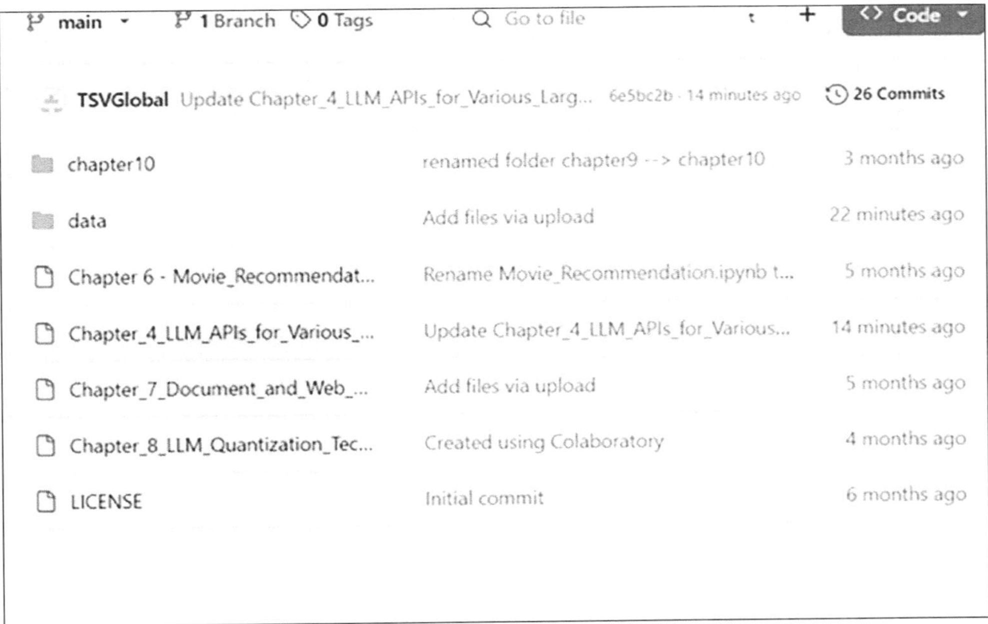

Figure 6.1: *GitHub Repo*

Setting up Redis

1. Create an account in redis cloud https://app.redislabs.com/#/login . We will be using Redis as our vector db service provider.

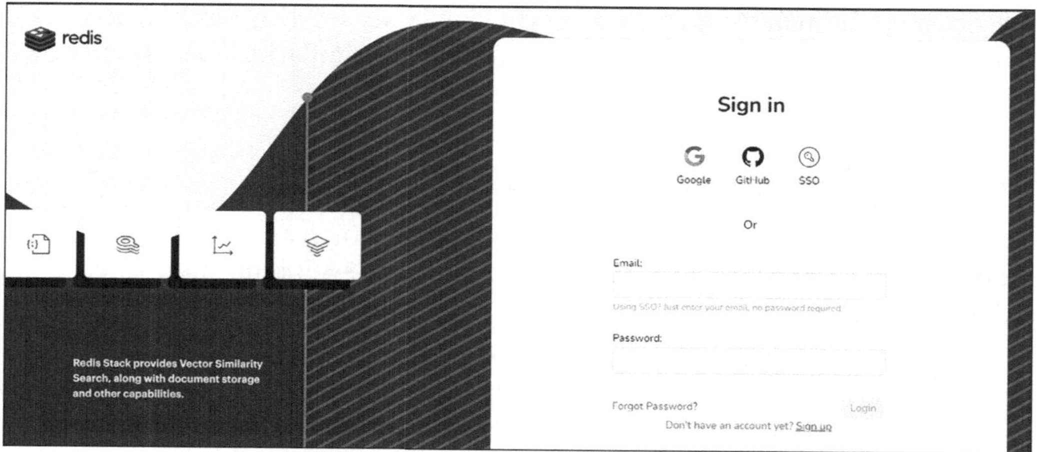

Figure 6.2: *Redis Cloud Login Console*

2. After logging in, you will be taken to the page to set up the database. AWS was selected for the infra support as an India-based region was available with it. Then, click Lets Start Free button:

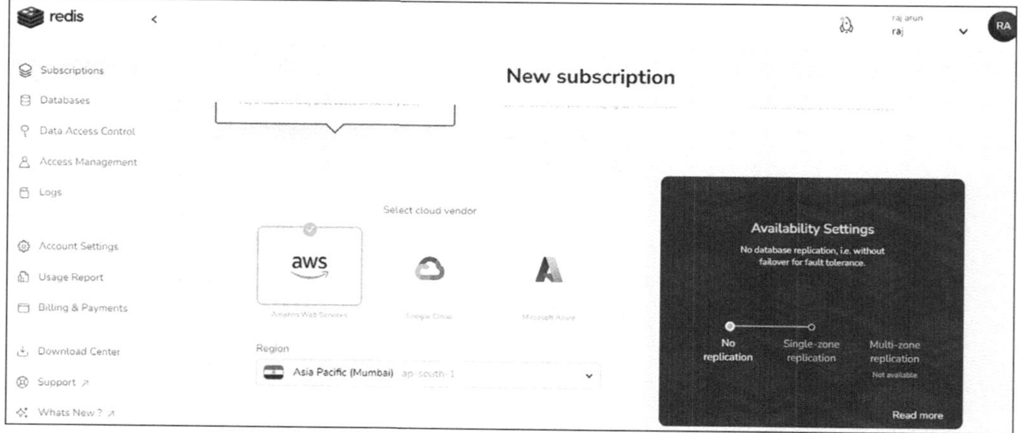

Figure 6.3: *DB Set Up*

3. Redis by default provides a free subscription for the user to try out its services, and we will be using the same for demonstration here.
4. A free subscription gets created, as shown in the following figure:

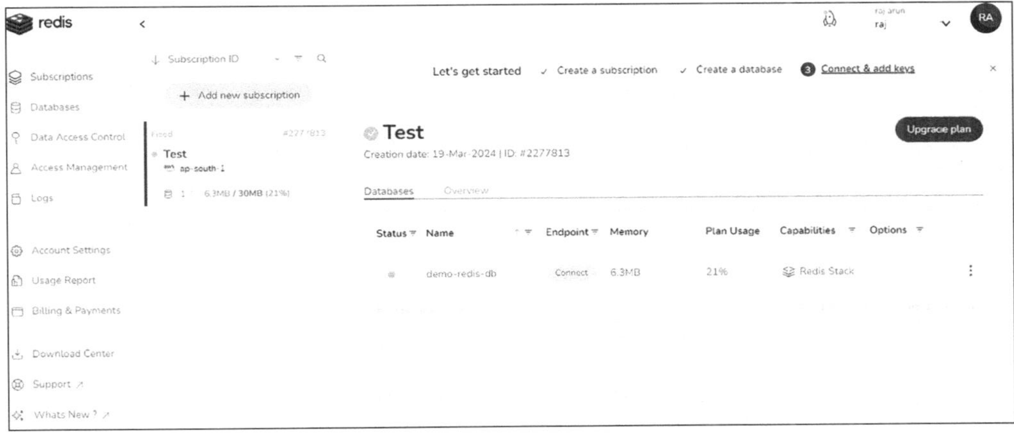

Figure 6.4: *DB Creation Landing Page*

5. To connect to this instance of the database we need the connection details. Click the connect button, as shown in *Figure 6.5*:

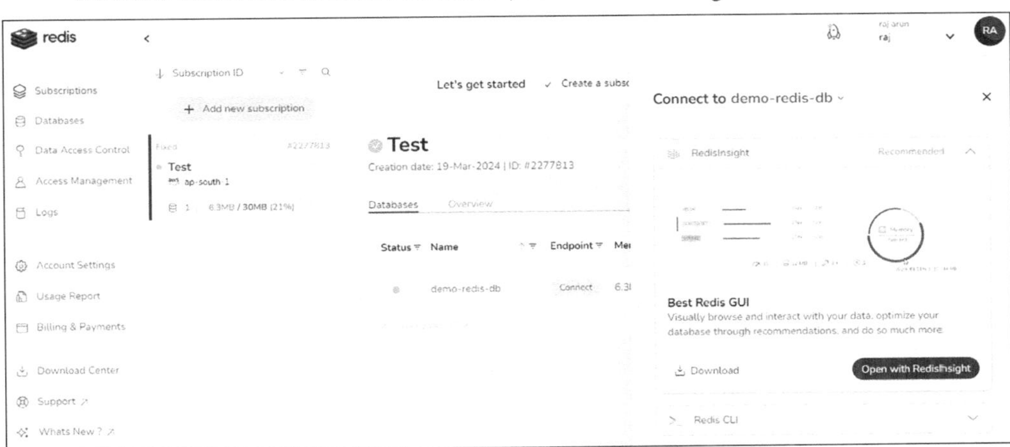

Figure 6.5: *Connection Pop-Up*

6. Select **`Redis Client`**, followed by the selection of the client, which is **`Python`**, as shown. Copy the code snippet and have it pasted in a notepad. We will be using this later to connect to this db for storing the embeddings (vectors).

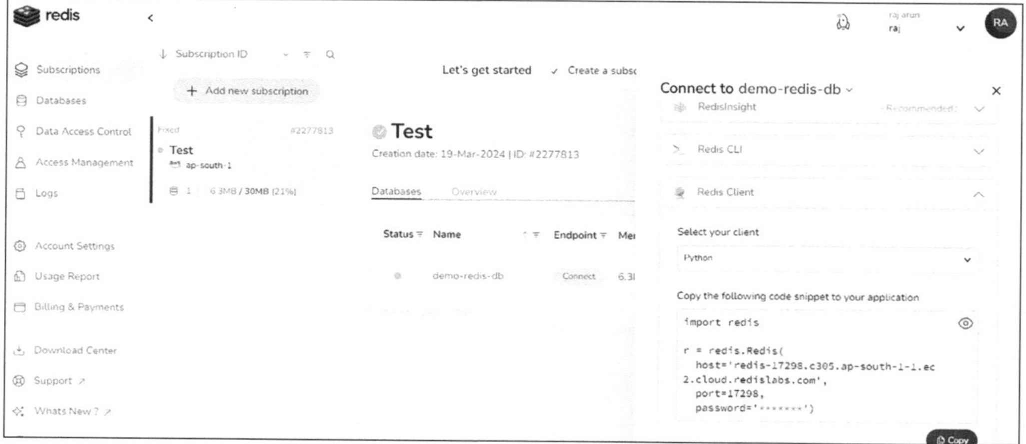

***Figure 6.6**: Connection Details*

7. In case the pop-up closed or did not appear, you can click **`Connect`**, as shown, to retrieve the details:

***Figure 6.7**: Connect Placeholder*

Setting up Google Colab:

1. Go to the URL: https://research.google.com/colaboratory/
2. On the landing page, click New notebook as shown:

***Figure 6.8**: Google Colab New Notebook*

3. This will open up a Jupyter notebook IDE which Google offers as a free version. We can upgrade as well but the free version should be sufficient.
4. A new notebook can also be created by clicking File and then selecting New notebook, as shown in *Figure* 6.9:

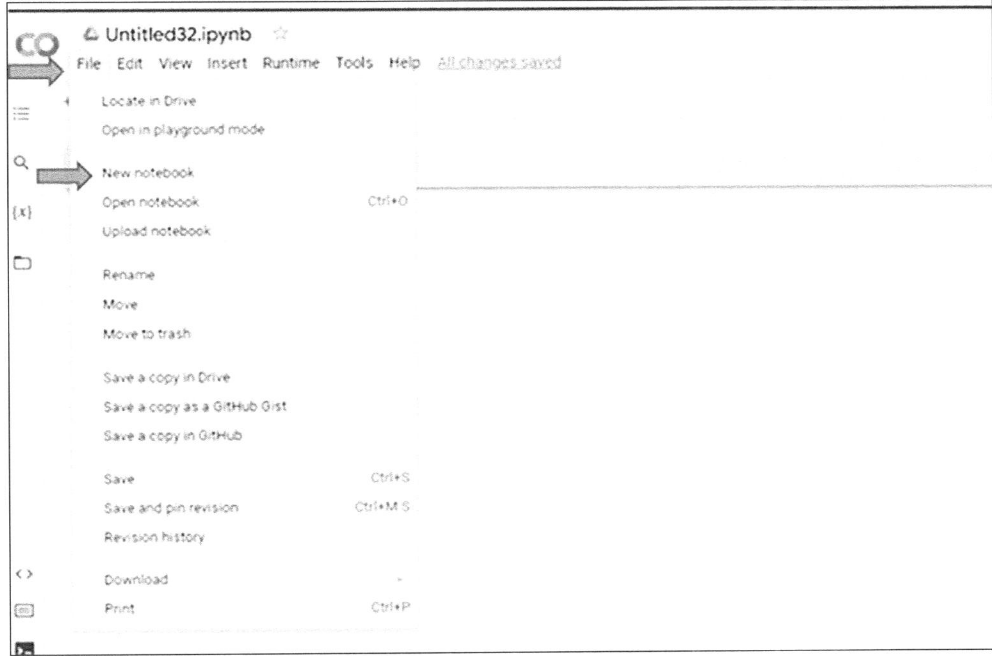

***Figure 6.9**: Google Colab Console New Notebook*

5. Once the notebook is created bring it online by clicking Connect on the top-right corner as shown:

Figure 6.10: *Google Colab Notebook Connect*

6. That's it. We are all set now to develop the recommendation service!

Environment Preparation in Google Colab

Google Colab uses pip, a package installer for Python, to manage and install additional Python libraries. You can use pip in Google Colab by prefixing your commands with an exclamation mark (!). Here's how you can install the required libraries:

```
!pip install pandas sentence_transformers redis
```

Pandas is a data analysis library, Sentence Transformers is for generating vector embeddings, and Redis is our choice of database for this task.

This command tells pip to install the three libraries. It might take a few moments to finish installing.

Upgrading Redis

It is a good practice to ensure that you are using the latest version of your libraries, as they would have the most up-to-date features and security updates. To upgrade the Redis library, use the following command:

```
!pip install --upgrade redis
```

Once you have run these commands, your Google Colab environment should have all the necessary libraries installed. You can verify this by trying to import these libraries in a new Python cell:

```
import pandas
import sentence_transformers
import redis
```

If these lines of code run without throwing an error, congratulations, your Google Colab environment is correctly set up and ready for the next steps!

Understanding the Dataset

We are dealing with a dataset taken from kaggle, "*IMDb Dataset Top-Rated films 1898-2022*", which includes a wealth of information about movies, including the title, director, star cast, IMDb rating, category, duration, censor-board rating, and release year. Here is a brief explanation of each field:

- Title: Name of the movie.
- Director: Director of the movie.
- Stars: Star cast of the movie.
- IMDb-Rating: Rating it received on IMDb's website.
- Category: Genre of the movie.
- Duration: Runtime of the movie.
- Censor-board-rating: Censor rating of the movie (for example, UA, R, A).
- Release year: The year in which the movie was released.

Understanding these fields allows us to comprehend the dataset structure, the type of data each field contains, and how it might be relevant to our task.

The `MovieRecommender` Class: An Overview

In this code snippet, we have implemented a movie recommendation system that uses natural language processing (NLP) to identify movies closely matching a user's query. Let us break down the various parts of the code and understand their functions.

This class, **`MovieRecommender`**, is the main implementation of our recommendation system. When initialized, it sets up a connection with a Redis server and loads a machine learning model for sentence embedding (a way of transforming sentences into meaningful numerical vectors). The class has several methods.

Let's first discuss the **`__init__`** method

```
def __init__(self, redis_host, redis_port, redis_password, csv_file_
path, model_name):
```

This is the definition of the **`__init__`** method. The self-parameter is a reference to the current instance of the class and is used to access class variables. The other parameters are explained in detail:

- **redis_host (str)**: The host address of the Redis server. This is the IP address or the domain name where the Redis server is running. For instance, if the Redis server is running on the same machine, this would be **'localhost'**.
- **redis_port (int)**: The port number where the Redis server is listening for connections. By default, the Redis server listens on port 6379.
- **redis_password (str)**: If the Redis server is protected by a password, you supply it here.
- **csv_file_path (str)**: The full path to the CSV file containing movie data, including the filename and its extension.
- **model_name (str)**: The name of the **SentenceTransformer** model to use for encoding the movie descriptions into vector format.

After defining the function, we will store these inputs as attributes of the class instance:

```
self.redis_host = redis_host
self.redis_port = redis_port
self.redis_password = redis_password
self.csv_file_path = csv_file_path
self.model_name = model_name
```

This means that these values are stored in the object and can be accessed later on in other methods by calling **self.attribute_name**.

```
self.model = SentenceTransformer(self.model_name)
```

Here, we are initializing a **SentenceTransformer** model. **SentenceTransformer** is a Python package for sentence, paragraph, and document embeddings, using BERT models specifically trained for this purpose. By passing **model_name** as a parameter, we are instructing it to use a specific pre-trained model for sentence encoding. The **self.model** object will now contain this model and can be used to transform sentences into their corresponding vector embeddings.

```
self.redis_client = redis.Redis(
    host=self.redis_host,
    port=self.redis_port,
    password=self.redis_password
)
```

Finally, we will establish a connection with the Redis server by initializing a **redis.Redis** object. We pass the Redis server's host address, port number, and password (if any) to do this. This object is used to interact with the Redis database throughout the rest of the class.

So, to summarize, the **__init__** method in the Movie Recommender class is used to initialize several important attributes and establish a connection with the Redis server. It takes in several parameters necessary for these tasks and creates a **SentenceTransformer** model for later use.

Data Preprocessing for Transformers

The model we have chosen for sentence embedding, **SentenceTransformer**, requires the input text to be in a certain format. Therefore, in the **load_data()** function, the relevant data about each movie (title, director, stars, IMDb rating, and more) is combined into a single string and then transformed into lowercase. The **SentenceTransformer** model then converts these strings into a meaningful vector representation. Let us go through it step-by-step.

```
def load_data(self):
```

The method name **load_data** suggests that this function is responsible for loading data from a source. self is a reference to the current instance of the class.

```
self.movie_df = pd.read_csv(self.csv_file_path)
```

This line is using the **read_csv** method from the pandas library to read the CSV file located at **self.csv_file_path**. It then assigns the resulting DataFrame to **self.movie_df**.

```
self.movie_df = self.movie_df.dropna(subset=['Category',
'Duration', 'Censor-board-rating'])
```

Here, the method **dropna** is used to remove rows with missing values in the **'Category'**, **'Duration'**, and **'Censor-board-rating'** columns. This helps ensure that the dataset we are working with does not contain incomplete data.

```
self.movie_df.reset_index(inplace=True)
```

This line resets the DataFrame index. The **inplace=True** argument means that the DataFrame is modified directly.

```
self.movie_df.drop(["index"],axis=1,inplace=True)
```

Here we drop the **'index'** column from the DataFrame that has been created from the resetting of the index in the previous step.

```
self.movie_df['formatted_text'] = (
            "The movie " + self.movie_df['Title'] + " directed by
" + self.movie_df['Director'] +
            " starring " + self.movie_df['Stars'] + " has an IMDb
rating of " + self.movie_df['IMDb-Rating'].astype(str) +
            " under the category " + self.movie_df['Category'] +
" with a duration of " + self.movie_df['Duration'] +
            ". It has a censor board rating of " + self.movie_
df['Censor-board-rating'] +
            " and was released in the year " + self.movie_df['Re-
leaseYear'].astype(str) + "."
        )
```

In this section, a new DataFrame column **'formatted_text'** is created by concatenating various fields from the dataset. This step creates a single string of text that contains most of the information about each movie. This will be the text that is encoded into a vector representation.

```
self.movie_df['formatted_text'] = self.movie_df['formatted_
text'].apply(lambda x: x.lower())
```

This line transforms all the text in the 'formatted_text' column to lowercase. This can help with consistency and can also affect the performance of some NLP models.

```
self.movie_df['row_vector'] = self.movie_df['formatted_text'].
apply(lambda x: self.model.encode(x))
```

Lastly, the apply method is used to apply the encoding method of the **SentenceTransformer** model to each row in the **'formatted_text'** column. This converts the text into a high-dimensional vector that captures the semantic information of the text. The resulting vectors are stored in a new column **'row_vector'**.

So, in summary, the **load_data** method reads a CSV file into a pandas DataFrame, removes rows with missing data, concatenates several fields into a single text column, converts this text to lowercase, and then transforms these strings into vector representations. These vector representations can then be used for similarity comparisons or other machine learning tasks.

Choosing the Right Transformer Model: MiniLM

We will use **MiniLM** for our sentence embeddings. **MiniLM** is a compact transformer model that achieves competitive results on various NLP tasks with fewer parameters. The name of this model, `'sentence-transformers/all-MiniLM-L12-v1'`, is passed when initializing the **`MovieRecommender`** class.

Defining Movie Data Loading and Vector Encoding

The **`load_vectors()`** method pushes the movie data into the Redis server. For each movie, it creates a unique key and a dictionary containing the movie details (title, director, stars, rating, and more). Notably, it also includes the vector representation of the movie, converted into bytes. This dictionary is stored in the Redis server under the unique key. Let us break down the code:

```
def load_vectors(self, _df, vector_data, vector_field_name):
```

Here, self refers to the instance of the class. **`_df`** is the DataFrame that contains the movie data. **`vector_data`** is the list of vectors generated by the SentenceTransformer model, and **`vector_field_name`** is the name of the field where these vectors will be stored in the Redis server.

```
p = self.redis_client.pipeline(transaction=False)
```

This line creates a Redis pipeline. Pipelines are a subclass of the base Redis class that provide support for buffering multiple commands to be executed as a group. The **`transaction=False`** argument means that the pipeline is not transactional - the commands in the pipeline are not atomic.

```
for index, row in _df.iterrows():
```

This line starts a loop that iterates over the DataFrame. For each row in the DataFrame, the loop will create a dictionary that maps field names to their values and then stores this dictionary in the Redis server.

```
key = 'title_id:' + str(index)
```

This line creates a unique key for each movie, using the format **`'title_id:'`** followed by the index of the row.

```
_data_mapping = {
    "Title": row['Title'],
    "Director": row['Director'],
    "Stars": row['Stars'],
    "Rating": row['IMDb-Rating'],
    "Category": row['Category'],
    "Duration": row['Duration'],
```

```
        "Censor_Rating": row['Censor-board-rating'],
        "ReleaseYear": row['ReleaseYear'],
        vector_field_name: vector_data[index].astype(np.float32).tobytes()
    }
```

Here, a dictionary **_data_mapping** is created to store all the relevant information from the DataFrame row. It also includes the transformed vector, converted to bytes using **tobytes()**. This is necessary because Redis cannot store complex data types like numpy arrays.

```
    p.hset(key, mapping=_data_mapping)
```

This command adds the **_data_mapping** dictionary to the Redis server under the key created earlier. The **hset** method is used to set the hash value.

```
    p.execute()
```

Finally, this line executes all the commands that have been buffered in the Redis pipeline. This is more efficient than executing each command individually, especially when dealing with large amounts of data.

In summary, the **load_vectors** method loads the vector representations of movie data into a Redis server for efficient storage and retrieval. The method creates a unique key for each movie and stores the movie data and vector under this key.

Defining the Vector Database Indexing Process

The **create_hnsw_index()** and **load_and_index_data()** methods are responsible for creating an index of vectors in the Redis server using the HNSW (Hierarchical Navigable Small World) method, an efficient algorithm for nearest neighbor search. This index allows for quick and efficient searching of similar vectors during the recommendation process. The method takes various parameters for index creation, like the **distance metric**, **number of vectors**, **vector dimensions**, and others.

This function takes in several parameters:

- **vector_field_name**: Name of the field where the vector data will be stored.
- **number_of_vectors**: The expected number of vectors to be stored in the index.
- **vector_dimensions**: The number of dimensions in each vector.

- **`distance_metric`**: The distance metric to be used in calculating the nearest neighbors.
- **`M`**, **`EF`**, **`EF_RUNTIME`**, and **`EPSILON`** are parameters of the HNSW algorithm.

Let us break down the method:

```
def create_hnsw_index(self, vector_field_name, number_of_vectors, vector_dimensions, distance_metric='COSINE', M=40, EF=200, EF_RUNTIME=100, EPSILON=0.2):
```

This line defines the method and its parameters. By default, it uses **`COSINE`** as the distance metric, which works well with high-dimensional data. The other parameters are set to common default values for HNSW.

```
create_command = [
    "FT.CREATE", "idx", "SCHEMA",
    ...
]
```

Here, **`create_command`** is a list that stores the command for creating the HNSW index. The **`FT.CREATE`** command is used to create a new index in Redis, and **`SCHEMA`** sets the schema of the index. The various fields (**`Title`**, **`Director`**, **`Stars`**, **`Rating`**, **`Category`**, **`Duration`**, **`Censor_Rating`**, **`ReleaseYear`**, and the **`vector field`**) are specified along with their respective data types.

The **`VECTOR`** field is set as the HNSW type. Then, the number of dimensions (DIM) for the vectors, the type of the vectors (TYPE), and the distance metric (**`DISTANCE_METRIC`**) are defined. The **`INITIAL_CAP`** parameter is used to specify the expected number of vectors.

Next, the parameters **`M`**, **`EF_CONSTRUCTION`**, **`EF_RUNTIME`**, and **`EPSILON`** for the HNSW algorithm are set. M is the maximum number of links created for a new element in the neighbors graph, **`EF_CONSTRUCTION`** is the size of the dynamic list used during the construction of the HNSW graph, **`EF_RUNTIME`** is the size of the dynamic list used during the search phase, and **`EPSILON`** is a trade-off between recall and precision.

```
self.redis_client.execute_command(*create_command)
```

Lastly, this line sends the command list to Redis for execution. The * operator unpacks the list into individual arguments for the **`execute_command`** method. It will create an HNSW index based on the given parameters, which allows efficient nearest neighbor search on the stored vectors.

Defining the Search Function

The **search()** method is where the recommendation takes place. It takes a user's query, encodes it using the same SentenceTransformer model, and then runs a KNN (k-nearest neighbors) query on the index in Redis server to find the most similar vectors (that is, the most relevant movie recommendations). It returns a list of these similar movies, which can then be printed or used in other ways.

Here are the parameters:

- **user_query**: A string that the user provides. This is what the system will use to find similar movies.
- **top_k**: The number of results to return. By default, it returns 4 results.
- **dist_field_name**: The name of the field where the distance scores will be stored. The default is set to **"__movie_vector_score"**.

Let us break down the method:

```
        def search(self, user_query, top_k=4, dist_field_name="__
movie_vector_score"):
```

This line defines the method and its parameters.

```
e = self.model.encode(user_query.lower())
```

This line uses the SentenceTransformer model to encode the user's query into a vector representation. The query is converted to lowercase to maintain consistency with the indexed data.

```
q = (
    Query(f'*=>[KNN $K @movie_vector $BLOB AS {dist_field_name}]')
    .return_fields('Title','Director','Stars','Rating',
'Category','Duration','Censor_Rating','ReleaseYear')
    .paging(0, top_k)
    .sort_by(dist_field_name)
    .dialect(2)
)
```

This block constructs a query using the Redisearch Python client's Query object.

- It uses the **KNN** syntax to search the **'movie_vector'** field (the HNSW index) with the encoded query vector (**$BLOB**) and requests the **top_k** results.
- The **return_fields** method specifies the fields that should be returned in the search results.

- The paging method specifies the offset (0) and the number of results to return (**top_k**).
- The **sort_by** method specifies that the results should be sorted by the distance field.
- The dialect(2) method specifies how to use the second version of the RediSearch Query Syntax.

```
params_dict = {"K": top_k + 1, "BLOB": e.astype(np.float32).
tobytes()}
```

This line creates a dictionary with parameters for the KNN query. The **top_k + 1** is used because the KNN search includes the query itself in the results. The vector representation of the user's query is converted to a bytes object using the numpy tobytes method, as required by the Redisearch client.

```
docs = self.redis_client.ft().search(q, params_dict)
```

This line executes the search query with the given parameters using the Redisearch client and stores the result in docs.

```
return docs
```

Finally, the method returns the search results.

So, in essence, the search method encodes a user's query into a vector using the SentenceTransformer, forms a KNN query, and then uses the Redisearch client to execute the query and retrieve the most similar movies from the Redis database.

The Load and Index and Search Functions

Finally, there are two standalone functions: **load_and_index()** and **search()**, which are used to initialize the MovieRecommender, load and index the data, and perform a search, respectively. These functions instantiate the MovieRecommender class with the necessary parameters like Redis server details, path to the CSV file, and model name. The **load_and_index()** function subsequently loads and indexes the movie data. The **search()** function performs a search based on a user's query and prints the results.

It has the following parameters:

- **num_movies**: The number of movie entries to load and index. The default is set to 800.
- **vector_field_name**: The name of the field where the vector data will be stored.

- **distance_metric**: The type of distance metric to use when creating the HNSW index. By default, it uses the **'COSINE'** metric.
- **dimensions**: The number of dimensions in the vectors. By default, it's set to 384, which could be the output size of the SentenceTransformer model.

Let us breakdown the method:

```
def load_and_index_data(self, num_movies=800, vector_field_
name='movie_vector', distance_metric='COSINE', dimensions=384):
```

This line defines the method and its parameters.

```
self.redis_client.flushall()
```

This line is used to delete all keys in the current database. It is used here to ensure that Redis starts with a clean slate, removing any previous data that might be in the database.

```
self.create_hnsw_index(vector_field_name, num_movies, dimensions,
distance_metric)
```

This line calls the **create_hnsw_index** method to create an HNSW index in Redis with the given parameters.

```
movie_vec = self.movie_df['row_vector'].tolist()
```

This line extracts the '**row_vector**' column from the movie dataframe (which contains the vector representation of the movie information) and converts it to a list.

```
self.load_vectors(self.movie_df.head(num_movies), movie_vec
[0:num_movies], vector_field_name)
```

Finally, this line calls the **load_vectors** method to load the vector representations of the movies into Redis. It passes the top **num_movies** rows from the dataframe and the corresponding vector data to the **load_vectors** method along with the **vector_field_name**.

In sum, **load_and_index_data** method is used to cleanse the Redis database, create an HNSW index, load the movie data into Redis, and then add the movie vectors to the index for efficient nearest neighbor searches.

Wrapper Functions

We have created the wrapper functions to create a pipeline that demonstrates the working of the different functionalities with different operations.

- **`load_and_index()` function**

The **`load_and_index`** function is responsible for initializing the MovieRecommender object and performing the necessary steps to load the movie data from the CSV file and indexing this data in the Redis server.

Here is a step-by-step walkthrough of what happens inside this function:

```
def load_and_index():
    # Note: Replace these values with your actual Redis server
details and CSV file path
    redis_host = 'redis-17820.c301.ap-south-1-1.ec2.cloud.redislabs.
    com'
    redis_port = 17820
    redis_password = ''
    csv_file_path = '/data/IMDb_Data_final.csv'
    model_name = 'sentence-transformers/all-MiniLM-L12-v1'
```

In this block, several configuration parameters are defined:

- **`redis_host`**, **`redis_port`**, and **`redis_password`** are used to connect to the Redis server.
- **`csv_file_path`** is the file path to the CSV data source.
- **`model_name`** is the name of the pre-trained SentenceTransformer model to use for encoding the movie descriptions.

```
    recommender = MovieRecommender(redis_host, redis_port, redis_
password, csv_file_path, model_name)
```

This line initializes the **`MovieRecommender`** class with the above-defined parameters. This creates a **`recommender`** object.

```
    recommender.load_data()
```

The **`load_data`** method of the **`MovieRecommender`** class is called, which loads and pre-processes the movie data from the CSV file, formats it, and encodes it into vectors using the SentenceTransformer model.

```
    recommender.load_and_index_data()
```

This calls the **`load_and_index_data`** method of the **`MovieRecommender`** class, which indexes the movie vectors in the Redis server.

- **`search()` function**

The search function is used to initialize the **`MovieRecommender`** object and perform a search operation based on a user's query.

Here is a detailed walkthrough of what happens inside this function:

```
def search(user_query, top_k=4):
    # Note: Replace these values with your actual Redis server
details and CSV file path
    redis_host = 'redis-17820.c301.ap-south-1-1.ec2.cloud.redislabs.
com'
    redis_port = 17820
    redis_password = ''
    csv_file_path = '/data/IMDb_Data_final.csv'
    model_name = 'sentence-transformers/all-MiniLM-L12-v1'
```

This block is similar to the one in the **load_and_index** function. It defines the same configuration parameters.

```
    recommender = MovieRecommender(redis_host, redis_port, redis_
password, csv_file_path, model_name)
```

This line is also identical to the corresponding one in the **load_and_index** function. It creates a MovieRecommender object with the defined configuration parameters.

```
    docs = recommender.search(user_query, top_k)
```

This line calls the search method of the **MovieRecommender** class, passing the user's query and the number of results to return. The method returns a list of the most similar movies, which is stored in docs.

```
    # print result
    for doc in docs.docs:
        print(doc)
```

This block loops through the search results and prints them out. The **docs.docs** accesses the **docs** attribute of the search results object, which is a list of documents (movies) returned by the search.

So, in sum, the search function takes a user query, creates a MovieRecommender object, performs a search on the indexed movie data, and prints the search results.

Results

```
# Load and index the data
load_and_index()


# User query
```

```
user_query="i want to watch movies under the comedy category with imdb rating of 7 and above"


# Search for the most similar movies
search(user_query, top_k=4)
```

- Document {'id': 'title_id:528', 'payload': None, 'Title': 'The King of Comedy', 'Director': 'MartinScorsese', 'Stars': 'RobertDeNiro, JerryLewis, DiahnneAbbott, SandraBernhard', 'Rating': '7.8', 'Category': 'Comedy,Crime,Drama', 'Duration': '109min', 'Censor_Rating': 'U', 'ReleaseYear': '1982'}
- Document {'id': 'title_id:15', 'payload': None, 'Title': 'The Goonies', 'Director': 'RichardDonner', 'Stars': 'SeanAstin, JoshBrolin, JeffCohen, CoreyFeldman', 'Rating': '7.7', 'Category': 'Adventure,Comedy,Family', 'Duration': '114min', 'Censor_Rating': 'U', 'ReleaseYear': '1985'}
- Document {'id': 'title_id:79', 'payload': None, 'Title': 'The Breakfast Club', 'Director': 'JohnHughes', 'Stars': 'EmilioEstevez, JuddNelson, MollyRingwald, AllySheedy', 'Rating': '7.8', 'Category': 'Comedy,Drama', 'Duration': '97min', 'Censor_Rating': 'UA', 'ReleaseYear': '1985'}
- Document {'id': 'title_id:468', 'payload': None, 'Title': 'Being John Malkovich', 'Director': 'SpikeJonze', 'Stars': 'JohnCusack, CameronDiaz, CatherineKeener, JohnMalkovich', 'Rating': '7.8', 'Category': 'Comedy,Drama,Fantasy', 'Duration': '113min', 'Censor_Rating': 'R', 'ReleaseYear': '1999'}

There we go. The search function recommends results that match the query. The response can be used in various ways and at different scales to accommodate a business use case involving data-driven decisions.

Summarizing the Use of Transformers and Vector Databases

Transformers, especially the SentenceTransformer model, have been instrumental in converting text data into a numeric form that can be processed efficiently. By generating sentence embeddings that capture the semantic content of the text, they allowed us to turn the details of each movie into a unique vector representation.

Vector databases like Redis play an essential role in storing these generated vectors and enabling efficient and fast similarity searches on top of them. Redis provides a powerful in-memory database that supports a wide variety of data structures and offers full-text and similarity searches through its RediSearch module.

In our case, using Hierarchical Navigable Small World (HNSW) indexing allowed us to perform quick nearest-neighbor searches. This feature is crucial for recommendation systems where the objective is to find items in the database that are most similar to a given item or query.

Discussion on Use Cases Beyond Movie Recommendations

While this case study focused on movie recommendations, the combination of Transformers and Redis can be used in a wide variety of applications. For example, this methodology can be applied to build recommendation systems for products, books, music, or any other item that can be described textually.

Further, it could be used to create a smart search engine that not only looks for keywords but understands the semantic meaning of a search query. In the field of customer support, it could help in automatically routing support tickets to the right department based on the semantic understanding of the issue described. Similarly, it can help in matching candidates to job descriptions in recruitment or in clustering news articles or social media posts based on their content.

Future Improvements and Scalability Considerations

As we look towards the future, there are several improvements and scalability considerations to keep in mind. One possible enhancement is to use more sophisticated transformers models or incorporate user feedback to improve the quality of recommendations. We could also experiment with different configurations of the HNSW index to optimize performance.

Regarding scalability, Redis scales well and can handle large amounts of data. However, as data grows, we might need to consider distributed databases or clustering solutions to handle the load. Furthermore, while our current implementation loads and indexes all data at the start, in a real-world there would be need for continually updated databases. Thus, we would need a strategy for incrementally updating our index.

Finally, while our current implementation is designed for a single server, in a production environment, we might need to design for redundancy and failover. This could include setting up a backup Redis server and developing a strategy for quickly switching to the backup in the event of a primary server failure.

This exploration of movie recommendation systems has shown us the power and potential of combining Transformers and Redis. The road ahead is exciting with endless possibilities to improve and adapt this approach to different use cases and larger datasets.

Conclusion

The combined use of Transformers and vector databases like Redis has demonstrated a powerful way to manage and utilize large amounts of data. Transformers, with their advanced understanding of language semantics, have been used effectively to convert movie information into representative vectors. Redis, on the other hand, provides a fast and efficient way to store and index these vectors. Together, they allow us to create an effective movie recommendation system.

In the next chapter, we will further explore the use of LLMs as chatbots, that is based on a private document and a website.

Chapter 7

Document-and Web-based QA Bots with Large Language Models

Introduction

The advent of artificial intelligence has revolutionized the way we interact with information. Today, we have access to a plethora of data, but the real challenge lies in extracting meaningful insights from this vast ocean of knowledge. This is where Document- and Web-based Question Answering (QA) bots, powered by Large Language Models (LLMs), come into play. These AI-powered bots are designed to understand, analyze, and interpret large volumes of text, providing precise answers to complex queries.

The code files and the data used in this chapter can be accessed at https://github.com/ava-orange-education/Hands-On-Large-Language-Models-for-Enterprise/blob/main/Chapter_7_Document_and_Web_based_QA_Bots_with_Large_Language_Models.ipynb

Structure

In this chapter, the following topics will be covered:

- LLM in the Context of Chatbots

- Semantic Search and How It Powers Context Understanding and Response Generation
- A Detailed Explanation of the Document-based QA Bot Use Case
- A Detailed Explanation of the Web-based QA Bot Use Case

Understanding Large Language Models in the Context of a Chatbot

Large Language Models (LLMs) like GPT-3 by OpenAI are a type of machine learning model that has been trained on a diverse range of internet text. This means that these models have been exposed to a vast amount of written content, from books and articles to websites and more. This extensive training allows them to understand and generate human-like text.

When we say that LLMs can "*understand*" text, we mean that they can identify patterns and relationships between words and phrases, allowing them to predict what comes next in a sentence. This is why they are so effective in generating human-like text - they can predict what a human would likely say next. It's important to note that these models are a type of transformer-based model, which is a key aspect of their ability to understand context in text.

In the context of Question Answering (QA) bots, this ability to understand and generate text is crucial. LLMs can parse complex queries, understand the context, and generate a response that accurately answers the question. They can handle a wide range of topics, making them versatile and adaptable. However, it's important to note that LLMs don't have real-time data access directly, so they can't provide current weather conditions or news updates. Instead, they excel at answering questions about complex topics based on the information they were trained on. For example, if a user asks a QA bot "What is the theory of relativity?", the LLM can understand that the user is asking about Einstein's theory and generate a detailed and accurate response accordingly.

Semantic Search and Its Role

Semantic Search is a process that understands the intent and contextual meaning of search phrases, delivering more accurate and relevant results. But how does it do this?

Traditional search engines match keywords in a user's query to keywords in a document. Semantic search goes a step further by understanding the context and intent behind the query. For example, if a user searches for "*apple*", a traditional search engine might return results about the fruit and the technology company. A semantic search engine, on the other hand, would try to understand what the user is likely looking for based on the context of their query.

In a QA bot, semantic search is used to find the most relevant documents or sections of documents that might contain the answer to a user's query. It does this by understanding the context and intent behind the query and then searching for documents that match this context and intent. This makes the QA bot more effective and efficient, as it can provide more accurate and relevant answers.

Building a Document- and Web-based QA Bot

Building a Document- and Web-based Question Answering (QA) Bot involves developing a sophisticated system that can understand user queries and provide accurate answers by extracting relevant information from various sources, including documents and web pages:

- **Query Understanding:** This is the process of understanding what the user is asking. The bot uses an LLM to parse the query, understand the context, and identify the key entities and relationships. For example, if a user asks, "*What is the capital of France?*", the bot needs to understand that the user is asking for information (the capital) about a specific entity (France).
- **Document Retrieval:** Once the bot understands the query, it needs to find the information to answer it. This is done using semantic search, which finds documents that match the intent behind the query. In our example, the bot would search for documents that contain information about the capital of France.
- **Answer Generation:** The final step is to generate a response. The bot uses the LLM to interpret the information in the retrieved documents and craft a response that accurately answers the user's query. In our example, the bot would generate a response like "*The capital of France is Paris.*"

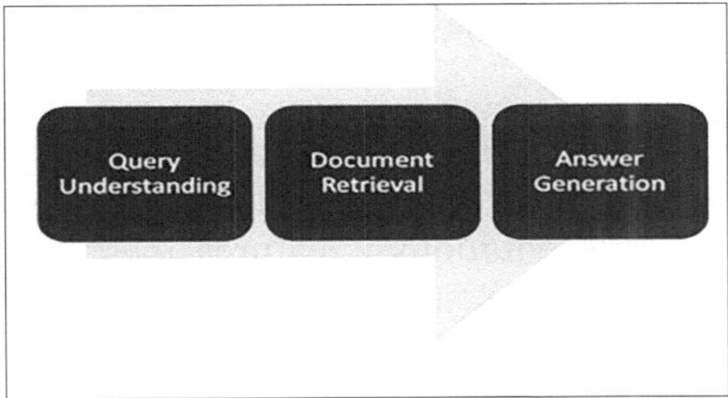

Figure 7.1: *QA Bot Approach*

Applications of Document- and Web-based QA Bots

QA bots powered by LLMs, and Semantic Search have a wide range of applications. They can be used in customer service to answer customer queries, in research to extract information from large volumes of text, and in education to provide students with precise answers to their questions.

In customer service, for example, a QA bot could assist in answering questions about a company's products or services, supplementing the efforts of human customer service representatives. They are particularly effective in handling routine queries, which can free up human representatives to address more complex or nuanced issues. In the context of research, a QA bot could sift through large volumes of academic papers to find relevant information, saving researchers valuable time. As for education, a QA bot could provide students with instant answers to their questions, enhancing their learning experience. However, it's important to stress that while QA bots are powerful tools, they are not yet capable of completely replacing the need for human expertise and judgment in these areas.

In summary, LLMs and Semantic Search are powerful tools that can greatly enhance the capabilities of QA bots. By understanding and generating human-like text and delivering accurate and relevant search results, these technologies can revolutionize the way we interact with information.

Transitioning to Vector Databases and Their Role in Semantic Search

As we delve deeper into the world of document-based QA bots powered by large language models, we encounter the need for efficient and effective ways to handle complex, high-dimensional data. This is where vector databases come into play.

Vector databases are a specialized type of database designed to handle high-dimensional data, such as text, images, audio, and video. They store data as vectors, mathematical representations of features or attributes, which can range from tens to thousands of dimensions. The vectors are typically generated by applying a transformation or embedding function to the raw data.

In the context of semantic search, vector databases play a crucial role. Semantic search seeks to improve search accuracy by understanding the searcher's intent and the contextual meaning of terms. It involves a variety of techniques from natural language processing, including word embeddings where words or phrases from the vocabulary are mapped to vectors of real numbers.

Vector databases provide an efficient way to store and retrieve these word embeddings, enabling fast and accurate similarity search and retrieval of data based on their vector distance or similarity. This is particularly important for document-based QA bots, which need to quickly and accurately retrieve relevant information in response to user queries.

The importance of vector databases in this context cannot be overstated. Traditional databases and search engines often struggle with the complexity and high dimensionality of modern data. Vector databases, however, are designed to handle this complexity, unlocking the potential for a wide range of applications, such as e-commerce recommendations, autonomous vehicle systems, and of course, natural language processing and document-based QA bots.

One such vector database that stands out in this domain is Pinecone. It's a fully managed, developer-friendly, and easily scalable vector database that enables efficient search, analysis, and unlocking of insights from high-dimensional data. But before we delve into the specifics of Pinecone and other vector databases, let's take a closer look at the benefits of vector databases over traditional databases and how they handle high-dimensional data.

Vector Databases and Pinecone: An In-Depth Look

Vector databases, a specialized breed of databases, are meticulously crafted to house data in the form of high-dimensional vectors. These vectors, which encapsulate mathematical representations of attributes or characteristics, span a spectrum from a handful to thousands of dimensions, adapting to the intricacy and refinement of the data at hand. This conversion into vectors is often achieved through transformation or embedding functions applied to raw data, spanning realms like text, images, audio, and video.

The predominant advantage of a vector database is its prowess in swiftly and precisely conducting similarity searches and data retrieval. This hinges on the concept of vector distance or similarity–measures that allow the database to discern how closely different vectors align. Traditional databases and search engines can falter when grappling with intricate, multi-dimensional data such as images, videos, or text embeddings. In stark contrast, vector databases excel by structuring data as vectors and employing specialized algorithms that adeptly scan and pinpoint similar data points. The criterion for similarity is gauged by the distance or likeness to a reference point.

The significance of this innovation lies in its capacity to accelerate and refine the analysis of high-dimensional data. This, in turn, lays the foundation for an array of applications that benefit from faster, more precise data exploration. The scope spans diverse domains, from empowering e-commerce recommendations by rapidly matching consumer preferences, to bolstering autonomous vehicle systems that rely on swift data assimilation, and even amplifying the capabilities of natural language processing techniques.

In essence, vector databases wield the power to revolutionize the landscape of data analysis and retrieval, redefining how we extract insights from intricate, multi-dimensional datasets across a plethora of industries and applications.

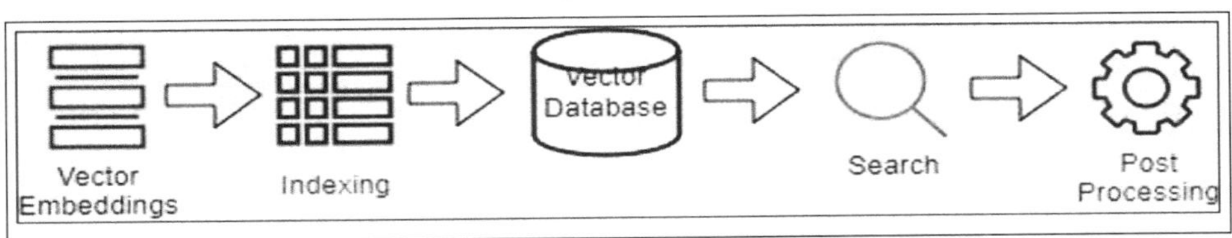

Figure 7.2: Vector DB Pipeline

Pinecone stands as a prime illustration of advanced technology–a fully managed, developer-centric, and effortlessly scalable vector database. This groundbreaking solution facilitates swift and effective searches, intricate data analysis, and the extraction of valuable insights from datasets with high dimensions. The core strength of Pinecone lies in its adeptness at indexing and storing vector embeddings–a form of mathematical representation–for the purpose of rapid retrieval and similarity-based searches. Its capabilities extend to encompass CRUD (Create, Read, Update, Delete) operations, metadata filtering, and horizontal scaling, while ensuring accuracy remains at the forefront.

Pinecone's prowess shines most notably in its capacity to gracefully tackle scaling challenges. For modest-scale use cases, conducting vector retrieval on a personal laptop with readily available sample code might suffice. As the scale of usage elevates, solutions like Redis and PostgreSQL, complemented by vector plugins, can fulfill the requirements. However, when the demands surge into large-scale territory, the need for a tailored, custom-designed system becomes paramount. Pinecone emerges as the go-to solution, enabling corporate giants to manage billions of vectors distributed across a multitude of machines.

In essence, Pinecone is a beacon in the realm of vector databases. Its significance stems from its meticulous approach to addressing the limitations inherent in standalone vector indices. This includes surmounting scalability hurdles, simplifying integration processes, and delivering real-time updates and built-in security features. This holistic approach ensures a seamless and potent data management experience. Pinecone's applications span a spectrum—from optimizing recommendation systems to identifying anomalies and bolstering the capabilities of natural language processing.

In summary, Pinecone's emergence marks a pivotal stride forward in the domain of vector database technology. Its capacity to harness vector embeddings while addressing challenges in scalability, integration, and security underscores its role as an invaluable tool for diverse applications, spanning fields that range from personalized recommendations to advanced language processing techniques.

Benefits of Vector Databases over Traditional Databases

Vector databases have gained popularity in recent years due to their ability to handle complex and high-dimensional data, such as images, videos, and text embeddings, which traditional databases and search engines are not designed to handle. Here are some benefits of using a vector database over a traditional database:

- **Vector indexing**: Vector databases use vector indexing to efficiently store and retrieve high-dimensional data. Vector indexing involves breaking down a document or website into smaller segments and converting these segments into vectors that can be stored in a vector database. This enables efficient similarity-based operations, such as approximate nearest neighbor (ANN) searches, which are useful for various applications, including recommendation systems, image and video search, natural language processing, and anomaly detection.

- **Efficient similarity search:** Vector databases utilize similarity search algorithms to swiftly retrieve data points that are similar to a given query point based on distance or similarity metrics. This approach enables efficient analysis of complex, multi-dimensional data, paving the way for applications like personalized e-commerce recommendations, autonomous vehicles, and natural language processing. The technology's impact spans diverse domains, streamlining data analysis and expanding possibilities across industries.
- **Flexibility**: Vector databases can handle a wide variety of data formats with flexible schemas, making them adaptable to changing business requirements. They are also designed for both search and data mining, making them suited for virtually all types of business use cases.
- **Scalability**: Vector databases can handle vast volumes of data and are designed to scale up and out. They are also horizontally scalable, meaning that they can be distributed across multiple servers to handle large datasets.
- **Handling complex data**: Vector databases excel in handling complex data like images, audio, and text by converting them into numerical vectors that computers can process. This transformation enhances data processing efficiency and supports applications such as image recognition, sentiment analysis, and sound analysis.
- **Spatial indexing**: Vector databases use spatial indexing techniques like R-trees and Quad-trees to enable data retrieval based on proximity. This allows for high-speed similarity searches and computations, essential for real-time applications and machine-learning tasks.
- **Approximate nearest neighbor search**: Vector databases excel at conducting fast approximate nearest neighbor (ANN) searches, identifying similar items in large datasets. They utilize techniques like dimensionality reduction and indexing algorithms for efficient searches, making them ideal for recommendation systems, anomaly detection, and natural language processing. These databases enhance application performance and responsiveness by swiftly finding relevant matches.

In summary, Vector databases excel in managing high-dimensional data efficiently by utilizing specialized indexing structures and advanced search algorithms. They have the unique ability to represent complex objects as embeddings, enhancing data processing. With unparalleled speed, scalability, and flexibility, vector databases offer versatile solutions for various applications and industries.

Introduction to the Use Case: Document-based QA bot

The use case we are discussing here is a private document-based Question-Answering (QA) bot. The bot is designed to answer questions based on the content of a specific document. In this case, the document is a PDF e-book by Cybrosys Limited Edition titled "BLOCKCHAIN". The bot reads the document, indexes its content, and then uses this index to answer queries related to the document's content.

Tech-Stack Walkthrough and Explanation

- **Llama-Index:** Llama-Index is a versatile tool that augments LLMs by ingesting and indexing private or domain-specific data, offering a natural language interface for accessing data distributed across various sources. It provides numerous tools ranging from data connectors for data ingestion to engines for data access. Llama-Index has the potential to empower not only beginners but also advanced users, offering high-level APIs for quick setup and low-level APIs for extensive customization. This flexibility makes it an ideal tool for a variety of applications, from chatbots to knowledge bases.
- **OpenAI**: OpenAI's models are used to convert the document's content and the user's queries into vectors. This process, known as embedding, allows the bot to compare the queries with the document's content and find the most relevant sections.
- **Pinecone**: Storing the document embeddings in a vector database like Pinecone allows the bot to quickly and efficiently retrieve the most relevant sections of the document when answering a query.
- **Transformers**: This library provides access to many pre-trained models for NLP tasks. These models can understand the semantic meaning of the text, making them ideal for a QA bot.

Pre-requisites

Before we embark on the journey to work on this use case, it's essential to thoroughly validate that all the required prerequisites have been successfully met and fulfilled. This will ensure a solid foundation as we move forward with our intended utilization.

OpenAI API Key

1. Login to https://platform.openai.com/
2. Click your profile icon and select **`View API Keys`**.

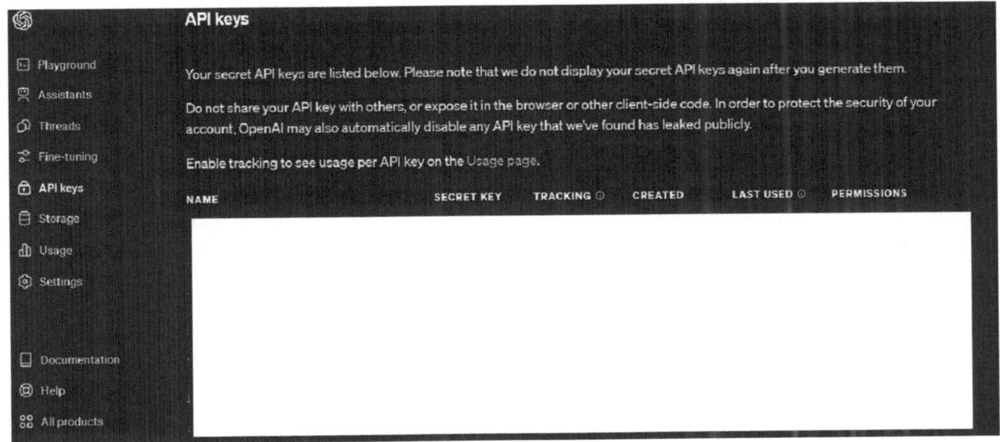

Figure 7.3: *OpenAI Navigate API Key*

3. Then select **`Create New Secret Key`**, provide a name for your key, and click Create Secret Key.

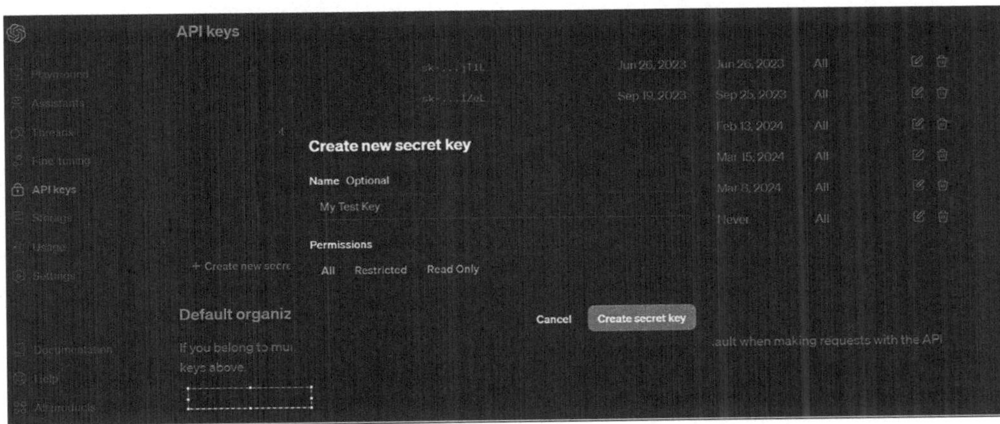

Figure 7.4: *Create API Key*

4. You can then copy the secret key and store it. We will be using it later in this exercise.

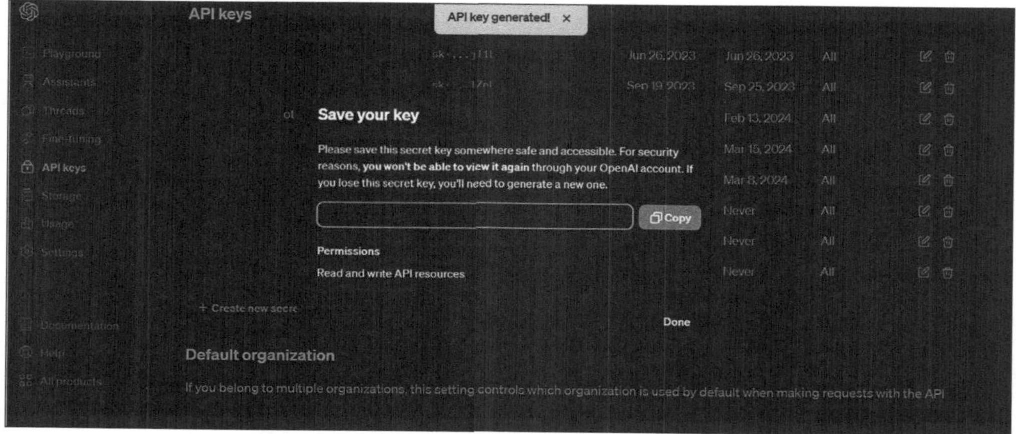

***Figure 7.5**: Copy API Key*

Pinecone API Key

1. Login into https://www.pinecone.io/

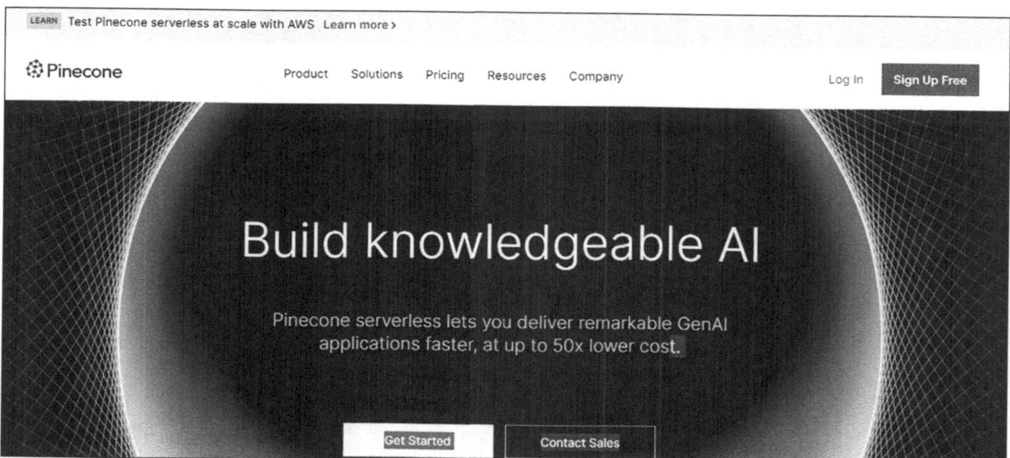

***Figure 7.6**: Pinecone Login*

2. On the landing page, select **`API Keys`**, and then copy both the Environment name and the hidden value, which is the API key.

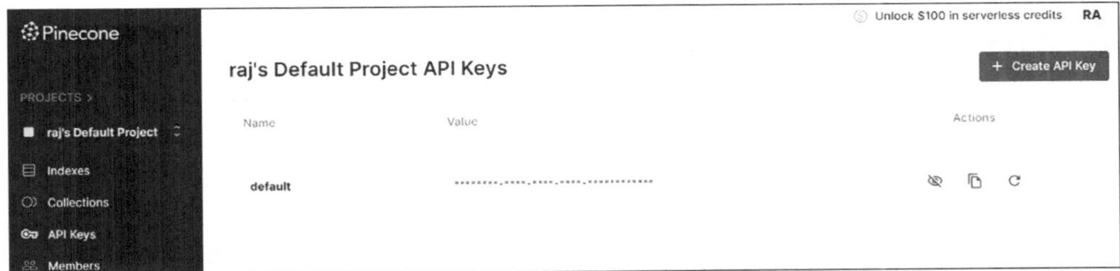

Figure 7.7: *Pinecone API Key*

3. We will be using this environment name and the API key later in the exercise.

Implementation Steps

The code provided performs the following steps:

1. **Import Required Libraries**: The necessary libraries are imported.
2. **Load Documents Using Llama-Index**: The PDF document is read and its content is stored.
3. **Setup OpenAI Environment**: The OpenAI environment is set up using the provided API key.
4. **Setup Pinecone Environment**: The Pinecone environment is set up using the provided API key and environment details. An index is created in Pinecone to store the document embeddings.
5. **Setup Vector Store with Pinecone**: A **`PineconeVectorStore`** is created to store the document embeddings.
6. **Setup Storage and Service Context: `StorageContext`** and **`ServiceContext`** are set up. The **`StorageContext`** specifies where the document embeddings will be stored (in this case, the **`PineconeVectorStore`**), and the **`ServiceContext`** specifies how the documents will be embedded (using OpenAI's text embedding model).
7. **Indexing Documents:** The documents are indexed using the **`GPTVectorStoreIndex`**. This involves embedding the documents and storing the embeddings in the vector store.
8. **Querying the Index:** The index is used to answer queries. The queries are embedded, and the embeddings are compared to the document embeddings to find the most similar documents.

Detailed Code Walkthrough

Let's go through the code in more detail as follows:

1. **Import Required Libraries:** The necessary libraries are imported. This includes **`Llama-Index`** for document indexing, OpenAI for text embeddings, Pinecone for vector storage, and Transformers for NLP tasks.

```
!pip install --quiet --no-cache-dir llama-index pinecone-client
openai transformers

# Step 1: Import required libraries

# --------------------------------

import os

from pathlib import Path

from llama_index import Document, download_loader, GPTVector-
StoreIndex, StorageContext, ServiceContext

from llama_index.embeddings.openai import OpenAIEmbedding

from llama_index.vector_stores import PineconeVectorStore

import openai

import pinecone
```

2. **Load Documents Using Llama-Index:** The **`PDFReader`** from Llama-Index is used to read the PDF document. The content of the document is stored in the **`'documents'`** variable.

```
# Step 2: Load documents using Llama-Index

# ---------------------------------------

PDFReader = download_loader("PDFReader")

loader = PDFReader()

documents = loader.load_data(file=Path('/content/blockchain-book.
pdf'))
```

3. **Setup OpenAI Environment:** The **`OpenAI API key`** is set as an environment variable. This key is used to authenticate with the OpenAI API and use their text embedding model.

```
# Step 3: Setup OpenAI environment

# ------------------------------

os.environ['OPENAI_API_KEY'] = "your_openai_api_key"

openai.api_key = "your_openai_api_key"
```

4. **Setup Pinecone Environment**: The Pinecone API key and environment details are set as environment variables. These are used to authenticate with the Pinecone service. A connection to Pinecone is initialized, and an index is created in Pinecone to store the document embeddings.

```
# Step 4: Setup Pinecone environment
# ----------------------------------
os.environ['PINECONE_API_KEY'] = 'your_pinecone_api_key'
os.environ['PINECONE_ENVIRONMENT'] = 'your_pinecone_environment'
pinecone.init(
    api_key=os.environ['PINECONE_API_KEY'],
    environment=os.environ['PINECONE_ENVIRONMENT']
)
index_name = 'docindex'
if index_name not in pinecone.list_indexes():
    pinecone.create_index(
        index_name,
        dimension=1536,
        metric='cosine'
    )
pinecone_index = pinecone.Index(index_name)
```

5. **Setup Vector Store with Pinecone:** The Pinecone index is used to create a **PineconeVectorStore**. This vector store will hold the document embeddings.

```
# Step 5: Setup Vector Store with Pinecone
# ----------------------------------------
vector_store = PineconeVectorStore(pinecone_index=pinecone_index)
```

6. **Setup Storage and Service Context:** The **StorageContext** is set up using the **PineconeVectorStore**. This context specifies where the document embeddings will be stored. The **ServiceContext** is set up using OpenAI's text embedding model. This context specifies how the documents will be embedded.

```
# Step 6: Setup Storage and Service Context
# ------------------------------------------
storage_context = StorageContext.from_defaults(
```

```
    vector_store=vector_store
)
embed_model = OpenAIEmbedding(model='text-embedding-ada-002',
embed_batch_size=100)
service_context = ServiceContext.from_defaults(embed_model=embed_
model)
```

7. **Indexing Documents:** The documents are indexed using the **`GPTVectorStoreIndex`**. This involves embedding the documents using the **`embed_model`** specified in the **`ServiceContext`** and storing the embeddings in the vector store specified in the **`StorageContext`**.

```
# Step 7: Indexing documents
# -------------------------
index = GPTVectorStoreIndex.from_documents(
    documents, storage_context=storage_context,
    service_context=service_context
)
```

8. **Querying the Index:** The index is used to answer queries. The queries are embedded using the same **`embed_model`**, and the embeddings are compared to the document embeddings in the vector store to find the most similar documents.

A simple query:

```
query_engine = index.as_query_engine()
res = query_engine.query("What is consensus in blockchain")
print(res)
```

Response

Consensus in blockchain is the process of reaching an agreement among all participants in a network on the validity of a transaction. It is achieved through a variety of consensus algorithms, such as Dev-Mode, PoET (Proof of Elapsed Time), and more. These algorithms are used to validate transactions and ensure that all participants in the network agree on the validity of the transaction.

A more complex query

```
res = query_engine.query("can you explain proof of work
and proof of stake")
print(res)
```

Response

> Proof of Work (PoW) is a consensus algorithm used by blockchain networks to validate transactions and create new blocks. It is an open challenge to all miners to solve a complex mathematical puzzle. The miner who solves the puzzle first is rewarded with a fixed amount of coins. PoW requires a lot of computational power and is used by Bitcoin and other cryptocurrencies. Proof of Stake (PoS) is an alternative consensus algorithm to PoW.
>
> In PoS, the validators are chosen based on the fraction of coins they own in the system. The nodes with more number of coins have more chance to be selected than the node with a lesser number of coins. In PoS, the reward is in the form of a transaction fee, new coins are not created for paying the validators. Presently, Blackcoin, NXT, and Peercoin blockchains use the PoS algorithm. Ethereum is also planning to shift to this method by 2018.

Please note that you should replace "`your_openai_api_key`", "`your_pinecone_api_key`", and "`your_pinecone_environment`" with your actual OpenAI and Pinecone API keys and environment details.

In summary, this code provides a robust and efficient way to create a private document-based QA bot. The use of Llama-Index, OpenAI, Pinecone, and Transformers allows the bot to understand the semantic meaning of the document's content and the user's queries, and to quickly and accurately find the most relevant sections of the document.

Introducing the Use Case: Web-based QA Bot

This use case involves the creation of a web-based QA bot. The bot is designed to answer questions based on the content of specified websites. This is achieved by indexing the content of the websites, and then using a language model to generate responses to queries based on this indexed content. This can be particularly useful for creating a customer support bot for a specific website, or a research assistant that can answer questions based on a set of academic papers or articles.

Tech-Stack Walkthrough and Explanation

- **`LangChain`**: `LangChain` is a framework that empowers developers to create language model-powered applications. It offers two main features: data awareness, enabling connections to external data sources, and agency, allowing interaction with the application's environment. The framework's key value propositions include modular components, making it user-friendly, and pre-configured off-the-shelf chains for quick application development. These chains simplify initial setup, while components provide flexibility for customizing or creating new chains for more complex use cases.
- **`FAISS`**: `FAISS` (Facebook AI Similarity Search) is a library developed by Facebook AI that allows for efficient similarity search and clustering of dense vectors. In the **`WebsiteQABot`** use case, FAISS is used as an in-memory vector store to store the embeddings of the text chunks. When a question is asked to the bot, the question is embedded into a vector, and this vector is compared with the vectors in the FAISS store to find the most similar text chunks.
- **Cohere**: Cohere is a platform that provides powerful language models that can be used for a variety of natural language processing tasks. In the **`WebsiteQABot`** use case, a Cohere language model is used to generate the answer to a question based on the most similar text chunks found by the FAISS vector store. The model takes the question and the text chunks as input and generates a coherent and contextually appropriate answer.
- **Sentence-Transformers**: Sentence-Transformers reshape the landscape of generating embeddings for text and images, offering a dynamic toolkit for semantic analysis and clustering. In real-world scenarios like the **`WebsiteQABot`** use case, this framework transforms the process of creating and utilizing embeddings, enhancing the precision and efficiency of tasks involving semantic similarity comparisons and search operations.

Understanding FAISS and Pinecone

In the earlier use case, we explored and used Pinecone, which is a vector database and provides search as a service. It will be beneficial to do a comparative study between FAISS and Pinecone before we proceed.

FAISS, an acronym denoting Facebook AI Similarity Search, emerges as a robust library crafted by Facebook AI, aimed at revolutionizing the landscape of efficient similarity search and clustering for dense vectors. This dynamic toolkit is designed to accommodate datasets comprising vectors of varying densities and dimensions, extending its capabilities even to datasets that exceed available RAM capacity. Beyond search algorithms, FAISS provides auxiliary code for evaluation and parameter optimization, establishing itself as a comprehensive resource. Developed in C++, the library seamlessly integrates with Python and NumPy through comprehensive wrappers, enhancing accessibility and ease of use. Notably, FAISS leverages GPU acceleration to execute pivotal algorithms with unparalleled efficiency.

In the context of the WebsiteQABot, FAISS is used as an in-memory vector store. This means that the embeddings (dense vectors) of the text chunks are stored in memory using FAISS. The advantage of this is that it allows for a very fast similarity search among the vectors. When a question is asked to the bot, the question is embedded into a vector, and this vector is compared with the vectors in the FAISS store to find the most similar text chunks. The bot then uses these text chunks to generate the answer.

Pinecone, on the other hand, is a vector database service that allows you to easily build and manage real-time vector search applications. It provides a fully managed, serverless, and scalable infrastructure for vector embeddings, and it supports large-scale vector search and machine-learning operations.

While both FAISS and Pinecone are used for storing and searching vector embeddings, there are some key differences as follows:

- **In-memory versus persistent storage:** FAISS is an in-memory vector store, which means that the vectors are stored in the RAM of the machine. This allows for very fast access and search, but the data is lost if the machine is turned off or crashes. Pinecone, on the other hand, provides persistent storage, which means that the vectors are stored in a way that survives machine restarts and crashes.
- **Scalability**: While FAISS can handle large datasets, it is limited by the amount of available RAM. Pinecone, being a cloud-based service, can scale to handle much larger datasets.
- **Management**: `FAISS` is a library, which means that you have to manage the infrastructure yourself. Pinecone is a fully managed service, which means that they take care of the infrastructure, scalability, and reliability for you.

In the context of the `WebsiteQABot`, FAISS is used because it provides a fast and easy-to-use in-memory vector store that is sufficient for the bot's needs. If the bot needed to handle much larger datasets or required persistent storage, Pinecone might be a better choice.

Pre-requisites

Before we embark on the journey to work on this use case, it's essential to thoroughly validate that all the required prerequisites have been successfully met and fulfilled. This will ensure a solid foundation as we move forward with our intended utilization.

Cohere API Key

1. Login to https://dashboard.cohere.ai/
2. Select **`API Keys`** and copy the default key or create a Trial or **`Production Key`**.

Figure 7.8: *Cohere API Key*

Implementation Steps

The implementation involves the following steps:

1. Load the documents from the web using LangChain's loaders.
2. Split the documents into smaller chunks using LangChain's text splitter.
3. Create embeddings of the chunks using LangChain's **`OpenAIEmbeddings`** class.
4. Store the embeddings in Pinecone.
5. Create a QA chain using LangChain's **`RetrievalQA`** class. This chain takes a query as input, retrieves the most relevant documents from Pinecone, and generates a response using OpenAI's language model.

Detailed Code Walkthrough

The code starts by installing the necessary libraries and setting up the OpenAI and Pinecone environments. It then loads the documents from a specified sitemap using Langchain's **`SitemapLoader`**. The documents are split into smaller chunks, and embeddings are created for each chunk. These embeddings are stored in Pinecone. Finally, a QA chain is created using Langchain's **`RetrievalQA`** class, and this chain is used to answer queries based on the indexed content of the websites.

1. **Importing Necessary Libraries**

   We import all the necessary libraries that we will use in the rest of the code. These libraries include:

   a. **`langchain`**: A library for building language models and retrieval-based question-answering systems.

   b. **`loguru`**: A library for logging.

```
from typing import Optional
from langchain.embeddings import HuggingFaceEmbeddings
from langchain.text_splitter import CharacterTextSplitter
from langchain.vectorstores import FAISS
from langchain.document_loaders import UnstructuredURLLoader
from langchain.llms import Cohere
from langchain.chains import RetrievalQAWithSourcesChain
import requests
from loguru import logger
import pickle
import os
```

2. **Defining the `WebsiteQABot` Class**

   We define the **`WebsiteQABot`** class, which represents a question-answering bot that can answer questions based on the content of specified URLs. The **`__init__`** method initializes the bot with a list of URLs, a chunk size, and a chunk overlap.

```
class WebsiteQABot:
    def __init__(
        self,
```

```
        urls: list,
        chunk_size: int,
        chunk_overlap: int,
    ):
        ...
```

3. **Loading the URLs Content**

   We load the content of the URLs using the **UnstructuredURLLoader** class from the **LangChain** library. This class loads the content of the specified URLs and returns it as a list of documents.

```
logger.info("Loading URLs content ...")
loader = UnstructuredURLLoader(urls)
data = loader.load()
```

4. **Splitting the Documents into Chunks**

   We split the documents into chunks using the **CharacterTextSplitter** class from the **LangChain** library. This class splits the documents into chunks of a specified size with a specified overlap.

```
logger.info("Splitting documents in chunks ...")
doc_splitter = CharacterTextSplitter(
    chunk_size=chunk_size, chunk_overlap=chunk_overlap
)
docs = doc_splitter.split_documents(data)
logger.info("{n} chunks created", n=len(docs))
```

5. **Building the Vector Database**

   We build the vector database using the **HuggingFaceEmbeddings** and FAISS classes from the **LangChain** library. The **HuggingFaceEmbeddings** class creates embeddings of the text chunks, and the FAISS class creates a vector database from the documents and their embeddings.

```
logger.info("Building the vector database ...")
embeddings = HuggingFaceEmbeddings()
docsearch = FAISS.from_documents(docs, embeddings)
```

6. **Building the Retrieval Chain**

   We build the retrieval chain using the Cohere and **RetrievalQAWithSourcesChain** classes from the **LangChain** library. The Cohere class creates a language model, and the **RetrievalQAWithSourcesChain** class creates a retrieval chain that uses the language model and the retriever.

```
logger.info("Building the retrieval chain ...")
os.environ["COHERE_API_KEY"] = ""
llm = Cohere(model="command-nightly", temperature=0)
self.chain = RetrievalQAWithSourcesChain.from_llm(llm=llm,
retriever=retriever)
```

7. **Asking a Query to the Bot**

   We define the ask method, which allows us to ask a question to the bot and returns the bot's response.

```
def ask(self, query: str):
    return self.chain({"question": query}, return_only_outputs=-
False)
```

8. **Main Function**

   We define the main function, which creates a **WebsiteQABot** object with a list of URLs, a chunk size, and a chunk overlap. It then asks a question to the bot and prints the bot's response.

```
if __name__ == "__main__":
    urls = [
        "https://blog.monsterapi.ai/what-is-falcon-7b-instruct-a-
better-alternative-to-gpt-3/"
    ]
    bot = WebsiteQABot(
        urls=urls,
        chunk_size=2000,
        chunk_overlap=100,
    )
    query ="why Is Falcon-7B Instruct a better alternative to GPT-3?"
    res = bot.ask(query)
    print(res)
```

Response: `{'question': 'why Is Falcon-7B Instruct a better alternative to GPT-3?', 'answer': ' Falcon-7B Instruct has been fine-tuned on instructions and conversational data, making it more suitable for popular`

```
assistant-style tasks. It requires less GPU memory, making it more accessible on consumer hardware. It offers a unique combination of affordability and performance, making it a compelling alternative to GPT-3.', 'sources': ''}
```

Conclusion

In this chapter, we have explored two distinct use cases of AI-powered question-answering bots, namely Document-based QA bot and Web-based QA bot. We delved into the details of how these bots work, the technologies they use, and how they can be implemented using Python.

In the first use case, we created a Document-based QA bot that uses OpenAI's GPT-3 model for language understanding and question answering. We utilized the Metaphor API to search for relevant documents and the Web Requests plugin to fetch the content of these documents. The bot was designed to answer questions based on the content of a specific document.

In the second use case, we developed a Web-based QA bot that uses the Cohere model for language understanding and question answering. This bot uses the **`LangChain`** library to load content from specified URLs, split the content into manageable chunks, create embeddings of these chunks, and store them in a FAISS **`vectorStore`**. The bot can answer questions based on the content of multiple web pages.

Throughout the process, we have seen how AI and machine learning technologies can be used to create intelligent bots that can understand and answer questions based on specific documents or web content. These bots have a wide range of applications, from customer service and technical support to education and research.

The field of AI is rapidly evolving, and the potential applications are vast. With the right tools and resources, we can harness the power of AI to create intelligent systems that can understand and respond to human language, providing valuable insights and solutions. Whether its answering questions based on a specific document or scouring the web for relevant information, AI-powered bots are transforming the way we access and interact with information.

In the upcoming chapter, we unearth the transformative potential of LLM quantization techniques. By deftly compressing these expansive models, we embark on a journey toward creating smaller yet equally potent models. This paradigm shift in AI deployment marks a significant stride towards efficient utilization of resources, enabling widespread accessibility and streamlined performance, catalyzing the democratization and adoption of LLMs.

CHAPTER 8

LLM Quantization Techniques and Implementation

Introduction

In the fast-paced world of natural language processing (NLP), large language models (LLMs) have emerged as a transformative force. Their ability to generate human-like text and understand complex language patterns has made them indispensable for a wide range of applications. However, this computational prowess comes with its own set of challenges, particularly in terms of storage, latency, and energy consumption. As these models continue to evolve, becoming more complex and data-hungry, the need for optimizing their resource efficiency has never been more critical.

One of the most promising solutions to this challenge is quantization. This technique involves the conversion of the model's parameters, such as weights and biases, from high-precision, floating-point numbers to more compact, low-precision formats. The result is a model that is not only smaller but also faster and more energy-efficient. For instance, weight in a neural network that is initially represented as a floating-point number like 3.14159 could be approximated to an integer like 3 through quantization. While this does introduce some level of error, the overall performance of the model often remains within an acceptable range.

The primary aim of this chapter is to provide a comprehensive understanding of quantization, exploring its various types and how they can be applied to LLMs. We will delve into specialized quantization strategies, such as 4-bit quantization and quantization with knowledge distillation, and provide practical guidelines for implementation. The chapter will also discuss the real-world implications of using quantized models, including the trade-offs in performance, deployment costs, and ethical considerations.

Organized into several key sections, this chapter will take you through the concept of quantization, its application in LLMs, and its real-world implications. By the end of this chapter, you will have a holistic understanding of the role and importance of quantization in the context of LLMs and will be equipped with the knowledge to implement these techniques in real-world scenarios.

The supporting code for this chapter can be found here:

https://github.com/ava-orange-education/Hands-On-Large-Language-Models-for-Enterprise/blob/main/Chapter_8_LLM_Quantization_Techniques_%26_Implementation_Making_the_Large_Models_Small.ipynb

Structure

In this chapter, the following topics will be covered:

- Understanding quantization in the context of large language models
- Types of quantization and specialized quantization strategies
- Selection criteria for quantization techniques
- Tradeoffs and challenges
- Implementation of 4-bit quantization using `bitsandbytes` and `auto-gptq`
- Relevance to real-world applications

Understanding Quantization

Quantization is a technique that maps a large set of continuous, infinite values to a smaller, finite set of discrete values. In mathematical terms, if you have a continuous function $f(x)$, quantization would map $f(x)$ to a set of discrete values within a certain range. This is particularly useful in the realm of machine learning models, where parameters like weights, biases, and activations are often represented as high-precision floating-point numbers. Through quantization, these continuous values are mapped to a more compact, lower-precision number format.

Quantizing Weights

Let us consider a simple example to illustrate this concept. Suppose a weight in a neural network is represented as 0.123456. In a quantized model, this could be approximated to 0.12 or even 0.1, depending on the level of precision you choose. This approximation makes the model smaller and faster, albeit at the cost of some accuracy.

Benefits and Importance of LLMs

The precision of the bits used to represent the parameters of a model can have a profound impact on both its performance and its memory footprint. This is where quantization comes into play, acting as a choreographer that helps the model make graceful moves within the constraints of memory and computational power. Let us delve into how bit precision and memory are intertwined in the realm of machine learning.

The Essence of Quantization

Quantization is the process of converting the high-precision floating-point numbers that represent a model's parameters—weights, biases, and activations—into lower-precision numbers. These could be lower-precision floating-point numbers or even integers. For instance, a 32-bit floating-point number could be converted into a 16-bit or 8-bit integer.

- **Reduced Memory Footprint:** Lower-precision representations significantly reduce the memory required to store the model's parameters. This is crucial for deploying LLMs on devices with limited storage capacity.
- **Improved Inference Performance:** Computations with lower-precision numbers are generally faster, which leads to quicker response times when the model is making predictions or inferences.
- **Increased Power Efficiency:** Using fewer bits for each calculation means less energy is consumed, making the model more power-efficient. This is particularly beneficial for mobile or IoT devices that operate on battery power.

Let us consider a practical example. Suppose you have a neural network model for image classification that uses 32-bit floating-point numbers for its weights. If you opt for 8-bit quantization, each weight would be represented as an 8-bit integer, ranging from 0 to 255. This simple step can reduce the memory usage of the model by up to 75%, making it four times more memory-efficient!

However, this comes at a cost. The model's accuracy might dip slightly, say from 95% to 93%. This is where the art of balancing comes in. You will need to decide if this slight dip in accuracy is acceptable for your specific application.

Quantization is a powerful tool in the machine learning toolkit, but it is not a one-size-fits-all solution. It requires a nuanced approach, taking into account the specific needs of the application, the limitations of the hardware, and the acceptable trade-offs in terms of accuracy and performance. By understanding the relationship between bit precision and memory usage, you can make more informed decisions, optimizing your models for your specific needs.

Types of Quantization Techniques

When it comes to the actual implementation, there are several types of quantization techniques commonly used in large language models (LLMs):

- **Fixed-Point and Floating-Point:** In fixed-point quantization, numbers are represented with a fixed number of digits after the decimal point. For example, 3.14159 could become 3.14. Floating-point quantization, on the other hand, allows for a variable number of digits after the decimal point, offering more flexibility but also more complexity.
- **Post-Training Quantization (PTQ):** This technique is applied after the model has already been trained. The high-precision weights, biases, and activations are converted to their lower-precision equivalents. This is often a straightforward way to reduce model size without retraining the model.
- **Symmetric and Asymmetric Quantization:** Symmetric quantization uses the same range for both positive and negative values. For example, if the range is [-3,3], then both positive and negative values are quantized within this range. Asymmetric quantization allows for different ranges for positive and negative values, providing more flexibility in how the values are quantized.

By understanding these techniques and their benefits, one can make informed decisions on how to effectively implement quantization in LLMs. This not only makes these models more accessible but also extends the range of platforms where they can be deployed efficiently.

Specialized Quantization Strategies for LLMs

As LLMs continue to grow in complexity and size, specialized quantization techniques have emerged to address their unique challenges. This section delves into these advanced strategies, each designed to optimize LLMs in terms of memory footprint, computational requirements, and accuracy.

Activation-aware Weight Quantization (AWQ)

- What is it?
  - AWQ is a technique that takes into account the distribution of activation values during the quantization process. In simpler terms, it looks at how neurons in the neural network are activated during inference and uses this information to optimize the quantization process.
- Why is it Important?
  - In traditional quantization methods, the focus is mainly on reducing the size of the weights. However, AWQ goes a step further by considering how these weights interact with activation values. This ensures that the quantized model maintains a high level of accuracy, which is crucial for LLMs that are often tasked with complex language understanding and generation.
- Example
  - Imagine a chatbot trained to assist in medical diagnoses. Using AWQ, the chatbot can maintain its ability to understand medical terminology and provide accurate information, while consuming fewer computational resources.

Data-Free Quantization Aware Training (LLM-QAT)

- What is it?
  - LLM-QAT allows for the fine-tuning of a quantized model without needing the original training data. This is particularly useful in scenarios where data privacy or data access is a concern.
- Why is it Important?
  - In industries like healthcare or finance, where data is sensitive, LLM-QAT offers a way to optimize models without risking data privacy. It is a significant advancement in making LLMs more accessible and secure.
- Example
  - A financial advisory chatbot can be fine-tuned using LLM-QAT to understand market trends and provide investment advice, all while adhering to data privacy regulations.

4-bit Quantization

- What is it?
  - 4-bit quantization is a radical approach that reduces the precision of the model's parameters to just 4 bits.

- Why is it important?
  - This results in a drastic reduction in the model's size and computational requirements. However, the trade-off is a potential loss in accuracy, which may or may not be acceptable depending on the application.
- Example
  - In IoT devices with very limited computational power, a 4-bit quantized LLM could be used for simple tasks like voice-activated commands.

Uniform Quantization

- What is it?
  - Uniform quantization is a method that divides the range of parameter values into equal intervals, simplifying the mapping process.
- Why is it Important?
  - It is a straightforward and effective method for reducing the computational requirements of an LLM while maintaining a reasonable level of accuracy.
- Example
  - A customer service chatbot deployed in a retail setting could use uniform quantization to balance performance and resource utilization effectively.

Quantization with Knowledge Distillation

- What is it?
  - This technique involves training a smaller "`student`" model to mimic the behavior of a larger "`teacher`" model. When combined with quantization, the student model is not only smaller but also quantized.
- Why is it important?
  - This is particularly useful for deploying LLMs in environments with limited resources, as it allows for the creation of efficient yet accurate models.
- Example
  - A mobile app that uses an LLM for real-time language translation could benefit from a distilled and quantized model, offering fast and accurate translations without draining the phone's battery.

Quantization with Fine-Tuning

- What is it?

- Fine-tuning is the process of taking a pre-trained model and adjusting its parameters to improve its performance on a specific task. When this is combined with quantization, you get a model that is both specialized and efficient.

- Why is it important?
  - This approach allows for the customization of the performance of the LLM for specific use cases, making it highly adaptable while still benefiting from reduced computational requirements.
- Example
  - In a legal advisory chatbot, fine-tuning a quantized LLM can result in a model that understands legal jargon and can provide accurate advice, all while being resource-efficient.

Post-Training Quantization (PTQ)

- What is it?
  - PTQ is a technique that quantizes a model after it has been fully trained. It converts the model's parameters from floating-point (FP32) to integer (INT8) format, thereby reducing the computational resources needed for inference.
- Why is it important?
  - The key advantage of PTQ is that you do not need to retrain the model on the full dataset, which can be both time-consuming and resource-intensive. This makes PTQ an efficient way to optimize large language models (LLMs) for deployment.
- Example
  - Consider a news summarization model running on a server. Using PTQ, the model can generate summaries more quickly and consume less memory, allowing for more concurrent users without compromising the quality of the summaries.
  - Tools like TensorRT
    - TensorRT uses a calibration step that runs the model with sample data to find the optimal mapping from FP32 to INT8, minimizing information loss during the quantization process.

Symmetric Quantization

- What is it?
  - In symmetric quantization, the same range is used for both positive and negative values. This simplifies the quantization process and can yield good results for many models.

- Why is it important?
    - Symmetric quantization is computationally simpler and can be more efficient in terms of memory usage. However, it may not be the best choice if the data is skewed or biased towards one side.
- Example
    - If an LLM is used for sentiment analysis and the range of activation values is evenly distributed around zero, symmetric quantization would be an effective choice.

Asymmetric Quantization

- What is it?
    - Asymmetric quantization allows for different ranges of positive and negative values. This is achieved by introducing an additional parameter called the zero-point or quantization bias.
- Why is it important?
    - This method can be more accurate when the data is skewed or biased towards one side. However, it may require additional computational resources due to the extra offset parameter.
- Example
    - In a machine translation model where the activation values are mostly positive, asymmetric quantization could provide a more accurate and efficient representation of the data.

Specialized quantization techniques offer a range of options for optimizing large language models. Whether you are constrained by data privacy issues, computational resources, or the need for high accuracy, there is likely a quantization strategy that fits your needs. By understanding and applying these advanced techniques, you can deploy more efficient and effective LLMs across a variety of applications.

Criteria for Quantization Strategy Selection

Quantization is a critical step in deploying LLMs efficiently, especially in resource-constrained environments. It involves converting the floating-point numbers that make up the model's weights to integers, thereby reducing the size and computational requirements of the model. However, choosing the right quantization strategy is crucial for balancing performance, latency, and accuracy. Following are some detailed guidelines to help you make an informed decision.

Evaluate Model's Performance at Different Bit Precisions

- What to do?
  - Start by evaluating your model's performance at different bit precisions. You can begin with a higher bit precision, such as 8-bit (INT8), and then experiment with lower bit precisions like 4-bit or 2-bit.
- Why is it important?
  - Different bit precisions offer various trade-offs between accuracy and memory usage. Lower bit precision will reduce the model size but may also degrade the model's performance.
- Example:
  - Suppose your LLM performs with 95% accuracy at 8-bit precision. When you reduce it to 4-bit, the accuracy drops to 92%, but the model size is halved. This information will help you decide whether the trade-off is acceptable.

Consider the Available Hardware Resources

- What to do?
  - Take into account the hardware resources you have at your disposal. This includes memory, processing power, and any hardware-specific optimizations for lower-precision arithmetic.
- Why is it important?
  - Your hardware capabilities will limit the size and complexity of the model you can deploy. For instance, edge devices may not have the computational power to handle higher-bit precisions.
- Example:
  - If you are deploying your model on a mobile device with limited memory, you might opt for a 4-bit quantization even if it slightly compromises accuracy.

Experiment with Different Quantization Techniques

- What to do?
  - Experiment with various quantization techniques like Post-Training Quantization (PTQ), Symmetric and Asymmetric Quantization, and specialized strategies like Activation-aware Weight Quantization (AWQ) or Data-Free Quantization Aware Training (LLM-QAT).
- Why is it important?
  - Different techniques have unique advantages and disadvantages.

For example, PTQ is easier to implement but may result in a more significant drop in accuracy compared to fine-tuned methods like LLM-QAT.

- Example:
  - You might find that using AWQ provides the best accuracy for your specific use case, even though it is more computationally intensive during the training phase.

Use a Representative Dataset for Calibration and Fine-Tuning

- What to do?
  - During the quantization process, use a dataset that closely represents the data your model will encounter in the real world for calibration and fine-tuning.
- Why is it important?
  - Using a representative dataset ensures that the quantization process minimizes the impact on accuracy.
- Example:
  - If your LLM is designed for natural language processing in medical transcripts, use a dataset comprising medical jargon and terminologies for calibration.

Consider Mixed-Precision Quantization

- What to do?
  - Consider using mixed-precision quantization, where different layers of the model use different bit precisions.
- Why is it important?
  - This approach allows you to optimize the balance between accuracy and memory usage further.
- Example:
  - The input layer might use 8-bit precision for higher accuracy, while the hidden layers could use 4-bit to save memory.

Trade Offs and Challenges

Deploying a large language model (LLM) is no small feat, especially when you are constrained by hardware limitations or aiming for real-time performance. Quantization offers a pathway to make your model more efficient, but it is a journey filled with trade-offs and challenges. Let us delve into these challenges and how to approach them.

- **Accuracy versus Model Size**
  - Quantization often forces you to choose between a smaller, faster model and a more accurate but resource-intensive one. For example, you might find that reducing your model to 4-bit precision cuts its size in half but also drops its accuracy by 3%. This is a crucial decision point: is the loss in accuracy acceptable for your specific use case?
- **Hardware Limitations**
  - Your available hardware significantly influences your quantization strategy. High-end servers with abundant memory and processing power can handle larger, more accurate models. In contrast, edge devices like smartphones or IoT devices may require you to be more aggressive in reducing model size, even at the cost of some accuracy.
- **Addressing Latency**
  - LLMs are not known for their speed, making latency a significant concern, especially for real-time applications. Your quantization strategy should aim to reduce latency while maintaining an acceptable level of accuracy. For instance, if you are developing a real-time translation service, even a small delay can make the conversation awkward, pushing you to find a quantization strategy that minimizes latency.
- **Development Complexity**
  - Quantizing an LLM is not just about reducing bit size; it is an intricate process that involves calibration, fine-tuning, and ongoing optimization. This complexity can extend development timelines and require specialized expertise. It's not a *set it and forget it* operation; think of it more like fine-tuning a high-performance engine.
- **Training Hurdles**
  - Training a quantized model presents its own set of challenges. Traditional training methods may not be directly applicable, requiring you to adopt specialized techniques to maintain performance. For instance, you might need to use quantization-aware training to ensure that the model's accuracy does not plummet during the quantization process.

Choosing the right quantization strategy for your LLM is a multifaceted challenge, requiring you to balance various factors like accuracy, model size, hardware limitations, latency, and complexity. By understanding these challenges and their implications, you can make more informed decisions, optimizing your model for your specific needs without unnecessary sacrifices.

Implementing 4-bit Quantization using `BitsandBytes` and GPTQ Libraries

Here we implement the 4-bit quantization discussed earlier, which can be a game-changer for deploying LLMs in resource-constrained environments. This section will guide you through the process of implementing 4-bit quantization using two Python libraries: `BitsandBytes` and `GPTQ`. We will break down the steps, explain the code snippets, and provide insights into best practices.

Quantization Using `BitsAndBytes`

The `BitsAndBytes` library is a Python-based tool designed to optimize the performance of LLMs. It serves as a lightweight wrapper around custom CUDA functions, focusing primarily on 8-bit optimizers and quantization functions. The library is particularly useful for those who are working with Hugging Face's Transformers library, as it offers seamless integration.

Key Features

- **8-bit Optimizers**: The library provides specialized 8-bit optimizers that are designed to work efficiently with LLMs. These optimizers help in speeding up the training process.
- **4-bit Post-training Quantization**: `BitsAndBytes` allows for 4-bit quantization after the model has been trained. This is particularly useful for models like BLOOM.
- **Memory and Computational Efficiency**: One of the main advantages of using `BitsAndBytes` is the reduction in memory and computational requirements. This makes deploying LLMs more feasible, especially in resource-constrained environments.
- **High Accuracy**: Despite the reduction in bit-width, the library ensures that there is no significant loss in the model's accuracy.

How it works

The library operates by quantizing the weights and activations of the model. Quantization is the process of constraining an infinite set to a finite range. In the context of neural networks, this means reducing the number of bits that represent the weights and activations. This results in a model that requires less memory and computational power, thereby making it more efficient for real-world applications.

Integration with Hugging Face Transformers

`BitsAndBytes` can be easily integrated with the Hugging Face Transformers library. The **`BitsAndBytesConfig`** class is used to apply the **`BitsAndBytes`** quantization methods to a pre-trained LLM. Here is a detailed example:

Connect to Google collab and set the run-time to T4 GPU:

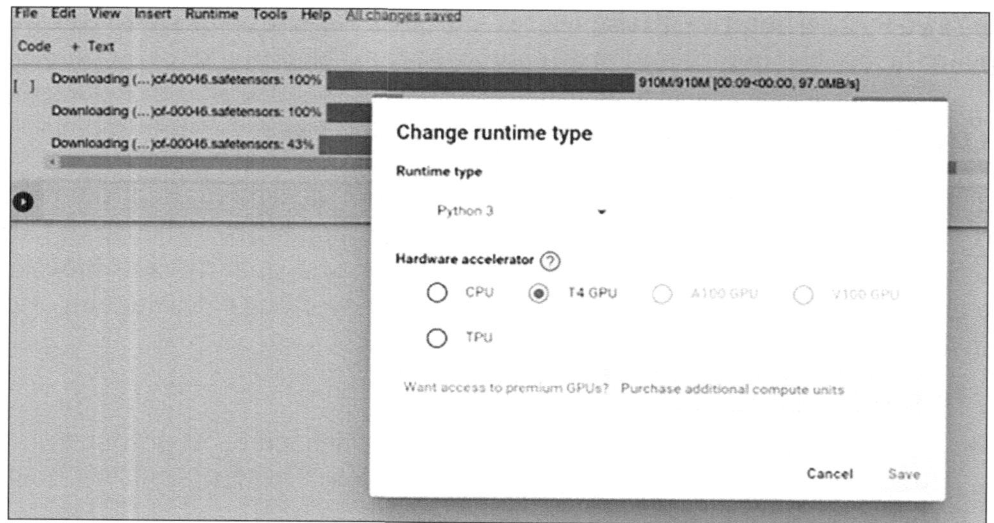

***Figure 8.1**: Set Colab Runtime Type*

Installing Required Packages

```
!pip install -q -U bitsandbytes
!pip install -q -U git+https://github.com/huggingface/transform-
ers.git
!pip install -q -U git+https://github.com/huggingface/peft.git
!pip install -q -U git+https://github.com/huggingface/accelerate.
git
```

The code installs the required Python packages using pip. The -q flag ensures quiet installation, and -U updates the package if it is already installed.

- **`bitsandbytes`**: The library for 8-bit optimizers and 4-bit quantization.
- **`transformers`**: Hugging Face's Transformers library for working with pre-trained language models.
- **`peft`**: Not explicitly used in the code but generally useful for performance evaluation.

- **accelerate**: A library for accelerating PyTorch code, especially useful for distributed training.

Importing Modules

```
from transformers import AutoModelForCausalLM, AutoTokenizer,
BitsAndBytesConfig

import torch

from transformers import pipeline
```

Here, the necessary Python modules are imported.

- **AutoModelForCausalLM**: Class for causal language models.
- **AutoTokenizer**: Tokenizer class for the language model.
- **BitsAndBytesConfig**: Configuration class for quantization.
- **torch**: The PyTorch library.
- **pipeline**: A utility from Transformers for creating common NLP pipelines.

Function Definitions –Load Model

```
# Define a function to load the Galactica model

def load_model(model_id, quantization_config=None, device_map="auto"):

    """

    Load a language model with optional quantization configuration and
device mapping.


    Args:

        model_id (str): The ID of the model to load.

        quantization_config (BitsAndBytesConfig, optional): Quantization
configuration. Default is None.

        device_map (str, optional): Device mapping for model loading.
Default is "auto".


    Returns:

        model (AutoModelForCausalLM): Loaded Galactica model.

        tokenizer (AutoTokenizer): Loaded tokenizer for the model.

    """

    model = AutoModelForCausalLM.from_pretrained(model_id, quantization_
config=quantization_config, device_map=device_map)
```

```
    tokenizer = AutoTokenizer.from_pretrained(model_id)
    return model, tokenizer
```

The **load_model** function serves as a streamlined utility for initializing and loading a language model and its associated tokenizer from the Hugging Face repository. It enhances flexibility by accepting optional parameters for model quantization and hardware mapping. Specifically, the function takes in a **model_id** to identify the model, an optional **quantization_config** for memory-efficient model loading, and a **device_map** to specify the hardware for model deployment. Internally, it employs **AutoModelForCausalLM.from_pretrained()** and **AutoTokenizer.from_pretrained()** to fetch the model and tokenizer, respectively. If quantization settings are provided, the model is quantized as per those configurations. The function returns the loaded model and tokenizer, thereby simplifying the setup process for various language model-based tasks.

Function Definitions –Generate Text

```
# Define a function to generate text using a loaded model and tokenizer
def generate_text(model, tokenizer, input_text, max_length=50, num_return_
sequences=1):
    “””
    Generate text using a loaded language model and tokenizer.

    Args:
        model (AutoModelForCausalLM): Loaded language model.
        tokenizer (AutoTokenizer): Loaded tokenizer for the model.
        input_text (str): Input text for text generation.
        max_length (int, optional): Maximum length of generated text.
Default is 50.
        num_return_sequences (int, optional): Number of generated sequences
to return. Default is 1.

    Returns:
        output_text (str): Generated text.
    “””
    text_generator = pipeline(“text-generation”, model=model, tokenizer
=tokenizer)
```

```
    output_text = text_generator(input_text, max_length=max_length, num_return_sequences=num_return_sequences)[0]["generated_text"]

    return output_text
```

The **generate_text** function serves as a streamlined utility for text generation, ideal for applications like text completion and chatbots. It takes a pre-loaded language model (**AutoModelForCausalLM**), a corresponding tokenizer (**AutoTokenizer**), an initial text string, and optional parameters for maximum text length and the number of sequences to generate. Internally, the function initializes a text-generation pipeline using Hugging Face's pipeline method and employs it to generate text based on the given input and settings. The generated text is then returned as the final output. This encapsulation makes it easier to execute text-generation tasks with a pre-loaded language model and tokenizer.

The main function

We begin with the declaration of the function:

```
def main():
    """
    Main function to demonstrate loading and generating text using Galactica models with different quantization configurations.
    """
```

We'll use a smaller model, **facebook/galactica-125m**, for demonstration. The load_in_4bit=True argument enables 4-bit quantization.

```
    model_id = "facebook/galactica-125m"
```

The **BitsAndBytesConfig** class allows you to customize various quantization settings. For example, you can change the compute dtype to **bfloat16** for speedups.

```
    # Load the Galactica model with 4-bit quantization and automatic device mapping

    quantization_config = BitsAndBytesConfig(

        load_in_4bit=True,

        bnb_4bit_compute_dtype=torch.bfloat16

    )

    galactica_model, galactica_tokenizer = load_model(model_id, quantization_config=quantization_config)
```

```
    # Define input text for generation
    input_text = "Generative AI is an exciting area of technology
[START_REF]"
```

After loading the model, you can run a prediction just like you would with a non-quantized model.

```
    # Generate text using the loaded model
    generated_text = generate_text(galactica_model, galactica_tokenizer,
input_text)
    print(f"Generated Text: {generated_text}")
```

You can switch between two 4-bit quantization types: FP4 and NF4. FP4 is a basic 4-bit float format, while NF4 is optimized for neural network quantization and generally shows better accuracy.

```
    # Load another model with different quantization configurations
    nf4_config = BitsAndBytesConfig(
        load_in_4bit=True,
        bnb_4bit_quant_type="nf4",
    )
    model_nf4, tokenizer_nf4 = load_model(model_id, quantization_config
=nf4_config)


    # Generate text using the nf4 quantization model
    generated_nf4_text = generate_text(model_nf4, tokenizer_nf4, input
_text)
    print(f"Generated Text (nf4): {generated_nf4_text}")
```

To save even more memory without sacrificing performance, you can enable nested quantization.

```
    # Load another model with double quantization and bfloat16 compute
dtype
    double_quant_config = BitsAndBytesConfig(
        load_in_4bit=True,
        bnb_4bit_use_double_quant=True,
    )
    model_double_quant, tokenizer_double_quant = load_model(model_id,
quantization_config=double_quant_config)
```

```
    # Generate text using the double quantization model
    generated_double_quant_text = generate_text(model_double_quant,
tokenizer_double_quant, input_text)
    print(f"Generated Text (double quant): {generated_double_quant_
text}")
```

You can combine multiple features in a single quantization config for optimal results.

```
    # Load a comprehensive quantization configuration model
    comprehensive_config = BitsAndBytesConfig(
        load_in_4bit=True,
        bnb_4bit_use_double_quant=True,
        bnb_4bit_quant_type="nf4",
        bnb_4bit_compute_dtype=torch.bfloat16
    )
    model_comprehensive, tokenizer_comprehensive = load_model(model_id,
quantization_config=comprehensive_config)

    # Generate text using the comprehensive quantization model
    generated_comprehensive_text = generate_text(model_comprehensive,
tokenizer_comprehensive, input_text)
    print(f"Generated Text (comprehensive): {generated_comprehensive_
text}")
```

This time let us use a larger model and put the free-tier GPUs of colab to test.

```
    # Example of loading and generating text with another model
    model_id_neox = "EleutherAI/gpt-neox-20b"
    neox_config = BitsAndBytesConfig(
        load_in_4bit=True,
        bnb_4bit_use_double_quant=True,
        bnb_4bit_quant_type="nf4",
        bnb_4bit_compute_dtype=torch.bfloat16
    )
    neox_model, neox_tokenizer = load_model(model_id_neox, quantization_
config=neox_config)
```

```
input_text_neox = "Once upon a time, there was a"
output_text_neox = generate_text(neox_model, neox_tokenizer, input_text_neox, max_length=50)
print(f"Generated Text (NEOX): {output_text_neox}")
```

The following code provides you with the size of the down-sized/quantized model:

```
# Display model size in MB
num_params = sum(p.numel() for p in neox_model.parameters() if p.requires_grad)
size_mb = num_params * 32 / 8 / (1024 * 1024)
print(f"Model size: {size_mb:.2f} MB")
```

Quantization Using GPTQ

GPTQ is a ground-breaking post-training quantization algorithm designed for LLMs. It enables these models to be quantized to 4-bit precision with minimal loss in performance. The algorithm is engineered to balance memory efficiency and computational speed, making it ideal for deploying large models on resource-constrained hardware.

Key Features of GPTQ

- **Hybrid Quantization Scheme**: GPTQ employs a hybrid approach where the model weights are quantized to 4-bits (int4), while activations remain at 16-bits (float16). During inference, these weights are dynamically dequantized, and the actual computation occurs in float16.
- **Efficient Block Quantization**: Unlike per-parameter methods that are slow, GPTQ uses approximate second-order information to quantize weights in large blocks. This speeds up the quantization process while maintaining model accuracy.
- **Memory and Speed Optimization**: GPTQ significantly reduces the memory footprint and accelerates inference times, making it possible to deploy large models like BLOOM-176B and OPT-175B on devices with limited resources.
- **Library Support**: The algorithm can be easily implemented using the `AutoGPTQ` library, simplifying the quantization process to just a few lines of code.
- **Research-Backed Performance**: Studies have shown that 4-bit GPTQ models perform almost identically to their full-precision counterparts. Even 3-bit models show minimal accuracy loss.

Comparative Analysis: GPTQ versus Other Algorithms

Performance

- **Accuracy**: GPTQ maintains near-full precision accuracy, with less than 1% performance drop on large models like OPT and BLOOM.
- **Speed**: GPTQ is faster than per-parameter methods and is competitive with state-of-the-art methods like **`SmoothQuant`** and `LLM.int8()`. However, newer methods like AWQ can outperform GPTQ in specific scenarios.

Memory Usage

- **Footprint**: GPTQ reduces memory usage by 4x compared to full-precision models by using 4-bit weights and 16-bit activations.
- **Comparison**: GPTQ has lower memory usage than 8-bit methods like `LLM.int8()` and is comparable to other 4-bit methods like **`SmoothQuant`**.

Specific Comparisons

- **`AWQ`**: Similar memory footprint but can outperform GPTQ in speed for certain models.
- **`SmoothQuant`**: Uses 8-bit weights and activations, resulting in higher memory usage compared to GPTQ.
- **`LLM.int8()`**: Also uses 8-bit quantization but has higher memory usage due to the quantization of both weights and activations.

GPTQ offers an excellent balance between accuracy, speed, and memory efficiency, making it a go-to choice for quantizing large language models. However, it is essential to consider newer algorithms like AWQ that may offer specific advantages in certain scenarios. We will further explore the implementation of the GPTQ algorithm using the AutoGPTQ library. GPTQ allows us to quantize large language models to 4-bit precision with minimal performance degradation. We will walk through the code step-by-step to understand each component.

Installing Required Packages

```
# Install the AutoGPTQ and transformers libraries
!BUILD_CUDA_EXT=0 pip install -q auto-gptq transformers
```

The first step is to install the required Python packages. We use pip to install the **`AutoGPTQ`** library for implementing the GPTQ algorithm and the transformers library for general functionalities like tokenization.

Importing Libraries

```
# Importing necessary libraries
import random  # For random number generation
from auto_gptq import AutoGPTQForCausalLM, BaseQuantizeConfig  # For GPTQ implementation
from datasets import load_dataset  # For loading datasets
import torch  # For tensor operations
from transformers import AutoTokenizer  # For tokenization
```

Here, we import all the necessary libraries. **AutoGPTQForCausalLM** and **BaseQuantizeConfig** are specific to the **AutoGPTQ** library and will be used for the quantization process.

Setting Up Model and Output Directory

```
# Define the base model (GPT-2 in this case) and the output directory for the quantized model
model_id = "gpt2"  # We are using GPT-2 as the base model
out_dir = model_id + "-GPTQ"  # Output directory for the quantized model
```

We specify the base model (gpt2) and the directory where the quantized model will be saved (gpt2-GPTQ).

Configuring and Loading the Model

```
# Define the quantization configuration using BaseQuantizeConfig
# bits=4 means we are quantizing to 4 bits
# group_size=128 specifies the size of the lazy batch for quantization
# damp_percent=0.01 is a parameter for the Cholesky reformulation
# desc_act=False means we are not sorting rows by decreasing activation


quantize_config = BaseQuantizeConfig(
    bits=4,  # 4-bit quantization
    group_size=128,  # Group size for lazy batch
    damp_percent=0.01,  # Cholesky reformulation parameter
    desc_act=False  # No sorting by decreasing activation
)
```

```
# Load the model and tokenizer
model = AutoGPTQForCausalLM.from_pretrained(model_id, quantize_
config)
tokenizer = AutoTokenizer.from_pretrained(model_id)
```

We set up the quantization configuration using **BaseQuantizeConfig**. The bits parameter specifies that we want 4-bit quantization. The **group_size** parameter is set to 128, which is the size of the lazy batch used during quantization. Then, we load the model and tokenizer using this configuration.

Preparing the Dataset

```
# Load and tokenize dataset
n_samples = 1024  # Number of samples for quantization
data = load_dataset("allenai/c4", data_files="en/c4-train.00001-
of-01024.json.gz", split=f"train[:{n_samples*5}]")
tokenized_data = tokenizer("\n\n".join(data['text']), return_ten-
sors='pt')
```

We prepare the dataset for the quantization process. We load 1024 samples from the C4 dataset and tokenize them using the tokenizer we loaded earlier.

Formatting Tokenized Examples

```
# Randomly select and format tokenized examples
examples_ids = []
for _ in range(n_samples):
    i = random.randint(0, tokenized_data.input_ids.shape[1] -
tokenizer.model_max_length - 1)
    j = i + tokenizer.model_max_length
    input_ids = tokenized_data.input_ids[:, i:j]
    attention_mask = torch.ones_like(input_ids)
    examples_ids.append({'input_ids': input_ids, 'attention_
mask': attention_mask})
```

We format the tokenized examples to be used in the quantization process. We create a list of dictionaries, each containing the **input_ids** and **attention_mask** for a particular sample.

Performing Quantization

```
# Perform the quantization using the model's quantize method
# examples_ids contains the tokenized text
```

```
# batch_size=1 means we are using a batch size of 1 for quantization

# use_triton=True enables the use of OpenAI Triton for GPU acceleration


model.quantize(
    examples_ids,  # Tokenized text
    batch_size=1,  # Batch size for quantization
    use_triton=True  # Use OpenAI Triton for GPU acceleration
)
```

We perform the actual quantization using the quantize method of the model. We pass in the formatted examples and specify a batch size of 1.

Saving and Reloading the Model

```
# Save the quantized model and tokenizer to the specified output directory
# use_safetensors=True saves the model in a format compatible with SafeTensors
model.save_quantized(out_dir, use_safetensors=True)
tokenizer.save_pretrained(out_dir)


# Reload the quantized model and tokenizer from the output directory
device = "cuda:0" if torch.cuda.is_available() else "cpu"
model = AutoGPTQForCausalLM.from_quantized(
    out_dir,
    device=device,
    use_triton=True,
    use_safetensors=True,
)
tokenizer = AutoTokenizer.from_pretrained(out_dir)
```

After quantization, we save the model and tokenizer using the **`save_quantized`** and **`save_pretrained`** methods, respectively.

Testing the Model

```
# Test the quantized model using Hugging Face's pipeline for text generation
from transformers import pipeline


generator = pipeline('text-generation', model=model, tokenizer=tokenizer)
result = generator("I have a dream", do_sample=True, max_length=50)[0]['generated_text']
print(result)
```

Finally, we test the quantized model to ensure it is working as expected. We use the pipeline from the transformers library to generate text based on the input I *have a dream.*

The Role of Quantization in Real-World Applications

In today's digital age, large language models (LLMs) like GPT-3 are revolutionizing various sectors, from healthcare and finance to entertainment and customer service. However, their enormous size and computational needs often make them challenging to deploy in real-world scenarios. This is where the magic of quantization comes into play. Let us explore how quantization techniques are making LLMs more accessible and efficient across different applications.

1. **Mobile and Edge Devices: A Pocket-Sized Revolution**
    a. **The Scenario**: Imagine you are developing a mobile app that uses GPT-3 to generate personalized workout plans. Deploying the full-sized model would be impractical due to hardware limitations.
    b. **Quantization to the Rescue**: By using an 8-bit quantized version of GPT-3, you can efficiently run the model on mobile phones and even IoT devices. This allows your app to offer sophisticated features without draining the resources of the device.
2. **Reduced Latency: Speeding Up Real-Time Applications**
    a. **The Scenario**: You are building a voice-activated search engine that needs to provide instant results.

   b. **Quantization to the Rescue**: Lowering the precision to INT8 or INT4 can significantly reduce computation time, enabling real-time applications like voice assistants and search engines to operate more swiftly.

3. **Efficient Inference Hardware: The Perfect Match**

   a. **The Scenario:** You are working with specialized AI accelerators or inference chips, like those from Qualcomm.

   b. **Quantization to the Rescue**: These hardware solutions are designed to work optimally with quantized models, enhancing both throughput and power efficiency.

4. **On-Device Personalization: Privacy Meets Efficiency**

   a. **The Scenario:** You want to offer personalized recommendations to users without sending their data to the cloud.

   b. **Quantization to the Rescue**: You can fine-tune a small, quantized version of GPT-3 right on the user's device, ensuring both efficiency and privacy.

5. **Democratization of Large Models: Making AI Accessible**

   a. **The Scenario**: You are an AI researcher who wants to make state-of-the-art language models accessible to a broader audience.

   b. **Quantization to the Rescue**: By reducing the memory and computational requirements, quantization allows more people to access and benefit from cutting-edge AI technologies.

6. **Commercial Viability: Cost-Effective Innovation**

   a. **The Scenario**: You are a startup aiming to offer AI-powered services but are concerned about the high infrastructure costs of deploying large models.

   b. **Quantization to the Rescue**: Quantization significantly lowers these costs, making it financially feasible to offer advanced AI services.

Quantization is not just a technical exercise; it is a catalyst for innovation and accessibility. By optimizing for latency, size, and hardware efficiency, quantization is breaking down barriers, making it feasible to deploy large language models in a variety of real-world applications. Whether it is enabling AI on a smartphone or powering a voice assistant that responds in the blink of an eye, quantization is the unsung hero making these advancements possible.

Conclusion

In this comprehensive chapter, we embarked on a journey through the multifaceted world of model quantization, with a special focus on large language models (LLMs). We began by laying the groundwork, discussing the fundamental *Understanding of Quantization* and its *Benefits and Importance in LLMs*. This set the stage for the technical depth that followed.

We explored the *Essence of Quantization*, dissecting its core components and how it serves as a cornerstone in optimizing machine learning models for performance and efficiency. This led us into a detailed discussion on *Types of Quantization Techniques*, where we examined various strategies and their applicability to LLMs. Specialized techniques like *Activation-aware Weight Quantization* (AWQ) and *Data-Free Quantization Aware Training* (LLM-QAT) were highlighted to showcase the advancements in this field.

The chapter then delved into the nitty-gritty of *4-bit Quantization*, a focal point in the realm of efficient computing. We explored various approaches like *Uniform Quantization*, *Quantization with Knowledge Distillation*, and *Quantization with Fine-Tuning*, each offering unique advantages and challenges. We also touched upon *Post-Training Quantization* (PTQ), *Symmetric Quantization*, and *Asymmetric Quantization*, providing a holistic view of the quantization landscape.

Choosing the right quantization strategy can be a daunting task, which is why we dedicated a section to *Criteria for Quantization Strategy Selection*. Here, we emphasized the importance of evaluating a model's performance at different bit precisions, considering the available hardware resources, and the need for representative datasets for calibration and fine-tuning. The section on *Trade Offs and Challenges* provided a balanced view, ensuring that the readers are well-informed about the complexities involved in quantization.

The latter part of the chapter was a hands-on guide to *Implementing 4-Bit Quantization using BitsAndBytes and GPTQ Libraries*. We meticulously walked through the code, breaking it down into lucid sections, each accompanied by detailed explanations and inline comments. This practical approach ensures that you not only understand the theory but also know how to implement it.

Finally, we touched upon *The Role of Quantization in Real-World Applications*, linking the technical aspects to tangible outcomes. This serves as a bridge to the real-world applicability of all the concepts discussed, making this chapter not just a theoretical guide but a practical handbook.

The world of quantization is ever-evolving, and the techniques and strategies discussed here provide you with a robust foundation. As you move forward, you can build upon this knowledge, experimenting with newer techniques and contributing to growth in the field. In the next chapter, we will look into Fine-tuning LLMs, which tailors pre-trained models to specific tasks or domains, optimizing their performance for particular applications. Evaluating these models relies on innovative metrics to ensure outputs meet desired standards of relevance and accuracy, as conventional ground truths are typically absent in such unsupervised scenarios.

CHAPTER 9

Fine-Tuning and Evaluation of LLMs

Introduction

Fine-tuning and evaluating large language models (LLMs) such as GPT-3 are essential steps for harnessing their full potential. The process of fine-tuning involves taking a pre-trained model and adapting it for a specific task by training it on a specialized dataset. This not only updates the neural network's weights but also allows the model to become more adept at the new task, leveraging the foundational knowledge it acquired during its initial training.

Evaluation is equally critical and employs a multi-pronged approach. Metrics like perplexity are used to gauge the model's ability to generalize, while human evaluations provide qualitative insights into the model's fluency and factual accuracy. Automated metrics such as BLEU and ROUGE offer a more quantitative assessment, focusing on aspects like grammaticality and semantic similarity. In addition, adversarial and behavioral testing methods are used to test the model's robustness and reasoning capabilities.

A comprehensive evaluation usually combines these different metrics to assess the model's reliability, quality, and safety, especially when it is deployed in real-world applications. It is important to note that creating robust frameworks for evaluation is still an area of active research.

Structure

In this chapter, the following topics will be covered:

- Foundation and Tuned Models: An Insight
- Model Size and Effective Practices
- GPUs in the Context of LLMs: A High-Level Overview
- Evaluation in Validating LLM Tasks: Key Concepts
- Evolving Landscape of Fine-Tuning LLMs

Insight into LLM Variants

Understanding the distinctions between the foundation, pretrained, and fine-tuned large language models (LLMs) is crucial for selecting the right model for your specific needs. These categories essentially represent different stages in the life cycle of an LLM, each with its own characteristics and applications.

Foundation LLM

Foundation models are the starting point in the LLM ecosystem. They are trained on vast datasets of unlabeled text using self-supervision techniques. This enables them to acquire a broad understanding of language, including syntax, semantics, and general linguistic patterns. However, they are not specialized for any particular task. Examples of foundation models include BERT and GPT-3.

Pre-trained LLM

Pre-trained models take foundation models as their starting point but go a step further. They are trained on domain-specific unlabeled data, allowing them to acquire more nuanced knowledge related to a particular field or genre of text. Despite this additional layer of training, they are still not specialized for any specific task.

Fine-Tuned LLM

Fine-tuned models begin with a pre-trained foundation model and are then trained further on labeled data specific to a particular task. This additional training specializes the model to perform well on that task. Examples of tasks for which models might be fine-tuned include question answering, text classification, and text summarization.

In essence, foundation models serve as a broad base, learning general language patterns. Pre-trained models build on this foundation by gaining domain-specific knowledge. Fine-tuned models take it a step further by specializing in particular tasks. Itis like a progression from a generalist doctor to a specialist; the foundation model is akin to a general practitioner, while the pre-trained model is comparable to a doctor with some specialized training, and the fine-tuned model is like a highly specialized surgeon.

Benefits of Using Pre-trained Over Foundation LLMs

When it comes to deploying LLMs for specific tasks, the question often arises: should you start with a foundation model or a pre-trained model? While foundation models offer a broad base of general language understanding, pre-trained models offer several advantages that make them more suitable for quick and efficient deployment.

Faster Training and Deployment

One of the most significant benefits of using pre-trained LLMs is the speed of training and deployment. Because these models have already been trained on domain-specific data, they require less computational time and resources to fine-tune for specific tasks. This enables faster iteration cycles and quicker deployment to production environments.

Better Performance on Specific Domains

Pre-trained models are tailored to specific domains or genres of text, which often results in better performance for tasks within those domains. This is because the additional layer of pre-training imbues the model with more relevant, domain-specific knowledge compared to general-purpose foundation models.

Requires Less Data for Fine-Tuning

Another advantage is that pre-trained models often require less data for effective fine-tuning. They provide a strong initialization point, which means you can achieve good performance even with smaller, task-specific datasets. In contrast, foundation models usually require massive datasets for fine-tuning.

Lower Risk

Using a pre-trained model is generally considered lower risk than training a foundation model from scratch. This is because pre-trained models have already proven their effectiveness and reliability in specific domains.

Access to State-of-the-Art Models

Pre-trained models often come from big tech companies that have invested heavily in research and development. As a result, these models are usually state-of-the-art, incorporating the latest advancements in machine learning and natural language processing.

Pre-trained LLMs offer several advantages over foundation models, including faster and more efficient training, better performance in specific domains, and lower risk. They are particularly beneficial when you have limited data for fine-tuning. The trade-off is that you have less flexibility and control compared to starting with a foundation model. However, for most applications, the benefits of using a pre-trained model outweigh the limitations, providing an efficient pathway to deploying cutting-edge NLP solutions.

Impact of Training Corpus on Performance

The size of the training corpus plays a pivotal role in shaping the performance of pre-trained LLMs. However, it is not just a matter of "*bigger is better*"; several factors come into play that can either enhance or limit the effectiveness of a pre-trained model based on the size of its training corpus.

More Data, More Knowledge

A larger training corpus allows an LLM to be exposed to a more extensive range of text data, enabling it to learn more linguistic patterns, knowledge, and representations. Generally, models pre-trained on larger datasets tend to outperform those trained on smaller datasets when applied to downstream tasks.

Model Scale and Architecture Matter

While a larger corpus can provide more data for the model to learn from, the scale and architecture of the model are also crucial. Training a small model on a massive dataset may not yield the desired performance improvements. Think of it like trying to pour a gallon of water into a small cup; the size of the cup limits how much it can hold.

Diminishing Returns

There is a point of diminishing returns when it comes to the size of the training corpus. Beyond a certain threshold, adding more data does not significantly improve the model's performance. This is akin to saturating a sponge with water; after a point, it cannot absorb any more.

Balancing Corpus Size with Compute Resources

Larger training corpora require more computational resources for effective pre-training. Therefore, the size of the training corpus needs to be balanced with available compute resources to ensure efficient training.

Corpus Relevance

The size of the corpus should align with the intended use cases. Training on a large but irrelevant corpus can limit the model's performance in the target domain. It is like training for a marathon by only doing sprints; the training does not align with the actual event.

Multi-domain Versatility

Using a multi-domain training corpus can improve the model's versatility across different tasks compared to a single-domain corpus. This is similar to a decathlete training in various sports to excel in a multi-event competition.

While larger and more diverse training corpora generally yield better-performing pre-trained LLMs, it is essential to consider other factors like model scale, diminishing returns, and corpus relevance. These elements collectively determine how efficiently a model can be pre-trained for optimal performance.

Best Practices for Fine-Tuning LLMs

Fine-tuning LLMs is an art that requires a nuanced approach. The process involves several steps, each with its own set of best practices. Following are some guidelines based on various aspects such as understanding the dataset, choosing the right pre-trained model, and employing advanced techniques like in-context learning.

Understanding the Dataset

- **Analyze Dataset Characteristics**: Before diving into fine-tuning, it is crucial to understand the dataset's size, balance, quality, and relevance to the target task.
- **Data Augmentation:** If the dataset is small, consider using techniques like in-context learning or data augmentation to improve its utility.
- **Data Pre-processing**: Clean and pre-process the data to ensure that the model is trained on high-quality information.

Choosing the Right Pre-trained Model

- **Task Relevance**: Choose a model that has been pre-trained on data similar to your target task. This ensures that the model already has some relevant foundational knowledge.
- **Resource Considerations**: Balance the model's size with the available compute resources and the performance needs of your specific application.
- **Advanced Pre-training Techniques**: Consider models that have been pre-trained using advanced techniques like multi-task learning, as they tend to be more versatile.

Targeted Parameter Fine-Tuning

- **Selective Fine-Tuning**: Instead of fine-tuning the entire model, you can choose to fine-tune only specific layers or parameters. This can be more computationally efficient.
- **Advanced Methods**: Use techniques like adapter modules, `BitFit`, or prompt tuning to fine-tune the model more effectively.
- **Resource Trade-offs**: Always consider the trade-off between the computational resources required and the level of customization you aim to achieve.

Customizing the Training Objective

- **Task-specific Objectives**: Incorporate task-specific loss functions or metrics to guide the fine-tuning process.

- **Staged Training**: Use techniques like intermediate fine-tuning and staged training to balance task performance while preserving the model's general capabilities.

In-Context Learning and Other Advancements

- **In-Context Learning**: This technique is particularly useful when the available data is limited. It allows the model to generalize better from a smaller dataset.
- **Prompting and Fine-Tuning**: Combining prompting techniques with fine-tuning can yield better performance.
- **Human Feedback and Reinforcement Learning**: Utilize reinforcement learning from human feedback to fine-tune the model in a more targeted manner.
- **Ensemble Methods**: Consider using an ensemble of fine-tuned models to improve performance and robustness.

Fine-tuning LLMs is a multi-step process that requires careful planning and execution. Each step, from understanding your dataset to choosing the right pre-trained model and employing advanced fine-tuning techniques, plays a crucial role in determining the model's final performance. By following these best practices, you can maximize the efficiency and effectiveness of your fine-tuning efforts.

Tips for Creating an Instruction Dataset

When it comes to fine-tuning large language models (LLMs), the quality and relevance of the dataset are paramount. While there are common datasets available for various tasks, creating a custom instruction dataset can be highly beneficial for specialized applications. Some tips for creating an effective instruction dataset for fine-tuning LLMs are as follows:

- **Gather Examples**: Start by collecting examples of the types of instructions and responses you want the model to generate. These could be sourced from existing human conversations, documentation, or support tickets.
- **Structure the Data**: Organize the data into instruction-response pairs. The instruction should be explicit about the task or request, and the response should provide the desired output.
- **Diversity in Phrasing**: Aim for variety in the phrasing of both instructions and responses. Uniformity in wording can limit the model's ability to generalize.

- **Include Positive and Negative Examples**: It is essential to show the model what good responses look like, but also include flawed examples to teach it what to avoid.
- **Multiple Valid Responses**: For open-ended tasks, consider including multiple valid responses per instruction to teach the model that there can be more than one correct way to complete a task.
- **Data Volume**: Aim to gather at least a few hundred examples, and ideally a few thousand, to teach nuanced behaviors effectively.
- **Data Splitting**: Divide your dataset into training, validation, and test sets. The test set will be crucial for evaluating the fine-tuned model's performance.
- **Crowdsourcing**: To scale up data collection, consider using platforms like Amazon Mechanical Turk.
- **Data Pre-processing**: Clean and pre-process the data to remove errors, biases, and to convert it into a standard format.

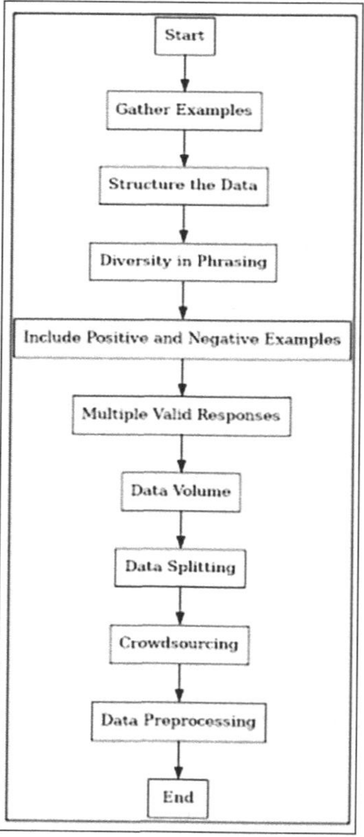

Figure 9.1: *Tips for Dataset Creation*

Creating a high-quality, diverse training dataset is crucial for fine-tuning LLMs effectively. The dataset should be structured, diverse, and large enough to teach the model nuanced behaviors. By following these best practices, you can create a dataset that enables your LLM to excel at the target task. Start small, iterate, and expand the dataset as needed to fine-tune your model successfully.

GPU Selection for LLM Training and Inference

Graphics Processing Units (GPUs) have evolved from their initial purpose of rendering graphics to becoming the linchpin in various high-performance computing tasks. They are particularly crucial in the training and deployment of LLMs due to their parallel processing capabilities. This section aims to provide a comprehensive guide on understanding the GPU architecture, its role in LLMs, and how to select the right GPU based on your specific needs.

GPU Architecture: Core Components

GPUs consist of several key components that work in tandem to execute complex tasks:

- **Core Computational Units**: These are the arithmetic units responsible for performing calculations.
- **Memory**: This is where data is stored for quick access. The larger the memory, the more data can be processed in parallel.
- **Caches**: These are smaller, faster types of memory that store frequently used data to speed up access.
- **Rendering Pipelines**: These are specialized pathways for graphics rendering tasks.
- **Interconnects**: These are the communication channels that allow different parts of the GPU to interact with each other and with the CPU.

Specialized Components

Modern GPUs also include specialized components like Tensor Cores designed to accelerate matrix multiplication operations, which are common in neural networks. These specialized components are particularly useful in LLM training where massive amounts of matrix calculations are required.

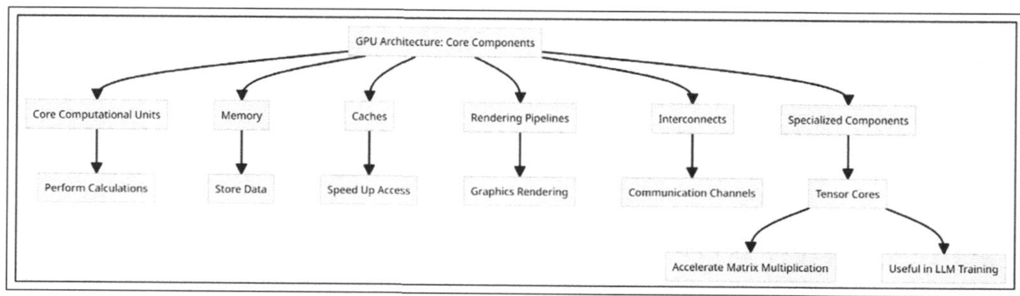

Figure 9.2: *GPU Functional Components*

Programming GPUs

To harness the power of GPUs, developers can use a variety of programming languages and frameworks. These include standard parallel programming languages like ISO C++, ISO Fortran, and Python, as well as specialized languages like CUDA C++, CUDA Fortran, OpenACC, PyCUDA, and OpenCL.

GPUs in LLMs

LLMs, such as GPT-3, require massive amounts of matrix calculations, which are highly parallel operations. This makes GPUs an ideal choice for two main reasons:

- **Speed**: The parallel architecture of GPUs allows them to perform multiple operations simultaneously, making them significantly faster than CPUs for specific tasks.
- **Memory Management**: GPUs generally have high-bandwidth memory, allowing them to handle large datasets more efficiently than CPUs.

NVIDIA, a leading name in the GPU market, has been instrumental in the development of LLMs. Their H100 Tensor Core GPU, for instance, is optimized for LLMs and provides significant performance improvements over previous generations like the A100 80GB.

Selecting the Right GPU for LLM Training

When it comes to choosing a GPU for training LLMs, several factors come into play:

- **Memory Capacity**: LLMs can have billions of parameters, requiring a significant amount of memory. GPUs like NVIDIA's A100 or H100, with 40-80 GB of RAM, are often suitable choices.

- **Compute Capability**: The speed of a GPU is often determined by the number of cores it has. More cores mean that the GPU can perform more calculations in parallel, speeding up the training process.
- **Memory Bandwidth**: This is the speed at which the GPU can read or write to its memory. Higher bandwidth allows for quicker data transfer, reducing bottlenecks in the training process.
- **Scalability**: For enterprise-level models, you may need to scale your resources. Look for GPUs that support technologies like SLI or NVLink, which allow for multi-GPU configurations.

Let's say you are working on a project that requires training a language model with 13 billion parameters. In this case, a single consumer-grade GPU will not suffice due to memory limitations. You would likely need to opt for multiple high-end GPUs like the NVIDIA A100, each with at least 40GB of memory, and employ model parallelism techniques to distribute the model across these GPUs.

GPU for Model Inference

While training is a critical aspect, inference is where the trained model is put to use. The factors to consider for inference are slightly different:

- **Speed**: GPUs can provide significant speedups for inference compared to CPUs due to their parallel architecture.
- **Model Size**: Larger models with more parameters will benefit more from parallel GPU processing. For small models, a CPU may be sufficient.
- **Batching**: GPUs achieve the highest throughput with batched inference of multiple inputs. If latency and throughput are less important, CPU inference of single inputs may suffice.
- **Cost and Power Consumption**: GPUs add hardware costs and require more power, which increases operating costs. CPUs are more efficient for low throughput use cases.

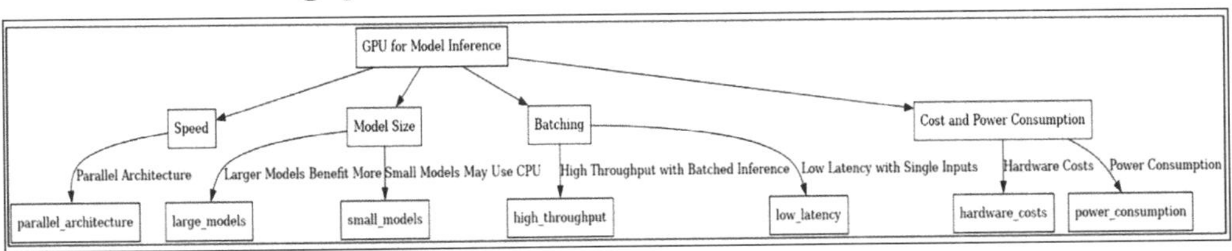

***Figure 9.3**: GPU Model Inference Benefits*

GPUs have become an indispensable tool in the field of machine learning and, more specifically, in the training and inference of large language models. Their architecture is uniquely suited to handle the parallelizable nature of machine learning algorithms. As LLMs continue to grow in size and complexity, the role of GPUs will only become more significant. Whether you are a researcher pushing the boundaries of natural language understanding or a business looking to deploy a chatbot, understanding the capabilities and limitations of your GPU resources is crucial.

By diving deep into the architecture of GPUs and understanding their role in the ecosystem of large language models, one can make informed decisions that balance performance, time, and cost, thereby unlocking new possibilities in the realm of artificial intelligence.

Selecting the Right Model for Fine-Tuning

Selecting the right LLM for fine-tuning is a critical decision that can significantly impact the success of your project. Various factors come into play, ranging from the type of task you are tackling to the computational resources at your disposal. Following are some key considerations and recommendations for choosing an LLM for fine-tuning.

Key Factors to Consider

- **Compute Resources**: Larger models like GPT-3 require more computational power and memory. Assess your hardware capabilities before making a choice.
- **Dataset Size**: Some models require massive datasets for effective fine-tuning, while others can work well with smaller datasets. Evaluate the volume of task-specific data you have.
- **Task Type**: Different models excel at different types of tasks. For instance, GPT-3 is geared towards text generation, BERT is good for encoding, and T5 is suitable for sequence-to-sequence tasks.
- **Pre-training Data**: Choose a model that has been pre-trained on data similar to your target task for better performance.
- **Performance Needs**: While larger models generally perform better, smaller models may suffice for simpler tasks.
- **Customizability**: Some models offer more architectural or pre-training customization options.
- **Cost**: Consider the financial aspect, especially if you are using cloud-hosted models. Open-source models can be more cost-effective.

Task-Specific Recommendations

- **Text Classification:** BERT and RoBERTa are strong choices for this task. ALBERT can also be a good option if you have model size constraints.
- **Question Answering:** BERT and ALBERT are effective for extractive QA tasks. For abstractive QA, consider using T5 or BART.
- **Text Generation:** GPT-2 and GPT-3 are ideal for text generation tasks. T5 and BART can also be used in an encoder-decoder framework for this purpose.

General Guidelines

- **Start Small**: Ideally, pick the smallest model that meets your requirements and scale up as needed.
- **Empirical Testing**: Whenever possible, evaluate multiple models on a small dataset to determine the best fit for your specific needs.
- **Ensemble Models**: Combining multiple models can sometimes yield better performance by leveraging their individual strengths.

Choosing the right LLM for fine-tuning involves a careful consideration of various factors like task type, dataset size, and computational resources. BERT and RoBERTa are generally good starting points for classification and QA tasks, while GPT-3 excels in text generation but comes with higher computational costs. T5 and BART offer a balanced approach for both understanding and generation tasks. Always consider running empirical tests to make an informed decision.

Challenges in Fine-Tuning Pre-trained Models

Fine-tuning pre-trained LLMs is not without its challenges. While these models offer a head start by leveraging pre-existing knowledge, several issues can arise during the fine-tuning process. Here is a detailed look at these challenges and some strategies to mitigate them:

- **Overfitting**
  - **Problem**: Fine-tuning on a small dataset can lead to overfitting, where the model performs well on the training data but poorly on unseen data.
  - **Solution**: Techniques like regularization, dropout, and freezing some layers can help mitigate overfitting.

- **Degradation**
  - **Problem**: The fine-tuning process can cause the model to forget the knowledge it gained during pre-training, leading to a loss of generalization ability.
  - **Solution**: Experimenting with different learning rates, optimization strategies, and regularization techniques can help mitigate this issue.
- **Computational Costs**
  - **Problem**: Fine-tuning large models can be computationally expensive, requiring significant hardware resources.
  - **Solution**: Using smaller models like DistilBERT can reduce computational costs without a significant loss in performance.
- **Hallucination**
  - **Problem**: When fine-tuned on tasks with limited data, models may generate outputs that are not grounded in the input data, a phenomenon known as hallucination.
  - **Solution**: Techniques like embedding hallucination, which involves generating additional training examples during fine-tuning, can help address this issue.
- **Quality of Data**
  - **Problem**: The effectiveness of fine-tuning is highly dependent on the quality and relevance of the dataset used.
  - **Solution**: Ensuring that the dataset is representative of the problem domain and is well-preprocessed can improve the performance of the fine-tuned model.

Addressing the challenges of fine-tuning pre-trained models requires a multi-faceted approach. It involves not just selecting the right model and dataset, but also carefully monitoring performance and applying specialized techniques to mitigate issues like overfitting and degradation. By being aware of these challenges and proactively addressing them, you can maximize the benefits of fine-tuning and deploy more robust and effective models.

Sneak Peek into Efficiency in LLMs

Large language models such as GPT-3 and GPT-4 have ushered in a transformative phase in the field of natural language processing (NLP). These models are no longer just tools in a developer's toolkit; they are integral parts of business strategies, aiding in decision-making, customer interactions, and even creative tasks. However, navigating the labyrinth of efficiency and cost metrics associated with these behemoths is non-trivial. This section aims to provide a comprehensive and industry-relevant guide to the key metrics crucial for deploying LLMs effectively.

Token Economics

Tokens are the fuel that powers the LLM engine. These are discrete pieces of text, usually words or characters, that the model reads as input and provides as output. Each model has a specific token limit, and once you hit that limit, the interaction abruptly ends.

Best Practices

- Limit the number of tokens in both input and output to avoid unnecessary costs.
- Design your application to truncate or summarize text dynamically to reduce token usage.

Art of Prompt Optimization

Every token counts, even those in the questions or prompts you pose to the model. A more concise and direct prompt will use fewer tokens, leaving room for more expansive answers.

Best Practices

- Test multiple prompt variants to identify the most efficient phrasing.
- Implement A/B testing to scientifically determine the prompt that maximizes efficacy while minimizing token consumption.

GPT Versions Cost Ratio

While newer GPT versions like GPT-4 offer incredible capabilities, they can cost up to 50 times more than their predecessors for certain tasks. It is essential to balance the features you need against the budget you have.

Best Practices

- Compare the performance of different GPT versions on your specific tasks before making a choice.
- Be willing to use older versions if they fulfil your requirements at a fraction of the cost.

Embedding and Fine-Tuning Costs

Vector stores can perform specific tasks at a much lower cost than a full-fledged LLM invocation. Moreover, fine-tuning, while beneficial for specific tasks, adds another layer of cost.

Best Practices

- Assess whether a vector store could perform the task adequately before invoking an LLM.
- Always conduct a cost-benefit analysis when considering fine-tuning.

Training and Fine-Tuning Costs

While it is tempting to consider training your own LLM, the costs are prohibitive for most. Estimates indicate that training a 13-billion parameter model can exceed $1 million, not including other overheads like electricity and maintenance.

Best Practices

- Opt for pre-trained models whenever possible.
- If specialization is needed, fine-tuning is often more economical than training a model from scratch.

GPU Memory Requirements

Your choice of GPU will directly affect your ability to deploy LLMs. GPUs come with varying memory capacities, affecting both costs and capabilities.

Best Practices

- Know your model's memory requirements beforehand.
- Choose a GPU that not only has sufficient computational power but also aligns with your model's memory needs.

Areas for Innovation

- **Cost-Effective Model Selection**: Innovate in machine learning techniques that dynamically select the most cost-effective model based on the task.
- **Token Optimization Algorithms**: Develop algorithms that can automatically optimize token usage.
- **Dynamic Batching and Scheduling**: Employ adaptive techniques that can handle varying workloads efficiently.

As LLMs increasingly become a mainstay in both industry and academia, understanding the intricacies of their deployment is critical. This section has aimed to provide you with pragmatic and actionable insights that will serve as your compass in this rapidly evolving landscape.

By mastering these elements, you are not only contributing to more efficient and economical model deployment but are also positioning yourself at the forefront of this exciting field. Welcome to the future of NLP, where the confluence of technical acumen and strategic planning sets the stage for unprecedented advancements.

Validating LLMs

Validation is a critical phase in the life cycle of powerful AI models like LLMs. It serves as a crucial checkpoint, ensuring that a trained LLM can perform effectively and reliably on specific tasks or a range of tasks, even when faced with unfamiliar data. Validation plays a pivotal role in identifying potential issues within the model's operation, such as overfitting or underfitting, and provides developers with the means to adjust model parameters and architecture for improved performance.

The choice of validation metrics depends on the specific LLM task and desired outcomes, offering a multifaceted view of the model's capabilities, whether it is accurate text prediction, high-quality translations, or precise text classification. Typically, the validation process involves partitioning data into training, validation, and test sets. The training set allows the model to learn from data, while the validation set assesses its performance during training. The ultimate test occurs on the unbiased test set, evaluating the model's true ability to generalize.

Beyond numerical metrics, human evaluation plays a vital role in assessing aspects like fluency, coherence, and meaning preservation in the LLM's output, offering qualitative insights that complement quantitative measurements. In the broader context of LLM development and deployment, validation stands as a guardian, ensuring these AI marvels are not only reliable and accurate but also well-equipped to handle real-world challenges.

Evaluation Metrics

This comprehensive section aims to delve deep into the metrics and methodologies used for evaluating LLMs and general NLP tasks. By understanding these metrics, software engineers, data scientists, and NLP practitioners can make informed decisions, ensuring the development of high-scale, state-of-the-art solutions.

Perplexity: The Speedometer of Language Models

Perplexity measures how well a language model predicts the next word in a sequence. A lower perplexity score indicates better predictive capabilities.

While perplexity serves as a good initial metric, akin to a car's top speed, it does not provide a complete picture. It lacks the ability to measure the model's coherence or factual accuracy. Therefore, it should be considered alongside other metrics for a holistic evaluation.

Example: Imagine you are reading a book, and you are trying to guess the next word. If you can guess it easily, the "*perplexity*" is low. If it is hard to guess, the "perplexity" is high.

Language Fluency: The River's Flow

Language fluency evaluates the grammatical correctness, naturalness, and clarity of the generated text. Fluency can be thought of as the "*readability*" or the flow of a river. It should be smooth and natural. Human ratings often serve as the gold standard, but automated metrics like BLEU can also offer quick approximations.

Example: A sentence like *The cat sat on the mat* would score high on fluency, while *Cat the sat mat on* would score low.

Coherence: The Structured Essay

Coherence assesses the logical consistency and unity of the text. A coherent text is like a well-structured essay, maintaining a single topic or theme throughout. Incoherence would be akin to a random collection of sentences, lacking logical flow.

Example: A coherent text would maintain a single topic or theme throughout, such as an article solely about climate change.

Contextual Understanding: The GPS System

This metric evaluates the model's ability to understand and respond to the context in which it is placed. Contextual understanding is similar to a GPS system; it needs to comprehend the current location (context) to provide accurate directions. Specialized QA datasets often serve as benchmarks.

Example: If given a paragraph about climate change, the model should generate responses related to that context.

Factual Accuracy: The Journalist's Fact-Check

Factual accuracy measures the validity of the information in the generated text.

This metric is akin to a journalist fact-checking an article before publication. Human annotators or adversarial datasets are commonly used for verification.

Example: If asked, *Who was the first President of the United States*, the model should accurately respond with *George Washington.*

Let us understand some of the metrics before we proceed to link these metrics with specific tasks:

Metric	Definition	Example
Accuracy	The proportion of correct predictions made by the model.	If a model correctly identifies 9 out of 10 spam emails, its accuracy is 90%.
Precision	Measures the proportion of true positive predictions among all positive predictions made.	If a model identifies 8 spam emails but 2 are false alarms, its precision is 8/10 or 80%.
Recall	Measures the proportion of true positives among all actual positive instances.	If there are 10 spam emails and the model identifies 8, its recall is 8/10 or 80%.
F1 Score	The harmonic mean of precision and recall, balancing both metrics.	If precision is 80% and recall is 90%, the F1 score would be approximately 85%.
ROC-AUC	Measures the area under the Receiver Operating Characteristic curve, indicating class separation.	A ROC-AUC score close to 1 indicates excellent class separation.
BLEU	A metric for evaluating the quality of machine-generated translations.	If a machine translation closely matches a human translation, it will have a high BLEU score.

ROUGE	A metric for evaluating text summaries based on recall.	If a generated summary captures most of the important points of the original text, it will have a high ROUGE score.
METEOR	A more advanced metric for machine translation that considers linguistic features.	METEOR takes into account synonyms, stemming, and word order to evaluate translations.
Cosine Similarity	Measures the angle between two non-zero vectors to gauge similarity.	Used in document retrieval to find the most relevant documents based on keyword vectors.
Task Completion Rate	Measures how often a system, like a chatbot, successfully completes tasks it is designed for.	If a chatbot successfully books a table 9 out of 10 times, its task completion rate is 90%.

Table 9.1: *Overview of Evaluation Metrics*

Evaluating General NLP Tasks

Now, let us delve into the notion of evaluation from a task-oriented standpoint.

Text Classification

Metrics like accuracy, precision, recall, and F1 score serve as basic tools in the toolbox, each with a specific purpose. They are foundational for tasks like sentiment analysis and spam detection. For example, in sentiment analysis, "*Accuracy*" would measure the percentage of reviews correctly classified as positive or negative. In a spam filter, accuracy would measure how many emails are correctly labeled as spam or not spam, while precision would focus on the correctness of only those labeled as spam.

Text Generation

BLEU, ROUGE, and METEOR act like different lenses to view the quality of a photograph. Each offers a unique perspective on the generated text, commonly used in machine translation and summarization. For example, in machine translation, BLEU would compare the n-grams in the translated text to those in a reference translation. In a news article summarization tool, BLEU could measure how well the summary captures the essence of the original article, while ROUGE could focus on the recall of key points.

Information Extraction

Precision, recall, and F1 score are akin to a miner sifting through dirt to find valuable gems (entities). These metrics are pivotal for named entity recognition tasks. For example, in extracting names from a text, "*Precision*" would measure how many of the extracted names are actually correct. In a legal document scanner, precision would measure how many of the extracted legal terms are correct, while recall would measure how many of the actual legal terms were captured by the model.

Question Answering

Metrics such as exact match accuracy and F1 score are used, resembling a game show where the model is scored based on the accuracy of their answers. For example, in a dataset like SQuAD, *exact match accuracy* would measure how many answers exactly match the ground truth.

Text Similarity

Cosine similarity and mean reciprocal rank act like matchmakers, finding the most compatible documents based on keyword vectors. For example, in document retrieval, *mean reciprocal rank* would average the ranks of the first relevant document in a list of ranked items. In a dating app algorithm, cosine similarity could be used to match profiles based on shared interests and attributes.

Dialogue Systems

Task completion rate is crucial for goal-oriented dialogue agents. It is akin to a customer service representative, where the primary goal is to resolve the customer's issue successfully. For example, in a virtual assistant, task completion rate would measure how often the assistant successfully sets reminders, sends emails, or performs other tasks itis designed for.

In summary, a comprehensive evaluation of LLMs and NLP tasks requires a multi-faceted approach, combining various metrics and frameworks to fully assess capabilities, safety, and use-cases. By understanding and applying these metrics and frameworks, you can make informed decisions about model selection and improvement, aligning with the goal of achieving high-scale, state-of-the-art solutions in software engineering and development.

Challenges

The evaluation of large language models (LLMs) and their tasks (LLMTs) is far from straightforward. With the plethora of dimensions to consider, it is crucial to have a systematic evaluation framework. Let us dissect the intricacies of evaluating LLMs, highlighting the key challenges and proposing avenues for overcoming them.

Metrics are Only Part of the Story

While quantitative metrics like BLEU, F1-score, and perplexity offer a standardized approach for comparing LLMs, they are not a silver bullet. Metrics can offer a glimpse into language quality and task performance but often miss out on nuances like coherence and creativity. Thus, relying solely on them is like seeing just the tip of the iceberg.

Human Factor in Evaluation

Human evaluation adds the much-needed depth to our understanding of a model's capabilities. However, this method is fraught with inconsistency and potential bias. Training human evaluators to adhere to a standard set of guidelines can lend more reliability to qualitative assessments.

Ethical Dimension

Evaluation is not merely a technical exercise but an ethical obligation as well. LLMs can inadvertently produce harmful or biased outputs, making the ethical alignment of these models a critical evaluation dimension. A well-rounded evaluation framework will thus also involve a thorough ethical impact assessment, which goes beyond simple metrics to include broader societal considerations.

No model is perfect, and every evaluation framework has its limitations. Metrics often focus only on surface-level attributes and fail to capture the semantic richness of a language. Furthermore, these evaluations can vary depending on the dataset used, the human judges involved, and even the specific tasks the LLMs are trained for. To navigate these challenges, an ideal evaluation framework needs to be comprehensive and multi-dimensional:

- **Quantitative Metrics**: For numerical comparisons and progress tracking.
- **Qualitative Human Evaluation**: To capture the richness and complexity of language tasks.

- **Ethical Audits**: For assessing the social and ethical implications of the model's output.
- **Task-specific Benchmarks**: To test the model's efficacy in specific domains.
- **Adversarial Evaluations**: To test how the model performs under challenging and unexpected scenarios.

Evaluating an LLM is not merely a question of how well it performs but also how safely, ethically, and comprehensively it aligns with human values and expectations. As we move towards increasingly sophisticated models, our evaluation frameworks must evolve in tandem, adopting a holistic approach that merges the quantitative with the qualitative and the ethical with the functional. Only then can we hope to make informed decisions in the selection and deployment of these powerful language models.

Now that we have a thorough grasp of fine-tuning and evaluation, let us explore a few practical implementations that will illustrate the concepts we have covered.

Future of Fine-Tuning LLMs

The future of fine-tuning LLMs holds significant promise as we enter a more AI-driven era. This involves several key trends:

- **Few-Shot Learning**: Researchers are exploring the concept of few-shot learning, which involves fine-tuning LLMs with minimal examples. This approach could reduce data requirements for training and enhance the model's ability to generalize.
- **Intermediate-Task Fine-Tuning**: Another emerging trend is intermediate-task fine-tuning. LLMs are first fine-tuned on an intermediate task before specialization for the final task, which helps the model focus its knowledge and improve performance.

These advancements are expected to have a substantial impact on various industries:

- **Healthcare**: Fine-tuned LLMs could revolutionize healthcare, aiding in drug discovery and disease diagnosis through better understanding of medical language and literature.
- **Finance**: In the financial sector, fine-tuned LLMs could analyze economic trends and financial reports, contributing to market prediction.
- **Education**: Fine-tuned LLMs in education could act as personalized tutors, adapting to individual learning styles and needs.

Looking ahead, as LLMs continue to grow in size and capabilities, effective fine-tuning methods will be crucial. Specialized and fine-tuned models will become more prevalent, democratizing AI across various tasks and languages. The future of fine-tuning LLMs holds promise for cutting-edge research and transformative applications across multiple sectors. Continuous evolution in this field is set to redefine how AI is leveraged, making fine-tuning an integral part of the AI development lifecycle.

Conclusion

In this comprehensive chapter, we embarked on a journey through the intricate landscape of LLMs and their fine-tuning. We navigated various aspects, from understanding the differences between foundation LLMs, pre-trained LLMs, and fine-tuned LLMs, to delving into the benefits and challenges of employing pre-trained LLMs. We also explored the critical factors influencing the performance of pre-trained LLMs, emphasizing the significance of corpus size and relevance. Our exploration extended to best practices for fine-tuning these behemoths, stressing the importance of dataset understanding, model selection, and parameter customization.

The chapter ventured into GPU selection for LLM training and inference. We discussed in detail GPU architectures, components, and programming nuances, ensuring that you are well-equipped to make informed choices in GPU selection. We also offered guidance on choosing the right LLM model for fine-tuning, considering task-specific recommendations and general guidelines.

Fine-tuning pre-trained models came with its set of challenges, including token economics, prompt optimization, and cost considerations across different LLM versions. We explored these intricacies to help you navigate the fine-tuning process effectively.

As we delved into the evaluation of LLMs, we examined various metrics and their implications, shedding light on how these models perform in tasks like text classification, generation, and information extraction. Challenges in evaluation, including the human factor and ethical dimensions, were also highlighted.

The chapter closed with a glimpse into the future of fine-tuning LLMs. We explored ongoing research and advancements, envisioning their impact on industries and research. As we looked ahead, the road was filled with opportunities and innovations, promising a dynamic future for LLMs.

In conclusion, this chapter served as a comprehensive guide through the intricate realm of LLMs and fine-tuning. Armed with knowledge, practical insights, and an eye on the horizon, you are well-prepared to navigate this ever-evolving landscape and harness the power of large language models for your endeavors.

In the next chapter, we will be leveraging the concepts learnt to implement diverse fine-tuning techniques.

References

https://github.com/ray-project/llm-numbers?search=1

CHAPTER 10

Recipes for Fine-Tuning and Evaluating LLMs

Introduction

In this comprehensive chapter, we will work on the implementation of fine-tuning with OpenAI and various other platforms, designed to empower you with the knowledge and skills to harness the full potential of state-of-the-art language models. In this chapter, we will embark on an extensive journey through the intricate process of fine-tuning models for diverse tasks and platforms. From Colab to Cohere and Kaggle GPUs, we will explore the entire landscape of model optimization and customization.

In the first part of our journey, we will focus on Colab, Google's collaborative platform, to fine-tune models with OpenAI. We will follow a step-by-step guide, from installing essential libraries and setting up the OpenAI key to creating and validating training data. As we progress, we will explore data upload, fine-tuning job initiation, and result retrieval. Our journey culminates with inference using the finely tuned model and understanding how to delete it when necessary.

Next, we will venture into the Cohere platform, where we will guide you through the process of fine-tuning LLMs for classification tasks. We will start by accessing the platform's dashboard, creating custom models, and configuring header information. After uploading training and validation data and reviewing data distribution, we will name the model and monitor its training progress. Finally, we will explore how to access the model, classify text, and manage API details.

The Kaggle GPUs for Text Classification in the IMDB Reviews section will provide insights into leveraging Kaggle's powerful GPUs for fine-tuning T5 models. Starting with environment setup and data loading, we will dive into model training and the main execution block. We will also examine the output and resource consumption to ensure efficient usage of resources.

In the Environment Preparation for DeepSpeed section, we will explore how to optimize your environment for efficient deep learning with DeepSpeed. We will discuss plugging in the DeepSpeed optimizer and analyze the resulting output.

For those interested in evaluation, the Evaluation Of LLMs on Summarization task section will guide you through the steps of installation, data sampling, batch generation, ROUGE score computation, and summarization using T5 and GPT-2 models. We will also cover how to display the results effectively.

Finally, we will dive into fine-tuning on Colab using quantization techniques. This advanced topic will require a solid foundation in the previous sections. We will walk through the installation, initialization, data loading, and quantization processes, ensuring you can effectively train and use quantized models.

Throughout this chapter, we aim to provide you with in-depth knowledge, practical guidance, and hands-on experience, empowering you to create unique and innovative solutions using state-of-the-art language models. Let's embark on this journey together and unlock the full potential of fine-tuning with OpenAI and beyond.

The codebase for this chapter can be accessed from https://github.com/ava-orange-education/Hands-On-Large-Language-Models-for-Enterprise/tree/main/chapter10

Structure

In this chapter, we will cover the following topics:

- Fine-tuning using OpenAI APIs
- Fine-tuning using the Cohere Platform
- Fine-tuning T5 models on Kaggle for classification tasks using DeepSpeed
- Evaluation of LLMs for summarization task

Fine-Tuning with OpenAI on Colab

Fine-tuning with OpenAI on Google Colab refers to the process of adapting OpenAI's extensive language models, like GPT-3, for particular tasks or applications. Google Colab offers a cloud-based development environment with

GPU capabilities, which is advantageous for training large models efficiently. Fine-tuning entails training a pre-existing model on a smaller, task-specific dataset to enhance its performance for that specific task. In this particular setup, we will utilize the CPU runtime, which is adequate for fine-tuning OpenAI Language Models (LLMs), given that they are API-based and do not require the extensive computational power of a GPU.

Prerequisite

1. Connect to Google Colab https://research.google.com/colaboratory/ and select runtime as CPU.

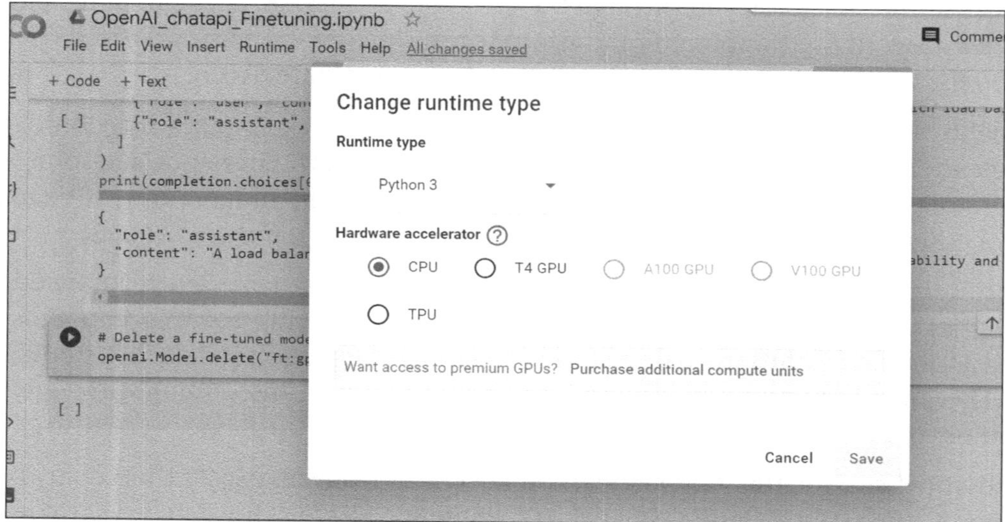

Figure 10.1: *Colab CPU Runtime*

2. Login to https://platform.openai.com/ and generate an API Key. Click on your profile.

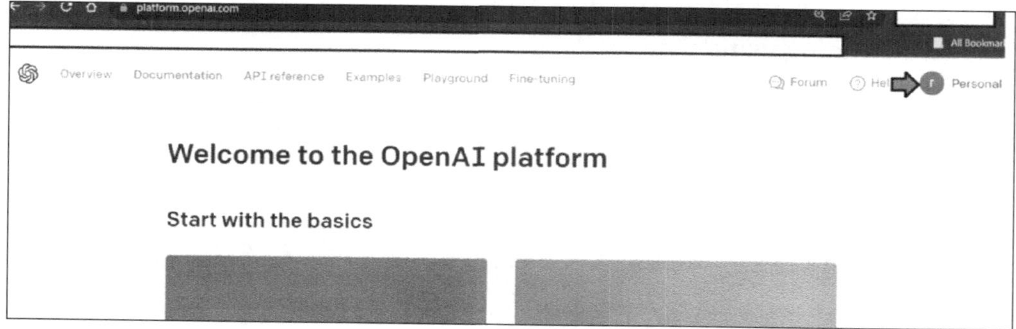

Figure 10.2: *OpenAI Profile*

3. Select **`View API keys`** from the options.

Figure 10.3: *API Keys navigation screen*

4. Click on **`Create new secret key`** and complete the creation of a new key. Please copy the key and store it securely as we will be using it in our implementation.

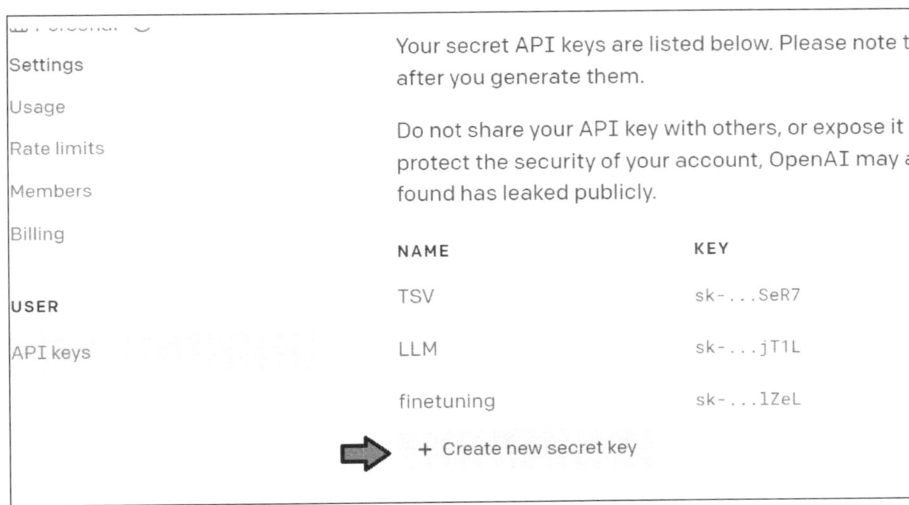

Figure 10.4: *API Keys creation screen*

Implementation Walkthrough

We are all set. Now let's get into the code walkthrough and understand how we can fine-tune a ChatGPT 3.5 turbo model.

The code for this implementation can be accessed from https://github.com/ava-orange-education/Hands-On-Large-Language-Models-for-Enterprise/blob/main/chapter10/OpenAI_chatapi_Finetuning.ipynb

Step 1: Installing Required Libraries

First and foremost, you will need to install some Python libraries in your environment. These libraries facilitate the various operations required for fine-tuning the model. To install the libraries, run the following command:

```
# This command installs openai, tiktoken, and matplotlib libraries.
!pip install openai tiktoken matplotlib -quiet
```

- **`openai`**: This is the core library that allows us to interact with OpenAI's GPT models.
- **`tiktoken`**: A library by OpenAI for counting tokens in text strings. Useful for keeping track of how many tokens are being processed.
- **`matplotlib`**: A plotting library for Python that will help us in visualization.
- Using **`--quiet`** suppresses the verbose output, making the installation look cleaner.

Step 2: Initializing Packages and Setting Up the OpenAI Key

After installing the required libraries, the next crucial step is to set the OpenAI API key and initialize the necessary Python packages for our implementation:

```
# Importing the required libraries
import json
import openai
import os
# Defining the OpenAI API key
api_key = "sk-***"
# Setting the API key for the openai library
openai.api_key = api_key
# Also setting the API key as an environment variable
os.environ['OPENAI_API_KEY'] = api_key
```

In preparation for interacting with OpenAI's API, we follow a series of essential steps. Initially, we import necessary libraries, including 'json' for handling JSON data commonly encountered in API responses, **`'openai'`** to facilitate interaction with OpenAI's API, and 'os' for managing environment variables. Subsequently, we define an API key as '**`api_key`**,' a critical element for authentication and accessing OpenAI's services. To ensure proper API key configuration, we set it in two ways: directly within the OpenAI library using '**`openai.api_key = api_key`**' and as an environment variable using '**`os.environ['OPENAI_API_KEY'] = api_key`**.'

These measures enable us to make authenticated requests to OpenAI's services effectively.

Step 3: Creating Training Data

The next significant step in fine-tuning a model is preparing your training data. This data should be formatted according to the specific requirements of the model you are fine-tuning. For OpenAI's chat models, training data often consists of a series of conversational exchanges.

The training data consists of JSON-formatted strings:

```
{
  "messages": [
    {"role": "system", "content": "You are a Software Engineering Mentor specialized in architecture and high-scale systems."},
    {"role": "user", "content": "Is there a specific technology stack you recommend for building high-scale web applications?"},
    {"role": "assistant", "content": "It depends on your requirements, but popular choices include using Node.js, React, and a NoSQL database for flexibility and scalability."}
  ]
}
```

The schema consists of three key components:

- **Messages**: This forms the parent container that holds the list of conversations
- **Role**: The **`'role'`** field designates the role of each entity in the conversation, which can be "**`system`**," "**`user`**," or "**`assistant`**":
    - **`System` Role**: The **`'system'`** message is used to set the context for the assistant. The provided example configures the assistant as a "*Software Engineering Mentor specialized in architecture and high-scale systems.*"
    - **`User` Role**: The **`'user'`** message represents the query or question posed by the user to the assistant. This can encompass a wide range of queries, such as technical questions or requests for information.
    - **`Assistant` Role**: The **`'assistant'`** message contains the model's response to the user's query. It represents the output that you aim to improve upon through fine-tuning.
- **Content**: The **`'content'`** field contains the actual text spoken or written by each entity in the conversation.

In the preceding snippet, the **'system'** message establishes the assistant's role as a Software Engineering Mentor specialized in high-scale systems.

The **'user'** message consists of a query regarding technology stacks for high-scale web applications.

The **'assistant'** message responds by recommending a technology stack that includes Node.js, React, and a NoSQL database, based on the user's requirements.

Step 4: Data Validation

Before proceeding with the actual fine-tuning, it's essential to validate your dataset. Data validation includes checking for inconsistencies, analyzing the token distribution, and estimating the computational cost.

Let's understand the functions used in this phase.

a. **num_tokens_from_messages Function**: This function serves the purpose of determining the total number of tokens within a collection of messages. You can provide a list of messages as input, and it also allows you to specify the token count associated with each message and name. By analyzing the content of these messages and considering role-specific token counts, it calculates the overall number of tokens present in the messages. The result is an integer, which signifies the total token count encompassed by the given messages.

```
def num_tokens_from_messages(messages, tokens_per_message=3, tokens_per_
name=1):
    """

    Calculate the total number of tokens in a list of messages.


    Parameters:

    messages (list): A list of dictionaries containing messages with
roles and content.

    tokens_per_message (int): The base number of tokens for each
message. Default is 3.

    tokens_per_name (int): Number of tokens for each name in the
message. Default is 1.


    Returns:

    int: The total number of tokens for the list of messages.
    """

…
```

b. **`num_assistant_tokens_from_messages` Function:** This function is designed to quantify the number of tokens utilized in the responses generated by an assistant within a set of messages. When provided with a list of messages, it meticulously scans through them, identifying messages originating from the assistant. It then proceeds to count the tokens within the content of these assistant messages. The function ultimately provides you with an integer representing the total token count associated with the assistant's responses in the messages.

```
def num_assistant_tokens_from_messages(messages):
    """
    Calculate the number of tokens in assistant's messages within
a list of messages.


    Parameters:
    messages (list): A list of dictionaries containing messages
with roles and content.


    Returns:
    int: The number of tokens used in assistant's responses.
    """
...
```

c. **`print_distribution` Function:** This function offers a valuable tool for understanding the distribution of numerical values within a given list, accompanied by a descriptive name. It calculates essential statistical properties such as the minimum, maximum, mean, median, and percentile values for the provided numerical values. By doing so, it enables you to gain insights into the distribution characteristics of the data. This can be particularly useful in data analysis and decision-making.

```
def print_distribution(values, name):
    """
    Print statistical distribution information for a list of values.


    Parameters:
    values (list): List of numerical values for which distribution
is calculated.
```

```
        name (str): Descriptive name for the list of values.
        """

    ...
```

d. **`check_for_duplicates` Function**: In the context of managing datasets, this function plays a crucial role in identifying and addressing duplicate conversations. It accomplishes this task by comparing serialized representations of conversations within a dataset. As it encounters duplicate conversations, it keeps a count of them. This function is instrumental in maintaining data quality and ensuring that each conversation is unique.

```
def check_for_duplicates(dataset):
    """

    Check for duplicate conversations in the dataset.


    Parameters:
    dataset (list): List of conversation data.


    Prints:
    Number of duplicate conversations found in the dataset.
    """

    ...
```

e. **`analyze_data_and_tokens` Function**: When working with datasets containing conversational data, it's essential to assess their quality and characteristics. This function takes a dataset as input and conducts an exhaustive analysis. It examines whether any system or user messages are missing, calculates token counts for individual conversations, and provides valuable statistics and warnings about the dataset. This comprehensive analysis aids in gaining a deep understanding of the dataset's attributes and potential issues.

```
def analyze_data_and_tokens(dataset):
    """

    Perform a comprehensive analysis on the dataset to ensure its
quality.


    Parameters:
```

```
    dataset (list): List of conversation data.

    Prints:
    Various warnings, token counts, and other statistics for the
dataset.
    """

...
```

f. **`estimate_cost` Function**: For those considering fine-tuning a model with a given dataset, estimating the associated cost is a critical step. This function facilitates that by taking into account factors such as the dataset's size, target epochs for training, and token limits. By multiplying these factors with the cost per 1000 tokens for model training, it provides an approximate cost for the entire training process. This estimation is essential for budgeting and planning purposes.

```
def estimate_cost(dataset, price_per_1k_token=0.0005):
    """
   Estimate the cost of fine-tuning the model based on dataset
size and token count.

    Parameters:
    dataset (list): List of conversation data.
    price_per_1k_token (float): Cost per 1,000 tokens for training
the model.

    Prints:
    Estimated cost for training the model.
    """
...
```

Output:

The section begins by indicating that there are no examples of missing system or user messages in the dataset, which is a positive sign as it ensures completeness.

```
### Data Analysis and Token Counts ### Num examples missing system mes-
sage: 0 Num examples missing user message: 0
```

The minimum and maximum values are both 3, suggesting that each example in the dataset comprises exactly 3 messages on average. The **`mean`** and **`median`** values, both at 3.0, reaffirm this consistency. The 5th and 95th percentile values also align closely with the mean and median, further emphasizing the uniformity in the number of messages per example.

```
#### Distribution of num_messages_per_example: min / max: 3, 3 mean /
median: 3.0, 3.0 p5 / p95: 3.0, 3.0
```

Analyzing the distribution of the total number of tokens per example. Here, the minimum and maximum values span from 50 to 79 tokens, indicating some variability in the length of conversations. The **mean** (66.65) and **median** (68.0) values suggest that, on average, each example contains around 66 to 68 tokens. The 5th and 95th percentile values (58.5 and 74.2) provide a broader perspective on the distribution, indicating that the majority of examples fall within this range.

```
#### Distribution of num_total_tokens_per_example: min / max: 50, 79
mean / median: 66.65, 68.0 p5 / p95: 58.5, 74.2
```

The distribution of tokens specific to the assistant's messages per example is explored. The range spans from 14 to 28 tokens, showcasing variability in the length of assistant responses. The **mean** (22.85) and **median** (24.0) values suggest that, on average, the assistant's messages contain approximately 22 to 24 tokens. The 5th and 95th percentile values (17.6 and 26.1) offer insights into the distribution's tails. None of the examples appear to exceed the 4096-token limit, meaning they won't need to be truncated during the fine-tuning process.

```
#### Distribution of num_assistant_tokens_per_example: min / max: 14,
28 mean / median: 22.85, 24.0 p5 / p95: 17.6, 26.1 0 examples may be
over the 4096 token limit and will be truncated during fine-tuning
```

It estimates the cost associated with training a model using the dataset. It begins by indicating that the dataset comprises approximately 1333 tokens that will incur charges during training. The default training plan is set to 2 epochs on this dataset, which means the model will undergo two complete training cycles using this data. It then calculates the cost estimate, considering the number of tokens charged during training. By multiplying the total tokens (2666) by the cost per 1000 tokens for training ($0.0005), it provides an estimated cost for this training, which amounts to approximately $0.001333.

```
### Cost Estimation ### Dataset has ~1333 tokens that will be charged for
during training. By default, you'll train for 2 epochs on this dataset.
By default, you'll be charged for ~2666 tokens. Estimated cost for this
training is approximately $0.001333 ### Duplicate Conversations Check
```

Here, the analysis checks for duplicate conversations within the dataset. Fortunately, it reports that there are no duplicate conversations, indicating that each conversation in the dataset is unique.

```
### Number of duplicate conversations: 0
```

Step 5: Training Data Upload

The following code snippet is designed to upload a file, in this case, **`chat_data.jsonl`**, to your OpenAI account. The purpose of the file is specified as **`'fine-tune'`**, indicating that the data in the file will be used for fine-tuning a large learning model.

```
# Define the path to the file you want to upload
file_name = "/content/chat_data.jsonl"


# Use OpenAI's File.create method to upload the file for the purpose of
fine-tuning
# The file is opened in binary read mode ("rb")
upload_response = openai.File.create(
  file=open(file_name, "rb"),  # Open the file in binary read mode
  purpose='fine-tune'  # Specify that the file is intended for fine-tuning
a model
)


# Output the upload response to see the details of the uploaded file
Upload_response
```

Output:

After running the code, you get a JSON object as output, containing details about the uploaded file.

- **`object`**: Indicates the type of object, which is a "**`file`**".
- **`id`**: Provides a unique identifier for the file.
- **`purpose`**: Indicates why the file was uploaded, in this case, for "**`fine-tune`**".
- **`filename`**: Shows the name of the file.
- **`bytes`**: Indicates the file size in bytes.
- **`created_at`**: Unix timestamp indicating when the file was created.
- **`status`**: States the upload status, which is "**`uploaded`**" in this case.
- **`status_details`**: Provides additional details about the status, if any (here it's null).

```
<File file id=file-xsa036zTL32wxy5eGSUzjwpE at 0x7d7ec0ccb6f0> JSON: {
"object": "file", "id": "file-xsa036zTL32wxy5eGSUzjwpE", "purpose":
"fine-tune", "filename": "file", "bytes": 8474, "created_at": 1695643341,
"status": "uploaded", "status_details": null }
```

Step 6: Initiating the Fine-Tuning Job

In this step, we are initiating the fine-tuning process for a specific model version, which in this case is gpt-3.5-turbo. You are using the previously stored **`file_id`** as the training file. Fine-tuning customizes the pre-trained model according to the data provided.

```
# Call the FineTuningJob.create method to initiate the fine-tuning process
# Provide the training_file using the previously saved file_id and specify
the model to use
openai.FineTuningJob.create(training_file=file_id, model="gpt-3.5-turbo")
```

Output:

The output contains details about the fine-tuning job, encapsulated in a **`FineTuningJob`** object. Here are some key fields:

- **`id`**: A unique identifier (**`ftjob-3MKXBj9VV4Q5xtUuJkDz0pEn`**) for this specific fine-tuning job.
- **`model`**: The model version being used (**`gpt-3.5-turbo-0613`**).
- **`status`**: Current status of the fine-tuning process (**`validating_files`**), indicating that the file validation is in progress.
- **`training_file`**: Shows the file ID (**`file-xsa036zTL32wxy5eGSUzjwpE`**) being used for training.
- **`hyperparameters`**: Parameters like **`n_epochs`** are set to "**`auto`**", indicating that the model will automatically decide the number of epochs to train.

```
<FineTuningJob fine_tuning.job id=ftjob-3MKXBj9VV4Q5xtUuJkDz0pEn at 0x7d-
7ec0d199e0> JSON: { "object": "fine_tuning.job", "id": "ftjob-3MKXBj9V-
V4Q5xtUuJkDz0pEn", "model": "gpt-3.5-turbo-0613", …
```

Step 7: Retrieving the State of a Fine-Tuning Job

This step is used to fetch the current state of a running or completed fine-tuning job. You are querying the status of the job using its unique identifier.

```
# Using the FineTuningJob.retrieve method to fetch the current status
# of the fine-tuning job with ID "ftjob-3MKXBj9VV4Q5xtUuJkDz0pEn"
openai.FineTuningJob.retrieve("ftjob-3MKXBj9VV4Q5xtUuJkDz0pEn")
```

Output:

Key information contained in this output are as follows:

- `fine_tuning.job id=ftjob-3MKXBj9VV4Q5xtUuJkDz0pEn at 0x7d7e8b3e6890`: This appears to be a unique identifier for the fine-tuning job.
- `object: fine_tuning.job`: Indicates that this is a fine-tuning job object.
- `id: ftjob-3MKXBj9VV4Q5xtUuJkDz0pEn`: The specific ID associated with this fine-tuning job.
- `model: gpt-3.5-turbo-0613`: Specifies the base model used for fine-tuning, in this case, "gpt-3.5-turbo-0613."
- `created_at: 1695643358`: Indicates the timestamp when the fine-tuning job was created, which might need conversion to a readable date and time.
- `finished_at: null`: This field is likely to be updated once the fine-tuning job is completed, showing the timestamp when it is finished.
- `fine_tuned_model: null:` Indicates that the fine-tuned model hasn't been created yet or specified.
- `organization_id: org-Fw23HNdOBixFvYL3rPmDB7Or`: This could be an identifier for the organization or entity that initiated the fine-tuning job.
- `result_files: []`: This likely represents a list of result files associated with the job. It's empty, indicating there may be no specific result files at this stage.
- `status: running:` Indicates the current status of the fine-tuning job, which is "`running`" at the moment.
- `validation_file: null`: Suggests that there might be a validation file associated with the fine-tuning, but it hasn't been specified yet.
- `training_file: file-xsa036zTL32wxy5eGSUzjwpE`: This appears to be the file used for training the model.
- `hyperparameters: { "n_epochs": 5 }:` Specifies the hyperparameters used for fine-tuning, in this case, the number of epochs is set to 5.
- `trained_tokens: null`: Indicates that the number of trained tokens hasn't been determined or specified yet.
- `error: null`: Suggests that there have been no errors or issues reported in the fine-tuning job at this point.

```
<FineTuningJob fine_tuning.job id=ftjob-3MKXBj9VV4Q5xtUuJkDz0pEn at 0x7d7e-
8b3e6890> JSON: { "object": "fine_tuning.job", "id": "ftjob-3MKXBj9VV4Q5x-
tUuJkDz0pEn", "model": "gpt-3.5-turbo-0613", "created_at": 1695643358, "fin-
ished_at": null, "fine_tuned_model": …
```

Step 8: Retrieving Events Associated with the Job

This code snippet utilizes **`openai.FineTuningJob.list_events()`** to retrieve events linked to a specific fine-tuning job identified by its unique ID, "**`ftjob-3MKXBj9VV4Q5xtUuJkDz0pEn`**." Additionally, it sets a limitation to display the most recent 30 events from the job, enhancing the control over the event history.

```
# List events associated with a fine-tuning job using OpenAI's API.
openai.FineTuningJob.list_events(id="ftjob-3MKXBj9VV4Q5xtUuJkDz0pEn",
limit=30)
```

Output:

The output represents a list of events associated with the specified fine-tuning job. Each event provides information about the progress and status of the fine-tuning process. Here is an explanation of the output schema:

- "**`object`**": "**`list`**": Indicates that this is a list of events.
- "**`data`**": Contains an array of event objects, each representing a specific event in the fine-tuning process.
    - Each event object includes the following information:
        - **`"object": "fine_tuning.job.event`**": Specifies that this is an event associated with a fine-tuning job.
        - "**`id`**": A unique identifier for the event.
        - "**`created_at`**": A timestamp indicating when the event occurred.
        - "**`level`**": Indicates the level or severity of the event (e.g., "**`info`**" for informational events).
        - "**`message`**": Describes the event or provides information about what happened during the fine-tuning process.
        - "**`data`**": Contains additional data related to the event. It can vary depending on the type of event.
        - "**`type`**": Specifies the type or category of the event (e.g., "**`message`**" for general messages, "**`metrics`**" for training metrics).
    - The events listed in the output include information about the job's progress, such as training steps, losses, and model creation.
- **`"has_more": false`**: Indicates whether there are more events beyond the ones listed in this response. In this case, it's set to false, suggesting that these are the most recent events.


```
<OpenAIObject list at 0x7d7ec0f0d5d0> JSON: { "object": "list", "data": [
{ "object": "fine_tuning.job.event", "id": "ftevent-1B9qQC6Nteq4T2BfqZLx-
KgiR", "created_at": 1695643362, "level": "info", "message": "Fine-tuning
```

```
job started", "data": null, "type": "message" }, { "object": "fine_tuning.
job.event", "id": ..
```

Step 9: Downloading the Report for Inspection

The process begins with importing key libraries: 'openai' for downloading a file from OpenAI, 'csv' for handling CSV data, and **'tabulate'** for formatting and displaying data in a table form. Using the **'openai.File.download()'** function, a file is downloaded from OpenAI, the raw content of which is stored in the **'content'** variable. This raw content, being in bytes, is stored in **'output_bytes'** for further proceedings. The bytes are then decoded into a UTF-8 string, resulting in **'output_string'**. Any leading 'b' and extra spaces from **'output_string'** are subsequently removed. The **'output_string'** is then fragmented into lines, forming a list. These lines are interpreted as CSV data using the **'csv.reader'**, and this parsed data is converted into a list of lists, each sub-list being a data row. The process culminates with the data being displayed in a tabulated format using the 'tabulate' library, facilitating easy comprehension of the file's content.

```
# Import the necessary libraries
import openai  # For downloading the file from OpenAI
import csv  # For parsing CSV data
from tabulate import tabulate  # For tabulating the data


# Download the file from OpenAI and store its content in a variable
...
print(tabulate(data, headers="firstrow", tablefmt="grid"))
```

Output:

The output is a table that shows various metrics across different epochs (ep) of a machine learning model training process. The metrics include:

- **train_loss**: The loss on the training set.
- **train_accuracy**: The accuracy of the training set.
- **valid_loss:** The loss on the validation set (appears to be empty in this case).
- **valid_mean_token_accuracy**: The mean token accuracy on the validation set (also empty in this case).

Each row represents one epoch, and the metrics are displayed for that epoch. For example, in epoch 1 (**`ep = 1`**), the training loss (**`train_loss`**) is approximately 0.21473, and the training accuracy (**`train_accuracy`**) is approximately 0.95652.

```
+------+-------------+-----------------+-------------+--------------
--------------+ | ep | train_loss | train_accuracy | valid_loss | val-
id_mean_token_accuracy | +======+=============+=================+=====
=========+============================+ | 1 | 2.28782 | 0.68966 | | |
+------+-------------+-----------------+-------------+--------------
--------------+ | 2 | 2.88231 | 0.42308 | | | +------+-------------+---
--------------+-------------+----------------------------+
```

Step 10: Inference Using the Fine-Tuned Model

The following code snippet is designed to interact with a specifically trained OpenAI GPT-3.5 Turbo model, with the intention to simulate a chat environment. It employs the **`ChatCompletion.create`** method to facilitate a chat-like interaction with an AI assistant. The code includes a model specification that indicates the custom-trained GPT-3 model to be used for completing the chat. The context for the chat is set by defining a system message that presents the model as a "*Software Engineering Mentor specialized in architecture and high-scale systems.*" The user interaction in this setup involves a query about the role of a load balancer in high-scale systems and the common algorithms used for load balancing. A placeholder is provided for the assistant's response, which will be filled by the model based on the input query. Ultimately, the assistant's response, derived from the **`completion.choices`** array is printed out.

```
# Initialize a chat-based completion with the custom-trained GPT-3.5 model
completion = openai.ChatCompletion.create(
  # Specify the model to use
  model="ft:gpt-3.5-turbo-0613:personal::82efbhJ6",


  # Set up the messages for the chat
...
```

Output:

The assistant responds with a brief but accurate explanation regarding the role of a load balancer in high-scale systems and mentions common algorithms used such as "**`round-robin`**" and "**`least connections`**."

```
{ "role": "assistant", "content": "A load balancer distributes incoming traffic across multiple servers to ensure availability and optimize resource utilization. Common algorithms include round-robin and least connections." }
```

Step 11: Deleting a Fine-Tuned Model

This code snippet is designed to delete a custom-trained GPT-3 model from an OpenAI account. The specific model to be deleted is identified through its unique identifier. The operation, which is sensitive in nature, must be performed by an owner of the organization under which the model was originally created, ensuring appropriate ownership and authority for such an action.

```
# Execute the delete operation for the specified fine-tuned model
# Note: You must be an owner of the organization under which the model
was created to perform this action
openai.Model.delete("ft:gpt-3.5-turbo-0613:personal::82efbhJ6")
```

Fine-Tuning LLM on the Cohere Platform

In this example, we will use the Cohere Platform to fine-tune LLM models for specific tasks. We will use the dashboard and understand the process of fine-tuning a model. The process involves preparing a dataset with at least 250 examples relevant to the target task, which is then uploaded to the Cohere dashboard to initiate the fine-tuning process. The model learns the specific nuances of the target domain during training, after which the refined model is deployed for use. The effectiveness of the fine-tuned model can be evaluated using metrics such as accuracy, loss, F1 score, precision, and recall on a holdout set. Comparing these metrics between the original and fine-tuned models provides a quantitative measure of the improvements gained through fine-tuning. Once fine-tuned, the model can be used via the Cohere API just like the original, but with enhanced performance in the target domain due to its specialized training. However, fine-tuning Cohere models involve substantial data, effort, and expertise, and can be time-consuming. The platform doesn't currently offer ready-to-use fine-tuned models for different domains, so the process of setting up data and pipelines can involve considerable work. Despite these challenges, fine-tuning is a potent way to customize Cohere models for specific tasks.

Step 1: Accessing the Dashboard

a. Begin by visiting https://dashboard.cohere.com/.

b. On the left panel, locate and select "**`Fine-tuning`**"

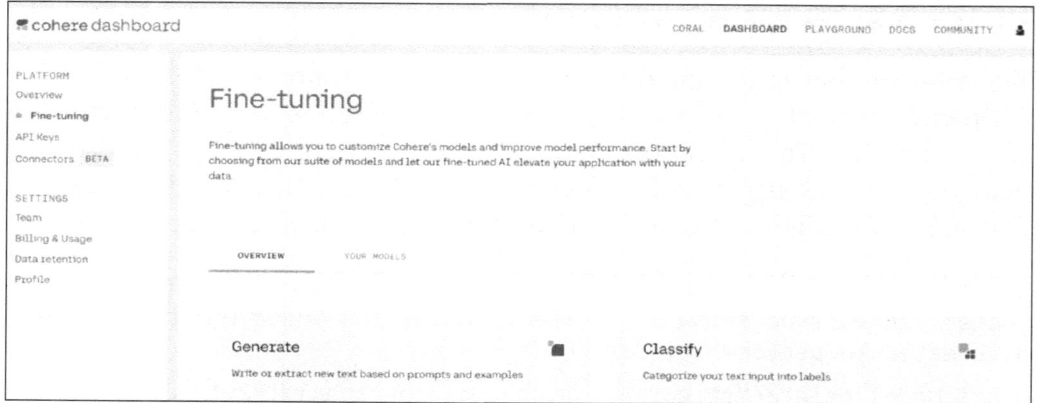

Figure 10.5: *Cohere Fine-Tuning Dashboard*

Step 2: Selecting Classification

In the next window, look for the "`Classify`" tile. This is where we will fine-tune a language model for classification purposes.

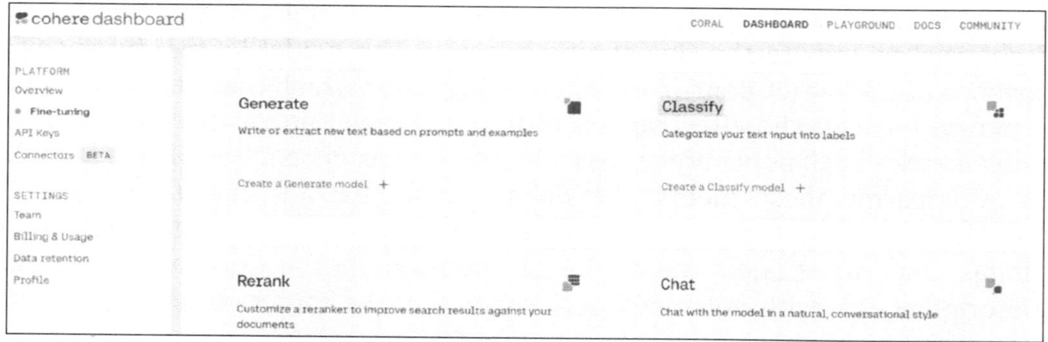

Figure 10.6: *Model Selection*

Step 3: Uploading Training Data

a. Scroll down and find the "**`Training Set - Upload Training Set`**" button.

   - The training data can be accessed from https://github.com/ava-orange-education/Hands-On-Large-Language-Models-for-Enterprise/blob/main/data/cohere_training_sample.csv

b. Upload your training dataset, which should be named "**`cohere_training_sample.csv`**". Select the check box since the first line is a header in the training file.

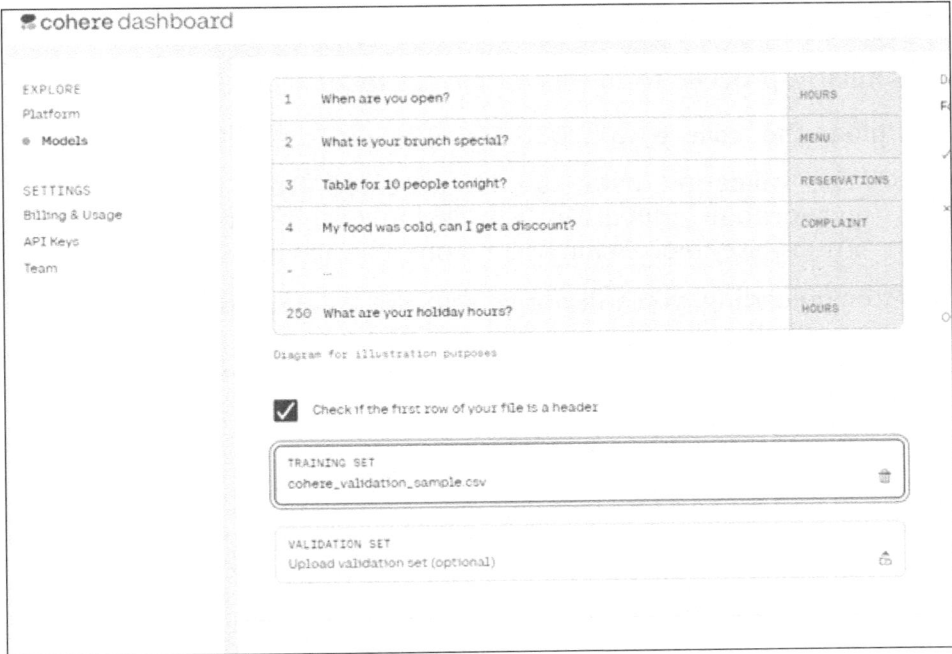

Figure 10.7: *Training Data upload*

Step 4: Training Data Requirements Check

a. Cohere performs a validation on the uploaded training data as per the platforms data requirements to fine-tune the model

b. Our data has been curated to meet these requirements as shown below:

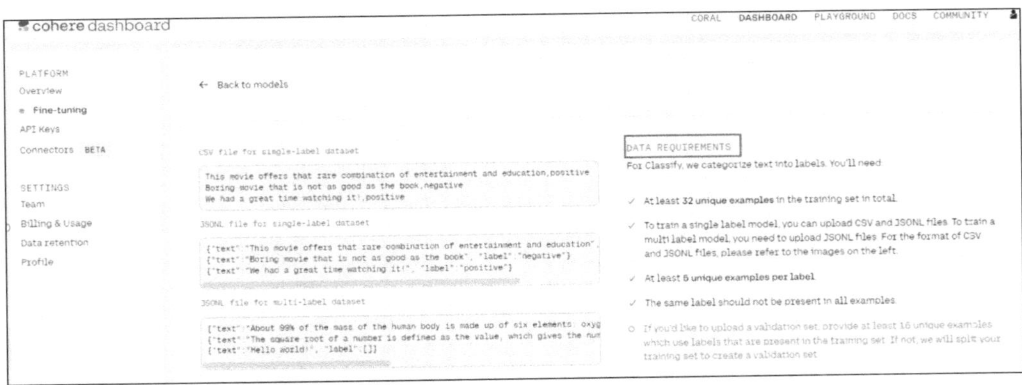

Figure 10.8: *Training Data Validation Requirements*

Step 5: Uploading Validation Data

a. Similarly, proceed to the validation set section.

b. Upload the "**`cohere_validation_sample.csv`**" dataset.

  - The validation data can be accessed from https://github.com/ava-orange-education/Hands-On-Large-Language-Models-for-Enterprise/blob/main/data/cohere_validation_sample.csv

c. After uploading, you will notice that the "**`Review Data`**" button becomes active. Click on it.

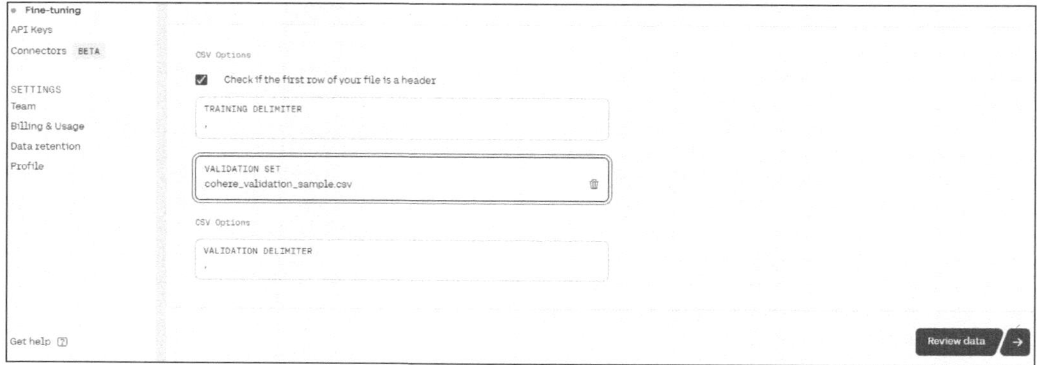

Figure 10.9: *Validation Data Upload*

Step 6: Reviewing Data Distribution

a. The next page presents the proportions of classes in your dataset.

b. This information helps you decide whether to retain, increase, or decrease the weightage of classes.

c. Once you have reviewed this data, proceed by clicking "**`Continue`**."

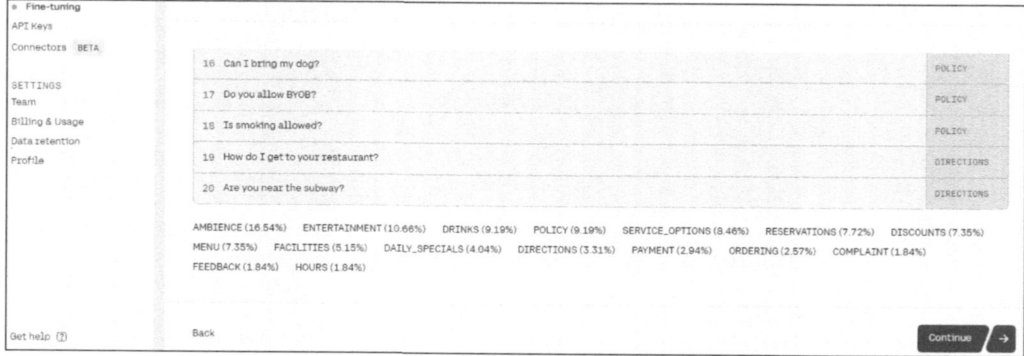

Figure 10.10: *Dataset Review*

Step 7: Naming the Model

a. Provide a unique nickname for your model.

b. Select Base Model as English.

c. Afterwards, click on "`Start training`."

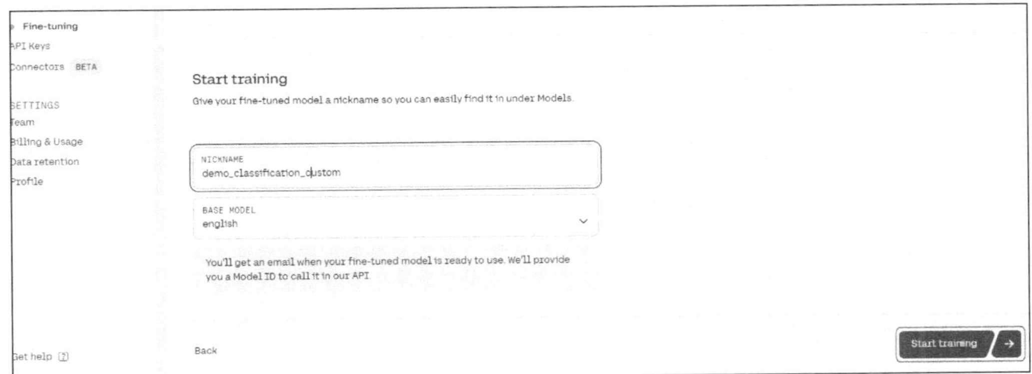

Figure 10.11: *Model Training Screen*

Step 8: Monitoring Training Progress

a. While the model is being trained, you can monitor its progress in the "`Overview`" section, which displays important metrics.

Figure 10.12: *Progress Monitoring*

Step 9: Accessing the Model

a. Once the model is trained, you have two options: using it in a playground or through APIs.

b. To access it via the playground, click on "`Try in Playground`" located at the top-right corner.

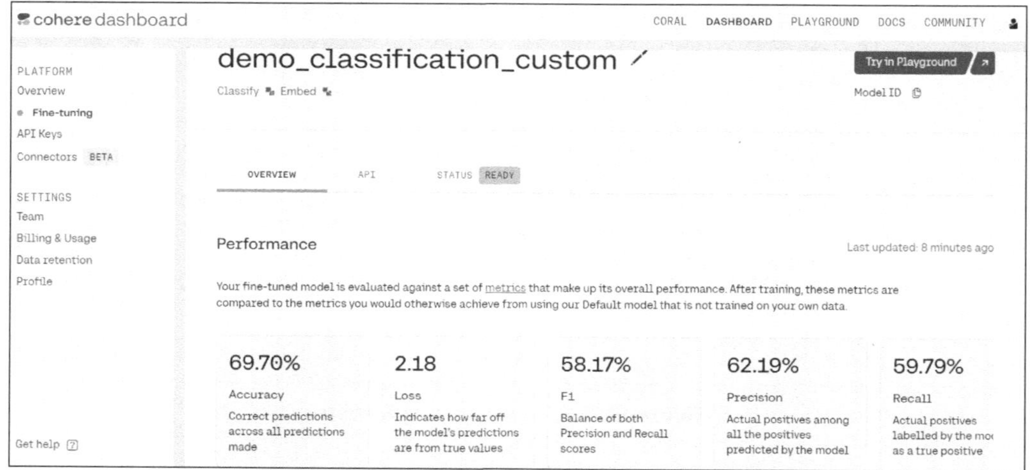

Figure 10.13: *Training Complete*

Step 10: Classifying Text

a. Within the playground, input the text you want to classify into the provided input box.

b. Click "`Run`." The output terminal will display the results along with the confidence level of the label.

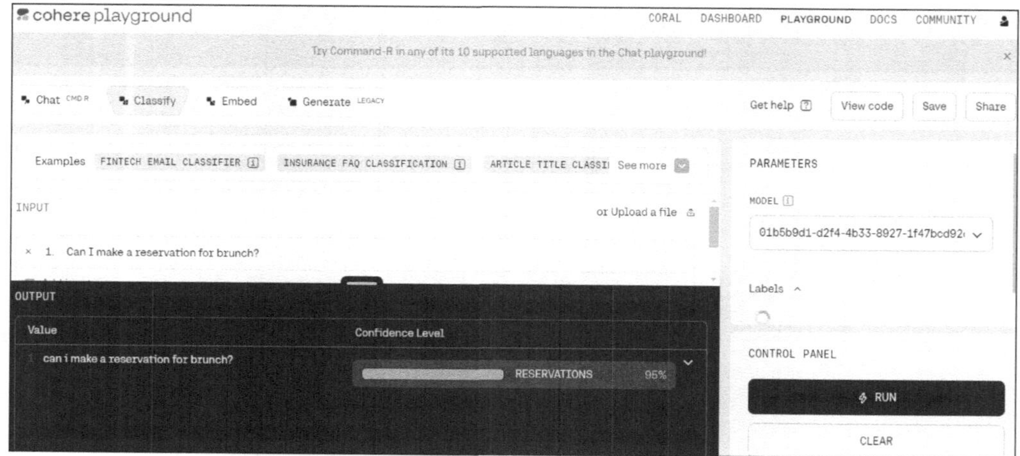

Figure 10.14: *Trying the Model in the Playground*

Step 11: API Details

a. If you need to integrate the model programmatically, click on the "**`View Code`**" button to access the API details.

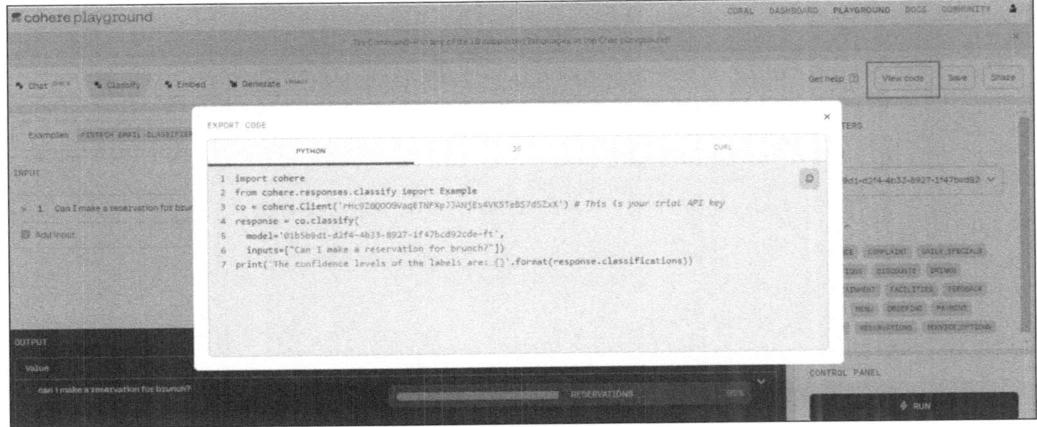

Figure 10.15: *Model API Details*

Step 12: Cleaning Up

a. After you have completed your experimentation, you can clean up by going back to the dashboard.

b. Select "**`Fine-tuning`**" on the left panel and select STATUS on the right , then click on "**`Delete Model`**". This will remove the model when it's no longer needed.

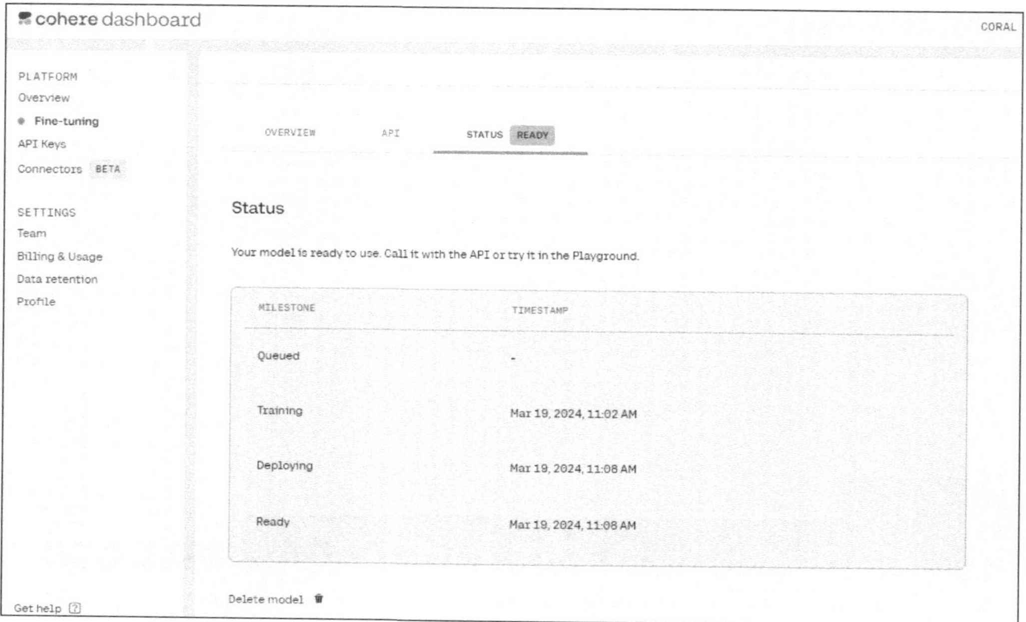

Figure 10.16: *Model Cleanup*

Fine-Tuning T5 Models on Kaggle GPUs for Text Classification on IMDB Reviews

In this implementation, we will fine-tune T5 models without DeepSpeed and with DeepSpeed. We will also be covering evaluation metrics by comparing them against different flavors of T5.

The code for this implementation can be accessed from https://github.com/ava-orange-education/Hands-On-Large-Language-Models-for-Enterprise/blob/main/chapter10/t5-finetuning-with-deepspeed.ipynb

DeepSpeed is an innovative open-source deep learning optimization library designed for PyTorch. Its primary aim is to drastically reduce computational and memory demands, enabling the training of large distributed models on existing hardware. A standout feature is the Zero Redundancy Optimizer (ZeRO), facilitating training with over 1 trillion parameters. It supports various training scenarios, from single-GPU to multi-GPU and multi-node setups, with mixed precision training and robust custom model parallelism.

Developed by Microsoft, DeepSpeed simplifies distributed training complexities while maximizing efficiency. It achieves exceptional performance and rapid model convergence through efficiency optimizations covering computing, communication, memory, and I/O. Key techniques include ZeRO, 3D-Parallelism, mixed precision training, and overlapping communication and computation. This elevates deep learning model performance, enabling researchers to train larger models with fewer resources.

DeepSpeed seamlessly integrates with PyTorch models and empowers model parallelism, accommodating diverse model types like CNNs, RNNs, and Transformers. It has successfully optimized models such as BERT and GPT-2, even enabling the training of models with over 13 billion parameters on a single GPU. Its versatility spans domains like NLP, computer vision, speech recognition, and more.

Implementing DeepSpeed into PyTorch code requires minimal adjustments, making it accessible for researchers and practitioners seeking efficient deep learning model training.

In summary, DeepSpeed's suite of optimizations and features exhibits broad compatibility with deep learning models of varying sizes and types developed using PyTorch. It serves as a potent tool to expedite and scale up the training process for virtually any model.

Prerequisite

Kaggle is a renowned online platform and community in the fields of data science and artificial intelligence. Founded in 2010 and now a subsidiary of Google, it's based in San Francisco. Kaggle is known for its extensive dataset hub and web-based data science environment for collaborative model creation. It hosts competitions sponsored by major companies, offering significant prizes.

Login to https://www.kaggle.com/account/login, click on the "+" icon from the left panel and select new notebook.

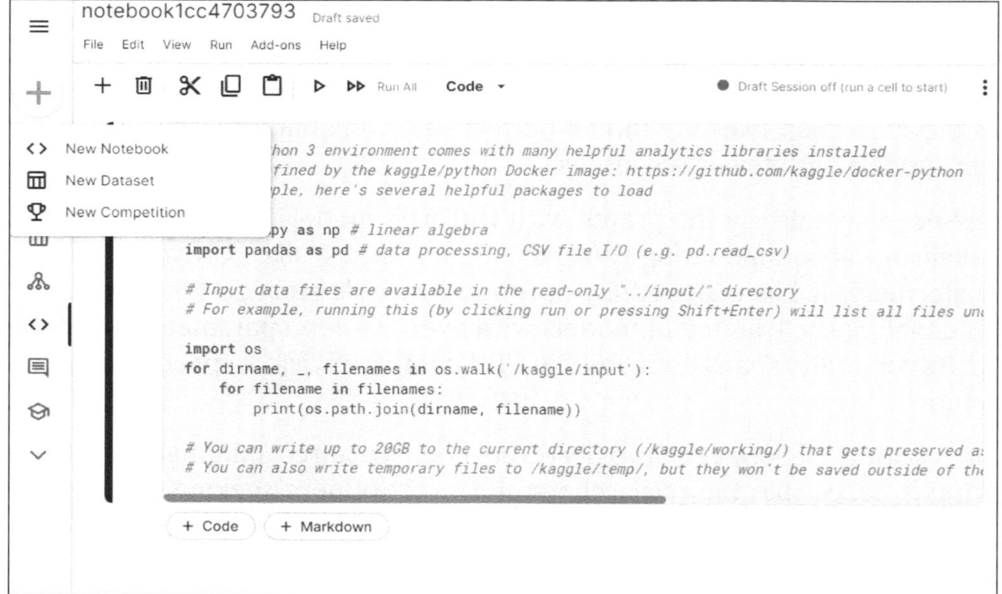

Figure 10.17: *Kaggle Notebook*

On the right-hand side panel, under Notebook Options, turn on the internal. This will enable the selection of accelerators for the kernel, which is the GPUs. Select GPU 100 for this exercise.

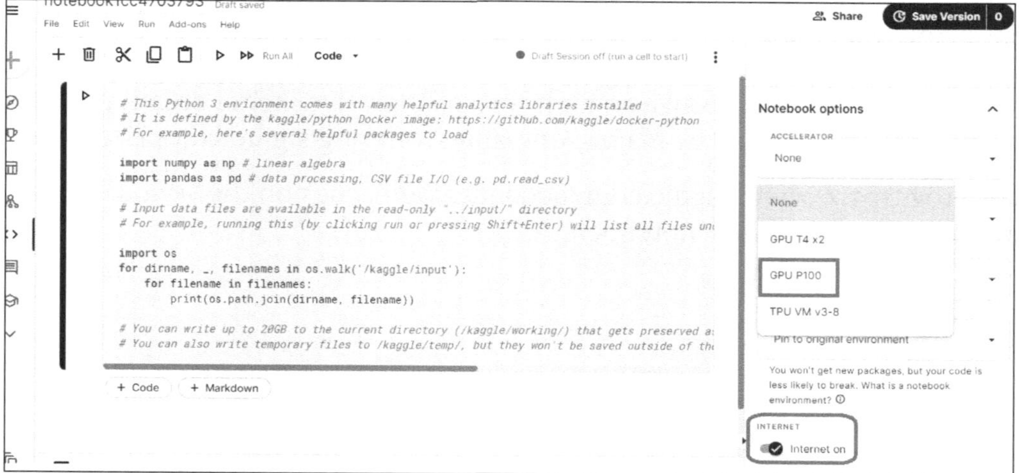

Figure 10.18: *Enabling GPU*

The exercise notebook can also be uploaded by selecting the upload notebook option under the file.

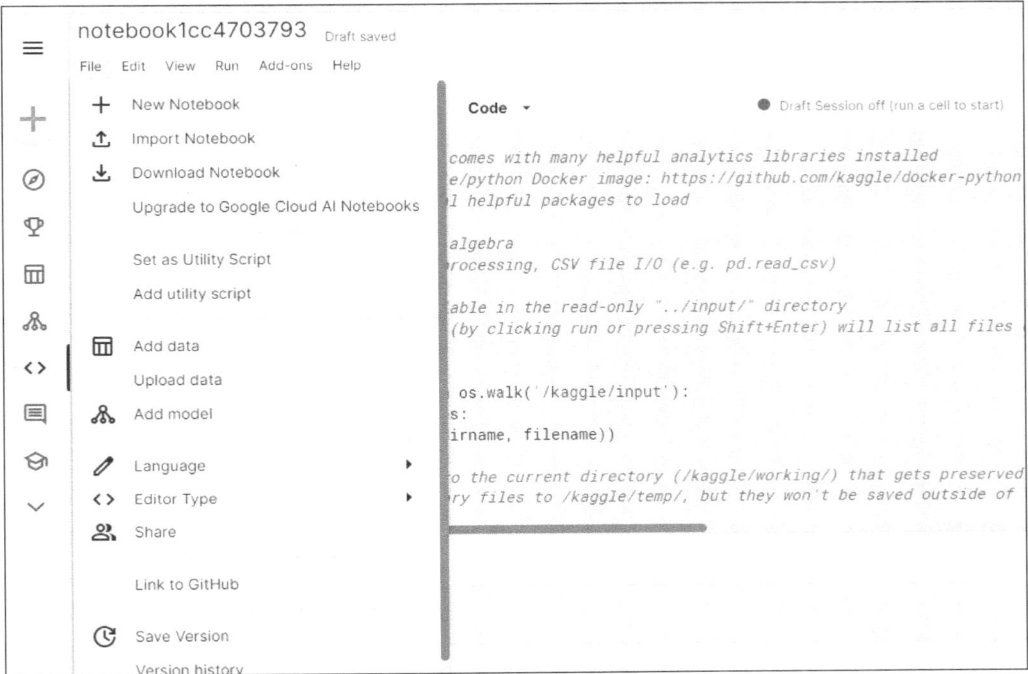

Figure 10.19: Notebook Upload

Implementation Walkthrough

Alright. The ground is set. Let's code!

Step 1: Initialization: Logging Setup

The code starts by setting up logging to capture events and errors. This is crucial for debugging and monitoring. The logging level is set to INFO, which means it will capture all the essential events and display them on the console. This is done using Python's built-in logging library.

```
import os
import logging
import pandas as pd
import transformers as tr
from datasets import load_dataset
import sys

# Initialize logging
```

```
logging.basicConfig(level=logging.INFO)

# Create a stream handler and set it to display log messages on the console
console_handler = logging.StreamHandler(sys.stdout)
logging.getLogger().addHandler(console_handler)
```

Step 2: Environment Setup

The **`setup_environment()`** function is responsible for preparing the computational environment. It updates the system's package lists, fixes any broken dependencies, and installs necessary libraries. This ensures that all the prerequisites for running the machine learning model are met. If any step fails, an error message is logged.

```
def setup_environment():
    """
    Sets up the environment by installing necessary packages and libraries.
    """
    ...
```

Step 3: Data Loading and Tokenization

The objective of this function is to load and tokenize the IMDB dataset, making it ready for further processing. It takes a single input, which is the name of the pre-trained model (**`model_checkpoint`**), and its output is the tokenized dataset. To achieve this, the function utilizes the **`load_dataset`** function from the datasets library to load the IMDB dataset. It also initializes a tokenizer that matches the specified pre-trained model. A nested function **`called to_tokens()`** is defined within the function, responsible for the actual tokenization of individual data points in the dataset. Ultimately, the function returns the fully tokenized dataset, ensuring it's prepared for subsequent operations.

```
def load_and_tokenize_data(model_checkpoint):
    """
    Loads and tokenizes the IMDB dataset.

    Parameters:
        model_checkpoint (str): The model checkpoint name.

    Returns:
```

```
        tokenized_dataset: The tokenized dataset.
    """

    ...
```

Step 4: Model Training

The primary aim of this function is to perform fine-tuning of a language model using the tokenized IMDB dataset. It takes three inputs: the model checkpoint (**`model_checkpoint`**), the tokenized dataset, and the **`local_training_root`** directory where the fine-tuned model will be stored. The function doesn't return any output, but it does save the fine-tuned model in the specified directory.

To accomplish this, the function first configures various training parameters such as the number of epochs, batch size, and optimizer type. It then initializes both the model and a trainer object for the training process. The model is trained using the provided tokenized dataset. Once the training is complete, the fine-tuned model is saved in the designated directory, making it ready for further usage.

```
def train_model(model_checkpoint, tokenized_dataset, local_training_root):
    """
    Trains the model on the tokenized dataset.

    Parameters:
        model_checkpoint (str): The model checkpoint name.
        tokenized_dataset: The tokenized dataset.
        local_training_root (str): The local directory for training.
    """
```

Step 5: Making Predictions

This function serves the purpose of utilizing the fine-tuned model to generate predictions on a given set of data, which in this case is a list of reviews provided as input. While the function doesn't produce any formal output, its primary function lies in displaying the results in a structured DataFrame format. This presentation includes both the original reviews and the labels predicted by the model. To achieve this, the function first loads the pre-trained and fine-tuned model, then proceeds to tokenize the input list of reviews to prepare them for model processing. Subsequently, it employs the model's "**`generate`**" method for making predictions based on the tokenized reviews. These predictions are then decoded to render them in a human-readable format. Finally, the function compiles the reviews and their corresponding predicted labels into a DataFrame, enabling users to conveniently review and analyze the results.

```
def predict_and_display(reviews,model_checkpoint):
    """
    Makes predictions on sample reviews and displays the results.

    Parameters:
        model_checkpoint (str): The model checkpoint name.
        reviews (list): The list of reviews for prediction.
    """
```

…

Step 6: Main Execution Block

The if **`__name__ == "__main__":`** block is the driver code that calls all these functions in a sequential manner. It sets some constants and then proceeds to set up the environment, load and tokenize the data, train the model, and finally make predictions on sample reviews.

By breaking down the code into these modular functions, it becomes easier to understand, debug, and extend. Each function has a single responsibility, making the code adhere to clean code principles.

```
if __name__ == "__main__":
    # Define constants
    local_training_root = "/kaggle/temp/"
    model_checkpoint = "t5-small"
```

…

Output:

The following output shows the training loss at different steps or iterations during the training of a model. Let's break down what this output means:

a. **Step**: This column represents the training step or iteration number. A training step is one complete pass through the entire training dataset. These steps are used to update the model's parameters (weights and biases) to improve its performance.

b. **Training Loss**: This column represents the value of the training loss function at each step. The training loss is a measure of how well the model is performing on the training data. It quantifies the difference between the model's predictions and the actual target values in the training dataset. The goal during training is to minimize this loss, as a lower loss indicates better alignment between the model's predictions and the true values.

   i. At step 500, the training loss was 0.614800. This means that after 500 training iterations, the model's performance, as measured by the loss function, was still relatively high.

   ii. At step 1000, the training loss decreased to 0.137100. This indicates that the model improved significantly, and its predictions became closer to the actual training data.

   iii. At step 1500, the training loss further decreased to 0.127100. This suggests continued improvement in the model's performance, although the rate of improvement may be slowing down.

In general, during training, you want to see the training loss decrease over time, as this indicates that the model is learning and becoming better at its task. However, it's important to monitor other metrics, such as validation loss or accuracy on a separate dataset, to ensure that the model is not overfitting the training data and that its performance generalizes well to unseen data.

Step	Training Loss
500	0.614800
1000	0.137100
1500	0.127100

Figure 10.20: *Training Progress*

The following output shows the predictions we have received captured in the classification column for the review.

	review	classification
0	In 'Whimsical Wonders,' the whimsy truly shine...	positive
1	'Midnight Mystery' is a gripping thriller that...	positive
2	While 'Galactic Odyssey' boasts stunning visua...	negative
3	In 'Whispering Shadows,' the cinematography is...	positive

Figure 10.21: *Output Inference*

Let's now look at how DeepSpeed optimization can be applied to the same implementation. Most of the code remains the same except for the config for DeepSpeed and plugging it into the trainer.

Environment Preparation for DeepSpeed

The setup is required because DeepSpeed uses distributed training even when only one process is in use. This means the model training is designed to be spread across multiple GPUs or even machines (nodes), and this setup emulates a distributed environment.

```
os.environ["MASTER_ADDR"] = "localhost"
os.environ["MASTER_PORT"] = "9994"  # modify if RuntimeError: Address already in use
os.environ["RANK"] = "0"
os.environ["LOCAL_RANK"] = "0"
os.environ["WORLD_SIZE"] = "1"
```

Here's a breakdown of what each environment variable means:

- **MASTER_ADDR**: This variable specifies the address of the master node. In this local training setup, we use "**localhost**" as the master address.
- **MASTER_PORT**: This variable defines the port number at which the master node listens. It's essential to choose an available port on your system to avoid conflicts (such as "**RuntimeError: Address already in use**"). If conflicts arise, you should select a different, unused port.
- **RANK**: The **RANK** variable indicates the rank of the current process within a distributed training setup. It serves as a unique identifier for each process within the set of all processes involved.
- **LOCAL_RANK**: The **LOCAL_RANK** represents the rank of the process on the current node. This ranking is particularly useful when training on a machine equipped with multiple GPUs, as it helps identify which GPU a process should utilize.
- **WORLD_SIZE**: The **WORLD_SIZE** specifies the total number of processes participating in distributed training. In a single-machine setup, it is typically set to 1. However, in configurations with multiple GPUs, you adjust this variable to match the number of GPUs in your system.

These environment variables play a crucial role in managing distributed training efficiently with **DeepSpeed**. For instance, in a two-GPU setup, you would set **WORLD_SIZE=2, assign RANK=0** to the first process, and **RANK=1** to the second process. This configuration enables DeepSpeed to facilitate communication between the two GPUs seamlessly.

In cases where DeepSpeed does not accurately detect the number of GPUs on your system, manual adjustment of these environment variables may be necessary. If you encounter this issue, it is advisable to verify your GPU configuration and ensure DeepSpeed's compatibility with your hardware and software environment.

Next, upload the **`deepspeed-config.json`** into the workspace as shown by clicking on the upload icon of Data under the Notebook section on the right panel. The file can be accessed from

https://github.com/ava-orange-education/Hands-On-Large-Language-Models-for-Enterprise/blob/main/chapter10/deepspeed.json

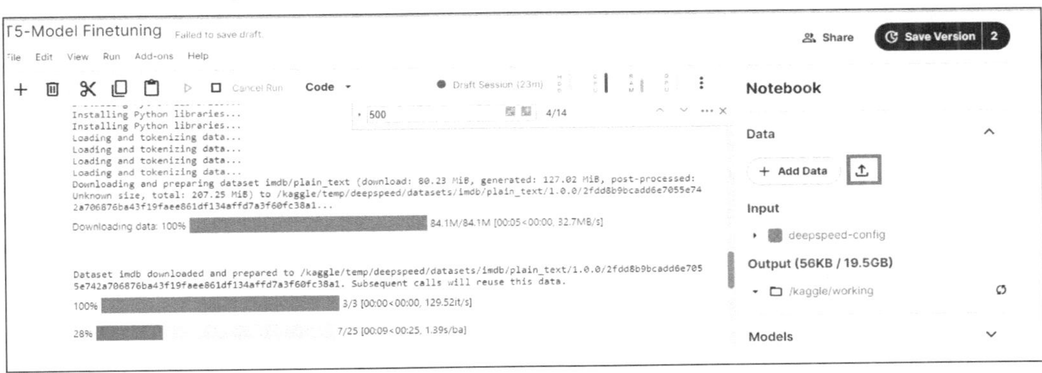

***Figure 10.22:** DeepSpeed config file upload*

This DeepSpeed configuration is specifically designed for fine-tuning large language models (LLMs). Let's break down the main components:

```
{
  “train_batch_size”: 8,
  “train_micro_batch_size_per_gpu”: 8,
  “gradient_accumulation_steps”: 1,
  “optimizer”: {
    “type”: “AdamW”,
    …
```

a. **`train_batch_size`**: This is the total batch size for training. Here, it is set to 8. The batch size can have a significant impact on your model's performance during training. Larger batch sizes can lead to faster training but also use more memory.

b. **`train_micro_batch_size_per_gpu`**: This is the per-GPU batch size. It's also set to 8 in this configuration. In the context of gradient accumulation (see below), this would be the "**`micro-batch`**" size.

c. **`gradient_accumulation_steps`**: This is the number of steps for which to accumulate gradients before performing an optimization step. It is set to 1, meaning that an optimization step is performed after each batch. If you have limited GPU memory, increasing the number of gradient accumulation steps allows you to effectively train with larger batch sizes.

d. **`optimizer`**: This section configures the optimizer used for training. The type of optimizer is AdamW, a variant of the Adam optimizer that includes weight decay. The parameters of the optimizer (**`learning rate`**, **`betas`**, **`epsilon`**, and **`weight decay`**) are also specified here.

e. **`scheduler`**: This section configures the learning rate scheduler. The type of scheduler is **`WarmupLR`**, which starts from a low learning rate (**`warmup_min_lr`**) and gradually increases to a maximum learning rate (**`warmup_max_lr`**) over a certain number of steps (**`warmup_num_steps`**). In this case, since **`warmup_num_steps`** is set to 0, the learning rate should be **`warmup_max_lr`** from the beginning.

f. **`fp16`**: This section controls whether to use mixed precision training. It is set to disabled (false) here. Mixed precision training can significantly reduce memory usage and increase the training speed by performing operations in a half-precision format.

g. **`zero_optimization`**: This part configures the ZeRO (Zero Redundancy Optimizer) settings. ZeRO is a memory optimization strategy that allows you to train much larger models and batch sizes with the same amount of memory.

   i. **`stage`**: ZeRO has three stages (1, 2, and 3), each with increasing levels of memory optimization and computational overhead. Here, it is set to stage 2.

   ii. **`offload_optimizer`**: This specifies whether and where to offload the optimizer's states. Here, the optimizer states are offloaded to the CPU (**`device: cpu`**), and **`pin_memory`** being true means that the optimizer will use pinned (or page-locked) memory, which can speed up CPU-to-GPU transfers.

iii. **allgather_partitions** and **allgather_bucket_size**: These control the gathering of updated parameters from all GPUs after each step.

iv. **overlap_comm**: When set to true, this allows overlapping communication with computation during backward propagation, which can lead to speedups.

v. **reduce_scatter**: If true, use reduce/scatter instead of reduce for communication. This can sometimes be faster.

vi. **reduce_bucket_size**: The bucket size for reduction.

vii. **contiguous_gradients**: If true, make the gradient's memory layout contiguous, which can improve speed.

Plugging the DeepSpeed Optimizer

As mentioned, the entire pipeline remains the same except for a few modifications in the "**train_model**" function bolded. We read the parameters from the json file and store them in a variable. This configuration variable is then plugged into the **TrainingArguments()** module as an argument. As you might have noticed, we have received the optimizer argument, which we had earlier used with DeepSpeed, now being available, taking charge of the optimization process. That's it. The pipeline is now ready to run.

```
def train_model(model_checkpoint, tokenized_dataset, local_training_root):
    """

    Trains the model on the tokenized dataset.


    Parameters:
        model_checkpoint (str): The model checkpoint name.
        tokenized_dataset: The tokenized dataset.
        local_training_root (str): The local directory for training.
    """

    ...
```

Output:

a. At step 500, the training loss is 0.883100. This is relatively high, suggesting the model is not yet performing very well.

b. At step 1000, the training loss has significantly decreased to 0.154200.

This indicates the model is learning and improving its ability to predict the correct output.

c. Between steps 1000 and 3000, the training loss continues to decrease, but at a slower rate, moving from 0.154200 to 0.121700. It shows that the model is still improving, but the rate of improvement is slowing down.

This pattern is common as they continue to learn from the data. Initially, the model learns quickly and makes big improvements (shown by a large decrease in training loss), but as it gets closer to its optimal performance, the improvements become smaller. This is because the model is starting to converge to a point where it can't learn much more from the data.

Remember, while lower loss values indicate better model performance on the training data, they do not necessarily mean the model will perform well on unseen data. It's crucial to also evaluate the model on a separate validation or test dataset to ensure it can generalize its predictions to new data.

Step	Training Loss
500	0.883100
1000	0.154200
1500	0.142000
2000	0.138700
2500	0.127900
3000	0.121700

Figure 10.23: *Training Steps vs. Training Loss*

The inference for the review has been generated and is as follows:

	review	classification
0	While 'Galactic Odyssey' boasts stunning visua...	negative
1	In 'Whispering Shadows,' the cinematography is...	positive

Figure 10.24: *Review Inference results*

Evaluation of LLMs on Summarization Task

Evaluating LLMs in summarization tasks is intricate because it requires assessing how effectively they can comprehend and condense extensive textual content into a more digestible form.

Summarization tasks can be categorized into two main types: extractive and abstractive.

- **Extractive Summarization**: In this approach, LLMs are tasked with identifying and selecting the most pertinent sentences or phrases from the source text to create a summary. The challenge here lies in determining which portions of the text are most crucial or relevant.
- **Abstractive Summarization**: This is a more intricate task where the model must comprehend the entire document and generate a summary, potentially using new phrasing or sentences not present in the original text. Essentially, it creates a shorter document that conveys the same information as the original.

Evaluating LLMs in summarization tasks involves considering various criteria:

- **Quality of Summary**: The summary should be concise, coherent, and faithfully represent the primary ideas of the original text without introducing incorrect information.
- **Readability**: The summary should be easily readable and comprehensible, maintaining grammatical correctness and logical flow.
- **Relevance**: It should focus on the most critical and pertinent points from the original text.

Several metrics are employed for evaluation, including ROUGE for assessing quality, BLEU for measuring relevance, and manual human evaluation for readability and coherence.

However, challenges persist in the domain of automatic text summarization, such as preserving the accuracy and context of the original text, addressing subjectivity in defining a 'good' summary, and ensuring the summary is free from bias.

In conclusion, evaluating LLMs in summarization tasks is a pivotal step in advancing NLP. While these models hold promise, there remains ongoing work to enhance their performance and overcome their limitations.

We will be using a Kaggle notebook as our IDE to demonstrate this implementation.

Prerequisite

We can use the same notebook instance and kernel as set earlier for the implementation. Because we are performing an inference task, a CPU with good RAM should also be sufficient.

Step 1: Installation and Imports

We begin by setting up the essential Python packages via %pip install, encompassing libraries and tools vital for the correct functioning of our code. These packages play a pivotal role in our workflow. We then proceed to import several Python libraries, each with its unique purpose:

- **`Torch`**: This is a fundamental library for harnessing the capabilities of PyTorch, a prominent deep-learning framework.
- **`gc`**: The **`gc`** library takes charge of memory management within the Python environment, ensuring efficient utilization.
- **`Pandas`**: **`Pandas`** takes the stage for data manipulation and efficient handling of DataFrames.
- **`nltk`**: The Natural Language Toolkit empowers us with an array of tools and resources for working with human language data.
- **`Datasets and transformers`**: These components, integral to the Hugging Face Transformers library, provide access to pre-trained models and datasets designed for natural language processing tasks.
- **`TorchMetrics`**: Serving as our metric computation companion, **`TorchMetrics`** is utilized in this code to compute ROUGE scores, an essential aspect of text summarization evaluation.

In addition to this setup, we enhance our toolkit by downloading the CNN/Daily Mail dataset using the **`load_dataset`** function from the datasets library. This dataset acquisition marks a significant step in our data-driven journey.

```
# Install the necessary packages

%pip install rouge_score==0.1.2 datasets transformers evaluate nltk
torchmetrics --quiet


# Import the necessary libraries

import torch

import gc

import pandas as pd

import nltk

from datasets import load_dataset

from transformers import AutoTokenizer, T5ForConditionalGeneration,
GPT2LMHeadModel, GPT2Tokenizer

from torchmetrics.functional.text.rouge import rouge_score
```

```
# Download the CNN/Daily Mail dataset
full_dataset = load_dataset("cnn_dailymail", version="3.0.0", cache_
dir="./datasets")
```

Step 2: Data Sampling

Our objective is to create a representative subset of the CNN/Daily Mail dataset by randomly selecting 100 articles. The process unfolds as follows: Initially, we set the sample size to 100 to determine the number of articles we intend to sample. Next, we employ the filter method to isolate articles with titles beginning with "**CNN**," effectively narrowing our focus on content associated with CNN. To ensure randomness in our selection, we shuffle the dataset using a seed value of 42. Ultimately, we utilize the select method to cherry-pick the initial 100 articles from the shuffled dataset, forming a diverse and unbiased subset for our further analysis and processing.

```
# Select a small random sample of 100 articles from the CNN/Daily Mail
dataset
sample_size = 100
sample = (
    full_dataset["train"]
    .filter(lambda r: "CNN" in r["article"][:25])  # Select articles
starting with "CNN"
    .shuffle(seed=42)  # Shuffle the dataset to ensure random selection
    .select(range(sample_size))  # Select the first 100 articles after
shuffling
)
```

Step 3: Batch Generator Function

The primary role of this function is to facilitate the creation of batches from a given data list. The function operates with two crucial parameters: "**data**," representing the input data to be batched, and "**batch_size**," specifying the desired batch size for data division. Inside the function, a while loop is employed to iterate through the data, generating batches of the specified size. It meticulously manages start and end indices to ensure precise slicing of the data into batches. This function serves as a foundational tool for future endeavors, enabling efficient batch processing of data as required.

```
# Function to create batches from a list
def batch_generator(data: list, batch_size: int):
    """
```

```
    Generate batches from a list of data.

    Args:
        data (list): The input data to create batches from.
        batch_size (int): The desired batch size.

    Yields:
        list: A batch of data.
    """
    s = 0
    e = s + batch_size
    while s < len(data):
        yield data[s:e]  # Yield a batch of data
        s = e
        e = min(s + batch_size, len(data))  # Update the start and end
indices for the next batch
```

Step 4: ROUGE Score Computation

The "**compute_rouge_score**" function plays a pivotal role in assessing the quality of text summaries through the calculation of ROUGE scores. This function takes two inputs: "**generated**" and "**reference**," which are lists containing generated and reference texts, respectively. Within the function, both the generated and reference texts undergo preprocessing, specifically being tokenized into sentences using NLTK's "**sent_tokenize**" function, a critical step for precise ROUGE score computation. Subsequently, the function employs the "**rouge_score**" function from the torchmetrics library to calculate the **ROUGE** scores. These scores provide valuable insights into the degree of overlap and similarity between the generated and reference texts, serving as a key metric for evaluating the effectiveness of text summarization.

```
# Function to compute ROUGE scores
def compute_rouge_score(generated: list, reference: list) -> dict:
    """
    Compute ROUGE scores between generated and reference texts.

    Args:
        generated (list): List of generated texts.
```

```
        reference (list): List of reference texts.

    Returns:
        dict: Dictionary containing ROUGE scores.
    """
```

...

Step 5: Summarization Using the T5 Model

The "**summarize_with_t5**" function streamlines the process of summarizing a list of articles using the T5 model. It accepts several parameters, including "**model_checkpoint**," a string specifying the pre-trained T5 model checkpoint, "**articles**," a list of articles to be summarized, and an optional "**batch_size**" parameter (defaulting to 8) for batch control during inference. The function first checks for GPU availability for accelerated computation and selects the appropriate device (GPU or CPU). It then loads the pre-trained T5 model and tokenizer based on the provided checkpoint. Within the function, an inner function called "**perform_inference**" manages the inference process, which involves article tokenization, summary generation using the T5 model, and decoding of the generated summaries. The resulting summaries are collected on a list named "**res**." The function concludes by performing resource cleanup, releasing GPU memory, and deleting model objects before returning the generated summaries, simplifying the task of producing summaries with the T5 model.

```
# Function to summarize using T5 model
def summarize_with_t5(model_checkpoint: str, articles: list, batch_size:
int = 8) -> list:
    """
    Summarize a list of articles using the T5 model.

    Args:
        model_checkpoint (str): The pre-trained T5 model checkpoint.
        articles (list): List of articles to summarize.
        batch_size (int, optional): Batch size for inference. Defaults
to 8.
```

```
    Returns:
        list: List of generated summaries.
    """
...
```

Step 6: Summarization Using GPT-2 Model

The "**summarize_with_gpt2**" function is designed for summarizing a list of articles using the GPT-2 model, offering a similar structure to the T5 summarization function. It accepts key parameters: "**model_checkpoint**" specifies the pre-trained GPT-2 model checkpoint, "**articles**" contains the articles to be summarized, and an optional "**batch_size**" parameter (defaulting to 8) for controlling inference batch sizes. The function starts by checking for GPU availability and selecting the appropriate device. It proceeds to load the pre-trained GPT-2 model and its corresponding tokenizer. The heart of the function is the "**perform_inference**" inner function, responsible for tokenizing input, generating summaries with GPT-2, and decoding these summaries. The decoded summaries are gathered in the "**decoded_summaries**" list. Subsequently, the function extracts summaries from "**decoded_summaries**," conducts resource cleanup, and finally returns the generated summaries. This function simplifies the task of summarization using the GPT-2 model, ensuring efficient summary extraction from the generated content.

```
# Function to summarize using GPT-2 model
def summarize_with_gpt2(model_checkpoint: str, articles: list, batch_size: int = 8) -> list:
    """
    Summarize a list of articles using the GPT-2 model.

    Args:
        model_checkpoint (str): The pre-trained GPT-2 model checkpoint.
        articles (list): List of articles to summarize.
        batch_size (int, optional): Batch size for inference. Defaults to 8.

    Returns:
        list: List of generated summaries.
    """
    ...
```

Step 7: Model Summarization and ROUGE Score Calculation

The functions previously defined for T5 and GPT-2 summarization are applied to generate summaries from input articles using both models. Additionally, these functions calculate ROUGE scores to assess the quality of the generated summaries. This comprehensive approach enables a thorough evaluation of the summarization capabilities of T5 and GPT-2, providing insights into their performance in comparison to reference summaries. It offers a systematic and data-driven method to determine which model excels in summarization tasks, contributing to informed decision-making in natural language processing applications.

```
# Generate summaries using T5 model
t5_small_summaries = summarize_with_t5("t5-small", sample["article"])


# Compute ROUGE scores for T5 model
t5_rouge_scores = compute_rouge_score(t5_small_summaries, sample
["highlights"])


# Generate summaries using GPT-2 model
gpt2_summaries = summarize_with_gpt2("gpt2", sample["article"])


# Compute ROUGE scores for GPT-2 model
gpt2_rouge_scores = compute_rouge_score(gpt2_summaries, sample
["highlights"])
```

Step 8: Results Display

Pandas DataFrame is crafted to present the summarization results effectively. This DataFrame encompasses ROUGE scores for both the T5 and GPT-2 models, offering a comprehensive view of various ROUGE metrics, such as F1, Precision, and Recall, specifically for unigrams and bigrams. The tabular format of the DataFrame provides a structured and easily interpretable presentation of the summarization performance metrics, facilitating seamless analysis and comparison between the two models' summarization capabilities.

```
# Construct a DataFrame to display the results
results_df = pd.DataFrame({
    "Model": ["T5-Small", "GPT-2"],
    "ROUGE-1 F1": [t5_rouge_scores["rouge1_fmeasure"].item(), gpt2_
```

```
rouge_scores["rouge1_fmeasure"].item()],
    "ROUGE-1 Precision": [t5_rouge_scores["rouge1_precision"].item(),
gpt2_rouge_scores["rouge1_precision"].item()],
    "ROUGE-1 Recall": [t5_rouge_scores["rouge1_recall"].item(), …
```

Output:

The output is a comparison of two models, T5-Small and GPT-2, using several variations of the ROUGE (Recall-Oriented Understudy for Gisting Evaluation) metric. ROUGE is a set of metrics used for evaluating automatic summarization and machine translation software in natural language processing. The metrics compare an automatically produced summary or translation against a reference or a set of reference summaries.

The variations of the ROUGE metric used here are ROUGE-1, ROUGE-2, and ROUGE-L (or ROUGE-Lsum in some sources). Each variation measures different aspects of the models' performance.

a. **ROUGE-1**: This measures the overlap of unigrams (individual words) between the system-generated summary and the reference summary. The F1, precision, and recall scores for this measure are provided for both models.

b. **ROUGE-2**: This measures the overlap of bigrams (two-word sequences) between the system-generated summary and the reference summary. Again, the F1, precision, and recall scores for this measure are provided.

c. **ROUGE-L (or ROUGE-Lsum)**: This measure is based on the Longest Common Subsequence (LCS) between the system-generated summary and the reference summary. The LCS is the longest sequence of words (not necessarily consecutive, but still in order) that is shared between both. The F1, precision, and recall scores for this measure are provided.

Here's a breakdown of what each of the output numbers means:

a. **F1 Score**: The F1 score is the harmonic mean of precision and recall. It provides a single metric that balances both the concerns of precision and recall in one number. The higher the F1 score, the better.

b. **Precision**: Precision is a measure of the number of correct positive results divided by the number of all positive results returned by the model.

c. **Recall**: Recall is a measure of the number of correct positive results divided by the number of all relevant samples.

The output shows that for every metric, the T5-Small model outperforms the GPT-2 model. This means, that according to these metrics and the specific test set, T5-Small is better at generating summaries that are similar to the reference summary.

Remember, these metrics are not the absolute measure of a model's performance. They are just one way to compare models, and the "best" model may depend on the specific task and requirements at hand. For instance, in some cases, you might care more about precision (you only want very accurate summaries, even if you miss some information), while in others, you might care more about recall (you want all the information, even if some of it isn't quite right).

	Model	ROUGE-1 F1	ROUGE-1 Precision	ROUGE-1 Recall	ROUGE-2 F1	ROUGE-2 Precision	ROUGE-2 Recall	ROUGE-L F1	ROUGE-Lsum Precision	ROUGE-Lsum Recall
0	T5-Small	0.293450	0.390506	0.241019	0.112200	0.150521	0.091911	0.224367	0.362700	0.222510
1	GPT-2	0.184629	0.259675	0.154533	0.044773	0.065962	0.036355	0.144070	0.242341	0.141547

Figure 10.25: *Output Scores for Summarization*

Fine-Tuning on Colab Using Quantization Techniques

This implementation focuses on fine-tuning the "`NousResearch/Llama-2-7b-chat-hf`" model, which belongs to Meta's Llama 2 family of large language models. Llama 2 models range from 7 billion to 70 billion parameters and are optimized for dialogue-oriented applications. The fine-tuned variant, '`NousResearch/Llama-2-7b-chat-hf`,' is specifically tailored for chat applications, while pre-trained Llama 2 models are versatile for various natural language generation tasks.

Llama-2-Chat models exhibit exceptional performance in benchmark assessments, rivalling proprietary models like ChatGPT and PaLM in human evaluations, especially in terms of helpfulness and safety.

The script starts by installing essential packages like PyTorch and Transformers from Hugging Face, along with other machine learning libraries. It focuses on loading a dataset, initializing a tokenizer and model, and training the model using customized routines and configurations. Best practices such as gradient accumulation and learning rate scheduling are followed, with robust error handling and logging for debugging and monitoring.

After training, the script prepares the model for inference, showcasing text generation from prompts and saving the trained model for future use. It also integrates TensorBoard for visualizing training progress, providing insights into model performance.

In summary, this script provides a comprehensive approach to fine-tuning large language models, emphasizing efficiency, modularity, and accessibility while incorporating advanced techniques and best practices for effective training and text generation.

Prerequisite

1. Login to Google Colab and select the runtime as T4 GPU.

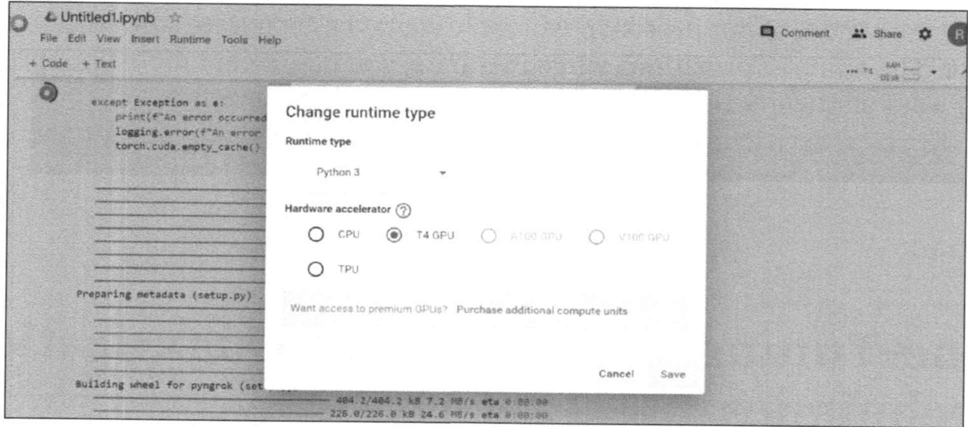

Figure 10.26: *Google Colab runtime setup*

Implementation Walkthrough

Now that the environment is set, let's implement it. The code for this implementation can be accessed from https://github.com/ava-orange-education/Hands-On-Large-Language-Models-for-Enterprise/blob/main/chapter10/Quantization_Training_of_LLM.ipynb

Step 1: Installation

The script starts by installing necessary Python packages using pip, including packages for PyTorch, Hugging Face Transformers, and other libraries for machine learning and optimization.

```
# # -*- coding: utf-8 -*-
"""Fine-tune Custom Large Language Model in Google Colab

Updated for best practices, modularity, and readability. Last update: 25
Sep 2023
"""
```

```
# Install required packages
!pip install -q torch torchvision torchaudio
!pip install -q accelerate peft bitsandbytes transformers trl xformers
peft datasets pyngrok
!pip install -q optuna  # For hyperparameter tuning
```

Step 2: Initialization

The code then begins by importing essential libraries and modules for various functionalities. Here's a summary of the imported libraries and their purposes:

- **`os`**: Used for performing operating system-related functions.
- **`torch`**: The primary library for working with PyTorch, a popular deep-learning framework.
- **`warnings`**: Utilized to suppress warning messages that might be generated during script execution.
- **`logging`**: Enables the script to log error messages, providing a record of any issues that occur during execution.
- **`optuna`**: A library specialized in hyperparameter tuning, which can be used to optimize model parameters.
- **`datasets`**: This library facilitates the loading of datasets, making it easier to work with various data sources.
- **`transformers`**: A library specifically designed for working with pre-trained models, including fine-tuning them for specific tasks.
- **`pipeline`**: A module within the transformers library that streamlines text generation tasks.
- **`tqdm`**: An essential library for creating progress bars, enhancing the user's visibility into the progress of long-running tasks.

Furthermore, the code imports specific modules needed for training and fine-tuning models, such as SFTTrainer from the **`trl`** library and **`LoraConfig`** and **`get_peft_model`** from the peft library. These modules are instrumental in implementing the TRL (Text Response Learning) and PEFT (Planning and Exploration in Fine-Tuning) methods, respectively.

The code also configures logging to capture error messages in a log file named **`training_errors.log`**, which helps in troubleshooting issues during script execution.

Additionally, it enables cuDNN benchmarking, a feature of the CUDA Deep Neural Network library, to optimize deep learning model performance on NVIDIA GPUs.

Lastly, the code takes measures to suppress any warning messages that might be generated during its execution, ensuring a smoother experience.

```
# Import libraries
import os
import torch
import warnings
import logging
import optuna  # For hyperparameter tuning
from datasets import load_dataset
from transformers import (
    AutoModelForCausalLM,
    AutoTokenizer,
    BitsAndBytesConfig,
    TrainingArguments,
)
…
```

Step 3: Loading Data

The function **`load_training_dataset(dataset_name, split="train")`** takes two arguments. **`dataset_name (str)`**: The name of the dataset to be loaded. **`split (str)`**: The name of the split within the dataset to load. The default value is "**`train`**." It uses the **`load_dataset`** function from the datasets library and passes the dataset_name and split arguments to the **`load_dataset`** function. Additionally, it specifies a **`cache_dir`** argument with the value of **`CACHE_DIR`**. The function then returns the loaded dataset split.

```
# Function to load dataset
def load_training_dataset(dataset_name, split="train"):
    """
    Load and return a training dataset split.

    Args:
        dataset_name (str): Name of the dataset.
        split (str): Split name (e.g., "train").

    Returns:
```

```
        Dataset: The loaded dataset split.
    """
    return load_dataset(dataset_name, split=split, cache_dir=CACHE_DIR)
```

Step 4: Initializing Tokenizer

This function, **`initialize_tokenizer`**, creates and configures a tokenizer for a specified language model. It takes the **`model_name`** as input, initializes the tokenizer, sets specific tokenizer properties, saves it to a directory, and then returns the initialized tokenizer.

```
# Function to initialize tokenizer
def initialize_tokenizer(model_name):
    """
    Initialize and return a tokenizer for a given model.

    Args:
        model_name (str): Name of the model.

    Returns:
        AutoTokenizer: The initialized tokenizer.
    """
    ...
```

Step 5: Initializing Model

The **`initialize_model`** function prepares and provides a model for fine-tuning. It takes inputs such as the pre-trained model's name, quantization configuration, and device mapping. It initializes the model, configures it for quantization, assigns devices for training, and returns the initialized model. This function streamlines the process of setting up a model for fine-tuning while allowing customization in model choice, quantization, and device mapping.

```
# Function to initialize model
def initialize_model(model_name, bnb_config, device_map={"": 0}):
    """
    Initialize and return a model for fine-tuning.

    Args:
```

```
        model_name (str): Name of the model.
        bnb_config (BitsAndBytesConfig): Configuration for quantization.
        device_map (dict): Mapping of devices for multi-GPU training.

    Returns:
        AutoModelForCausalLM: The initialized model.
    """
...
```

Step 6: Quantization Process

The **shrink_model** function reduces the memory footprint of a given neural network model by applying two techniques: Gradient Checkpointing and LoRA (Lossless Rectified Activation) compression. It takes the input model, enables Gradient Checkpointing to reduce memory usage during training, configures LoRA compression with specific parameters (reduction factor, alpha parameter, target modules, dropout rate, bias handling, and task type), and applies LoRA compression to the model. The output is the shrunk model with a reduced memory footprint, making it more memory-efficient for training and inference.

```
def shrink_model(model):
    """
    Shrink a given neural network model using Gradient Checkpointing and
LoRA (Lossless Rectified Activation) compression.

    Args:
        model (nn.Module): The model to be shrunk.

    Returns:
        nn.Module: The shrunk model with reduced memory footprint.
    """
...
```

Step 7: Printing Utility

The **print_trainable_parameters** function analyzes a given neural network model. It takes the model as input and performs the following functionality: it counts the number of trainable parameters and the total parameters in the model by iterating through all named parameters. It then calculates the percentage of trainable parameters relative to the total parameters. Finally, it prints the results, including the count of trainable parameters, total parameters, and the trainable percentage.

```
# Function to print trainable parameters


def print_trainable_parameters(model):
    """

    Print the number of trainable parameters in the model.


    Args:
        model (nn.Module): The model to analyze.
    """

...
```

Step 8: Train

The **train_model** function trains a language model with specified training data and settings. It takes as input the model to be trained, the training dataset, a text tokenizer, and training configuration. The function initializes a trainer with these inputs and trains the model for a specified number of epochs, displaying a progress bar. If an error occurs during training, it handles and logs the error, clearing the GPU cache. The function returns the trainer object, encapsulating the training process for the language model.

```
# Function to train model
def train_model(model, dataset, tokenizer, training_arguments):
    """

    Train a language model using the specified dataset and training argu-
ments.


    Args:
        model (AutoModelForCausalLM): The model to train.
        dataset (Dataset): The training dataset.
        tokenizer (AutoTokenizer): The tokenizer for text encoding.
        training_arguments (TrainingArguments): Training configuration.
    """

    ...
```

Step 9: Inference

The **prepare_for_inference** function is responsible for configuring a trained language model for text generation and demonstrating its capabilities. It takes three inputs: a model trainer (**trainer**), a trained language model (**model**), and a text tokenizer (**tokenizer**).

First, it saves the trained model to a specified directory. Then, it loads the configuration for Lossless Rectified Activation (LoRA) compression from that directory and prepares the model for inference using this configuration. Finally, the function generates text based on a given prompt using the configured model and tokenizer and prints the generated text.

We provide the input in the following format: "f"<s>[INST] {text} [/INST]"" because the dataset is an instruction dataset with the following format:

```
<s>[INST] How to own a plane in the United States? [/INST] To own a plane in the United States, you will need to follow these general steps: 1. Obtain a pilot's license: Before you can legally fly your own plane, you will need to obtain a pilot's license. This involves completing flight training and passing both a written and...
```

```
# Function to prepare for inference
def prepare_for_inference(trainer, model, tokenizer):
    """
    Prepare the model for inference and demonstrate text generation.


    Args:
        trainer (SFTTrainer): The model trainer.
        model (AutoModelForCausalLM): The trained model.
        tokenizer (AutoTokenizer): The tokenizer for text encoding.
    """
...
```

Step 10: The pipeline

This main code segment begins by loading a dataset named "**mlabonne/guanaco-llama2-1k**." Next, it initializes a text tokenizer for a language model with the identifier "**NousResearch/Llama-2-7b-chat-hf**." It also sets up the model with specific quantization configurations and enables gradient checkpointing to reduce memory usage.

The model is then further shrunk using quantization techniques. After this, the code prints the number of trainable parameters in the model. Training arguments, such as the number of training epochs and batch size, are configured.

The model is trained using the specified dataset, tokenizer, and training arguments. Following training, the code prepares the model for inference by saving it and loading Lossless Rectified Activation (LoRA) compression configurations.

The script generates text based on a given prompt using the trained and configured model. In case of any errors during this process, the script handles exceptions, logs error messages, and clears the GPU cache.

```
# Main code
if __name__ == "__main__":
    try:
        # Load dataset
        dataset = load_training_dataset(dataset_name="mlabonne/guana-
co-llama2-1k")


        # Initialize tokenizer
        tokenizer = initialize_tokenizer(model_name="NousResearch/Llama-
2-7b-chat-hf")
…
```

Resource consumption

As noticed from the following figure, the fine-tuning has utilized a max of 5.5 GPU RAM from the allocated free tier of 15 GB.

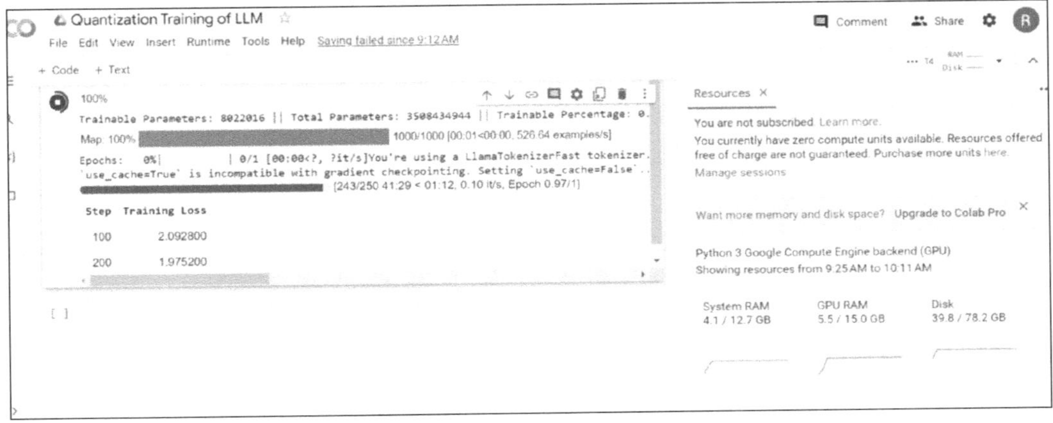

Figure 10.27: Resource Utilization

Output:

The output contains key observations and information about the number of trainable parameters in a model, training loss at specific steps, and text generated during inference.

a. **Trainable Parameters**: The model has 8,022,016 trainable parameters out of a total of 3,508,434,944 parameters, which represents only 0.23% of the total parameters being trainable.

```
Trainable Parameters: 8022016 || Total Parameters: 3508434944 || Trainable Percentage: 0.23%
```

***Figure 10.28**: Trainable Parameters of the Model*

b. **Training Progress**: During training, the script displays the training loss at certain steps. At step 100, the training loss is 2.092800, and at step 200, it reduces to 1.975200.

Step	Training Loss
100	2.092800
200	1.975200

***Figure 10.29**: Training Progress*

c. **Inference Text**: The generated text during inference is in response to the prompt "**`What is a large language model?`**" It describes a large language model as a type of AI model trained on a substantial dataset to produce coherent and natural-sounding language outputs. The generated text also mentions that while many people have heard of large language models, only a few understand what they are and how they function. It briefly discusses the definition and applications of large language models but is cut off.

```
text = "What is a large language model? "
device = "cuda:0"
inputs = tokenizer(f"<s>[INST] {text} [/INST]", return_tensors="pt").to(device)
outputs = model.generate(**inputs, max_new_tokens=100)
print(tokenizer.decode(outputs[0], skip_special_tokens=True))

[INST] What is a large language model?  [/INST]  A large language model is a type of artificial intelligence (AI) model that is trained on a large da

A large language model is a type of neural network that is trained on
```

***Figure 10.30**: Model Inference*

Conclusion

This comprehensive guide has taken you on an illuminating journey through the intricate world of fine-tuning with OpenAI and various other cutting-edge platforms. We embarked on this expedition with the goal of empowering you with the knowledge and skills to unlock the full potential of state-of-the-art language models.

Our journey commenced by establishing a solid foundation in the "*Prerequisite*" section, ensuring that you possessed the essential knowledge to navigate the complexities of model optimization and customization. Armed with this foundational understanding, we then delved into the practical aspects of the process in the "Implementation Walkthrough" section.

Throughout our exploration, we traversed a diverse landscape of platforms and techniques. We began by focusing on Colab, Google's collaborative platform, where we fine-tuned models with OpenAI. We meticulously followed step-by-step guides, installing crucial libraries, configuring OpenAI keys, and creating and validating training data. Our journey culminated in mastering the art of model inference and management, including the deletion of models when necessary.

Venturing further, we explored the Cohere platform, where we demystified the process of fine-tuning LLMs for classification tasks. We delved into Cohere's dashboard, customized models, and meticulously managed data. With precision and care, we monitored training progress and learned how to access models and leverage their capabilities.

In the Kaggle GPUs section, we harnessed the power of Kaggle's GPUs to fine-tune T5 models for text classification. Our journey encompassed environment setup, data loading, model training, and resource optimization, ensuring efficiency and effectiveness in our endeavors.

For those with a penchant for evaluation, the "*Evaluation Of LLMs on Summarization task*" section provided a comprehensive guide. We explored data sampling, batch generation, ROUGE score computation, and the application of T5 and GPT-2 models for summarization tasks, culminating in the effective display of results.

Our expedition reached its zenith with a deep dive into fine-tuning on Colab using quantization techniques, an advanced topic that required a solid foundation in the preceding sections. We navigated through installation, initialization, data loading, quantization processes, and model training, ensuring mastery of these intricate techniques.

Throughout this chapter, our aim has been to provide you with profound knowledge, pragmatic guidance, and hands-on experience. Our mission was to empower you to craft unique and innovative solutions using state-of-the-art language models. As you conclude this journey, remember that your path as a software engineer and developer is an ongoing one, filled with ever-evolving challenges and opportunities.

With the knowledge and skills you have acquired, you are well-prepared to make a significant impact in the dynamic field of software engineering and development. We encourage you to continue pushing the boundaries of innovation, solving problems with originality, and creating differentiating factors in your work. As you move forward, may you unlock the full potential of fine-tuning with OpenAI and beyond, shaping the future of technology and software engineering with creativity and expertise. In the next chapter, we will discuss the key components and data management in LLMOps, economics of LLMOps, and deployment and security considerations.

References

- https://github.com/ray-project/llm-numbers?search=1
- https://openai.com/
- https://cohere.com/
- https://github.com/databricks-academy/large-language-models/tree/published
- https://huggingface.co/datasets/mlabonne/guanaco-llama2-1k

CHAPTER 11
LLMOps - Operationalizing LLMs at Scale

Introduction

Large Language Model Operations (LLMOps) is a comprehensive set of practices, techniques, and tools that are employed to manage the lifecycle of large language models (LLMs). This lifecycle spans from data management and model development to deployment and ethics. The field of LLMOps is a subset of MLOps (Machine Learning Operations), which is a set of best practices for operationalizing machine learning models. However, LLMOps introduces additional challenges, such as managing large amounts of data and ensuring the safe and responsible use of LLMs.

LLMOps is an emerging field, driven by the recent prevalence of large language models. These models, with their seemingly limitless applications, are poised to revolutionize the world as we know it. Companies like Hugging Face, Humanloop, and NVIDIA are at the forefront of this change, paving the way for the adoption of LLMOps.

As LLMOps continues to evolve, there is a growing trend toward its convergence with other AI domains such as computer vision and speech recognition. This amalgamation will equip organizations to construct multifaceted AI ecosystems capable of tackling a broader spectrum of tasks. Adhering to industry best practices and overcoming LLMOps-related challenges enables businesses to proficiently oversee the entire lifecycle of applications driven by large language models. This sets the stage for a future where AI is even more deeply woven into the fabric of our daily experiences.

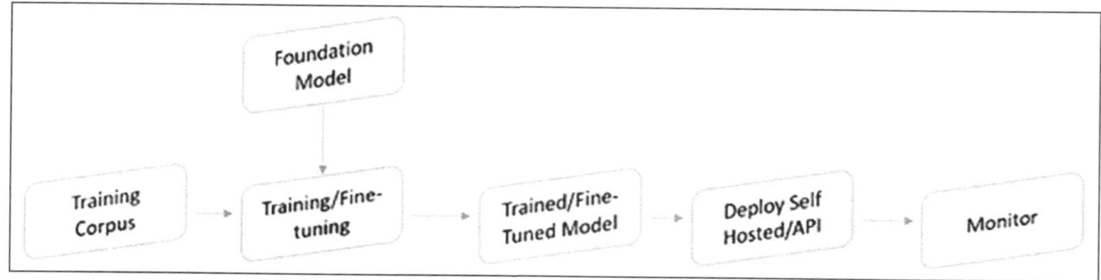

Figure 11.1: *LLMOps Workflow*

Structure

In this chapter, the following topics will be covered:

- Key Components and Data Management in LLMOps
- Difference between MLOps and LLMOps
- Key Challenges, Benefits, and Best Practices
- Deployment and Security Considerations
- Economics of LLMOps

Key Components of LLMOps

Large Language Model Operations (LLMOps) is a comprehensive set of practices, techniques, and tools designed to manage the lifecycle of large language models (LLMs) in production environments. The lifecycle of an LLM includes several key stages, each of which plays a crucial role in the successful implementation and operation of these models. This section will delve into these key components, providing an understanding of their importance and the best practices associated with each stage.

Data Preparation

The first stage in the LLMOps lifecycle is data preparation. This involves the collection, cleaning, and labeling of data for training and testing LLM models. The quality of the data used in this stage can significantly impact the performance of the model, making it a critical component of LLMOps. Best practices in data preparation include implementing robust data cleaning and validation processes to ensure the quality and reliability of the data used for training and testing.

Model Training

Once the data has been prepared, the next stage is model training. This involves using the prepared data to train LLM models. The choice of model and the training techniques used can significantly impact the model's performance and the resources required for training. Therefore, selecting the appropriate model and understanding your tool stack are crucial aspects of this stage.

Model Evaluation

After the model has been trained, it needs to be evaluated. This stage involves assessing the performance of the LLM models using various metrics. The evaluation process helps identify any issues or weaknesses in the model, allowing for adjustments and improvements to be made before deployment. Techniques such as SHAP values and LIME can be used to explain the predictions of LLM models, aiding in the interpretability of the model.

Model Deployment

The next stage is model deployment, which involves deploying the LLM models in production environments. This stage requires careful planning and execution to ensure the model operates effectively and securely in a live environment. Security patching and support are crucial aspects of this stage, ensuring the deployed model is secure and reliable.

Model Monitoring

The final stage in the LLMOps lifecycle is model monitoring. This involves tracking the performance of the LLM models in production environments and making necessary adjustments. Monitoring helps identify any issues early and allows for timely interventions to maintain optimal performance. Cloud computing services or distributed computing frameworks such as Apache Spark can be used to aid in the scalability of the model monitoring process.

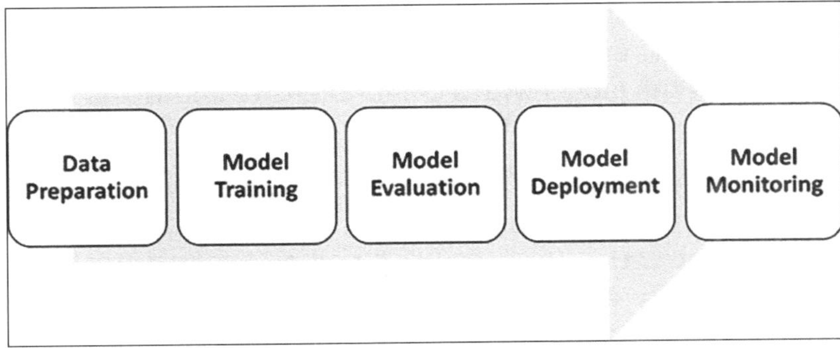

***Figure 11.2**: LLMOps Key Components*

By understanding and effectively managing these key components of LLMOps, organizations can successfully manage the lifecycle of LLM-powered applications. However, it's important to note that implementing LLMOps also comes with its challenges, such as a lack of talent, poor data quality, security, model interpretability, and model scalability. Addressing these challenges requires strategic planning, resource allocation, and continuous learning and adaptation.

Data Management in LLMOps

Meticulous data management plays a pivotal role in shaping the development of large language models, as it fundamentally influences their functionality and behavior. Essentially, how you curate and handle the data not only determines the model's accuracy but also its operational characteristics in various applications.

Importance of Data Management

LLMOps is a comprehensive set of practices, techniques, and tools designed to manage the lifecycle of LLMs. This lifecycle spans from data management and model development to deployment and ethics. A key component of LLMOps is data management, which involves the collection, cleaning, labeling, storage, and organization of data for training and testing LLMs. The quality of data is crucial in LLM training as it directly influences the quality and performance of the model.

Data Collection and Preprocessing

The cornerstone of a robust LLM lies in the caliber and variety of the data used to train it. Gathering information from an array of sources, fields, and languages is crucial for crafting a versatile LLM capable of handling diverse tasks. Such a diverse dataset arms the model with a comprehensive knowledge base, allowing it to be more adaptable across different scenarios.

Nonetheless, the initial data is often cluttered and disorganized, requiring meticulous refinement before it can be used for training the LLM. Standardization techniques like tokenization, transforming text to lowercase, and eliminating stopwords help simplify and streamline the text. Additionally, processes like spell-checking, removing duplicates, and identifying outliers further elevate the quality of the training data, thereby laying the groundwork for a more effective LLM.

Data Labeling and Annotation

For tasks that rely on supervised learning, having precise and reliable labeled data is crucial. Engaging domain experts in the data annotation process significantly boosts the quality of these labels. The use of a human-in-the-loop strategy is particularly beneficial for cases that are intricate, specialized to a certain domain, or rife with ambiguity, as they demand expert interpretation. Annotation platforms designed for scalability and cost-efficiency facilitate the gathering of these high-quality labels. These platforms have the capability to disperse labeling assignments among a broad pool of annotators, often with varied expertise, thereby enhancing both the quality and scope of the annotations.

Data Storage, Organization, and Versioning

Managing extensive data sets is a pivotal aspect of LLMOps. The choice of appropriate databases and storage solutions enables efficient data storage, access, and modification throughout the lifecycle of large language models. Version control is indispensable in this context, as it helps keep track of data alterations and its progressive development. Utilizing data version control systems, AI teams can systematically record different versions of datasets, thereby encouraging teamwork and enabling reproducibility in experiments. Maintaining a structured record of data history allows for smoother iterations on LLM development and facilitates performance improvements over time.

By adhering to industry standards and tackling the inherent challenges in data management specific to LLMOps, organizations can proficiently oversee the entire lifecycle of applications powered by LLMs. This strategy not only streamlines the data pipeline for training, thereby accelerating the process and reducing overhead costs, but also guarantees that the data is readily available for the model during the training phase.

Traditional Development Process

Before the advent of LLMOps platforms, the process of developing applications based on LLMs was often cumbersome and time-consuming. Developers had to manually handle tasks at each stage, leading to inefficiencies, scalability issues, and potential security vulnerabilities. Here's a snapshot of the traditional development process:

- **Data Preparation**: Developers had to manually collect and preprocess data, which often involved complex data cleaning and annotation work. This process required a significant amount of code and time.

- **Prompt Engineering**: Developers could only write and debug prompts through API calls or Playgrounds, lacking real-time feedback and visual debugging.
- **Embedding and Context Management**: Developers had to manually handle the embedding and storage of long contexts, which can be difficult to optimize and scale. This process required a fair amount of programming work and a deep understanding of model embedding and vector databases.
- **Application Monitoring and Maintenance**: Developers had to manually collect and analyze performance data, which could lead to an inability to detect and address issues in real time. In some cases, there might even be a lack of log records.
- **Model Fine-tuning**: Previously, developers were tasked with individually overseeing the data preparation and model training processes for fine-tuning, a situation that could result in operational inefficiencies and an increase in code volume.
- **System and Operations**: The necessity for technical staff engagement in the creation of a management backend added layers of complexity, driving up both development and upkeep expenses. This approach also fell short in facilitating collaboration and wasn't particularly user-friendly for those lacking technical expertise.

Platform LLMOps Approach

The introduction of LLMOps platforms revolutionizes the process of developing applications based on LLMs, making it more efficient, scalable, and secure. Here are the advantages of developing LLM applications using an LLMOps platform:

- **Data Preparation**: LLMOps platforms provide data collection and preprocessing tools, simplifying data cleaning and annotation tasks, and minimizing or even eliminating coding work.
- **Prompt Engineering**: LLMOps platforms offer a WYSIWYG (What You See Is What You Get) prompt editing and debugging environment, allowing for real-time optimization and adjustments based on user input data.
- **Embedding and Context Management**: LLMOps platforms automate key tasks such as integrating long textual contexts into the model, storing them for future use, and managing them efficiently. This automation eases the burden on developers by reducing the amount of code they need to write, while also making the system more scalable and efficient.

- **Application Monitoring and Maintenance**: LLMOps platforms come equipped with tools that allow for the immediate observation of how well the system is running. This enables quick identification of any problems, leading to faster resolutions that help maintain a stable operating environment. In addition, these platforms provide detailed logs that record all actions and events, serving as a valuable resource for troubleshooting and analysis.
- **Model Fine-tuning**: LLMOps platforms come with a user-friendly function that allows for model optimization at the click of a button. This is made possible by using data that has already been annotated based on actual usage scenarios. This feature streamlines the fine-tuning process, making the model more accurate while simultaneously reducing the coding effort needed.
- **System and Operations**: LLMOps platforms are designed with user interfaces that are simple enough for people who may not have the technical expertise to navigate. This inclusivity promotes a collaborative environment among team members with varied skill sets. As a byproduct of this ease of use and collaboration, the costs associated with the development and ongoing maintenance of the platform are also reduced.

Compared to traditional development methods, LLMOps platforms offer more transparent and easy-to-monitor application management, allowing team members to better understand the application's operation. By leveraging the power of LLMOps, organizations can harness the power of large language models to drive innovation and growth.

Difference Between LLMOps and MLOps

Large Language Model Operations (LLMOps) and Machine Learning Operations (MLOps) are both subsets of Development Operations (DevOps), focusing on the operational aspects of machine learning. While they share common ground, they cater to different types of models and thus have unique challenges and requirements. This section will explore the differences between LLMOps and MLOps, highlighting the unique aspects of managing large language models.

Computational Resources

Training and fine-tuning large language models typically involve performing a significantly larger number of calculations on extensive datasets. This process requires specialized hardware like GPUs for faster data-parallel operations. The cost of inference can also necessitate model compression and distillation techniques. Thus, access to these specialized compute resources becomes essential for both training and deploying large language models, a requirement not as pronounced in traditional MLOps.

Transfer Learning

Traditional machine learning models are usually built from the ground up for specific tasks. However, large language models typically commence with a 'base' or 'foundation' model. This foundation is then specialized or "fine-tuned" for particular applications using additional, specific data. This approach – known as transfer learning – permits the model to achieve high levels of performance in specialized domains without needing as much data or computational power. This is a unique benefit when managing these models through LLMOps platforms.

Human Feedback

Many tasks performed by large language models don't have a single correct answer, which makes performance evaluation challenging. In such cases, end-user feedback becomes crucial for determining how well the model is doing its job. By embedding this human-feedback loop directly into your LLMOps infrastructure, not only is the model's performance evaluation simplified, but the gathered feedback can also be used for future fine-tuning. This approach to incorporating real-world user feedback is not as commonly seen in traditional MLOps, making it a distinguishing aspect of LLMOps.

Hyperparameter Tuning

Both traditional machine learning operations (MLOps) and large language model operations (LLMOps) employ hyperparameter tuning to improve model performance. However, in LLMOps, this tuning takes on an additional role: it's not just about performance but also about efficiency. Adjusting specific settings, like the size of the data chunks (batch sizes) being processed simultaneously, or the step sizes in the learning algorithm (learning rates), can have a considerable impact on how quickly a model can be trained and at what cost. This optimization for both speed and resource allocation sets LLMOps apart from traditional MLOps.

Performance Metrics

Evaluating large language models requires a different set of standard metrics and scoring, such as bilingual evaluation understudy (BLEU) and

Recall-Oriented Understudy for Gisting Evaluation (ROUGE). These metrics require extra consideration when implementing, unlike the straightforward calculation of metrics like accuracy, AUC, F1 score, and more, in traditional ML models.

Prompt Engineering

The practice of designing specific queries or directives for instruction-based models is pivotal for eliciting precise and dependable outputs from LLMs. This activity, referred to as prompt crafting, minimizes the likelihood of model-based errors like false output generation (hallucination) and vulnerabilities like sensitive data exposure or unauthorized command injections.

Building LLM Chains or Pipelines

In contrast to creating new LLMs, much of the development focus in LLM applications is on crafting intricate workflows, known as LLM pipelines. These workflows might involve a series of calls to one or multiple LLMs, and could even integrate with external databases or search platforms. This enables LLMs to undertake complex functions such as responding to user inquiries based on document collections or pulling from knowledge databases.

Both LLMOps and MLOps aim to facilitate the practical use of machine learning. However, LLMOps has unique concerns like prompt crafting and specialized workflows because it is designed to manage the peculiarities and complexities of large language models. Understanding these differences helps in better operationalizing LLMs for enterprise use.

Best Practices for LLMOps

LLMOps is a rapidly evolving field, and as such, best practices are continually being refined and expanded. This section outlines some of the current best practices for each stage of the LLMOps lifecycle, from exploratory data analysis to model monitoring.

Exploratory Data Analysis (EDA)

- **Detailed data exploration**: This establishes that the first crucial action in the LLMOps process is to delve deeply into your data. This is not a one-time activity but an ongoing effort to understand what your data contains and what it can offer.

- **Investigation**: The idea here is that data exploration isn't just about looking at data; it's about making it ready for the steps that follow in the machine learning lifecycle. Also, the data is not kept siloed but shared among various teams to get a multidimensional view.
- **Centralization and Modularization**: The emphasis here is on creating a data environment that is not only rich in insights but also flexible and collaborative. The goal is to make sure that the work done during this phase can be easily replicated or adjusted by other team members, thus fostering a more collaborative and efficient work environment.

Data Preparation and Prompt Engineering

- **Data Curation and Preprocessing**: The meticulous work involved in making the raw data useful. Transforming could mean converting the data into a format more suitable for modeling. Consolidation refers to aggregating data from different sources to create a unified dataset. The removal of duplicates is self-explanatory and is done to maintain data integrity.
- **Data Orchestration**: This is important for ensuring a streamlined workflow. Having data that can be easily accessed and shared by different teams reduces bottlenecks and enhances collaboration.
- **Crafting well-structured and reliable prompts for LLMs**: Prompt engineering essentially involves creating well-thought-out queries or instructions that the language model can comprehend and respond to effectively. This is especially critical for LLMs, which are designed to handle a wide range of complex tasks.

Model Fine-Tuning

- **Adjusting Model Parameters in LLMOps:** One of the critical activities in managing large language models effectively involves making incremental changes to the model's parameters to optimize its performance. This is a typical step after the model has been initially trained and is tailored to more specific tasks or datasets.
- **Renowned Open-Source Frameworks**: Hugging Face Transformers, DeepSpeed, PyTorch, TensorFlow, and JAX are widely used libraries in machine learning and natural language processing. They provide a variety of tools and functionalities that can assist in the fine-tuning process.
- **Substantially Elevate the Efficacy**: The utilization of these frameworks can lead to marked improvements in the model's capabilities, making it more accurate, efficient, or faster. In summary, leveraging these advanced libraries can be a catalyst for enhancing the performance metrics of a large language model.

Model Review and Governance

- **Monitoring Model Lineage and Versions for Governance**: This implies that it's crucial to have a well-documented record of how models and pipelines have evolved over time, including changes made and versions created. This information is vital for compliance, auditing, and responsible AI usage.
- **Utilizing an open-source platform for MLOps, such as MLflow**: MLflow is a well-known, open-source platform specifically designed for machine learning operations (MLOps). Its use enables efficient management of models, pipelines, and their various versions.
- **Seamless Management of Digital Artifacts from Inception to Decommissioning**: MLflow is designed to handle these digital assets throughout their lifecycle, from creation to eventual retirement, providing an organized way to track changes and performance metrics.
- **Encourages Visibility, Sharing, and Team Collaboration**: MLflow also has features that support the sharing of models and pipelines, making it easier for team members to collaborate, replicate experiments, and build upon each other's work.

Model Inference and Serving

- **Overseeing model update rates and production metrics in QA testing**: This stresses the importance of paying close attention to how often your models are updated and how quickly they respond to inference requests. These factors are crucial for the model's performance once it is deployed in a production environment.
- **DevOps-inspired tools like version control repositories and orchestration platforms**: DevOps principles, which aim to streamline software development and operation processes, have influenced CI/CD tools used in machine learning. Repositories for version control and orchestration tools can help automate various steps in the pre-production pipeline, ensuring smoother transitions and fewer manual errors.
- **Automate the pre-production process**: The automation enabled by these tools helps to standardize and streamline pre-production tasks, reducing the risk of manual errors and making the process more efficient.
- **Activating REST API endpoints for models, optimized by GPU acceleration**: By enabling REST API endpoints that leverage GPU acceleration, you make the model more scalable and capable of handling multiple requests simultaneously, enhancing its performance metrics.

Model Monitoring with Human Feedback

- **Setting up real-time monitoring pipelines for both the model and data**: Organizations should have a continuous tracking mechanism to supervise both the data that feeds into the model and the model's performance itself. Real-time tracking can identify issues as they arise, enabling quicker resolution.
- **Built-in alerts and notifications:** These alerts act as an immediate flagging system. If the model starts to behave in an unexpected manner (known as model drift) or if questionable user behavior is detected, the system will alert the responsible teams for immediate action.
- **Integrating human oversight**: While automation is valuable, human judgment is still essential to assess the model's performance critically and make adjustments as needed. This ensures that the model aligns with what the organization aims to achieve and satisfies its quality criteria.

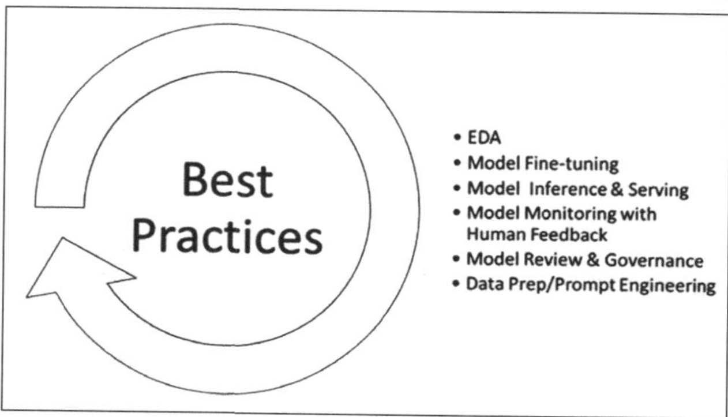

***Figure 11.3**: LLMOps Best Practices*

General Best Practices

In addition to the stage-specific best practices, there are several general best practices to consider as follows:

- Identify the right use case that can benefit from LLMs.
- Choose the appropriate model for your use case, such as GPT-3, T5, or BERT.
- Collect, clean, and label data for training and testing LLM models.
- Define clear project goals, roles, responsibilities, and timelines.
- Select the right tools for each stage of the project.
- Keep track of the costs associated with each stage of the project.
- Establish standards for data formats, model architectures, and deployment environments.

- Assess the skills of your team members and provide necessary training to fill any gaps.

By following these best practices, organizations can effectively manage the lifecycle of LLM-powered applications, ensuring their successful implementation and operation.

Benefits of LLMOps

LLMOps is a burgeoning field that concentrates on the comprehensive management of LLMs. This includes everything from data management and model development to deployment and ethical considerations. LLMOps offer a plethora of benefits that can empower organizations to utilize LLMs more effectively to achieve their business objectives. This section delves into the benefits of LLMOps in a detailed manner.

Efficiency

Efficiency is one of the primary benefits of LLMOps. It enables data teams to expedite model and pipeline development, leading to cost savings and enhanced productivity. By automating the processes involved in LLM development, LLMOps can diminish the time and effort required to train and deploy LLMs. This allows organizations to bring LLM-powered applications to the market faster, thereby gaining a competitive edge.

Scalability

Scalability is another significant advantage of LLMOps. It allows organizations to scale large language models effectively and deploy them in production, which can enhance the quality of the models and minimize the risk of errors. By leveraging LLMOps, organizations can train and deploy LLMs at scale. This enables them to handle large volumes of data and consistently deliver high-quality results, which is crucial in today's data-driven world.

Risk Reduction

Risk reduction is a key benefit of LLMOps. It enhances the reliability of LLMs by providing a framework for monitoring and maintaining the models in production environments. By monitoring the performance of LLMs in production environments, LLMOps can detect and prevent model drift, which refers to the degradation of an LLM's predictive ability over time due to changes in the digital environment. This proactive approach reduces the risk of ethical issues and negative consequences, ensuring that LLMs are used safely and responsibly.

Enhanced Customer Experience

LLMOps can also significantly enhance the customer experience. It powers natural language interfaces, leading to improved customer engagement and satisfaction. By utilizing LLMs, organizations can develop chatbots, virtual assistants, and other conversational interfaces that can understand and respond to customer queries and requests in natural language. This leads to faster and more personalized support, thereby improving the overall customer experience.

LLMOps offers several benefits, including efficiency, scalability, risk reduction, and enhanced customer experience. By addressing the challenges of LLM development through effective monitoring practices and data management, LLMOps can help organizations leverage the power of large language models to achieve their business goals more effectively. By adopting LLMOps, organizations can train and deploy LLMs at scale, reduce the risk of errors and ethical issues, and improve the customer experience.

Challenges of LLMOps

While LLMOps offer a multitude of benefits, it also presents a unique set of challenges. These challenges range from managing large model sizes and complex datasets to continuous monitoring, evaluation, and scalability. This section aims to provide a comprehensive understanding of these challenges and potential solutions.

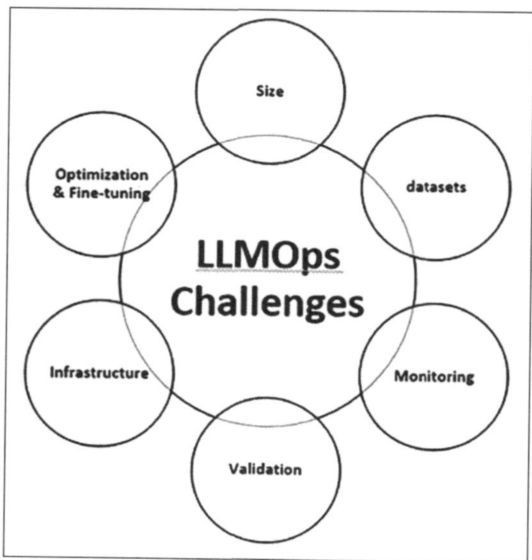

Figure 11.4: LLMOps Challenges

Large Model Size

One of the primary challenges in operationalizing LLMs is their large model size. LLMs often have billions of parameters, requiring specialized computational resources and capabilities. Consequently, managing LLMs can become time-consuming and expensive. Organizations need to invest in robust infrastructure and efficient resource management strategies to handle these large models effectively.

Complex Datasets

The management of complex and large datasets is another critical challenge. The development of LLMs involves a massive amount of data for training, requiring a lot of parallel processing and optimization. Organizations need to implement effective data management strategies and use advanced data processing tools to handle these complex datasets.

Continuous Monitoring and Evaluation

Similar to machine learning models, LLMs require a persistent cycle of oversight and evaluation based on various performance metrics. A diligent and continuous supervisory system is crucial for detecting any slump in performance or irregularities in how the model functions. To manage models successfully, organizations should allocate resources for sturdy monitoring utilities and devise a well-organized evaluation framework.

Scalability

The increasing adoption of LLMs places a demand for powerful, scalable infrastructure. Cloud-based platforms offer a compelling solution to accommodate the scaling needs of these language models. However, maintaining this scalable environment without ballooning costs remains a complex task.

Model Optimization

LLMs are not *'set-and-forget'* systems; they require ongoing adjustments and cycles of feedback for refinement. Utilizing LLMOps, the process specialized for managing LLMs, you can fine-tune these sizable base models via transfer learning techniques, thereby enhancing their applicability for specific tasks. Establishing these feedback mechanisms and assuring effective transfer learning, however, is not straightforward.

Infrastructure Optimization

LLMs are computational powerhouses that demand substantial resources. For efficient operation, organizations must fine-tune their existing infrastructure. This could include leveraging specialized computing units like GPUs or TPUs and adapting data centers to support high-performance computing needs.

Security and Privacy

Given that LLMs often process sensitive or confidential data, safeguarding this information is imperative. Compliance with legal norms and implementing protective mechanisms such as access controls and data encryption are non-negotiable aspects.

Integration

For LLMs to be genuinely useful, they should be seamlessly incorporated into existing data and analytics workflows. This integration might require linking with data lakes, warehouses, or other data management solutions.

Automation

In line with practices in MLOps, LLMOps also demands a degree of automation to guarantee the rapid and reliable deployment of LLMs. Utilizing orchestration tools like Kubernetes, Docker, or Ansible could automate many tasks, including deployment and scalability.

Monitoring

Active monitoring tools are essential to ensure the LLM is functioning within expected parameters. Tools like Prometheus or Grafana can be employed to monitor various metrics, such as computational resources consumed and the model's overall accuracy and efficacy.

Validation

Since LLM technology is relatively nascent, robust validation measures are needed. Companies must also consider the 'Hallucination' risk associated with LLMs, which, if not managed, could compromise user trust.

Though LLMOps presents considerable challenges, they are not insurmountable barriers. With meticulous planning, resource allocation, and a culture of ongoing improvement, companies can navigate these challenges effectively, reaping transformative business benefits from operationalized LLMs.

Deployment Strategies for Large Language Models

Deploying LLMs in a production environment presents a unique set of challenges. The optimal deployment strategy will vary based on the specific use case and the problem that the model is intended to solve. This section will delve into the various deployment strategies, their pros and cons, and the factors to consider when choosing a strategy.

Latency Considerations

Different applications have varying latency requirements. The desired inference speed should be assessed prior to deployment, and the appropriate hardware choices should be made to meet these requirements. For instance, Graphics Processing Units (GPUs) and Tensor Processing Units (TPUs) are key when optimizing inference speed, although they are more expensive than Central Processing Units (CPUs), which are generally slower.

Cost Management

Building your own model or leveraging open-source models necessitates hosting the model. Due to their substantial size, LLMs require a lot of computational power and memory, which can increase infrastructure costs. Additionally, to reduce latency, you might need to leverage GPUs or TPUs. Therefore, optimizing resources is paramount to manage costs effectively.

Resource Management

Deploying a machine learning model, be it a proprietary one or an open-source variant, is resource-intensive. The idea of stowing such a model on a singular storage unit quickly becomes unfeasible given its storage demands, which usually outstrip those of more traditional models. Memory allocation is another vital consideration.

To mitigate the storage conundrum, you have several options: deploying across multiple servers, implementing model parallelism, or utilizing distributed inference techniques. Furthermore, certain hardware specifications, such as

Graphics Processing Units (GPUs), Random Access Memory (RAM), and high-velocity storage solutions, could be requisites for enhancing the speed of model inference.

However, securing this robust infrastructure isn't just logistically complex; it's also financially demanding. As such, an exhaustive and meticulous planning phase focused on infrastructure is imperative for successfully hosting an LLM.

Deployment Options: Cloud-based or On-premise

Selecting an optimal strategy for deploying a model involves multiple variables such as financial constraints, data protection needs, and infrastructural prerequisites. Cloud solutions from providers like AWS, Google Cloud AI, and Microsoft Azure provide an adaptable, easy-to-scale, and user-friendly environment. Conversely, an on-site deployment could be the go-to choice for those prioritizing stringent data security and more granular control over their systems.

Continuous Integration and Delivery (CI/CD)

Continuous Integration and Continuous Deployment (CI/CD) pipelines serve as the backbone for automating model development cycles, making the processes of testing and rolling out models more streamlined. Utilizing orchestration tools such as Jenkins, GitLab CI/CD, and GitHub Actions contributes to a fluid and optimized operational flow. A strategically planned CI/CD pipeline not only facilitates easy updates and reversions of models but also ensures minimal interruptions for end-users. Implementing version control for models coupled with rigorous testing procedures allows for early detection of issues, making sure only the models that meet performance criteria go live.

Monitoring and Maintenance

Constant vigilance on how a model performs and is utilized is crucial for both spotting potential problems and discovering opportunities for refinement. A specific concern to watch out for is model drift, a phenomenon where the model's efficacy diminishes as the data it was trained on becomes outdated or changes in its distribution. By continually scrutinizing model performance and rejuvenating it with up-to-date data, you can counteract the effects of model drift.

Scalability and Performance Optimization

To effectively manage high-traffic scenarios, it may be necessary to scale your models either horizontally by incorporating additional instances, or vertically through the enhancement of existing resources. Technologies such as Kubernetes and serverless architectures make this type of scalability straightforward, adapting to variable workloads. Ensuring low model latency is also critical for delivering a seamless user experience. Platforms like NVIDIA TensorRT and ONNX Runtime furnish a suite of tools aimed at optimizing a wide array of deep learning models.

Deployment Strategies

There are several strategies for deploying LLMs, each with its own set of advantages and disadvantages. Here are three common strategies:

- **Building an In-House ML Platform with Your Existing Team's Expertise (K8 + Docker)**: This approach allows you to have full control over your ML platform, deploy in your infrastructure of choice, and leverage your team's existing knowledge of K8 and Docker. However, it requires a team of engineers to build and maintain, can be time-consuming, and is limited to the existing team's knowledge.

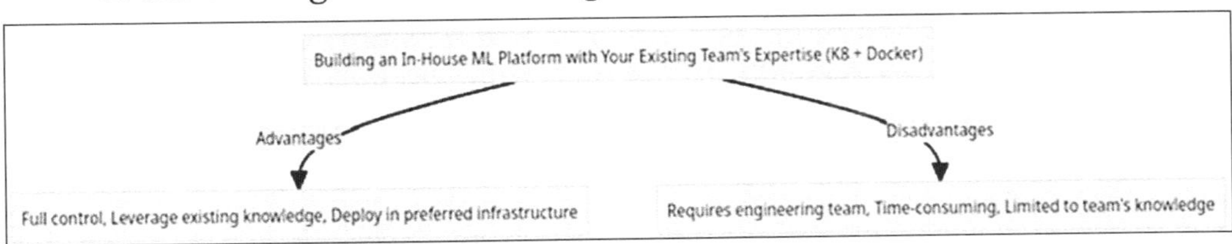

Figure 11.5: *LLMOps Deployment Strategy In-House*

- **Selecting a Cloud Provider and Building around their LLM Tooling**: This strategy allows for faster deployment than building in-house, access to advanced technologies, scalability, and flexibility. However, it may lead to cloud lock-in, requires expertise on the cloud of choice, and requires careful cost management.

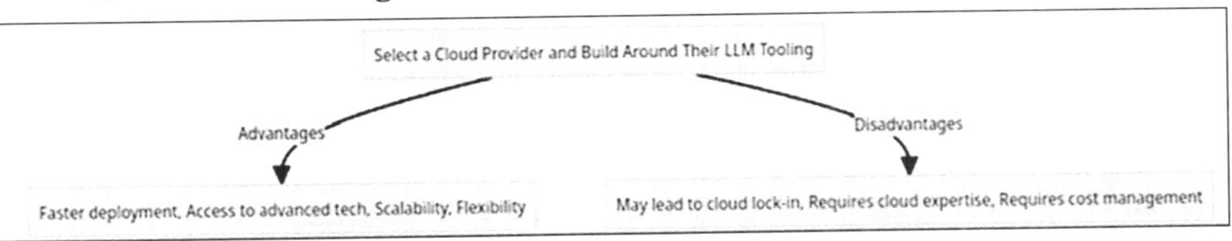

Figure 11.6: *LLMOps Deployment Strategy On-Cloud*

- **Purchasing a Pre-Built Solution for Hosting LLMs:** Purchasing a pre-built solution can significantly reduce the time it takes to deploy your ML models, is often more affordable than building in-house or relying on a cloud provider's services, and is proven and reliable. However, it offers limited customization, creates a dependency on an external provider, and can hamper the in-house expertise required to build and manage ML infrastructure.

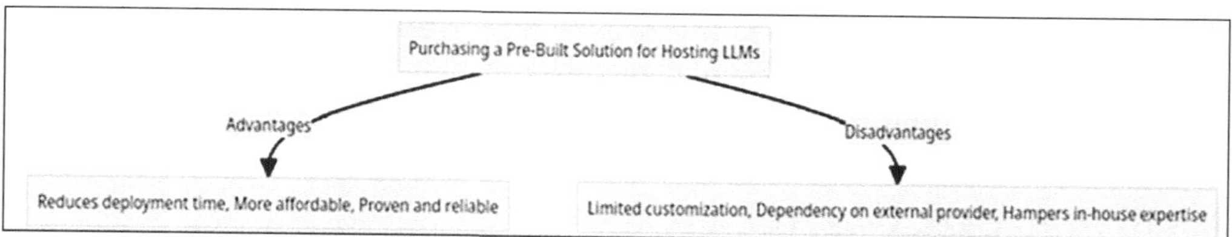

***Figure 11.7**: LLMOps Deployment Strategy On-Cloud-Pre Build*

The choice of deployment strategy for LLMs depends on a variety of factors including cost, latency requirements, resource management, and the specific use case. It is crucial to carefully consider these factors and choose the strategy that best aligns with your organization's needs and capabilities.

Security and Privacy in LLM Deployment

As we navigate the realm of LLMs, it becomes increasingly evident that security and privacy are not mere considerations, but rather, they are integral components of successful deployment. The vastness of data processed and generated by these models necessitates stringent measures to ensure its protection and the preservation of privacy.

Data Privacy and Protection

The first line of defense in preserving data privacy is the implementation of robust data management strategies. This involves the application of techniques such as anonymization and pseudonymization, which work to remove or obscure personally identifiable information (PII) from datasets. By doing so, we can significantly reduce privacy risks and ensure data confidentiality.

MachEye, a platform specializing in providing businesses with decision-making intelligence, underscores the critical nature of having the right infrastructure in place. The platform highlights that without well-designed structural frameworks, LLMs can be bereft of essential control mechanisms for data access. This absence of proper guardrails can elevate concerns about adhering to industry-specific data compliance regulations, particularly when dealing with sensitive data.

Data Encryption and Access Controls

Beyond anonymization and pseudonymization, data encryption serves as a crucial layer of protection for data both at rest and in transit. By encrypting data, we can safeguard it from unauthorized access, thereby bolstering our security measures.

Complementing encryption, the implementation of access controls, such as role-based access control (RBAC), ensures that only authorized personnel can access sensitive data. This contributes to a secure and compliant data management environment, further fortifying our defenses against potential breaches.

Model Security

In the world of LLMs, safeguarding isn't limited to just the data; it also involves the protection of the model architecture itself. These extensive text models can be susceptible to targeted attacks, known as adversarial attacks, which can adversely affect their operational effectiveness and data integrity. To mitigate these risks, various strategies such as adversarial learning and defensive distillation can be utilized. These methods serve to enhance the model's ability to withstand external threats and maintain its performance stability.

Additionally, it's essential to continuously track how the model is functioning in real time. Anomaly detection is vital in spotting any unusual behaviors that could signify a breach or performance issue. By taking a proactive approach in locating and resolving these issues, teams focused on artificial intelligence can assure that their large language models continue to be dependable, precise, and secure.

Regulatory Compliance

In the field of data security, adhering to legal regulations like the General Data Protection Regulation (GDPR) and the California Consumer Privacy Act (CCPA) is a mandatory element when deploying LLMs. Following these guidelines is not merely a legal necessity but also an essential factor in building confidence among consumers and key stakeholders.

One valuable tool for gauging privacy threats in AI initiatives is the Privacy Impact Assessment (PIA). PIAs facilitate the process of pinpointing and counteracting potential privacy vulnerabilities within your LLM-related projects. When paired with routine compliance audits, these assessments contribute to ongoing data protection and model security, setting a high benchmark for both.

Managing LLMs involves a complex set of tasks that require a multi-faceted approach towards ensuring both security and privacy. A rigorous data security framework, robust model defenses, and strict regulatory adherence all serve to mitigate the challenges that come with the deployment of LLMs. By taking these comprehensive measures, we can safely unlock the immense possibilities offered by LLMs without compromising on security or privacy.

Joint Recommendation for Language Model Deployment: Cohere, OpenAI, and AI21 Labs

In the rapidly evolving landscape of LLMs, the collaborative efforts of leading organizations such as Cohere, OpenAI, and AI21 Labs have resulted in a set of key principles aimed at mitigating the risks associated with this technology. These principles, while developed based on their collective experience with providing LLMs through APIs, are designed to be universally applicable, regardless of the release strategy employed.

Prohibit Misuse

The first core principle stresses the necessity of preventing any improper use of LLMs. It advocates for creating transparent guidelines and terms of service that spell out acceptable and unacceptable uses of the technology, aiming to avoid harm to individual users, specific communities, or society in general. Harmful activities like spamming, fraudulent actions, or astroturfing should be explicitly mentioned as forbidden. The guidelines should also delineate areas where the application of LLMs should be closely reviewed, banning any uses that could involve high-risk scenarios, like categorizing individuals based on legally protected traits.

To implement these guidelines effectively, it's advisable to construct an underlying architecture and systems that incorporate specific preventive mechanisms. These could include rate-limiting capabilities, content screening functionalities, a requirement for pre-approval before accessing production environments, and continuous monitoring for any unusual or potentially harmful activities.

The second foundational principle emphasizes the importance of taking steps to actively reduce unintended negative impacts from model behavior. This involves thoroughly evaluating the model to identify any limitations and seeking to minimize biases present in the training datasets. Methods to reduce unsafe conduct, including iterative refinement through human feedback, should also be implemented.

Moreover, it's essential to maintain comprehensive documentation that outlines any known shortcomings and vulnerabilities of the model. This should consist of safety best practices that are tailored to both the specific model and its intended applications. This acknowledges the reality that no matter how thorough the preventive actions are, there is no way to completely negate the possibility of unintended harm occurring.

Thoughtfully Collaboration with Stakeholders

The third principle encourages thoughtful collaboration with stakeholders. This involves building teams with diverse backgrounds and soliciting broad input to ensure that the models operate effectively and fairly in the diverse real world.

Public disclosure of lessons learned regarding LLM safety and misuse is also encouraged to enable widespread adoption and facilitate cross-industry iteration on best practices. Furthermore, it is essential to treat all labor in the language model supply chain with respect, ensuring high standards for working conditions and well-specified standards for vendors.

These principles represent a significant first step in collaboratively guiding safer large language model development and deployment. As LLM providers, Cohere, OpenAI, and AI21 Labs are committed to working together and with other parties to identify further opportunities to reduce unintentional harms from and prevent malicious use of language models. This collaborative approach is a testament to their commitment to harnessing the potential of LLMs in a secure and responsible manner.

Confidence Checklist for Deploying Large Language Models in Production

When deploying LLMs in a production environment, there are several key considerations to ensure optimal performance, security, and user experience. This section provides a comprehensive checklist to guide you through the process, covering aspects such as output validation, DDoS attack preparation, user limit implementation, latency considerations, log and monitoring practices, and data privacy implementation.

Output Validation

Output validation is a crucial step in productionizing LLMs. It ensures the accuracy and reliability of the model's outputs. The stages of validation are as follows:

- **Basic Validation:** Start with simple checks such as looking for empty strings and character lengths.
- **Advanced Validation:** Progress to more complex validation techniques like checking for relevance and ranking results.
- **Expert Validation:** For a more in-depth analysis, use model-based checks. This involves using metrics such as perplexity and BLEU scores to evaluate the model's performance.

Prepare for DDoS Attacks

DDoS attacks can significantly impact the performance and availability of your LLM system. The steps to prepare for DDoS attacks are as follows:

- **Basic Preparation**: Implement a Captcha system to prevent automated bots from sending a large number of requests.
- **Advanced Preparation**: Implement rate-limiting and geo-blocking to manage the flow of incoming requests and block or limit access from known sources of DDoS attacks.
- **Expert Preparation**: Use IP-based monitoring, fingerprinting, Intrusion Detection and Prevention Systems (IDPS), and specialized DDoS protection services to proactively identify and mitigate potential DDoS attacks.

Building User Limits

User limits ensure that LLMs are used appropriately and protect users from potential misuse or abuse. The strategies for implementing user limits are as follows:

- **Basic Limits**: Implement client-side rate-limiting and debounce techniques.
- **Advanced Limits**: Set different limits for different users, organizations, or segments of users.
- **Expert Limits:** Implement dynamic rate-limiting, exponential decrease in limits for identified abuse, and fingerprinting. Also, start with lower limits and increase as trust increases.

Care About Latency

Low latency is essential for applications that require fast response times. The strategies to achieve low latency are as follows:

- **Basic Measures**: Implement streaming and use correct HTTP headers for efficient data transmission.
- **Advanced Measures**: Implement backoff techniques and caching to manage rate-limits and reduce latency.
- **Expert Measures**: Build fallbacks, use queues for storing requests, and implement semantic caching for optimal latency.

Avoid Retrofitting Logs and Monitoring Records for LLMs

Retrofitting can lead to inaccurate results as it relies on time-stamped log records, which may be incomplete or out of date. The strategies are as follows:

- **Basic Measures:** Live with poor visibility or pay for a monitoring service like Datadog or CloudWatch.
- **Expert Measures**: Build your own monitoring layer using tools like Elasticsearch, Kibana, and Grafana to collect and visualize your logs and metrics.

Implement Data Privacy

LLMs can potentially reveal private information, so it's essential to implement measures to protect customer privacy. The measures are as follows:

- **Basic Measures**: Use encryption, limit data access, and monitor your systems for signs of unauthorized access.
- **Advanced Measures**: Amend GDPR, Cookie, and Privacy Policies, and implement PII masking with tools like LangChain or LLamaIndex.
- **Expert Measures**: Use services like Microsoft/Presido or Azure that provide features such as data encryption, data masking, and data access control.

By following this comprehensive checklist, you can ensure the successful and secure deployment of your large language models in a production environment.

Understanding the Economics of Large Language Models

The journey from development to deployment of LLMs is not without its costs, which include expenses related to hardware, storage, and infrastructure. This section provides an in-depth analysis of the economics of LLMs, discussing the costs, optimization strategies, and necessary trade-offs.

Costs

The financial commitment involved in developing and deploying LLMs can be substantial. This is primarily due to the need for high-performance resources such as Graphics Processing Units (GPUs) or Tensor Processing Units (TPUs) to ensure low latency and high throughput during inference.

The cost of training an LLM can fluctuate based on several factors such as the model's size, the volume of training data, and the hardware used for training. For instance, it is estimated that the training of GPT-3 cost OpenAI around $5 million.

Moreover, the deployment of the model also incurs significant costs, including expenses related to hosting, maintenance, and updates. It's important to note that fine-tuning models like those from OpenAI can be approximately 7 times more expensive compared to around 1.6 times for open-source models.

Optimization

Several techniques can be employed to optimize the cost of LLM development and deployment. One of the most effective strategies is the judicious use of cloud computing for computational resources. Cloud computing offers cost-effective access to high-performance computing resources, enabling organizations to train and deploy LLMs at scale.

Additionally, techniques such as model compilation, model compression, and model sharding can be utilized to reduce the model's size while preserving its accuracy. These techniques can help decrease the deployment cost and enhance the model's performance.

Trade-offs

When developing and deploying LLMs, organizations need to consider several trade-offs. One of the most significant trade-offs is between cost and accuracy.

While more accurate LLMs require more data and computational resources, making them more expensive, less accurate LLMs may not deliver the desired performance level, potentially leading to decreased customer satisfaction and engagement.

Another trade-off to consider is between open-source and closed-source LLMs. While open-source LLMs may be less expensive to deploy, they might not offer the same performance level as their closed-source counterparts. Additionally, open-source LLMs may not be suitable for all use cases due to potential limitations in customization and support for specific applications.

Interestingly, lower parameter models can sometimes outperform larger models when fine-tuned for a specific use case. Moreover, the cost of using the model increases with an increase in the number of parameters of the model and with an increase in the context window, approximately by a factor of 2.

The economics of LLMs can be complex, encompassing costs, optimization techniques, and trade-offs. By optimizing the cost of LLM development and deployment, organizations can leverage the power of LLMs more effectively to achieve their business goals. However, it is crucial to consider the trade-offs involved in LLM development and deployment, including those between cost and accuracy, and between open-source and closed-source LLMs. By carefully considering these factors, organizations can develop and deploy LLMs that meet their specific needs and provide the desired level of performance at an optimal cost. Significant cost savings are possible without much harm to performance if the right trade-off is established between cost and performance.

LLMOps Adoption Blueprint

The "*LLMOps Adoption Blueprint*" is used as a guide designed to help organizations effectively implement and manage Large Language Models (LLMs). This blueprint provides a structured approach to navigate the complexities of LLM deployment, from assessing organizational readiness and identifying suitable use cases, to planning for implementation and adopting best practices. It also addresses crucial aspects such as security and ethical considerations, and provides strategies for scaling and optimizing LLM applications. By following this blueprint, organizations can harness the power of LLMs in a secure, ethical, and efficient manner, thereby enhancing their operations and maintaining a competitive edge in the market.

1. **Assess Organizational Readiness**
    - Capability Assessment
        - Evaluate the existing skills and expertise within the organization in areas such as data science, machine learning, natural language processing, and software engineering.
        - Identify skill gaps and create a plan to bridge them through training, hiring, or partnering with external experts.
        - Establish a dedicated LLMOps team with clearly defined roles and responsibilities.
    - Infrastructure Evaluation
        - Assess the current IT infrastructure's capacity to support large-scale LLM deployments, including storage, computing power, and network bandwidth.
        - Identify necessary hardware and software upgrades or additions to ensure optimal performance and scalability.
        - Consider cloud-based solutions for flexibility and cost-efficiency.
    - Security and Compliance
        - Review the organization's data security and privacy policies to ensure compliance with relevant regulations (for example, GDPR, HIPAA, CCPA).
        - Develop a comprehensive security framework for LLM deployments, including data encryption, access controls, and monitoring systems.
        - Establish a governance structure to oversee the ethical use of LLMs and ensure adherence to organizational values and legal requirements.
2. **Identify Suitable Use Cases**
    - Needs Analysis
        - Conduct a thorough analysis of the organization's processes, workflows, and challenges to identify areas where LLMs can provide significant value.
        - Engage with stakeholders from various departments to gather insights and understand their specific needs and pain points.
        - Prioritize use cases based on their potential impact, alignment with business objectives, and feasibility of implementation.

- Feasibility Study
  - Assess the technical feasibility of implementing LLMs for each identified use case, considering factors such as data availability, model complexity, and integration with existing systems.
  - Evaluate the financial viability of each use case by estimating the costs associated with development, deployment, and maintenance, as well as the expected return on investment (ROI).
  - Identify potential risks and challenges associated with each use case and develop mitigation strategies.
- Pilot Projects:
  - Select one or two high-priority use cases for pilot projects to validate assumptions, test the LLMOps pipeline, and gather user feedback.
  - Establish clear objectives, success metrics, and timelines for each pilot project.
  - Allocate necessary resources, including personnel, budget, and infrastructure, to ensure the success of the pilot projects.

3. **Plan for Implementation**
   - Data Management
     - Develop a comprehensive data management strategy that covers data collection, cleaning, labeling, storage, and governance.
     - Ensure the quality, diversity, and representativeness of the training data to minimize bias and improve model performance.
     - Implement data version control and lineage tracking to maintain data integrity and reproducibility.
   - Model Development and Training
     - Select the most appropriate LLMs for each use case based on factors such as performance, scalability, and ease of integration.
     - Develop a standardized pipeline for model training, testing, and evaluation, leveraging automation tools and best practices.
     - Establish a framework for model versioning, experiment tracking, and hyperparameter optimization to facilitate continuous improvement.
   - Deployment Strategy
     - Evaluate the pros and cons of different deployment options, such as cloud-based, on-premise, or hybrid, considering factors such as cost, scalability, and security.

    - Design a deployment architecture that ensures high availability, fault tolerance, and efficient resource utilization.
    - Develop a plan for continuous deployment and rollback mechanisms to minimize downtime and ensure smooth updates.

4. **Adopt LLMOps Best Practices**
    - Collaborative Development
        - Foster a culture of collaboration and knowledge sharing among data scientists, ML engineers, and software developers.
        - Establish clear communication channels and workflows to facilitate seamless collaboration and reduce silos.
        - Encourage the use of version control systems, code reviews, and documentation to maintain code quality and reproducibility.
    - Continuous Integration and Delivery (CI/CD)
        - Implement a robust CI/CD pipeline that automates the building, testing, and deployment of LLM applications.
        - Integrate code quality checks, unit tests, and integration tests into the CI/CD pipeline to catch issues early and ensure the stability of the deployed models.
        - Establish a release management process that includes staging environments, canary releases, and rollback mechanisms.
    - Monitoring and Maintenance
        - Implement comprehensive monitoring systems to track the performance, health, and usage of deployed LLMs in real-time.
        - Set up alerts and notifications to proactively identify and address issues, such as model drift, data anomalies, or system failures.
        - Establish a maintenance schedule for regular model updates, data refreshes, and infrastructure optimizations to ensure optimal performance and relevance.

5. **Address Security and Ethical Considerations**
    - Security Measures
        - Implement a multi-layered security approach that includes data encryption, secure communication protocols, and access controls.
        - Regularly conduct security audits and penetration testing to identify and address vulnerabilities.

  - Develop an incident response plan to effectively handle security breaches or data leaks.
- Ethical Guidelines
  - Establish a set of ethical principles and guidelines for the development, deployment, and use of LLMs within the organization.
  - Ensure transparency in the decision-making processes involving LLMs, and provide clear explanations to users about the limitations and potential biases of the models.
  - Implement fairness and non-discrimination measures to prevent the perpetuation of societal biases and ensure equitable treatment of all users.
- Privacy Protection
  - Develop and enforce strict data privacy policies that comply with relevant regulations and protect user data.
  - Implement data anonymization and pseudonymization techniques to minimize the risk of re-identification.
  - Provide users with clear information about data collection, usage, and sharing practices, and obtain explicit consent when required.

6. **Scale and Optimize**
   - Scalability Planning
     - Anticipate future growth and increased demand for LLM applications, and plan for scalability accordingly.
     - Design the infrastructure and architecture to support horizontal and vertical scaling, leveraging technologies such as containerization and orchestration.
     - Conduct load testing and performance benchmarking to identify bottlenecks and optimize resource allocation.
   - Performance Optimization
     - Continuously monitor and analyze performance metrics, such as response times, throughput, and resource utilization, to identify opportunities for optimization.
     - Implement caching mechanisms, data compression, and efficient data retrieval techniques to reduce latency and improve overall performance.
     - Explore advanced techniques such as model compression, quantization, and pruning to reduce the computational and memory footprint of LLMs.

- Cost Optimization
    - Monitor and analyze the costs associated with LLM deployments, including infrastructure, data storage, and API usage.
    - Identify cost-saving opportunities, such as rightsizing resources, using spot instances, or negotiating better pricing with service providers.
    - Implement cost allocation and budgeting mechanisms to ensure the financial sustainability of LLM initiatives.

Checklist for LLMOps Deployment

1. Organizational Readiness Assessment
    - Capability Assessment Completed
    - Infrastructure Evaluation Completed
    - Security and Compliance Review Completed
2. Suitable Use Cases Identification
    - Needs Analysis Conducted
    - Feasibility Study Completed
    - Pilot Projects Selected
3. Implementation Planning
    - Data Management Strategy Developed
    - Model Development and Training Pipeline Established
    - Deployment Strategy Chosen
4. Best Practices Adoption
    - Collaborative Development Processes Implemented
    - CI/CD Pipeline Set Up
    - Monitoring and Maintenance Systems Established
5. Security and Ethical Considerations
    - Security Measures Implemented
    - Ethical Guidelines Developed
    - Privacy Protection Mechanisms in Place

6. Scalability and Optimization
    - Scalability Planning Completed
    - Performance Optimization Measures Identified
    - Cost Optimization Strategies Implemented

By following this comprehensive LLMOps adoption blueprint and utilizing the provided checklist, organizations can systematically assess their readiness, identify suitable use cases, plan for implementation, adopt best practices, address security and ethical considerations, and scale and optimize their LLM deployments. This structured approach ensures that all critical aspects are considered and addressed, maximizing the chances of successful LLMOps adoption and realizing the full potential of large language models within the organization.

Conclusion

In this comprehensive exploration of LLMOps, we have delved into the intricate details of their operations, deployment strategies, and economic considerations.

We started with an introduction to LLMOps, and then moved on to the key components of LLMOps, including data preparation, model training, evaluation, deployment, and monitoring.

We discussed the importance of data management in LLMOps, highlighting the steps involved such as data collection, preprocessing, labeling, annotation, and storage. We compared the traditional development process with the platform LLMOps approach, emphasizing the unique aspects of LLMOps that set it apart from MLOps, such as the use of computational resources, transfer learning, human feedback, and hyperparameter tuning.

We then explored the best practices for LLMOps, from exploratory data analysis to model fine-tuning, review, governance, inference, serving, and monitoring. We also discussed the benefits of LLMOps, such as efficiency, scalability, risk reduction, and enhanced customer experience, along with the challenges it presents, including handling large model sizes, complex datasets, continuous monitoring, and evaluation.

We delved into the strategies for deploying LLMs, considering factors like latency, cost management, resource management, and the choice between cloud-based or on-premise deployment. We also discussed the importance of continuous integration and delivery (CI/CD), monitoring, maintenance, scalability, and performance optimization.

Security and privacy in LLM deployment were also addressed, emphasizing data privacy, protection, encryption, access controls, model security, and regulatory compliance. We also discussed the joint recommendations for LLM deployment by leading organizations like Cohere, OpenAI, and AI21 Labs.

Finally, we explored the economics of LLMs, discussing the costs involved, optimization techniques, and the trade-offs to consider. We highlighted the need for output validation, preparation for DDoS attacks, building user limits, and the importance of data privacy.

The journey through the world of LLMs, LLMOps, and their economics has provided us with a comprehensive understanding of these complex models. This knowledge is crucial for leveraging the power of LLMs effectively and responsibly, enabling us to harness their potential to transform various applications and industries. As we continue to innovate and explore in this field, this understanding will serve as a guiding light, leading us towards more efficient, effective, and ethical use of LLMs.

In the next chapter, we will perform a hands-on implementation of LLMOps by leveraging popular tech stacks.

Chapter 12

Implementing LLMOps in Practice Using MLflow on Databricks

Introduction

As the landscape of artificial intelligence (AI) continues to evolve, one of the most transformative advancements is the development and deployment of large language models (LLMs). These models, capable of understanding and generating human-like text, are revolutionizing numerous sectors from customer support to content creation. However, the management and operationalization of these LLMs in production environments present unique challenges, giving rise to a new field known as large language model operations, or LLMOps.

LLMOps is an amalgamation of practices, techniques, and tools aimed at the efficient and scalable management of LLMs. It aims to automate various stages of the LLM life cycle, including experimentation, iteration, deployment, and continuous improvement. By streamlining these processes, LLMOps not only enhances efficiency but also reduces risks associated with manual interventions.

The adoption of LLMOps allows data teams to expedite model and pipeline development, paving the way for efficient utilization of resources. Moreover, it provides a framework for managing and monitoring thousands of models, enabling continuous integration, delivery, and deployment at a scale previously unimaginable.

While LLMOps draws parallels with MLOps (machine learning operations), it also addresses unique challenges posed by LLMs. These include handling vast volumes of data and ensuring the safe and responsible use of LLMs. Consequently, LLMOps necessitate collaboration among data scientists, DevOps engineers, and IT professionals, each playing a critical role in the successful deployment of LLMs.

The comprehensive solution showcased in this chapter, implemented in Python, serves as a robust demonstration of LLMOps in action. It embodies an end-to-end LLMOps process, encompassing every phase from data ingestion to text summarization, and culminating in the adept management of MLflow tasks. This solution effectively utilizes the MLflow tracking system for seamless experiment logging and model management and harnesses the power of Hugging Face transformers for insightful text summarization.

This is not just an assortment of disparate elements, but a tightly integrated, holistic workflow that mirrors real-world implementation of LLMOps. It is a tangible manifestation of LLMOps practices, methodologies, and tools, illustrating how they unite to orchestrate operations that are efficient, scalable, and risk-optimized.

In this chapter, we delve deep into these areas, utilizing this holistic workflow as a practical guide on the benefits and pragmatic aspects of LLMOps. As you navigate this chapter, you will gain a profound understanding of the operational management of LLMs. You will get an intimate look at how various tools, techniques, and practices come together in a real-world LLMOps workflow. This knowledge will empower you to implement LLMOps effectively in your projects, making the most of its potential.

The code for this exercise can be found here: https://github.com/ava-orange-education/Hands-On-Large-Language-Models-for-Enterprise/tree/main/Chapter12

Structure

In this chapter, the following topics will be covered:

- Understanding the LLMOps Technology Stack
- The LLMOps Process and Use Case Overview
- Setting Up and Configuring Pre-requisites for LLMOps
- Exploring LLMOps Code: A Detailed Walkthrough

Technological Stacks in LLMOps Implementation

Implementing large language model operations (LLMOps) efficiently involves leveraging various technological tools and platforms. These technologies are paramount in enabling a smooth and scalable LLMOps pipeline, from initial data ingestion to final model deployment and management. Here, we delve into these essential components in detail.

- **Azure Databricks**: Azure Databricks forms the core computational platform for our LLMOps implementation. As an Apache Spark-based analytics platform, Azure Databricks offers a unified and collaborative workspace conducive to large-scale data processing and machine learning tasks. Its seamless integration with other Azure services and built-in support for MLflow further adds to its utility in our LLMOps workflow.
- **Python**: As our primary programming language, Python brings simplicity, versatility, and a broad spectrum of library support to the table. Given its readability and widespread adoption in data science and machine learning, Python forms the coding backbone of our implementation.
- **MLflow**: MLflow, an open-source platform, is fundamental to managing the machine learning lifecycle. It handles tasks like tracking experiments, logging model parameters, and maintaining the model lifecycle, making it an indispensable part of our tech stack.
- **Hugging Face Transformers**: We use this state-of-the-art library to employ pre-trained models for text summarization tasks. Hugging Face Transformers provides us with a robust framework for analyzing and generating human-like text.
- **Pandas**: For data analysis and manipulation, we rely on the Pandas library. Its flexible data structures simplify data preprocessing and handling, ensuring efficient data flow through our pipeline.

Alongside these tools, our LLMOps implementation incorporates several best practices such as data sampling, model versioning, and model lifecycle management. These techniques, in conjunction with our chosen technologies, allow for an efficient, scalable, and robust LLMOps workflow.

By integrating these technologies into a comprehensive workflow, our LLMOps implementation exemplifies the operational management of large language models. Understanding these tools and techniques will empower you to leverage LLMOps' potential, driving efficiency, scalability, and risk reduction in your own projects.

High-Level Overview of the Implementation Pipeline

Let us first comprehend the foundational elements of the pipeline, making the subsequent implementation steps straightforward to understand and execute.

- **Data Ingestion and Pre-processing:** The pipeline begins with the ingestion of data, accomplished using the Pandas library. The data, stored in a CSV format, is loaded into a Pandas DataFrame. Depending on the requirements, pre-processing steps such as data cleaning and normalization might be undertaken.
- **Text Summarization**: The pre-processed data is then passed to the text summarization model, a pre-trained model from the Hugging Face Transformers library. This model analyzes the input text and creates a summarized output.
- **Experiment Tracking and Model Logging:** As the model generates summarized texts, these predictions, along with the model parameters and performance metrics, are logged using MLflow. This allows for robust experiment tracking, performance comparison, and a detailed record of the modeling process.
- **Model Registration and Lifecycle Management**: After the model is trained and evaluated, it is registered in the MLflow model registry. This registry serves as a collaborative hub where data science teams can share models, make comments, and transition models through various stages such as staging, production, and archived.
- **Model Serving with Databricks**: In the final stage of the pipeline, the registered model is served using the model serving capabilities of Azure Databricks. This enables the deployment of the model as a web service, which can be accessed and used to make predictions. The model-serving component of Databricks provides a robust, scalable, and efficient way to deploy models, making it an essential aspect of our LLMOps pipeline.

This pipeline presents a comprehensive LLMOps workflow, seamlessly integrating various stages of the large language model life cycle. From data ingestion to model serving, each stage plays a critical role in ensuring an efficient and scalable process, embodying the principles of LLMOps.

Step-by-Step Overview of the Implementation

This section provides a detailed, step-by-step overview of an LLMOps pipeline that leverages MLflow, a popular open-source platform designed to manage the entire machine learning life cycle.

The pipeline includes stages from initializing the MLflow handler, creating and logging a model instance, registering the model, transitioning the model through various stages ('Staging' and 'Production'), and making predictions at each stage.

Additionally, this pipeline incorporates a **`DataLoader`** class for loading and sampling data, and a Databricks serving component for model serving. This comprehensive walkthrough will help you understand the intricacies of managing ML models and the importance of each stage in a typical MLflow-based pipeline.

- **Data Loading**: The **`DataLoader`** class is used to load data from a specified file path. A random sample of the data is returned.
- **Initialize MLflow handler**: An instance of **`MLflowHandler`** is created. This handler is used to interact with the MLflow tracking server.
- **Create Model Instance**: An instance of the Summarizer model is created. This model is presumably a machine learning model for summarizing text.
- **Start MLflow Run and Log Parameters**: An MLflow run is started using the **`start_run`** method of the **`MLflowHandler`**. The parameters of the summarizer model are logged as part of this run.
- **Log the Model:** The summarizer model is logged to the MLflow tracking server. The model artifact is stored in a directory named **`_pipeline/summarizer`**.
- **Register the Model:** The logged model is registered in the MLflow Model Registry under the name "**`model summarizer`**".
- **Search for Registered Models**: The MLflow Model Registry is searched for models registered under the name "**`model summarizer`**".
- **Load Model Version 1**: The first version of the registered model "**`model summarizer`**" is loaded from the MLflow Model Registry.
- **Predict Using Model Version 1**: The loaded model is used to make a prediction on the first review in the reviews list.
- **Transition Model to `'Staging'` Stage**: The model's stage is transitioned to 'Staging' in the MLflow Model Registry.
- **Load Model from `'Staging'` Stage**: The model in the **`'Staging'`** stage is loaded from the MLflow Model Registry.
- **Predict Using the Model from `'Staging'`**: The loaded model from the 'Staging' stage is used to make a prediction on the first review in the reviews list.

- **Transition Model to `'Production'` Stage**: The model's stage is transitioned to 'Production' in the MLflow Model Registry.
- **Load Model from `'Production'` Stage**: The model in the 'Production' stage is loaded from the MLflow Model Registry.
- **Predict Using the Model from `'Production'`**: The loaded model from the 'Production' stage is used to make a prediction on the first review in the reviews list.
- **Databricks Serving Component**: The model is deployed to a Databricks cluster for serving. This allows for scalable, real-time predictions.

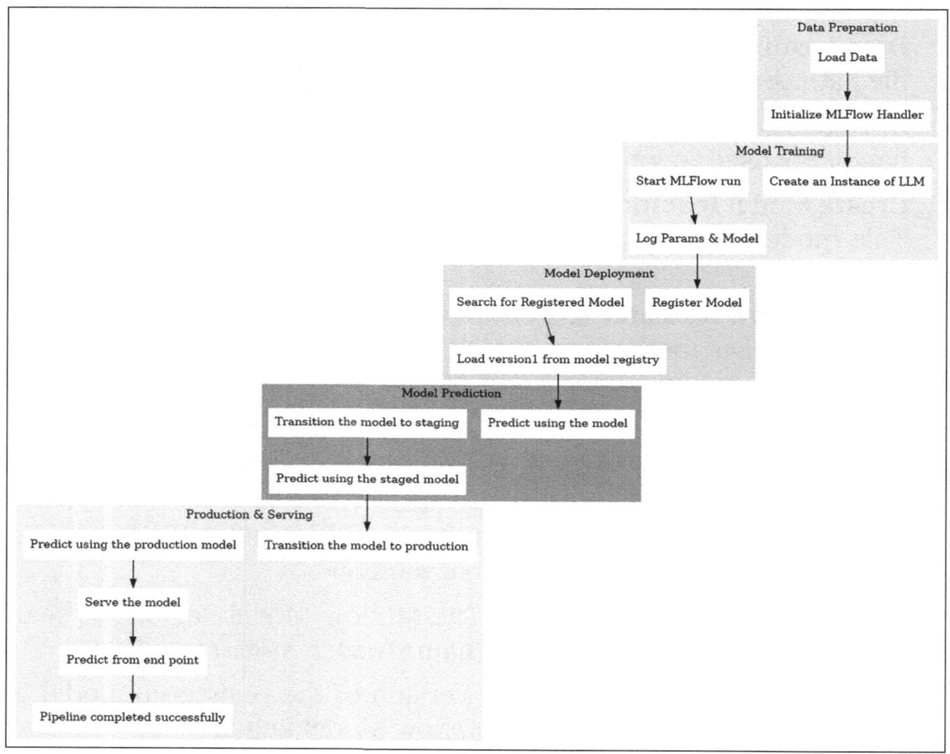

Figure 12.1: *A High-Level LLMOps Process*

Pre-requisite: Setup and Configuration

We are leveraging Azure Databricks for this implementation as it would be as close to a production system as possible for real-time large-scale production use cases.

1. Begin by signing up or logging in to Databricks through this link: https://www.databricks.com/try-databricks#account. Provide your details and click **`Continue.`**

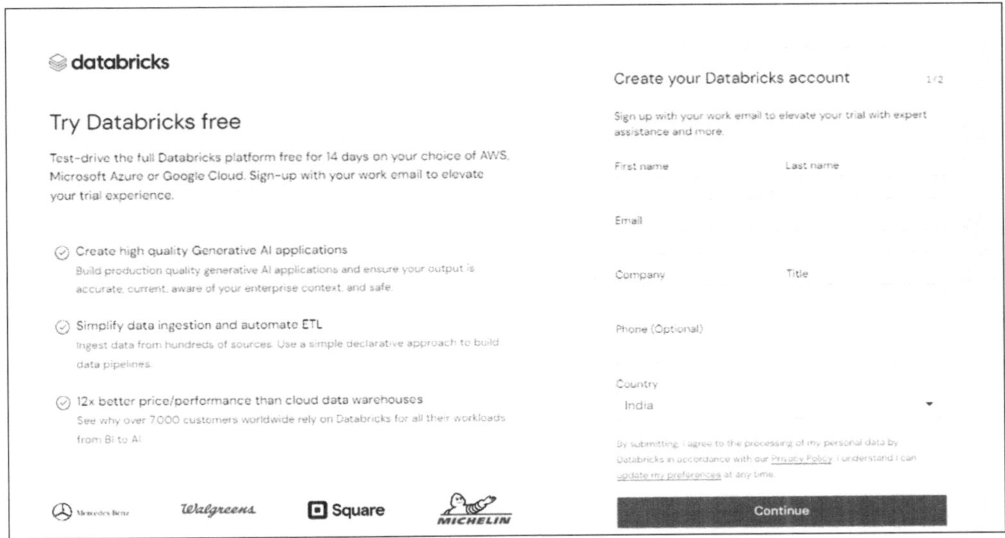

Figure 12.2: *Databricks Login Console*

2. Choose your desired cloud service provider for infrastructure support. In this instance, we are choosing Azure.

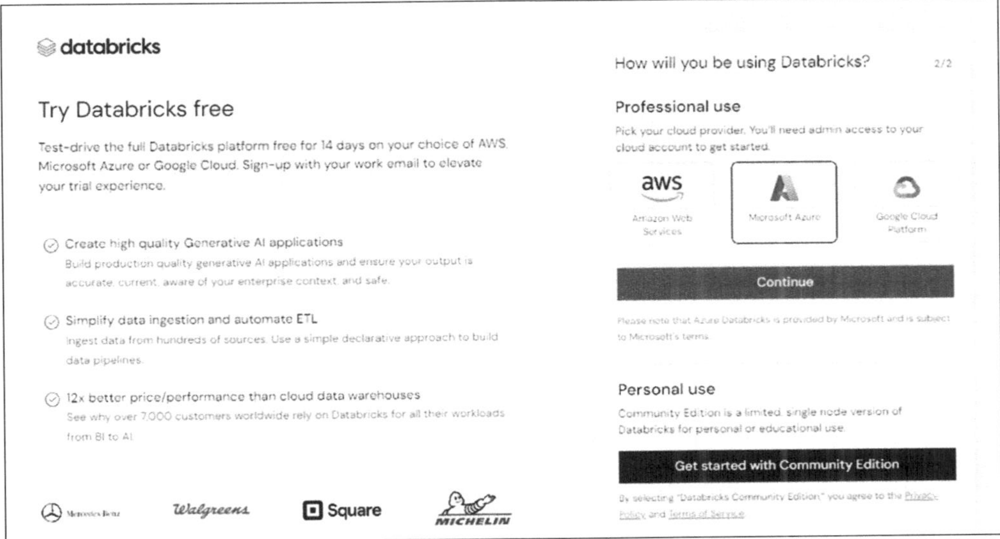

Figure 12.3: *Databricks: Choose Service Provider*

3. Once you have successfully signed up and selected Azure as your cloud service provider, you will be redirected to the landing page. Proceed by clicking the `Take me to Azure Databricks` button.

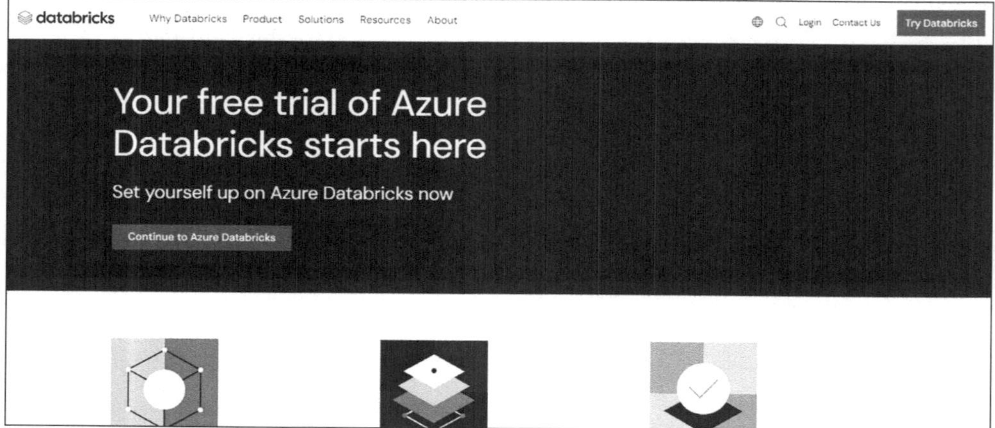

Figure 12.4: *Go to Azure*

4. You will be navigated to a new page. As a new Azure user, you can take advantage of the **`Try Azure for free`** offer. If not, you may need to **`Create a pay-as-you-go account`**.

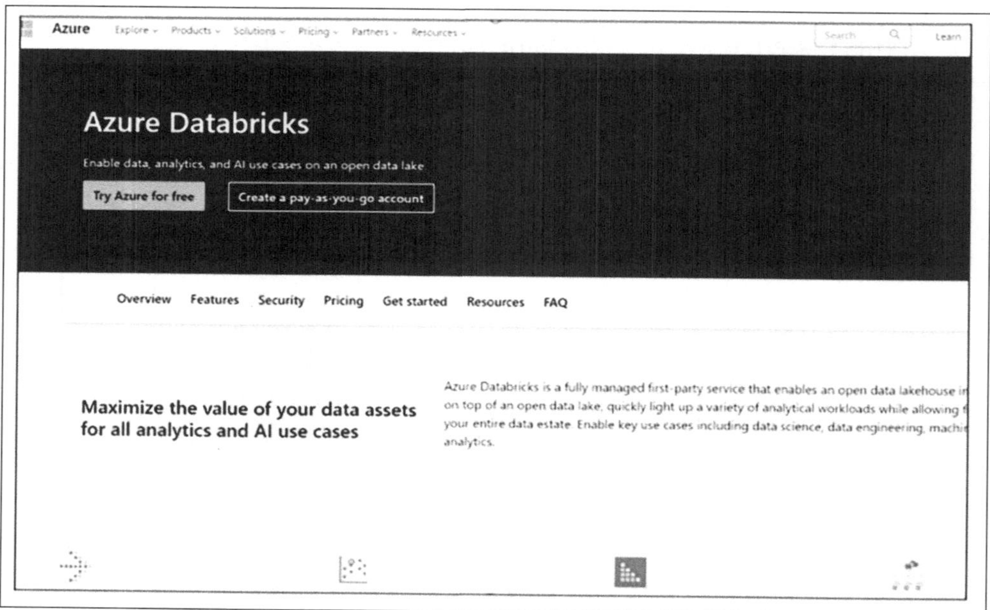

Figure 12.5: *Choose Subscription Type*

5. The process in the previous step also applies to the subsequent page.

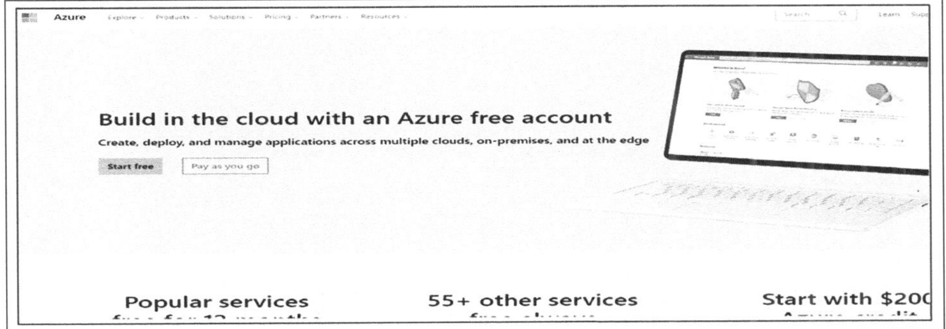

Figure 12.6: *Apply Subscription Type*

6. Navigate to the services search bar in Azure, input **`Azure Databricks`**, and select the **`Azure Databricks`** service from the dropdown options.

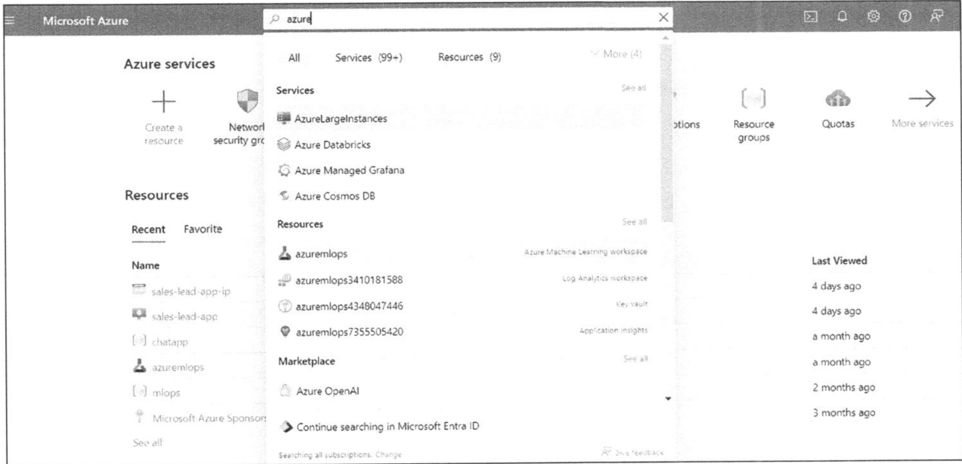

Figure 12.7: *Search Databricks Service*

7. You will then need to create an Azure Databricks workspace. Click **`Create`** located on the top left corner or select **`Create Azure Databricks Service`**.

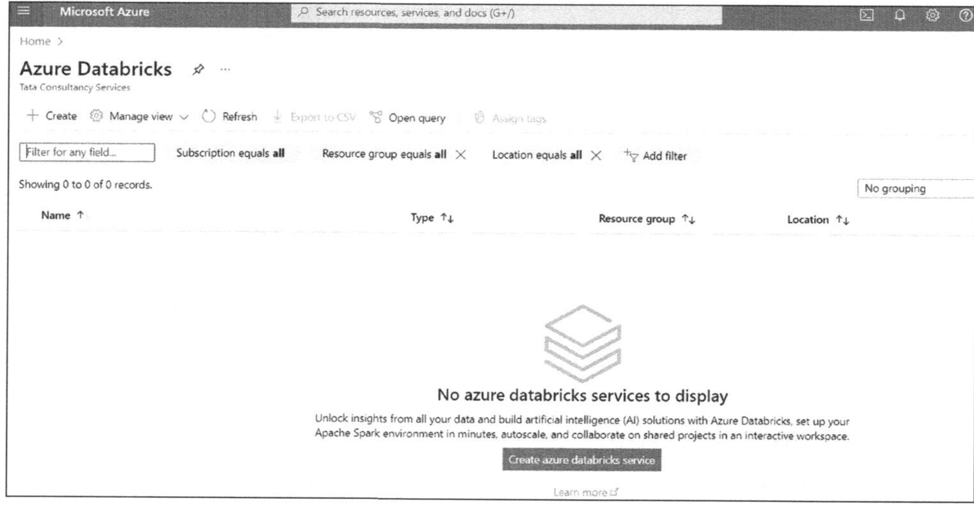

Figure 12.8: *Create Service*

8. Choose your subscription, either based on a free trial or a pay-as-you-go plan. Fill in the required fields. New users can utilize the 14-day trial offered by Azure and Databricks under the pricing tier. After completing the required fields, click "`Review + Create`" button.

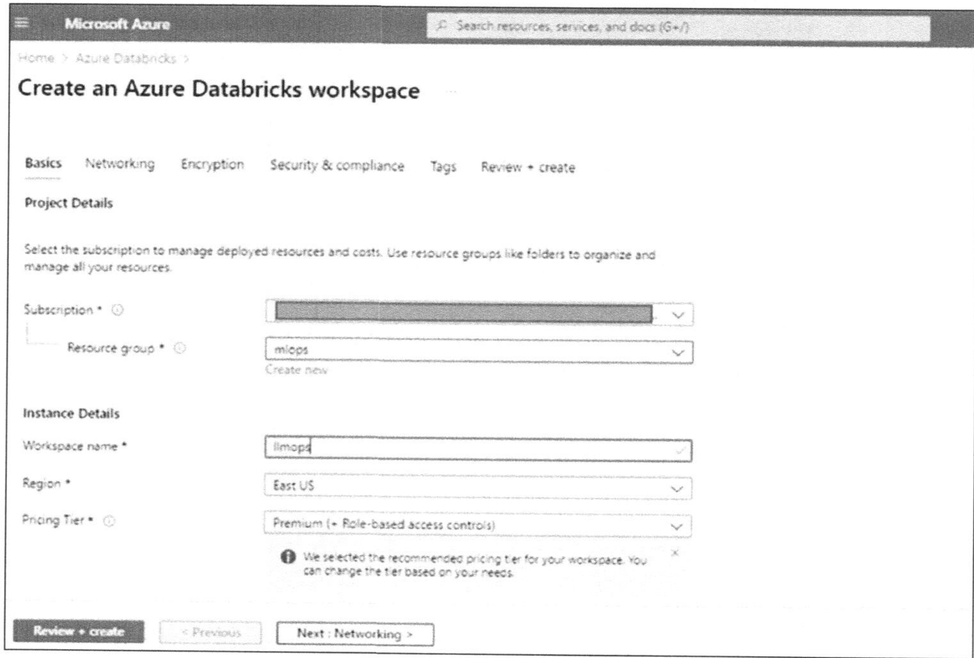

Figure 12.9: *Review Workspace*

9. Proceed by clicking **`Create`** and patiently wait for the deployment to complete.

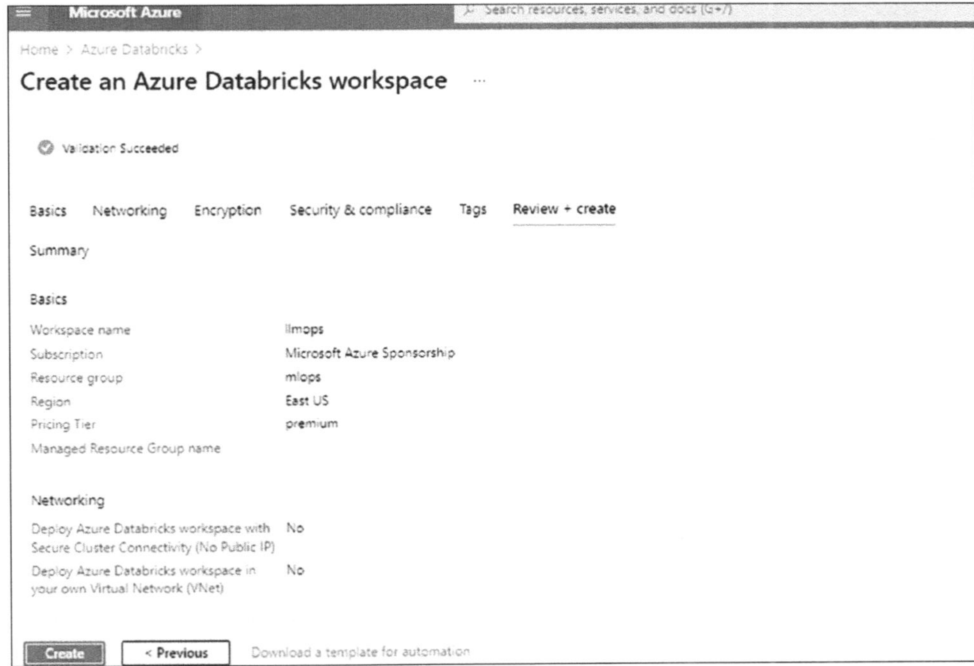

Figure 12.10: *Create Workspace*

The following figures shows that "**`...Deployment is in progress`**":

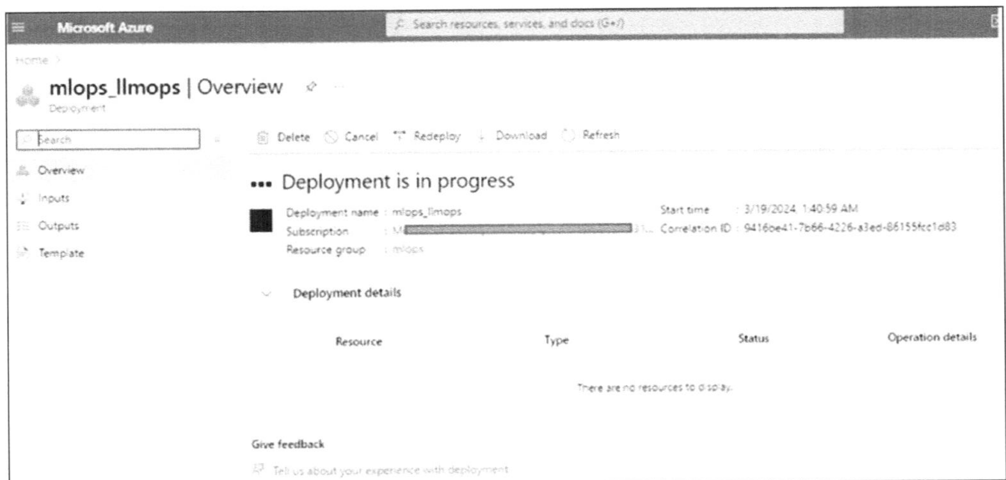

Figure 12.11: *Workspace Deployment in Progress*

10. After deployment, click **`Go To Resource`** button.

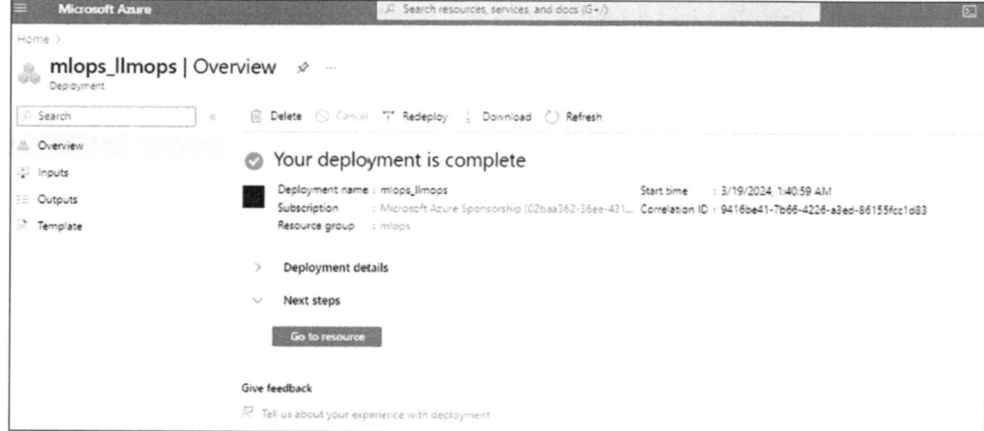

Figure 12.12: *Resource Navigation*

11. On the resource landing page, click **`Launch Workspace`**.

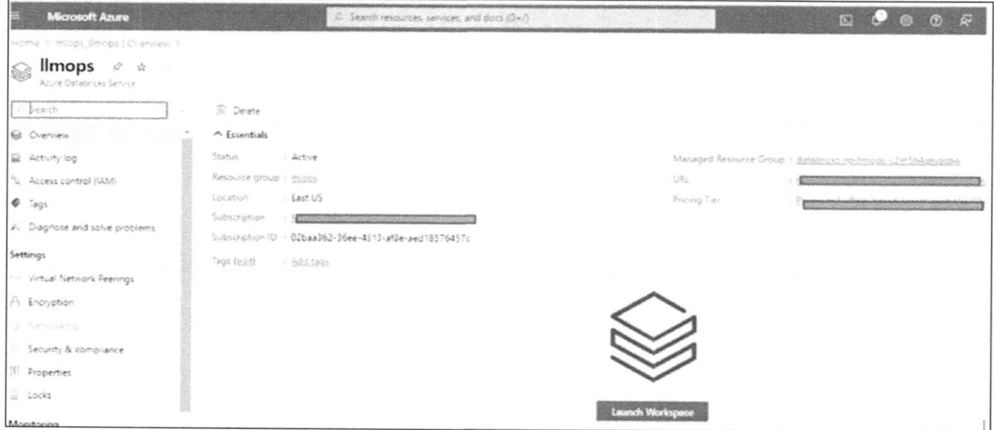

Figure 12.13: *Launch Workspace*

12. Clicking this button will automatically log you into the **`Azure Databricks`** workspace.

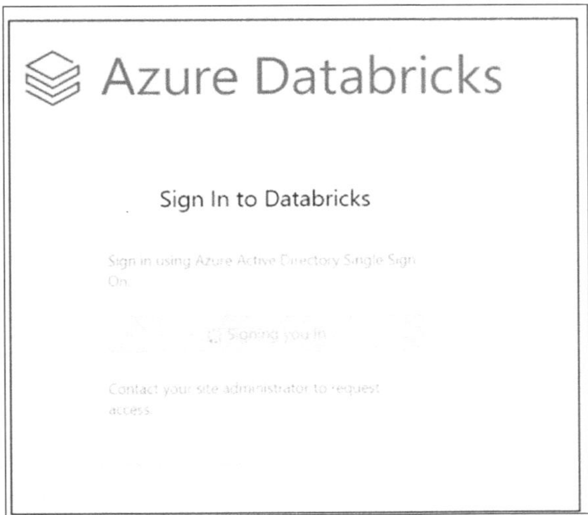

Figure 12.14: *Launch Workspace in Progress*

13. Within the Databricks console, choose **`Training ML Models`** from the dropdown as your preferred experience and click **`Finish.`**

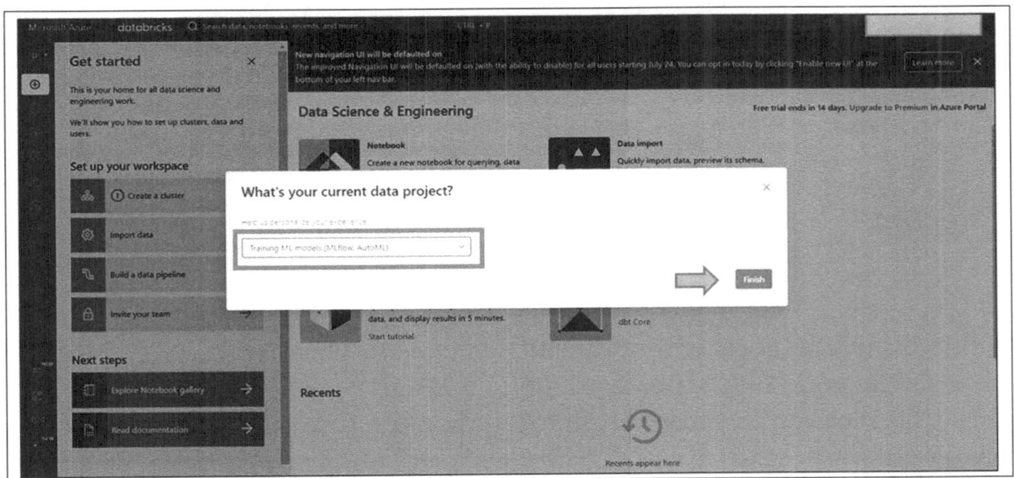

Figure 12.15: *Select Project Type*

14. This will take you to the **`Get Started`** page.

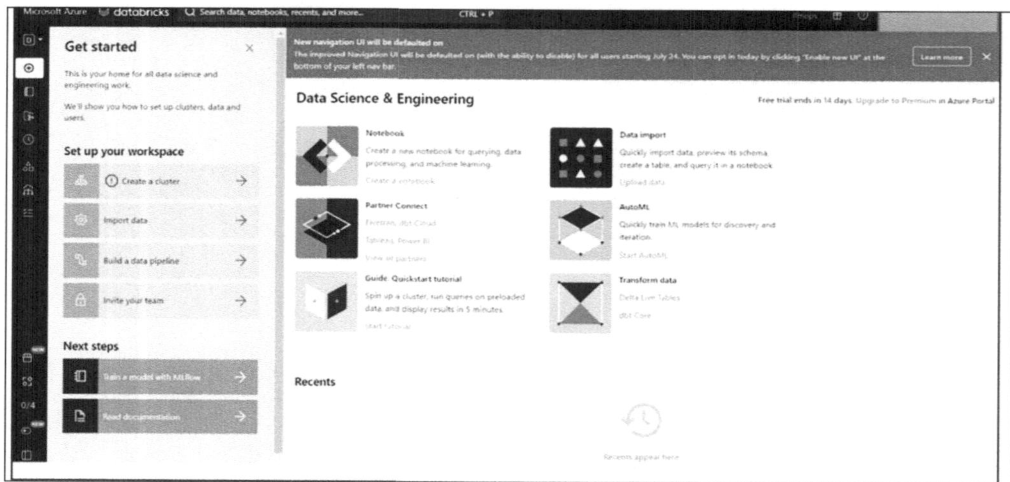

Figure 12.16: *Project - Get Started*

15. On the left side panel, select **`Machine Learning`** from the first dropdown to customize your settings and options.

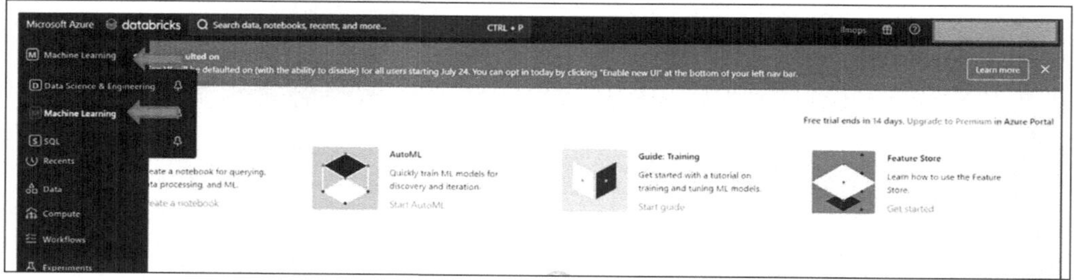

Figure 12.17: *Project Scope*

16. Next, click **`Compute`** from the left-side panel. This step involves creating a single-node machine infrastructure where we will run our experiments. Click **`Create Compute`** button located on the top-right corner.

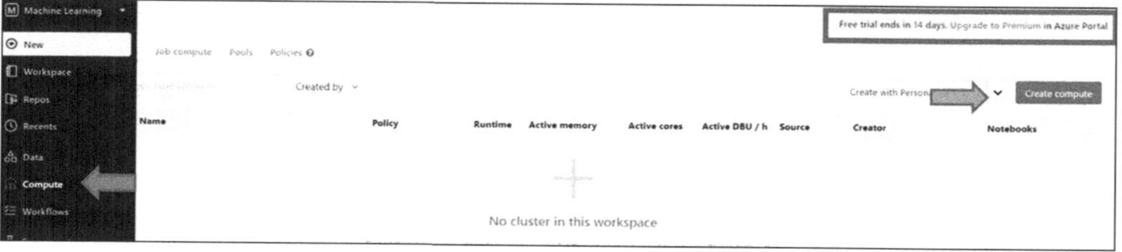

Figure 12.18: *Create Compute*

17. In the cluster creation UI, select **Single Node** for the node type, set Access mode as **Single User**, and specify a suitable time frame for termination. For faster computation, you can change the node type to **Standard_D8s_v3**, which provides 32GB memory with 8 cores. The remaining values can be set as default.

Figure 12.19: *Cluster Configuration*

18. After completing the configuration, click **Create Cluster** button located at the bottom left of the page.

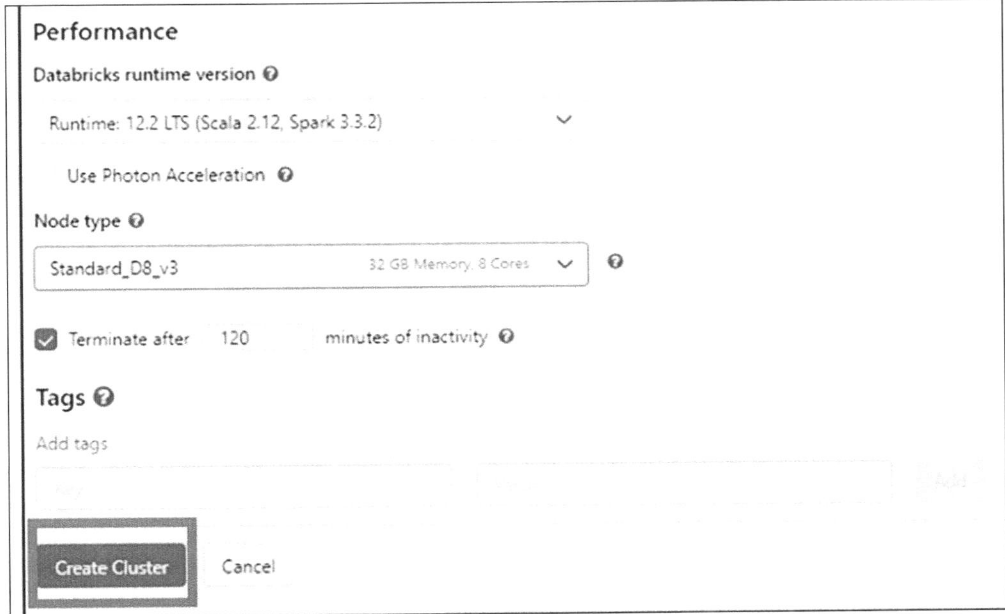

Figure 12.20: *Cluster Creation*

19. Allow a few seconds to minutes for the cluster to be created.

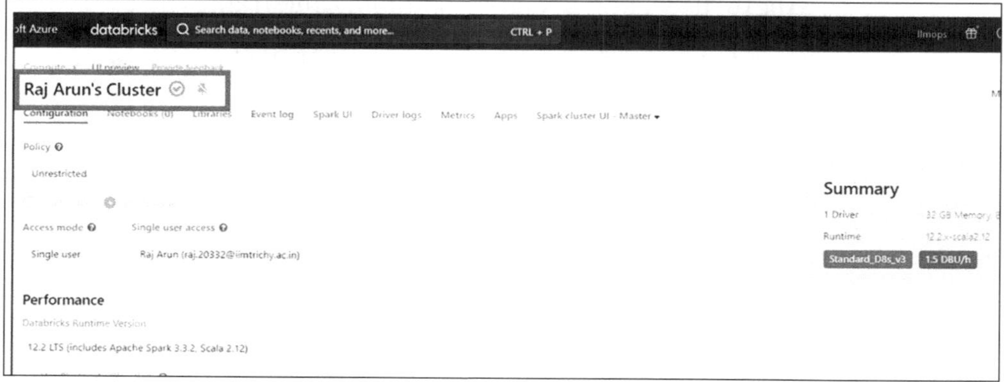

Figure 12.21: *Cluster Created*

20. Upon returning to the Compute section from the left-side panel, you should see the single-node cluster instance that was created.

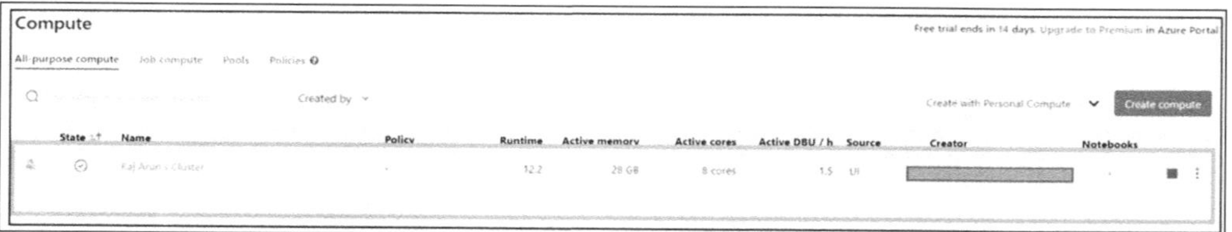

Figure 12.22: *List of Computes*

21. With the machine now created, it is time to create a Databricks notebook for running our LLMOps process code. From the left-hand side panel, select **`Workspace`**, and then from the user's tab, select your username. Click on the drop-down arrow, then click **`Create`** and select **`Notebook`**. This creates a Databricks notebook for running Python code, which will by default be attached to the cluster we created earlier. Name the notebook **`LLMOps`**.

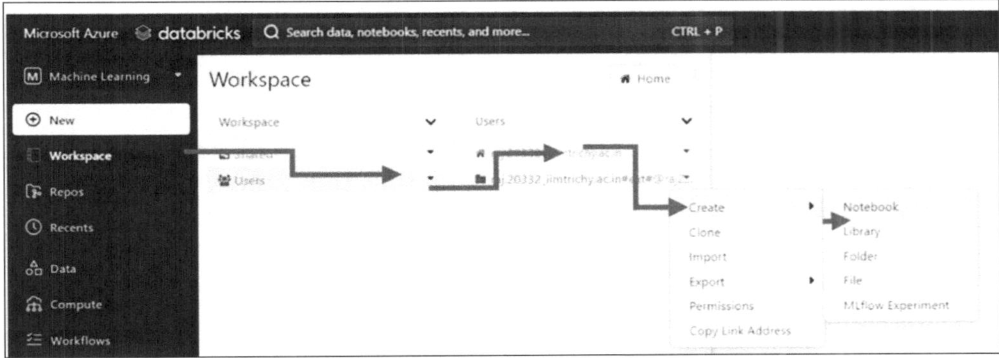

Figure 12.23: *Databricks Notebook Creation*

22. Additionally, create a folder for use during the exercise. Navigate to the **`Workspace`** from the left-side panel, select **`Users`**, and then the user under which the notebook was created. Click on the drop-down arrow, select **`Create`**, and then select **`Folder`**. Name this folder "**`LLM`**":

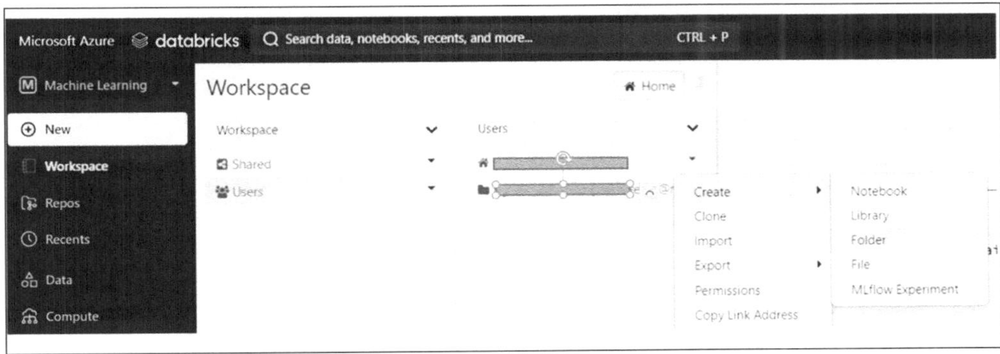

Figure 12.24: *Databricks Folder Creation*

23. Finally, both the **`LLMOps`** Databricks notebook and the **`LLM`** folder should now be visible under the user.

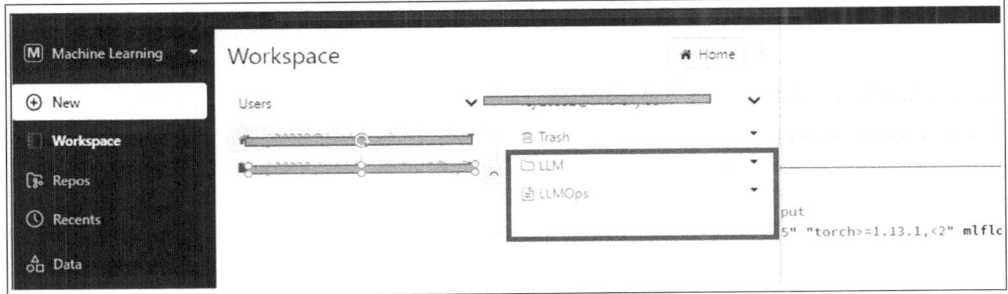

Figure 12.25: *Setup Verification*

Code Structure

We have created three classes for this use case:

- `DataLoader`: The `DataLoader` class provides a structured way to load and sample data from a file. By encapsulating this functionality in a class, the code becomes more organized, reusable, and easier to maintain, as the data loading logic is centralized in one place. This class can be instantiated and used wherever data needs to be loaded and sampled in the application, promoting code reusability.

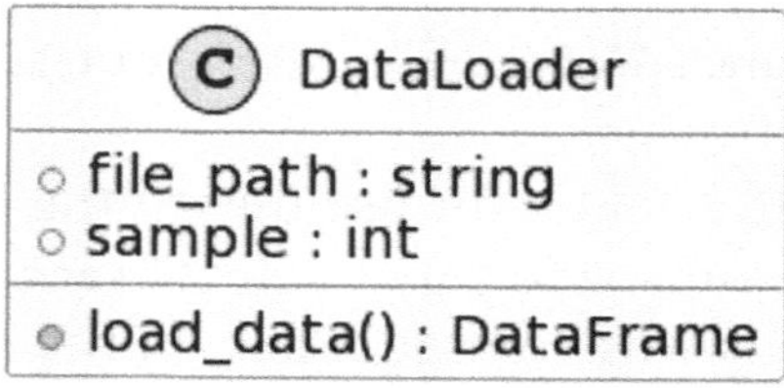

Figure 12.26: *DataLoader Class*

- `Summarizer`: The `Summarizer` class provides a structured approach to text summarization. It makes the summarization process reusable and maintainable by encapsulating the related functionality in a single class. This class can be instantiated wherever text summarization is required in the application, ensuring code reusability and organization.

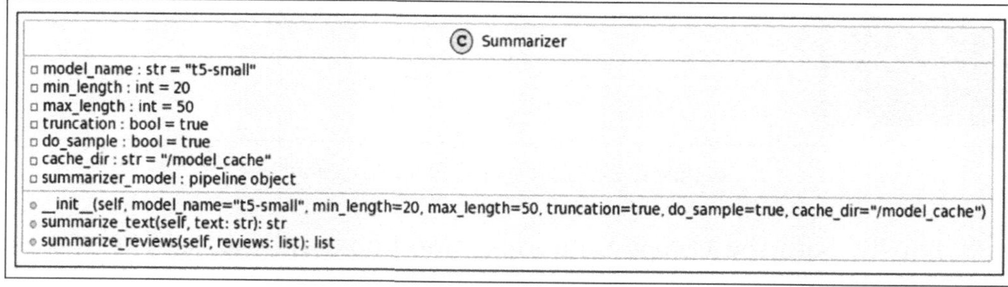

Figure 12.27: *Summarizer Class*

- `MLflowHandler`: The `MLflowHandler` class provides a structured way to manage MLflow experiments and models. By encapsulating the related functionality in a single class, the code becomes more organized, reusable, and easier to maintain. This class can be instantiated wherever MLflow experiment or model management is required in the application, promoting code reusability and organization.

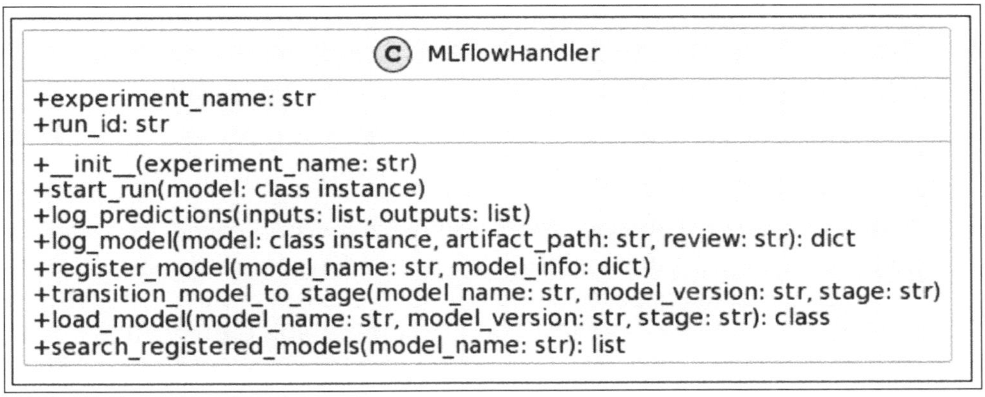

(C) MLflowHandler

+experiment_name: str
+run_id: str

+__init__(experiment_name: str)
+start_run(model: class instance)
+log_predictions(inputs: list, outputs: list)
+log_model(model: class instance, artifact_path: str, review: str): dict
+register_model(model_name: str, model_info: dict)
+transition_model_to_stage(model_name: str, model_version: str, stage: str)
+load_model(model_name: str, model_version: str, stage: str): class
+search_registered_models(model_name: str): list

Figure 12.28: *MLflowHandler Class*

Detailed Code Walkthrough

Now let us dive into the code specifics to gain a deep understanding of the pipeline's inner workings.

DataLoader

The `DataLoader` class encapsulates the functionality of loading data from a file and sampling a subset of that data. Its primary purpose is to abstract the process of data loading and sampling, making the operation reusable, organized, and more maintainable.

Here are the key components of this class:

Attributes:

- `file_path (string)`: This attribute stores the path to the data file from which data needs to be loaded.
- `sample (integer)`: This attribute specifies the number of random samples to be returned from the loaded data.

Methods:

- `__init__(self, file_path, sample)`: The `__init__` method is a special method in Python classes, also known as a constructor. This method is automatically called when an object of this class is instantiated. Here, it takes three arguments – self, file_path, and sample. `self` is a reference to the current instance of the class and is used to access variables and methods associated with that instance. `file_path` and `sample` are parameters provided at the time of object creation. file_path is expected to be a string representing the path to the data file. Sample is an integer that represents the number of random samples to extract from the data.

```
def __init__(self, file_path, sample):
    self.file_path = file_path
    self.sample = sample
```

- **`load_data(self)`**: This code block defines a method called **`load_data`**. This method loads the data from the file specified in **`file_path`**, prints the status of the data loading process, checks if the file exists at the given path, reads the data from the file into a Pandas DataFrame, and then returns a random sample from the DataFrame. The **`assert`** statement is used to continue the program only if the given condition returns True. If the condition returns False, it raises an **`AssertionError`** exception with the specified error message. In this case, it checks whether the file exists at the given path. **`pd.read_csv`** is a function from the Pandas library used to read a CSV file and convert it into a DataFrame. The **`df.sample`** function returns a random sample of items. The number of items is specified by **`self.sample`**.

```
def load_data(self):
    print(f"Starting data loading from {self.file_path}")
    assert os.path.exists(self.file_path), f"File not found at
{self.file_path}"
    df = pd.read_csv(self.file_path)
    print("Data loading completed")
    return df.sample(self.sample)
```

Summarizer

The **`Summarizer`** class encapsulates the functionality of text summarization using a model from the **`Hugging Face Transformers`** library. It serves to abstract the process of text summarization, making the operation reusable and organized.

Here are the key components of this class:

Attributes:

- **`model_name (string)`**: This attribute holds the identifier of the pre-trained model to be used for text summarization.
- **`min_length (integer)`**: This attribute specifies the minimum length of the summarized text.
- **`max_length (integer)`**: This attribute defines the maximum length of the summarized text.

- **`truncation (boolean)`**: This attribute determines whether the input text should be truncated to the maximum length specified.
- **`do_sample (boolean)`**: This attribute decides whether sampling should be used for text summarization.
- **`cache_dir (string)`**: This attribute specifies the directory where the models will be cached.

Methods:

- **`__init__(self, model_name="t5-small", min_length=20, max_length=50, truncation=True, do_sample=True, cache_dir="/model_cache")`**: The parameters specified in this method are used to initialize the object. Here, the summarizer class is taking several parameters such as **`model_name`**, **`min_length`**, **`max_length`**, **`truncation`**, **`do_sample`**, and **`cache_dir`**. The **`model_name`** is the name of the Hugging Face model used for summarization. The **`min_length`** and **`max_length`** parameters control the length of the summarized output. **`truncation`** and **`do_sample`** are boolean flags that affect how the model generates the summary. **`cache_dir`** specifies the directory to cache the model. These values are stored as attributes of the object (via **`self.attribute_name = value`**). A summarization pipeline from the Hugging Face Transformers library is then initialized using these parameters and stored as **`self.summarizer_model`**. This pipeline will be used to generate summaries.

```
def __init__(self, model_name="t5-small", min_length=20, max_
length=50, truncation=True, do_sample=True, cache_dir="/model_
cache"):
    self.model_name = model_name
    self.min_length = min_length
    self.max_length = max_length
    self.truncation = truncation
    self.do_sample = do_sample
    self.cache_dir = cache_dir
    self.summarizer_model = pipeline(
        task="summarization",
        model=self.model_name,
        min_length=self.min_length,
        max_length=self.max_length,
        truncation=self.truncation,
        do_sample=self.do_sample,
```

```
        model_kwargs={"cache_dir": self.cache_dir},
    )
```

- **summarize_text(self, text)**: This method takes a string text and returns a summarized version of it. It does this by calling the **Hugging Face summarizer** model on the text and retrieving the summarized text.

```
    def summarize_text(self, text):
        """
        Function to summarize a given text.
        Parameters:
        text (str): The text to be summarized.
        Returns:
        str: The summarized version of the text.
        """
        print(f"Summarizing the text: {text[:50]}...")  # Print-
ing the first 50 characters for brevity
        # Summarize the text
        summary = self.summarizer_model(text)[0]["summary_text"]
        print("Text summarized")
        return summary
```

- **summarize_reviews(self, reviews)**: This method takes a list of reviews and returns a list of their summarized versions. It does this by applying the **summarize_text** method to each review in the list.

```
    def summarize_reviews(self, reviews):
        """
        Function to summarize multiple reviews.
        Parameters:
        reviews (list): A list of reviews to be summarized.
        Returns:
        list: A list of summarized reviews.
            """
        print(f"Summarizing {len(reviews)} reviews")
        # Apply the summarize_text method to each review in the
list of reviews
        summaries = [self.summarize_text(review) for review in
reviews]
```

```
        print("Reviews summarized")
        return summaries
```

MLflowHandler

The **MLflowHandler** class serves to encapsulate the functionality of managing machine learning experiments and models using MLflow. It abstracts the process of starting an experiment, logging predictions and models, registering models, transitioning model stages, loading models, and searching registered models.

Here are the key components of this class:

Attributes:

- **experiment_name (string)**: This attribute holds the name of the MLflow experiment.
- **run_id (string)**: This attribute will hold the ID of the current MLflow run. It's initialized as None.

Methods:

- **__init__(self, experiment_name=f"/Users/<username>/LLMOps")**: This is the initializer (or constructor) of the MLflowHandler class. It initializes the experiment_name and run_id attributes.
- **start_run(self, model)**: The start_run method starts a new run in the MLflow experiment. It logs various parameters of the model used, such as model name, **min_length**, **max_length**, **truncation**, and **do_sample**.
    - o The method starts by logging the commencement of an MLflow run. This provides a record of the run being started, useful for monitoring and debugging.

      ```
      logging.info('Starting MLflow run')
      ```

    - o The method then checks if the input model has all the required attributes - "**model_name**", "**min_length**", "**max_length**", "**truncation**", and "**do_sample**". It uses Python's built-in **hasattr** function to do this. If any attribute is missing, an assertion error is raised.

      ```
      assert all(hasattr(model, attr) for attr in
      ("model_name", "min_length", "max_length",
       "truncation", "do_sample"))
      ```

The method then sets the current experiment using **MLflow's set_experiment** function. The experiment name is an attribute of the **MLflowHandler** instance (**self.experiment_name**).

```
mlflow.set_experiment(self.experiment_name)
```

- **log_predictions(self, inputs, outputs)**: This method logs predictions and corresponding inputs to the MLflow experiment. It takes two parameters, inputs and outputs, which are lists of input and output data, respectively. It calculates and logs parameters such as average **input/output** length, **max/min input/output** length. It then uses MLflow's **log_predictions** method to log the inputs and outputs.

```
def log_predictions(self, inputs, outputs):
        """

        Log predictions and corresponding inputs to the MLflow
experiment.


        Parameters
        ----------
        inputs : list
            List of input data.
        outputs : list
            List of output data.

        Returns
        -------
        None
        """


        # Log the prediction process
        logging.info('Logging predictions')


         # Start a new MLflow run and log parameters
        with mlflow.start_run(nested=True):
            mlflow.log_params(
                {
                    "average_input_length": sum(len(inp) for
inp in inputs) / len(inputs),
                    "average_output_length": sum(len(out) for
out in outputs) / len(outputs),
                    "max_input_length": max(len(inp) for inp
```

```
in inputs),
                    "max_output_length": max(len(out) for out
in outputs),
                    "min_input_length": min(len(inp) for inp
in inputs),
                    "min_output_length": min(len(out) for out
in outputs),
                }
            )
            # Log predictions using the LLM library
            mlflow.llm.log_predictions(
                inputs=inputs,
                outputs=outputs,
                prompts=["summarization of reviews" for _ in
outputs]
            )
```

- **`log_model(self, model, artifact_path, review)`**: This method logs the model to the MLflow experiment. It takes three parameters: **`model`**, **`artifact_path`**, and **`review`**. The method creates input and output dataframes, infers the model's signature, and logs the model using the **`log_model`** method from MLflow's transformers module. It also logs additional parameters such as the model's signature, the artifact path, and the chain type.

```
# Define method to log the model to the MLflow experiment
    def log_model(self, model, artifact_path, review):
        """
        Log the model to the MLflow experiment.


        Parameters
        ----------
        model : class instance
            An instance of a model class with necessary
attributes.
        artifact_path : str
            Path for the artifact.
        review : str
```

```
            Sample review for logging with the model.

        Returns
        -------
        dict
            Information about the logged model.
        """

        # Log the model logging process
        logging.info('Logging model')

        # Create dataframes for input and output
        input_df = pd.DataFrame({"review": [review]})
        output_df = pd.DataFrame({"summary": model.summarize_
reviews([review])})

        # Infer signature from input and output
        signature = infer_signature(input_df, output_df)

         # Log parameters
        mlflow.log_params(
            {
                'Model Signature': str(signature),
                'artifact_path': artifact_path,
                'Chain_Type': "Context Chain"
            }
        )

        # Define inference configuration and conda environment
        inference_config = {
            "min_length": model.min_length,
            "max_length": model.max_length,
            "truncation": model.truncation,
```

```
                "do_sample": model.do_sample,
            }

            conda_env = {
                'channels': ['defaults'],
                'dependencies': [
                    f'python={platform.python_version()}',
                    'pip',
                    {
                        'pip': [
                            'mlflow',
                            'torch',
                            'transformers',
                        ]
                    }
                ],
                'name': 'mlflow-env'
            }

             # Log the model with transformers
            model_info = mlflow.transformers.log_model(
                transformers_model=model.summarizer_model,
                artifact_path=artifact_path,
                task="summarization",
                inference_config=inference_config,
                signature=signature,
                input_example="This is an example of a long news
    article which this pipeline can summarize for you.",
            )
            return model_info
```

- **`register_model(self, model_name, model_info)`**: This method registers the model to the **`MLflow`** model registry. It takes two parameters: **`model_name`** and **`model_info`**. The method formats the model name and registers the model using the **`register_model`** method from **`MLflow`**.

```
    # Define method to register the model to the MLflow registry
    def register_model(self, model_name, model_info):
        """
        Register the model to the MLflow registry.

        Parameters
        ----------
        model_name : str
            Name of the model.
        model_info : dict
            Information about the model.

        Returns
        -------
        None
        """

        # Log the model registration process
        logging.info('Registering model')

        # Format model_name for registration
        model_name = model_name.replace("/", "_").replace(".",
"_").replace(":", "_")
        mlflow.register_model(model_uri=model_info.model_uri,
name=model_name)

    # Define method to transition a registered model to a specified stage
```

- **transition_model_to_stage(self, model_name, model_version, stage)**: This method transitions a registered model to a specified stage. It takes three parameters– **model_name**, **model_version**, and **stage**. The method creates an instance of MlflowClient and tries to transition the model version to the specified stage using the **transition_model_version_stage** method.

```
def transition_model_to_stage(self, model_name, model_version,
stage):
```

```
        """
        Transition a registered model to a specified stage.

        Parameters
        ----------
        model_name : str
            Name of the model.
        model_version : str
            Version of the model.
        stage : str
            The desired stage for the model.

        Returns
        -------
        None
        """

         # Log the model transition process
        logging.info('Transitioning model to stage')

        # Create an instance of MlflowClient
        mlflow_client = mlflow.tracking.MlflowClient()

        # Try to transition model version to the specified
stage
        try:
            mlflow_client.transition_model_version_stage(name=-
model_name, version=model_version, stage=stage)
        except Exception as e:
            logging.error(f"Error transitioning model version
to stage: {e}")
            raise RuntimeError(f"Error transitioning model
version to stage: {e}")
```

- **`load_model(self, model_name, model_version=None, stage=None)`**: This method loads a model from the MLflow model registry. It takes three parameters– **`model_name`**, **`model_version`**, and **`stage`**. The method tries to load the model from the specified stage or version using the **`load_model`** method from MLflow's **`pyfunc`** module.

```
# Define method to load a model from the MLflow model registry
    def load_model(self, model_name, model_version=None,
stage=None):
        " " "
        Load a model from the MLflow model registry.

        Parameters
        ----------
        model_name : str
            Name of the model.
        model_version : str, optional
            Version of the model, by default None
        stage : str, optional
            Stage of the model, by default None

        Returns
        -------
        class
            Class of the loaded model.
        " " "

         # Log the model loading process
        logging.info('Loading model')

        # Try to load the model from the specified stage or
version
        try:
            if stage:
                return pyfunc.load_model(model_uri=f"models:/
{model_name}/{stage}")
```

```
            else:
                return pyfunc.load_model(model_uri=f"models:/
{model_name}/{model_version}")
        except for Exception as e:
            logging.error(f"Error loading model: {e}")
            raise RuntimeError(f"Error loading model: {e}")
```

- **search_registered_models(self, model_name)**: This method searches for registered models in the **MLflow** model registry. It takes one parameter – **model_name**. The method creates an instance of **MlflowClient** and tries to search for registered models by **model_name** using the **search_registered_models** method.

```
# Define method to search for registered models in the MLflow
model registry
    def search_registered_models(self, model_name):
        " " "
        Search for registered models in the MLflow model registry.

        Parameters
        ----------
        model_name : str
            Name of the model.

        Returns
        -------
        list
            List of registered models.
        " " "

        # Log the model search process
        logging.info('Searching registered models')

        # Create an instance of MlflowClient
        mlflow_client = mlflow.tracking.MlflowClient()

        # Try to search for registered models by model_name
```

```
        try:
            return mlflow_client.search_registered_models
(filter_string=f"name='{model_name}'")
        except Exception as e:
            logging.error(f"Error searching registered models:
{e}")
            raise RuntimeError(f"Error searching registered
models: {e}")
```

Wrapping Up – The Pipeline

Here is how the pipeline works:

- **Data Loading**: The `DataLoader` class is used to load data from a file (reviews.csv) and take a random sample of 100 rows. The reviews are then extracted into a list.
- **Model Initialization**: The summarizer class is used to initialize a text summarization model. The model is a T5 transformer model, with a minimum summary length of 30 and a maximum summary length of 100.
- **Text Summarization**: The `summarize_reviews` method of the summarizer class is used to generate summaries for the reviews.
- **MLflow Setup**: An instance of the `MLflowHandler` class is created to handle interactions with MLflow. The experiment name is specified.
- **Logging Run**: The `start_run` method of the `MLflowHandler` class is used to start a new run in the `MLflow` experiment and log the parameters associated with the summarizer model.
- **Logging Predictions**: The `log_predictions` method of the `MLflowHandler` class is used to log the original reviews (inputs) and their summaries (outputs) to MLflow.
- **Logging Model**: The `log_model` method of the `MLflowHandler` class is used to log the model artifact along with an example review.
- **Registering Model**: The `register_model` method of the `MLflowHandler` class is used to register the model with the MLflow Model Registry.
- **Transitioning Model Stage**: The `transition_model_to_stage` method of the `MLflowHandler` class is used to transition the registered model to the "Production" stage in the Model Registry.
- **Loading Model**: The `load_model` method of the `MLflowHandler` class is used to load the model from the `MLflow Model Registry`.

- **Making Predictions**: Finally, the loaded model is used to make predictions on a sample review.

```
def run_pipeline(reviews):
    """
    This function executes a DevOps/MLOps pipeline with MLflow.

    Parameters
    ----------
    reviews : list
        List of reviews to process.
    """

    # Initialize MLflow handler
    mlflow_handler = MLflowHandler()

    logging.info('Pipeline initiated')

    # Create an instance of your model (change this according
to your model class)
    model = Summarizer()
    # Start an MLflow run and log the model parameters
    mlflow_handler.start_run(model)

    logging.info('MLflow run started and model parameters
logged')

    # Log the model
    artifact_path = "_pipeline/summarizer"
    model_info = mlflow_handler.log_model(model, artifact_path,
reviews[0])

    logging.info('Model logged')

    # Register the model
```

```
    mlflow_handler.register_model("model summarizer", model_
info)

    logging.info('Model registered')

    # Search for registered models
    model_results = mlflow_handler.search_registered_models
("model summarizer")

    logging.info('Registered models searched')

    # Load model (version 1) from the model registry
    modelpyV1 = mlflow_handler.load_model("model summarizer",
model_version=1)

    logging.info('Model Version 1 loaded')

    # Predict using the model
    modelpyV1.predict(pd.DataFrame({"review": [reviews[0]]}))

    logging.info('Prediction executed with Model Version 1')

    # Transition the model to 'Staging' stage
    mlflow_handler.transition_model_to_stage('model summarizer',
1, "Staging")

    logging.info('Model transitioned to Staging')

    # Load model from 'Staging' stage
    modelStaged = mlflow_handler.load_model("model summarizer",
model_version=1, stage="Staging")

    logging.info('Model loaded from Staging')

    # Predict using the model from 'Staging'
```

```
    modelStaged.predict(pd.DataFrame({"review": [re-
views[0]]}))

    logging.info('Prediction executed with Staging model')

    # Transition the model to 'Production' stage
    mlflow_handler.transition_model_to_stage('model summarizer',
1, "Production")

    logging.info('Model transitioned to Production')

    # Load model from 'Production' stage
    modelProduction = mlflow_handler.load_model("model
summarizer", model_version=1, stage="Production")

    logging.info('Model loaded from Production')

    # Predict using the model from 'Production'
    modelProduction.predict(pd.DataFrame({"review":
[reviews[0]]}))

    logging.info('Prediction executed with Production model')

    logging.info('Pipeline completed successfully')
```

You have the option to go to the 'Experiments' section to examine the various variables and artifacts that have been produced during the execution process. This feature is a standout offering from MLflow and serves to promote development practices that are both well-governed and controlled.

In simpler terms, the '*Experiments*' tab allows you to review and analyze different aspects of your machine learning model's performance and generated data. This is especially useful for understanding how the model is functioning and for making any necessary adjustments. MLflow provides this feature as a way to encourage responsible development practices, helping teams manage and monitor their machine learning projects more efficiently.

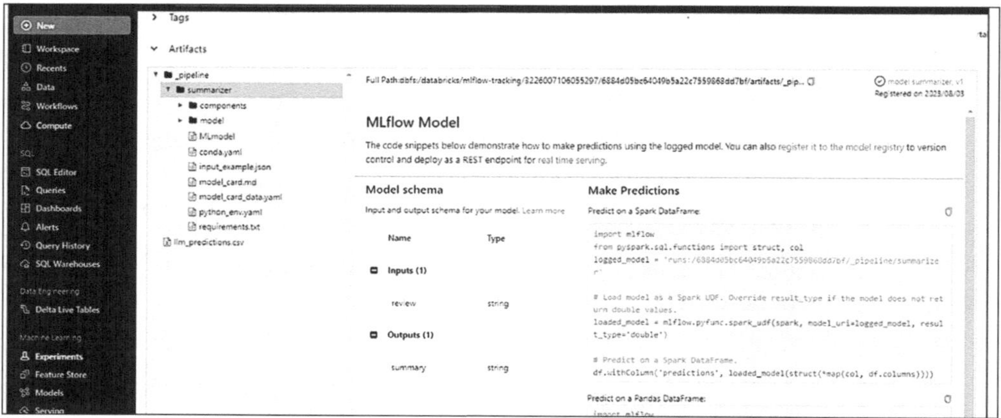

Figure 12.29: *MLflow Experiments*

The **MLflow** model registry can effectively be utilized to facilitate ModelOps. ModelOps, or Model Operations, refers to the practice of streamlining the deployment, monitoring, and governance of machine learning models in a production environment.

MLflow's model registry provides a centralized repository where you can manage and track different versions of your machine learning models. This feature can be particularly useful in a ModelOps framework, which aims to make the process of taking a machine learning model from the development stage to a fully operational state as efficient as possible. By leveraging the model registry, you can better manage the model's life cycle, ensuring that only validated and approved models are deployed. This contributes to a more organized and regulated approach to machine learning within a production setting.

Figure 12.30: *MLflow Model Registry*

Here is how the LLMOps steps map to DevOps and MLOps principles:

- **Data Loading**: This step is analogous to the data collection and pre-processing phase in an ML pipeline. In the context of DevOps, this could be compared to the process of gathering and validating requirements for a software project.
- **Model Initialization and Text Summarization:** These steps represent the development phase in the ML pipeline, where a model is chosen and trained on the available data. In DevOps, this is similar to the design and coding phases of software development.
- **MLflow Setup**: This is similar to setting up a CI/CD pipeline in DevOps. In this case, MLflow is used to create a pipeline for tracking experiments, storing model artifacts, and serving models.
- **Logging Run and Logging Predictions**: These steps represent the model evaluation and validation phases. In DevOps, this is similar to the testing phase, where the software is tested to ensure it meets all the requirements and works as expected.
- **Logging Model and Registering Model**: These steps correspond to the deployment phase in DevOps, where the software is delivered or deployed to production. In this case, the ML model is logged as an artifact and registered in the MLflow model registry.
- **Transitioning Model Stage**: This step represents the operation phase in DevOps, where the deployed software is monitored and maintained to ensure it runs smoothly in the production environment. Here, the ML model is transitioned to the "Production" stage in the model registry, indicating that it is ready for use in a production environment.
- **Loading Model and Making Predictions**: These steps are analogous to the user acceptance testing and operation phases in DevOps. The model is loaded from the registry and used to make predictions, demonstrating that it works as expected in a production-like environment.
- **Monitoring and Continuous Improvement:** Although not explicitly shown in the `main()` function, the principles of monitoring and continuous improvement are inherent in the MLOps process. Continuous monitoring of the model's performance in the production environment is crucial, and if the model's performance deteriorates, the entire process from data loading to making predictions is repeated to develop a new model. This is analogous to the continuous monitoring and improvement processes in DevOps.

Conclusion

As we have journeyed through the dynamic landscape of large language model operations (LLMOps), we have uncovered the potential of applying advanced NLP techniques and MLOps principles to streamline model life cycle management and amplify business value. Leveraging cutting-edge tools like Hugging Face's Transformers, Databricks, and MLflow, we have built an efficient and robust pipeline for training, evaluation, versioning, serving, and managing language models.

The use of LLMOps is not limited to creating summaries; it is an open avenue for a plethora of applications including translation, text generation, sentiment analysis, and more. Our journey began with training a transformer-based summarizer model using Hugging Face's Transformers library. This simplified the otherwise complex task of training large language models and provided access to pre-trained models and easy-to-use pipelines.

Subsequently, we delved into the operational side of things, utilizing MLflow and Databricks. We learned how to leverage MLflow's tracking capabilities to log model parameters, metrics, and artifacts. By doing so, we effectively created a centralized repository for our model's metadata, enabling easy access and comparison of different model versions.

Next, we explored how to register and version our models using MLflow's model registry. This critical component of our pipeline allowed us to manage the lifecycle of our models, transitioning them between various stages from 'Staging' to 'Production'. This way, we could ensure that the right model is used at the right time, minimizing the risk of errors.

Our journey did not stop at model management; we also investigated how to serve our models for real-time inference using Databricks and MLflow. We demonstrated how to transform our models into RESTful APIs that can be easily consumed by different applications, ensuring that the insights our models generate are readily available to drive decision-making processes.

Lastly, we touched upon the importance of interoperability in MLOps and how MLflow caters to this by supporting multiple ML frameworks. This ensures that our operations pipeline remains flexible and adaptable to the evolving needs of our projects.

In conclusion, the adoption of LLMOps signifies a step toward the future of machine learning operations. As businesses continue to realize the potential of large language models, the principles and techniques we have discussed in this chapter will become increasingly vital. By combining the power of NLP and MLOps, we can build solutions that are scalable, maintainable, and highly impactful. As the field continues to evolve, we can look forward to even more sophisticated tools and techniques to streamline our operations and maximize the value that we derive from our models.

In the upcoming chapter, we will explore the fascinating subject of prompt engineering within large language models. We will examine various strategies and techniques to excel at prompt engineering, empowering you to make LLMs more effective for your needs. This focus will help you to harness better the capabilities of LLMs by fine-tuning how you interact with them.

CHAPTER 13

Mastering the Art of Prompt Engineering

Introduction

As the pace of advancements in AI and Machine Learning continue to accelerate, language models, particularly those built on Transformer-based architectures like GPT-3 and GPT-4, have emerged as a focal point for innovation and research. Their ability to understand, generate, and transform human language opens up new possibilities for a multitude of applications, from chatbots and content creation to more complex tasks such as sentiment analysis, summarization, and translation.

Yet, one of the most intriguing aspects of these models lies in their use of prompts. A prompt, in the simplest terms, is an initial input given to the model to guide its output. This aspect of the technology is a game-changer because it gives the ability to guide and manipulate the model's output, thereby allowing for more control and direction in its functionality.

In this chapter, we will delve into the advanced techniques of prompt engineering, examining how we can harness their full potential in training and deploying language models. We will explore various methods, including hard and soft prompting, few-shot and zero-shot learning, prompt design, and the calibration of prompting methods. In each section, we will discuss the methodologies, their strengths and weaknesses, and their practical applications.

As we navigate through these topics, the chapter aims to provide a comprehensive understanding of prompt engineering, empowering researchers, data scientists, engineers, and AI enthusiasts to leverage these techniques in their AI projects. Let us embark on this journey to unlock the true potential of language models, and bring forth a new era of machine-human communication.

Structure

In this chapter, the following topics will be covered:

- Introduction to Prompt Engineering and its Applications
- Exploring Prompt Engineering Techniques and Approaches
- The Intersection of Prompt Engineering with Existing Learning Techniques
- Challenges Foreseen in the Area of Prompt Engineering Research and Development

Prompt Engineering

In AI, prompt engineering is a strategy of crafting prompts that enhance the model's performance in specific tasks. A prompt is essentially a question or instruction given to an AI model to perform a task. This process can be done either manually (manual template engineering) or using automated techniques (automated template learning).

For example, to create a language translation model, a simple prompt could be "`Translate the following English text to French: {text}`". The `{text}` is a placeholder into which actual English sentences will be inserted.

Prompt Shape

The structure of a prompt can vary based on its type. The two primary types are close prompts and prefix prompts. Close prompts have a blank in them that the model needs to fill. Prefix prompts, on the other hand, provide a starting point or context, after which the model generates the rest of the content.

To illustrate, a close prompt might look like this: "`Paris is the capital of` ________". A model receiving this prompt will need to fill in the blank, in this case, with "France". A prefix prompt might be: "`Write a short story that begins with 'Once upon a time`'". The AI model will then continue the text from that point.

Manual Template Engineering

This method involves designing prompts based on human intuition and expertise. While this method can be quite effective, it can also be time-consuming and demanding, especially for complex tasks.

As an example, in a question-answering task, a human expert might create a prompt such as "`What is the answer to the question: {question}?`", where `{question}` is a placeholder for any specific question.

Automated Template Learning

As the manual method can be labor-intensive, automated approaches are often utilized. These can be divided into two categories: discrete prompts and continuous prompts.

Discrete Prompts

Discrete prompts involve the automatic search for templates within a predefined space, typically made up of natural language phrases. The following methods fall under discrete prompts:

1. **Prompt Mining:** This process automatically discovers effective prompt templates given a set of training inputs and outputs. For example, given a database of questions and answers, prompt mining can help find effective question structures.
2. **Prompt Paraphrasing:** This method involves creating variants of an existing prompt and selecting the most effective one. For instance, if "Translate the following English text to French: {text}" does not yield good results, you might try "Give the French equivalent of the English phrase: {text}".
3. **Gradient-based Search:** This technique involves iteratively searching over tokens to find short sequences that result in desired predictions. It is like fine-tuning the prompt at the word level to enhance the performance.
4. **Prompt Generation:** This approach treats the creation of prompts as a text generation task, leveraging existing natural language generation models.
5. **Prompt Scoring:** This method involves designing a prompt template, filling it with input and answer slots, and then using a model to score the generated prompts, which aids in prompt selection.

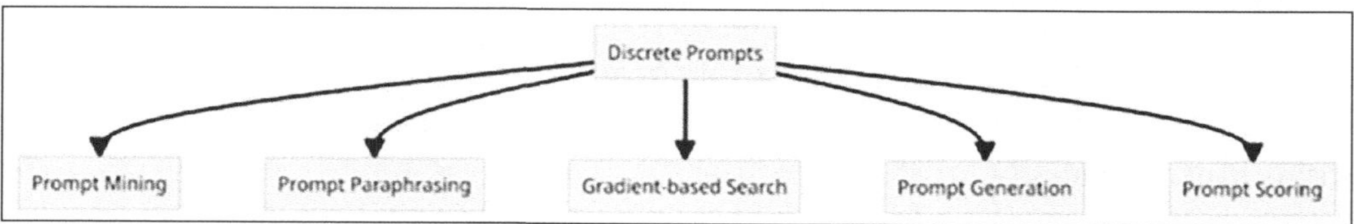

Figure 13.1: *Discrete Prompts*

Continuous Prompts

In a continuous prompting approach, the limitations associated with using the embeddings of natural language words for template terms are eased. Moreover, this technique detaches the template parameters from the ones that have been pre-trained in the language model itself. With continuous prompts, templates possess their own distinct parameters that can be fine-tuned according to the specific data related to the end-use task. The following are some notable techniques that leverage this approach:

1. **Prefix Tuning:** This involves adding a sequence of task-specific vectors to the input, thus allowing modification of the initial condition of the language model.
2. **Tuning Initialized with Discrete Prompts:** Here, the search for a continuous prompt starts with a prompt discovered through discrete prompt search methods.
3. **Hard-Soft Prompt Hybrid Tuning:** This method mixes fixed embeddings from a discrete prompt with adjustable embeddings to increase flexibility.

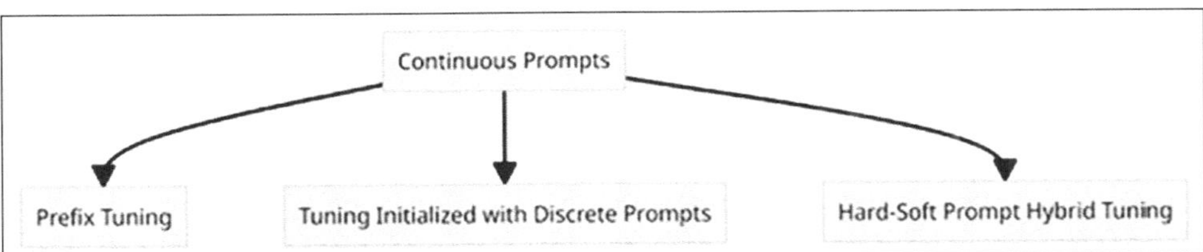

Figure 13.2: *Continuous Prompts*

This detailed exploration of prompt engineering techniques highlights the potential and variability of this strategic process. It is crucial to understand the specifics and implications of each method to decide the best approach for a given task. The effectiveness of a method could vary significantly based on the task, the model, and the available resources, making this decision an essential component of successful machine learning applications.

Answer Engineering

This is the method of improving the way a language model generates its output responses. It essentially focuses on refining how the model answers the prompts it receives, with the goal of optimizing accuracy and relevance.

For example, if you ask an AI model to translate a sentence from English to French, the response it provides is an "answer". Answer engineering refines how these answers are generated.

Answer Shape

This refers to the format or structure of the output provided by the language model. The shape of the answer can differ based on the task the model is performing. Some common answer shapes include:

- **Tokens**: These are single words or symbols that come from the model's vocabulary. For instance, if the task is to identify the sentiment of a sentence, the answer might be a single word such as "`positive`", "`negative`", or "`neutral`".
- **Span**: These are short segments made up of multiple tokens (words). They are often used with close prompts. For example, in a fill-in-the-blank task, the answer might be a phrase that fits in the blank.
- **Sentence**: These are full sentences or entire documents. They are often used with prefix prompts. For instance, if the task is to generate a paragraph continuing from a given sentence, the answer would be a series of sentences.

Answer Space Design Methods

This involves defining the possible answers (the "*answer space*"), and how those possibilities relate to the final outputs. The approach can vary, including the following:

- **Manual Design**: In this approach, the answer space and its mapping to outputs are created by hand. The space could be unconstrained (including all possible tokens or sequences) or constrained (limited to specific outputs). For instance, if the task is to categorize a text into predefined categories, the answer space will be the list of those categories.
- **Discrete Answer Search**: Here, the process automatically searches for possible answers, given that manually creating them might not always be optimal. Methods under this include:
    - **Answer Paraphrasing**: This technique begins with a set of initial answers and uses paraphrasing to expand it. So, for example, if an AI model is trained to respond to the prompt "*How's the weather*?" with "*It's sunny*", paraphrasing might expand the answer space to include synonyms such as "*It's bright out*".

- **Prune-Then-Search**: This involves first reducing the answer space to several plausible answers, then further searching within this reduced space to select the best answers.
- **Label Decomposition**: This method breaks down labels into constituent words and uses those as answers. For example, in a task to identify the color of an object in a sentence, the label "*red car*" might be decomposed into "*red*" and "*car*".

- **Continuous Answer Search**: This is a less explored approach in which soft answer tokens, which can be optimized using gradient descent, are used. This allows the answer space to be more flexible and adaptable. An example could be assigning a unique token for each category in a classification task, and then optimizing these tokens based on the training data of the task.

The goal of answer engineering is to fine-tune the way AI models produce responses, aiming for optimal performance and more accurate, relevant outputs. This is crucial as it directly influences the model's usefulness and effectiveness.

Multi-prompt Learning

Until now, we have been focusing on using a single prompt to guide the output from language models. A "prompt" is a kind of instruction that provides context to the language model, and hints at the format of the answer required. Multi-prompt learning, however, is a method that involves using more than one prompt, which can make the language model even more effective.

Prompt Ensembling

This approach involves using multiple prompts for a single input when the model is generating its predictions. It is similar to how a team of experts combine their insights to make a more accurate prediction. The various techniques in this method include:

- **Uniform Averaging:** This technique simply combines the predictions from different prompts by averaging them. For instance, if three prompts generate three different temperature forecasts, this method would average these three numbers to create a final forecast.
- **Weighted Averaging**: This technique is a refinement of uniform averaging and gives each prompt a weight based on its performance. So, if one prompt consistently produces better predictions, it is given a higher weight in the averaging process.

- **Majority Voting**: This is typically used for classification tasks. It works by choosing the result that comes up most often from different prompts. For example, if three prompts classify a text as "`positive`," "`positive`," and "`neutral`," the final prediction would be "positive."
- **Knowledge Distillation**: This is where the performance of a group of models is '`distilled`' into a single model, which results in a more robust and accurate model.

Prompt Augmentation

This approach is also known as demonstration learning. It involves supplementing the actual prompt with additional answered prompts that show the model how it should answer. The challenge lies in selecting and ordering the examples appropriately, and current research is working on using sentence embeddings and entropy-based methods to tackle this.

Prompt Composition

This method is used for composable tasks, which are tasks that can be broken down into smaller subtasks. It involves creating multiple sub-prompts for each subtask, and then defining a composite prompt based on these sub-prompts.

Prompt Decomposition

This is the opposite of prompt composition, and is used for tasks where multiple predictions should be made for one sample. It involves converting a single comprehensive prompt into different sub-prompts and answering each one separately.

The key takeaway here is that using multiple prompts can enhance the effectiveness of language models. This area of multi-prompt learning is expanding and becoming more sophisticated, promising better performance and more precise results in language model outputs.

Training Strategies for Prompting Methods

Prompting methods have emerged as a significant tool to harness the power of language models. While obtaining appropriate prompts is vital, it is equally crucial to train these models effectively to maximize their potential. In this chapter, we delve into strategies that train models in concert with prompting methods.

Training Settings

Prompting methods can be employed with or without explicit training of the LM for the downstream task. A language model trained to predict text probability, P(x), can be directly applied to fill the prompts defined to specify a task. This is known as a zero-shot setting, which means that no training data is used for the task of interest.

However, there exist methods that leverage training data to train the model along with prompting methods. These could be full-data learning (using a large number of training examples) or few-shot learning (using a minimal number of examples). Few-shot learning can particularly benefit from prompting methods as the scarcity of training examples might not fully define the desired behavior. Thus, using a prompt to direct the model is highly effective.

Although training samples are not explicitly used in training the downstream task model for many of the prompt engineering methods, they often contribute to the construction or validation of prompts for downstream tasks. Therefore, arguing for this to be true zero-shot learning might not be entirely accurate.

Parameter Update Methods

In prompt-based downstream task learning, two types of parameters usually exist. The first includes those from pre-trained models, and the second pertains to prompts. Deciding which parameters to update is crucial and can significantly impact the applicability in different scenarios. We will discuss five tuning strategies based on whether the parameters of the underlying LM are tuned, and whether there are additional prompt-related parameters.

Promptless Fine-Tuning

This strategy, widely used in NLP, involves updating all or some of the parameters of the pre-trained LM using gradients induced from downstream training samples. Typical examples of pre-trained models tuned this way include BERT and RoBERTa. While powerful and simple, it may overfit or destabilize learning on small datasets, and is prone to catastrophic forgetting where the model forgets previously learned abilities.

Example: You start with the pre-trained GPT-2 model and fine-tune it using a curated dataset of financial news articles paired with their summaries. During training, GPT-2 learns the specific language, style, and key points typically highlighted in financial summaries.

- **Advantages**:
  - **Simplicity:** There is no need for prompt design.
  - **Adaptability:** Tuning all the LM parameters allows the model to fit larger training datasets.
- **Disadvantages**:
  - **Instability:** LMs may overfit or not learn stably on smaller datasets.

Tuning-Free Prompting

This strategy involves generating answers directly based on a prompt without changing the parameters of the pre-trained LMs, also referred to as in-context learning when combined with prompt augmentation. Examples of tuning-free prompting include LAMA and GPT-3.

Example: Utilizing GPT-3 for generating educational content on historical events without further training. By crafting detailed prompts such as "*Explain the significance of the Battle of Hastings in shaping British history*", GPT-3 leverages its extensive pre-trained knowledge to produce informative content. The key is to design prompts that are specific and detailed enough to guide GPT-3 towards generating the desired educational output.

- **Advantages**:
  - **Efficiency:** No parameter update process.
  - **Stability:** No catastrophic forgetting as LM parameters remain fixed.
- **Disadvantages:**
  - Heavy engineering is necessary to achieve high accuracy. Providing many answered prompts can be slow at test time, and thus cannot easily use large training datasets.

Fixed-LM Prompt Tuning

This strategy updates only the parameters of the prompt using the supervision signal obtained from the downstream training samples, while keeping the entire pre-trained LM unchanged. Examples include Prefix-Tuning and WARP.

Example: Adjusting a model for restaurant review sentiment analysis using Prefix-Tuning. A sequence of tunable vectors is optimized and appended to inputs from a dataset of restaurant reviews to train the model in distinguishing between positive and negative sentiments. These tunable vectors (prefixes) act as a specialized lens, focusing the model's attention on sentiment indicators within the reviews.

- **Advantages**:
  - **Retention:** Can retain knowledge in LMs and is suitable in few-shot scenarios.
- **Disadvantages**:
  - Inapplicable in zero-shot scenarios and limited representation power in large-data settings.

Fixed-prompt LM Tuning

Fixed-prompt LM tuning tunes the parameters of the LM, along with using prompts with fixed parameters to specify the model behavior. Examples include PET-TC (Pattern-Exploiting Training - Text Classification), PET-Gen, and LM-BFF (Language Model as Best Friend Forever).

Example: GPT-2 is fine-tuned on a dataset comprising technical support exchanges, using prompts that structure the output as email responses. The training process involves learning from the structured exchanges to generate email responses that are coherent, polite, and informative.

- **Advantages**:
  - Efficient learning in few-shot scenarios due to more complete task specification via prompt or answer engineering.
- **Disadvantages**:
  - Prompt or answer engineering is still required. LMs fine-tuned on one downstream task may not be effective on another one

Prompt+LM Tuning

This method involves fine-tuning the prompt-relevant parameters, along with some or all of the parameters of the pre-trained models. Examples include PADA and P-Tuning.

Example: Developing a language model for personalized fitness advice. Both the language model parameters and a set of prompt-specific parameters are fine-tuned together on a dataset containing fitness queries and professional advice. The model learns not only to understand diverse fitness-related queries but also to generate personalized advice by adjusting both the prompt parameters and the model's internal parameters for optimal performance.

- **Advantages**:
  - **Expressiveness:** Suitable for high-data settings.
- **Disadvantages**:
  - May overfit to small datasets and requires training and storing all parameters of the models

These are just a few examples of parameter update methods and the variety of strategies that can be employed to train prompting methods in language models effectively. Understanding these strategies and their advantages and disadvantages can help guide the decision-making process when deploying a model for a specific task.

Prompt Engineering for Various Applications

Prompt engineering has emerged as a crucial technique for optimizing the performance of language models across diverse applications. Whether it is natural language processing tasks such as text summarization, machine translation, or more complex objectives such as sentiment analysis and question-answering, crafting the right prompt is key to eliciting the desired output from the model.

At its core, prompt engineering focuses on tailoring the input queries or "prompts" to evoke the most accurate and relevant responses from language models. This involves a blend of computational linguistics, psychology, and domain-specific knowledge to engineer prompts that can better guide the model towards generating appropriate and contextually accurate answers.

The versatility of prompt engineering makes it invaluable for various applications, ranging from automated customer service chatbots to complex data analysis tools. With a keen focus on fine-tuning, prompt engineering adapts to the specific demands and constraints of different applications, thereby serving as a bridge between the capabilities of general language models and the specialized needs of individual tasks.

Knowledge Probing

Knowledge probing is a critical application of prompt engineering. It serves as a method to quantify the factual knowledge embedded in a pre-trained language model's internal representations. The LM parameters are typically fixed, and knowledge is retrieved by transforming the input into a close prompt. Close prompts are the prompts that require filling in the blanks.

In the realm of factual probing, templates for close prompts could be manually crafted or automatically discovered. Datasets such as LAMA and X-FACTR are primarily used in this context. Both discrete template search and continuous template learning have been experimented with to optimize fact retrieval.

Moreover, LMs are also adept at handling linguistic phenomena such as analogies, negations, semantic role sensitivity, semantic similarity, context understanding, and rare word understanding. Such knowledge can be elicited by presenting linguistic probing tasks in the form of natural language sentences for the LM to complete.

Classification-based Tasks

Classification-based tasks, such as text classification and natural language inference, have seen wide usage of prompt-based learning. The key is to reformulate the task as an appropriate prompt. For instance, a prompt such as "`the topic of this document is [Z]`" is used in text classification. The document is then fed into mask pre-trained LMs for slot filling.

Prompt engineering and answer engineering have been extensively explored in the context of text classification tasks, primarily in few-shot settings with "fixed-prompt LM Tuning" strategies.

For natural language inference (NLI), the task is to predict the relationship between two given sentences. Close prompts are commonly used in this context as well. The research focus is primarily on the template search in a few-shot learning setting, with manually pre-selected answer space from the vocabulary.

Information Extraction

For information extraction tasks, the construction of prompts often requires greater finesse. For instance, in relation extraction, the task is to predict the relation between two entities in a sentence. The complexity arises from a larger label space, and the varying importance of different tokens in the input sentence.

Researchers have proposed adaptive answer selection methods to address the issue of larger label space and task-oriented prompt template construction to tackle the importance of differentiation among tokens.

"Reasoning" in NLP

The ability of deep neural networks to perform "*reasoning*" has been the center of numerous debates. There have been attempts to probe models' reasoning ability by defining benchmark tasks that span different scenarios.

Some of these tasks involve commonsense reasoning and mathematical reasoning. The latter has been explored in the context of pre-trained LMs for solving simple arithmetic operations. However, the models generally fail when the numbers become larger. Researchers are investigating more complex mathematical reasoning problems and improving LM performance through serializing reasoning for the question.

Question Answering

Question answering (QA) tasks involve answering a given input question, often based on a context document. These tasks can be of various formats such as extractive QA, multiple-choice QA, and free-form QA. A major benefit of solving QA problems with LMs, using prompting methods, is that different formats of QA tasks can be solved within the same framework.

Text Generation

The process of text generation is aimed at creating textual content, often based on some existing information or context. Using prefix prompts in tandem with autoregressive language models that have been pre-trained, one can effectively tackle text generation tasks. These types of models have shown remarkable proficiency in executing various text-related tasks, such as condensing larger pieces of text into summaries or translating text between different languages.

In conclusion, prompt engineering has proven to be an effective method for a wide range of NLP tasks, from knowledge probing and text classification to information extraction and question answering. As our understanding of prompt engineering deepens, we can expect even more refined and powerful applications in the future.

Unveiling the Intersections of Prompt Engineering with Existing Learning Techniques

Prompt engineering is an instrumental strategy for making the best use of pre-trained language models, a trend that is fast becoming a staple in the field of machine learning. However, it is essential to recognize that prompt-based learning does not exist in isolation. It shares striking similarities and contrasts with numerous established learning methodologies, which we will explore in this chapter.

Ensemble Learning

Ensemble Learning leverages the strengths of multiple models to improve the performance of a given task. It typically includes a combination of different architectures, training strategies, data ordering, and random initialization. A new dimension added to this mix is prompt ensembling, in which the choice of prompt templates acts as another parameter to generate varied results. This approach, particularly when using discrete prompts, allows for an alteration in the inference stage, negating the need to train the model multiple times.

Few-Shot Learning

Few-shot learning is a mechanism that enables a machine learning system to adapt to data-scarce scenarios with minimal training samples. Various methodologies facilitate few-shot learning, such as model-agnostic meta-learning and embedding learning. Prompt augmentation, often referred to as priming-based few-shot learning, can be seen as a new entrant in this domain. It allows the model to draw knowledge from pre-trained LMs without any parameter tuning, marking a considerable advantage over other methods.

Larger-Context Learning

Larger-context learning is about enhancing system performance by supplementing the input with additional contextual information. Prompt augmentation, in this context, can be viewed as integrating relevant labeled samples into the input. However, unlike larger-context learning, the context introduced is not necessarily labeled data.

Query Reformulation

Query reformulation is a technique commonly used in information retrieval and question-answering tasks to extract more relevant texts. The process shares similarities with prompt-based learning in terms of their goals, and the opaque nature of the knowledge bases they deal with. However, there are also differences, most notably in the form of the knowledge base and the modifications needed in task formulation and the modeling framework.

QA-based Task Formulation

QA-based task formulation aims to conceptualize various NLP tasks as a question-answering problem. This concept shares striking similarities with the prompting methods, as both use textual questions to specify the task. However, prompt methods put a stronger emphasis on using the knowledge in pre-trained LMs.

Controlled Generation

Controlled generation is about guiding the model beyond the input text. It shares commonalities with prompt-based learning methods. For instance, both add extra information to the input text for better generation. However, with controlled generation, the control usually revolves around the style or content of generation, while the underlying task remains the same. The primary motivation for using prompts for text generation is to specify the task itself, and to better use the pre-trained model.

Supervised Attention

Supervised attention and prompt learning share a common goal: to extract salient information based on given clues. Supervised attention methods have used additional loss functions to learn to predict gold attention on a manually labeled corpus. Prompt learning can borrow from this line of research.

Data Augmentation

Data augmentation is a well-known technique used to increase the amount of training data by modifying the existing dataset. Adding prompts to downstream tasks can produce similar accuracy improvement to that of adding hundreds of data points on average across classification tasks, which suggests a connection between prompts and implicit data augmentation.

While prompt engineering is a relatively recent field, its intersection with existing learning methods is apparent. By understanding these overlaps and distinctions, we can leverage them to improve the effectiveness of our models and continue to advance the field of machine learning.

Challenges in Prompt Engineering

Despite the significant potential exhibited by prompt-based learning across different tasks and scenarios, a variety of challenges still exist. Some of these challenges are as follows:

Prompt Design

In the sphere of prompt engineering, "*prompt design*" refers to the strategic crafting of input queries or statements commonly known as "prompts", that guide language models toward generating the desired output. The focus is not merely on creating any prompt, but on developing a query that is optimally suited to produce accurate, relevant, and contextually appropriate responses from the model.

The process involves a multidisciplinary approach, incorporating elements of computational linguistics, psychology, and domain expertise. It is about understanding both the capabilities and limitations of the language model you are working with, and tailoring your prompts to navigate these factors effectively.

Prompt design can also be an iterative process. Initial prompts are often tested and fine-tuned based on the quality of the model's responses. Variables such as the length, complexity, and specificity of the prompt can all be adjusted in a systematic way to improve the model's performance for a particular application, whether it is natural language understanding, text summarization, machine translation, or more specialized tasks.

Therefore, in the broader context of prompt engineering, prompt design serves as a pivotal component that translates the general abilities of a language model into targeted, effective solutions for specific tasks or applications.

Tasks Beyond Classification and Generation

The majority of existing research on prompt-based learning centers around tasks related to text classification or generation. The application to tasks such as information extraction and textual analysis is less explored, primarily due to the intricacy involved in creating prompts for these activities. The future might demand either a reconfiguration of these tasks to fit into classification or text generation methods, or the creation of effective answer engineering that can articulate structured outcomes in a text-compatible manner.

Prompting with Structured Information

In many natural language processing endeavors, inputs come with various structures, ranging from trees and graphs to tables and relational constructs. Crafting prompts or answers that optimally express these structures remains a considerable challenge. Some initial progress includes prompts with additional markers for encoding lexical data such as entity markers, and structuring prompts based on HTML for more nuanced web text generation. Still, further exploration of more complex structural varieties remains largely untapped.

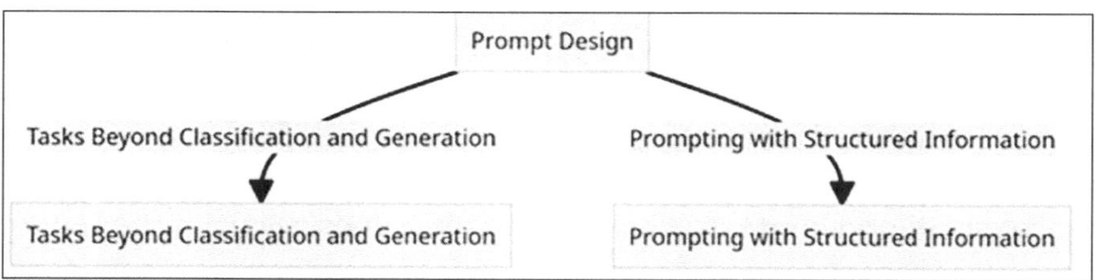

Figure 13.3: *Challenges – Prompt Design*

Answer Engineering

In the context of prompt engineering, "answer engineering" focuses on fine-tuning and optimizing the output generated by language models in response to carefully crafted prompts. While prompt engineering aims to refine the input queries to elicit the most accurate and relevant results, answer engineering zeroes in on improving the quality, relevance, and precision of the responses themselves.

This practice often involves a combination of techniques. For instance, you might analyze the generated answers to identify patterns of errors or biases, then modify the prompts or adjust model parameters to correct for these issues. Sometimes, additional logic or post-processing steps are introduced after the model generates its initial output to further refine the answer and make it more aligned with the specific requirements of the application.

In certain cases, answer engineering might involve ensemble techniques, where outputs from multiple models or configurations are combined to produce a more robust and accurate answer. Alternatively, the approach could be more interactive, involving a feedback loop where the model's responses are evaluated and used to refine subsequent prompts.

Overall, answer engineering complements prompt engineering by working on the other end of the language model pipeline. While prompt engineering seeks to initiate the most effective model interaction through optimized input, answer engineering strives to ensure that the resulting output meets the quality and contextual standards necessary for the application at hand. Together, these engineering techniques aim to maximize both the efficacy and efficiency of using language models for various specialized tasks.

Many-class and Long-answer Classification Tasks

For tasks based on classification, answer engineering faces two main challenges:

- **Large Answer Space**: One of the major hurdles in answer engineering for classification tasks is the optimization problem arising when you have an extensive range of possible classes. Determining the most appropriate set of answers becomes increasingly complex.
- **Multi-token Decoding**: When the correct answers comprise of multiple tokens, identifying the best method for decoding these multiple tokens with language models is still a gray area. Although some techniques for multi-token decoding have been suggested, a universally optimal method has not been established yet.

Multiple Answers for Generation Tasks

- **Multiple Valid Answers:** Text generation tasks often present a unique challenge where several answers may be semantically equivalent but differ in their syntax. Usually, the training process hinges on a single correct answer, despite the possibility of multiple correct variations.
- **Guiding Learning with Multiple References**: The question of how to effectively guide the learning process when multiple equally valid answers exist remains a largely untapped research area.

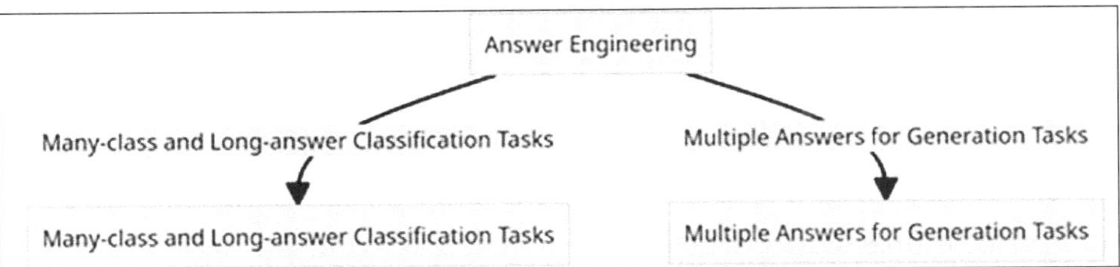

Figure 13.4: *Challenges – Answer Engineering*

Selection of Tuning Strategy

There is a spectrum of strategies for tuning the parameters of prompts, LMs, or both. However, a systematic comprehension of the trade-offs between these methods is still elusive. Systematic explorations, similar to the pre-train and fine-tune paradigm, can shed more light on these trade-offs.

Multiple Prompt Learning

Multiple prompt learning refers to a technique within prompt engineering in which various prompts are used to guide a language model in generating outputs for the same task or a set of related tasks. Unlike the single-prompt approach, which relies on one carefully crafted query to elicit a response, multiple prompt learning employs an array of different prompts, either simultaneously or sequentially, to improve the model's understanding and output quality.

The key advantage of this approach is its capacity to capture different facets of a problem, enabling a more nuanced and comprehensive response. For instance, if you are working on a text summarization task, using multiple prompts such as "*Summarize the text,*" "*What are the key points of the text?*", and "*Condense the main ideas of the text*" could provide different perspectives, making the final summary more robust and thorough.

Additionally, multiple prompt learning can be particularly useful for tasks that have ambiguous or subjective elements. By using a variety of prompts, you can mitigate biases and ensure that the model explores multiple interpretations of the input data, leading to a more balanced and accurate output.

Another benefit is the potential for increased model generalization. Multiple prompts can expose the model to a wider range of phrasing and context, making it more adaptable to varied real-world scenarios.

However, the approach does come with its own set of challenges, such as the need for a mechanism to aggregate or choose among the multiple outputs generated, and the computational overhead involved in managing and processing multiple prompts.

Prompt Ensembling

As more prompts are incorporated, the intricacies in time and space complexities escalate within prompt ensembling methods. While the concept of knowledge distillation from various prompts holds potential, it remains a realm that is largely untapped in current research.

Prompt Composition and Decomposition

The strategies of prompt composition and decomposition aim to simplify intricate tasks by introducing a set of sub-prompts. The pivotal decision between these techniques holds significance in practical applications. The choice between composing a complex prompt from smaller elements, or breaking down a large prompt into manageable parts, can influence the efficiency of the prompt engineering process.

Prompt Augmentation

Current prompt augmentation methods encounter limitations due to input length constraints, rendering it infeasible to input an excessive number of demonstrations. A significant challenge lies in selecting informative demonstrations and determining their optimal order within the input. This complex yet engaging problem adds an intriguing layer to prompt engineering efforts.

Prompt Sharing

Typically, prompt applications are tailored to singular tasks, specific domains, or particular languages. The concept of prompt sharing introduces a new perspective in which prompt learning principles are extended across multiple tasks, domains, and languages. The exploration of this approach remains at a relatively early stage, offering a realm of untapped potential to uncover.

Choosing Optimal Pre-trained Models

In the realm of prompt-based learning, the task of selecting an appropriate pre-trained language model among the diverse options available is both fascinating and challenging. The decision involves considering factors such as model capabilities, architecture, and suitability for the specific prompt engineering goals.

Analyzing Prompting Theoretically and Empirically

While the effectiveness of prompting techniques has been demonstrated across various scenarios, there remains a notable scarcity of theoretical analysis and formal guarantees in the context of prompt-based learning. This gap underscores the need for a deeper understanding of the underlying principles, and the potential for refining prompt strategies based on solid theoretical foundations.

Exploring Prompts' Transferability

A significant aspect to consider is the extent to which prompts are tied to a particular language model, and whether they can be applied across different models. Enhancing the transferability of prompts, that is enabling them to function effectively across diverse models, presents a valuable avenue of exploration to optimize prompt engineering practices.

Calibration of Prompting Methods

While prompt engineering has proven to be a potent technique in enhancing model performance, it is essential to understand the calibration of these methods to achieve optimal results. Like any machine learning model, tuning is a crucial part of the process and prompt-based models are no different.

Calibration, in the context of prompting methods, refers to the adjustment and optimization of the prompt's design, and its implementation to increase the efficiency and effectiveness of the model. This could involve the customization of the prompt language, length, complexity, and structure depending on the task at hand. It is about finding the 'sweet spot' between the complexity of the prompts and the performance of the model.

Some factors to consider during the calibration of prompt methods include:

- **Task Complexity:** The nature of the task greatly influences the design of the prompts. For instance, simple tasks may only require single-token prompts while more complex tasks may need multi-token or even structured prompts.
- **Pre-trained Model Compatibility:** The compatibility of the prompt with the pre-trained model is another significant factor. Some prompts may work better with certain models, therefore, understanding the model's characteristics is crucial in prompt design.
- **Number of Prompts:** The number of prompts used also plays a significant role in the model's performance. Using too few prompts might limit the model's learning, while too many prompts could lead to overfitting. Thus, it is essential to find a balance.
- **Prompt Variety:** The use of diverse prompts that approach the problem from various perspectives can help the model understand and generalize the task better.
- **Training Data:** Lastly, the nature of the training data also influences the calibration process. Depending on the data, some prompts might be more effective than others.

Combination of Different Paradigms

Much of the success of the prompting paradigm is built on pre-trained models developed for the pre-train and fine-tune paradigm. However, the pre-training methods best suited for one paradigm might not be optimal for the other, necessitating careful examination of how best to integrate these approaches.

Overall, while challenges are plenty, the potential rewards of mastering prompt engineering are even greater. It is a burgeoning field ripe for exploration, and we anticipate fascinating discoveries as we venture deeper into its intricacies.

Conclusion

This chapter thus provides a comprehensive view of the vast and dynamic field of prompt engineering, delving into its various aspects and applications. This cutting-edge area of research and development has emerged as a pivotal force in shaping the landscape of artificial intelligence and natural language processing.

Throughout this exploration, we have seen the intricate details and techniques involved in crafting effective prompts to guide the behavior and responses of AI models. Manual template engineering and automated template learning have been discussed as strategies to design prompts, with both discrete and continuous prompts highlighted for specific use cases. Additionally, answer engineering and answer space design methods play a crucial role in optimizing model outputs.

The concept of multi-prompt learning has been introduced, along with the significance of prompt ensembling, prompt augmentation, and prompt composition for enhancing AI model performance. The importance of considering various training strategies for prompting methods such as promptless fine-tuning and tuning-free prompting has been emphasized.

Prompt engineering finds extensive applicability across diverse domains, ranging from knowledge probing and classification-based tasks to information extraction and question answering. We have also explored how prompt engineering intersects with existing learning techniques such as ensemble learning, few-shot learning, and larger-context learning.

Challenges in prompt engineering have been addressed, including prompt design for different task types, prompting with structured information, and addressing tasks beyond classification and generation. Handling tasks such as many-class and long-answer classification tasks, as well as multiple answers for generation tasks, has presented unique complexities.

The selection of tuning strategies and pre-trained models is a crucial decision in prompt engineering, and theoretical and empirical analyses have been conducted to understand the transferability of prompts and the calibration of prompting methods.

As we conclude, the field of prompt engineering continues to evolve, offering immense opportunities and challenges. Researchers, practitioners, and industry leaders are encouraged to leverage the insights gained from this comprehensive study to foster innovation and advancement in the realm of AI and NLP. Through continuous learning, experimentation, and collaboration, we can push the boundaries of AI capabilities, and pave the way for a more intelligent and interconnected world. The future of prompt engineering holds potential to revolutionize industries and enhance human-machine interactions, making it an exciting and vital area of exploration for the years to come.

The next chapter will focus on applying the knowledge of prompt engineering to OpenAI models. This practical application will involve experimenting with various prompt design strategies and tuning methods to optimize the language models for specific tasks and domains.

CHAPTER 14

Prompt Engineering Essentials and Design Patterns

Introduction

In the age of conversational AI, the ability to interact effectively with large language models (LLMs) like ChatGPT is becoming increasingly important. However, the interaction is often only as good as the prompt provided to the model. This chapter aims to demystify the art and science of prompt design, drawing inspiration from the research paper "`A Prompt Pattern Catalog to Enhance Prompt Engineering with ChatGPT`", which presents a framework for documenting and applying a catalog of prompt patterns for LLMs.

The chapter aims to provide a comprehensive insight into the intricate world of prompt design patterns such as the Meta Language Creation Pattern, The Output Automater Pattern, and the Flipped Interaction Pattern, among others. Each pattern is discussed in detail, presenting its intent, context, structure, key ideas, example implementation, and potential consequences.

We will also cover advanced techniques such as Zero-Shot Prompting, Few-Shot Prompting, and Chain-of-Thought Prompting. We will delve into the complex scenario of controlling inconsistencies within LLMs and also explore the Tree-of-Thoughts Framework.

In addition to understanding these patterns, it is equally critical to follow best practices in prompt engineering. This chapter offers concrete advice on specifying instructions and context, being explicit about expectations, and avoiding vague descriptions.

Structure

In this chapter, we will cover the following topics:

- Purpose of Prompt Design Patterns
- Anatomy of Prompts: Stimulus, Direction, Constraints
- Advanced Techniques: Zero-Shot, Few-Shot, Chain-of-Thought Prompting
- Overview of Major Prompt Patterns Best Practices for Prompt Engineering

Essence of Prompt Patterns

Just like design patterns in software engineering serve as reusable solutions to common problems, prompt patterns serve a similar purpose for LLMs. They provide a structured way to discuss, identify, and classify prompts, guiding users to more efficient and effective interactions with LLMs.

Need for Prompt Design Patterns

- **Reusability**: Once a prompt pattern is identified, it can be reused across different tasks and domains.
- **Composability**: Patterns can be combined to solve complex problems.
- **Clarity**: They offer a clear mental model, helping both developers and end-users understand the capabilities and limitations of an LLM.

Anatomy of Prompts

Prompts are the linchpin of effective interaction with language models such as ChatGPT. They serve as the blueprint that guides the model in generating responses that are not only coherent but also contextually relevant and accurate. Understanding the anatomy of prompts is therefore not just beneficial but essential for anyone looking to harness the full potential of language models. In this comprehensive guide, we will dissect the anatomy of prompts into their core components and delve into why each is crucial for effective prompt engineering.

Three Pillars of Prompt Anatomy

The art of crafting effective prompts is often likened to steering a ship through uncharted waters. The quality of the journey and the final destination are heavily influenced by how well you navigate. At the core of this navigation are three fundamental pillars that constitute the anatomy of prompts: Stimulus, Direction, and Constraints. These elements serve as the compass, rudder, and guardrails of your interaction with the model, guiding it to generate responses that are coherent, contextually relevant, and within the bounds of specified guidelines. Understanding these three pillars is essential for anyone aiming to unlock the full potential of language models through the practice of prompt engineering.

Stimulus

The stimulus is the initial spark that ignites the interaction between the user and the language model. It can take various forms such as a question, a statement, or even a command. The stimulus serves as the contextual foundation upon which the language model constructs its response.

Understanding the role of the stimulus is akin to knowing the starting point of a journey. It sets the initial conditions and context for the model, thereby influencing the direction and relevance of the generated output. A well-crafted stimulus can make the difference between a response that is on point and one that misses the mark.

Direction

The direction component serves as the navigational aid for the language model. It can include explicit instructions about the desired format, tone, or even the content of the response. For example, asking the model to "`summarize the following text in bullet points`" provides clear directional cues.

Direction acts as the steering wheel that guides the model's output along the desired path. It helps eliminate ambiguity and focuses the model's computational prowess on generating a response that aligns closely with the user's expectations. In the absence of clear direction, the model might generate outputs that, while grammatically correct, could be contextually irrelevant or off-target.

Constraints

Constraints are the set boundaries or limitations imposed on the model's responses. These could range from word count limits and topic avoidance to more nuanced restrictions, such as maintaining a formal tone.

Constraints act as guardrails that keep the model's responses within the realm of acceptability and relevance. They are particularly useful in specialized or sensitive applications where the scope of the response needs to be tightly controlled. For example, in a customer service application, constraints could be used to ensure that the model avoids making unauthorized promises or guarantees.

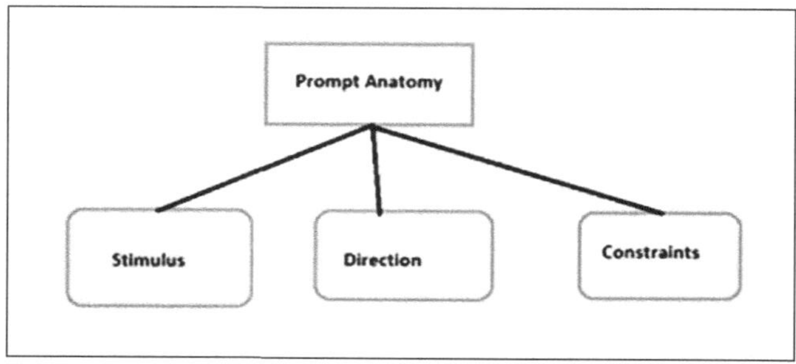

Figure 14.1: *Prompt Anatomy*

Significance of Understanding Prompt Anatomy

- **Improved Control**

  A nuanced understanding of the anatomy of prompts allows for a more controlled interaction with the language model. By meticulously crafting the stimulus, direction, and constraints, one can fine-tune the model's output to a high degree of precision.

- **Enhanced Relevance**

  Well-engineered prompts ensure that the model's responses are not just accurate but also contextually relevant. This is particularly important in applications like data analysis, content generation, and customer interaction where the value of the output is determined by its relevance to the task at hand.

- **Ethical and Responsible Use**

  Prompt engineering can serve as a first line of defense against the generation of biased or inappropriate content. By incorporating well-thought-out constraints and directions, one can mitigate the risks associated with the ethical use of AI language models.

The anatomy of prompts is a triad of stimulus, direction, and constraints. Each component plays a pivotal role in shaping the behavior and output of language models. A deep understanding of these elements not only allows for improved control and relevance but also promotes the responsible and ethical use of AI. As we continue to push the boundaries of what language models can do, effective prompt engineering will undoubtedly remain a cornerstone of this exciting field.

Advanced Techniques

In the field of prompt engineering for large language models, there are two common approaches: **Zero-Shot prompting** and **Few-Shot prompting**. Let's break down these concepts and explore them in more detail with illustrated examples.

Zero-Shot Prompting

In Zero-Shot prompting, the task is explained to the language model using natural language without providing additional context or examples. The model relies on its general intelligence and training to understand and generate a response. For example, if you ask the model to summarize a document, it will use its training data and understanding of what a "`summary`" means to generate a summary.

The main limitation of Zero-Shot prompting is that the model's understanding is limited to its training data. To improve Zero-Shot prompting, you can either fine-tune the model or provide examples that help the model better understand the task.

Few-Shot Prompting

Few-shot prompting involves providing the model with examples of the task at hand. This approach is useful for more complex tasks that require a specific format or style. By providing examples, you give the model a template to follow. For example, if you want the model to generate poetry, you can provide a few examples of poems to guide the model's output.

Flexibility and Popularity: Few-shot prompting is popular because it offers more flexibility and allows for nuanced output without requiring extensive model fine-tuning.

Chain-of-Thought Prompting

Chain-of-thought prompting involves making the thought process of the language model part of its output. By forcing the model to articulate its thought process, we can expect more accurate and reasoned outputs. For example, if you ask the model to solve a math problem step-by-step, it will break down the problem and provide a detailed solution.

Examples:

- **Zero-Shot**: Asking the model to break down a mathematical problem step-by-step.
- **Few-Shot**: Providing the model with similar problems and their step-by-step solutions as a guide.

Tree-of-Thoughts Framework

For more complex problems, the Tree-of-Thoughts framework can be employed. This involves branching out every thought generation into multiple possibilities and selecting the strongest thought at each level. It allows the model to explore different paths and choose the most promising one.

Various search techniques, such as Breadth-First Search, can be used to navigate through the thought tree and find the most desired path.

By understanding and applying these techniques in prompt engineering, we can effectively guide large language models to generate more accurate and relevant responses.

Controlling Inconsistencies: Temperature and Self-Consistency

Language models can produce inconsistent results due to their autoregressive nature. To control this, parameters like "`temperature`" can be adjusted. A lower temperature value will produce more deterministic results, while a higher value will introduce randomness.

This technique involves running the same prompt multiple times and then merging the results using a defined strategy. For example, for categorical outputs, you can use majority voting, and for numerical outputs, you can use averaging.

Prompt Engineering Design Patterns

Design patterns are reusable solutions to common problems that arise during software design and development. They provide a structured approach to solving these problems and help improve the quality, maintainability, and scalability of software systems. In the context provided, the chapter discusses various prompt patterns that can be used to enhance the interaction between a language model and the user. Let's explore these prompt patterns in more detail:

Prompt Pattern Catalog

Following is a bouquet of identified patterns of a prompt that has been classified and detailed with examples:

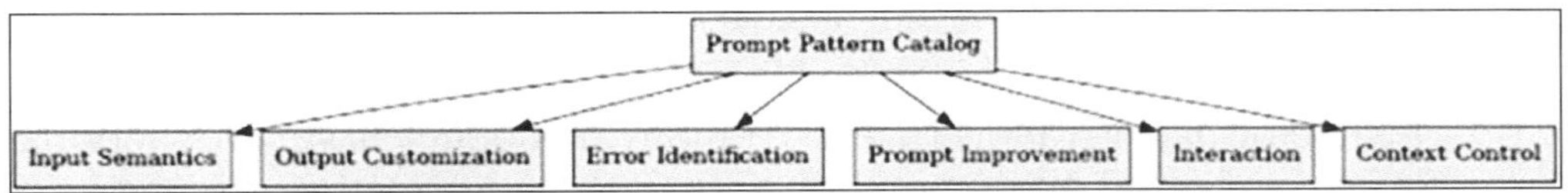

Figure 14.2: *Prompt Pattern Catalog*

Input Semantics

The Input Semantics category focuses on how a language model understands and translates input into something it can use to generate output. One of the prompt patterns in this category is the Meta Language Creation pattern. This pattern involves creating a custom language for the language model to understand. It can be useful when the default input language is not suitable for expressing the user's ideas to the model.

Suppose you are interacting with a language model that is trained to generate code snippets. However, the default input language of the model does not support a specific programming language feature that you want to include in the code. In this case, you can use the Meta Language Creation pattern to define a custom syntax or set of keywords that the model can understand and generate code accordingly.

- **Prompt Example**: "`When I say 'BS,' I mean 'Binary Search.' Now, how do I implement BS?`"
- **Outcome**: The LLM understands that "`BS`" refers to "`Binary Search`" and provides you with a code snippet for implementing a Binary Search algorithm.

Output Customization

The Output Customization category focuses on constraining or tailoring the output generated by the language model. Several prompt patterns fall under this category, including Output Automater, Persona, Visualization Generator, Recipe, and Template patterns.

- The Output Automater pattern allows users to create scripts that automate tasks suggested by the language model's output. For example, if the model suggests a series of steps to perform a task, the user can automate those steps using a script generated by the model.

- The Persona pattern gives the language model a specific persona or role to play when generating output. This can add a personalized touch to the generated content.
- The Visualization Generator pattern enables users to generate visualizations by producing textual outputs that can be fed into other tools, such as AI-based image generators.
- The Recipe pattern allows users to obtain a sequence of steps or actions to achieve a desired outcome, even with partial information or constraints.
- The Template pattern allows users to specify a template for the output, which the language model fills in with relevant content.

Let's say you are using a language model to generate blog post introductions. By applying the Output Customization patterns, you can automate the process of generating blog post outlines, assign a specific writing style or tone to the model, generate visualizations to accompany the text, follow a recipe-like structure for the introduction, and use a predefined template to ensure consistency.

- **Prompt Example**: "`Generate a workout routine for me and add it to my Google Calendar.`"
- **Outcome**: The LLM generates a workout routine and provides a script that, when executed, will add the routine to your Google Calendar.

Error Identification

The Error Identification category focuses on identifying and resolving errors in the output generated by the language model. Two prompt patterns in this category are the Fact Checklist and Reflection patterns.

- The Fact Checklist pattern requires the language model to generate a list of facts on which the output depends. This list can be used for fact-checking purposes.
- The Reflection pattern involves the language model introspecting on its own output and identifying any errors.

Suppose you are using a language model to generate scientific explanations. By applying the Error Identification patterns, the model can provide a list of facts it used in generating the explanation, allowing you to verify the accuracy of those facts. Additionally, the model can reflect on its own output and identify any inconsistencies or errors that may have occurred during the generation process.

- **Prompt Example**: "`Tell me about the American Revolution and list the facts that should be fact-checked.`"

- **Outcome**: The LLM provides an overview of the American Revolution and lists key facts like "`The war started in 1775`" for you to fact-check.

Prompt Improvement

The Prompt Improvement category focuses on improving the quality of both input and output. Several prompt patterns fall under this category, including Question Refinement, Alternative Approaches, Cognitive Verifier, and Refusal Breaker patterns.

- The Question Refinement pattern ensures that the language model suggests a better version of the user's question. It helps in clarifying and refining the user's input.
- The Alternative Approaches pattern requires the language model to suggest alternative ways of accomplishing a user-specified task.
- The Cognitive Verifier pattern instructs the language model to suggest a series of sub-questions for the user to answer. The model then combines the answers to these sub-questions to produce an answer to the overall question.
- The Refusal Breaker pattern requires the language model to reword the user's question when it refuses to produce an answer.

Imagine you are using a language model to assist with problem-solving. By applying the Prompt Improvement patterns, the model can refine and rephrase your initial question to make it more specific and actionable. It can also suggest alternative approaches to solving the problem, ask you relevant sub-questions to gather more information and rephrase your question if it initially refuses to provide an answer.

- **Prompt Example**: "`Good sci-fi?`"
- **Outcome**: The LLM refines your question to "`What are some good science fiction books?`" and provides a list of recommended titles.

Interaction

The Interaction category focuses on the interaction between the user and the language model. Three prompt patterns in this category are the Flipped Interaction, Game Play, and Infinite Generation patterns.

- The Flipped Interaction pattern requires the language model to ask questions instead of generating output. This can be useful in scenarios where the model needs more information from the user.

- The Game Play pattern involves the language model generating output in the form of a game. This can make the interaction more engaging and interactive.
- The Infinite Generation pattern allows the language model to generate output indefinitely without the user having to reenter the generator prompt each time.

Suppose you are using a language model to create a conversational chatbot. By applying the Interaction patterns, the model can ask follow-up questions to gather more context, engage the user in a game-like conversation, and generate continuous responses without requiring the user to provide prompts repeatedly.

- **Prompt Example**: "`Start a text-based adventure game.`"
- **Outcome**: The LLM transforms into a game master and starts narrating a quest. You find yourself choosing between exploring a dark cave or climbing a mysterious mountain.

Context Control

The Context Control category focuses on controlling the contextual information in which the language model operates. One prompt pattern in this category is the Context Manager pattern, which allows users to specify the context for the model's output.

Let's say you are using a language model to generate personalized recommendations based on user preferences. By applying the Context Control pattern, you can provide the model with specific contextual information, such as the user's previous interactions, preferences, or browsing history, to generate more accurate and relevant recommendations.

- **Prompt Example**: "`I want answers based on scientific research. Tell me about the benefits of exercise.`"
- **Outcome**: The LLM provides information on the benefits of exercise, citing scientific studies to back up each point.

Category	Description	Example Prompt	Outcome
Input Semantics	How the language model understands and translates input.	"`When I say 'BS,' I mean 'Binary Search.' Now, how do I implement BS?`"	The LLM understands that "`BS`" refers to "`Binary Search`" and provides a code snippet for implementing a Binary Search algorithm.

Output Customization	Tailoring the output generated by the language model.	"`Generate a workout routine for me and add it to my Google Calendar.`"	The LLM generates a workout routine and provides a script that adds the routine to your Google Calendar.
Error Identification	Identifying and resolving errors in the output.	"`Tell me about the American Revolution and list the facts that should be fact-checked.`"	The LLM provides an overview of the American Revolution and lists key facts for fact-checking.
Prompt Improvement	Improving the quality of both input and output.	"`Good sci-fi?`"	The LLM refines the question to "`What are some good science fiction books?`" and provides a list of recommended titles.
Interaction	Managing the interaction between the user and the language model.	"`Start a text-based adventure game.`"	The LLM transforms into a game master and starts narrating a quest, allowing the user to make choices.
Context Control	Controlling the contextual information in which the model operates.	"`I want answers based on scientific research. Tell me about the benefits of exercise.`"	The LLM provides information on the benefits of exercise based on scientific research.

Table 14.1: *Prompt Patterns Overview*

Meta Language Creation Pattern

The Meta Language Creation pattern is a design pattern that allows you to create a customized language or notation for interacting with a large language model (LLM), such as the AI model you are communicating with right now. This pattern is particularly useful when you want to define specific meanings for words, symbols, or statements in a way that the LLM understands.

The structure of this pattern is simple: it involves defining the meaning of one or more symbols, words, or statements. For example, you might decide that whenever you type "`X`", you want the LLM to interpret it as "`Y`". Or, you might define a particular phrase to trigger a specific action from the LLM.

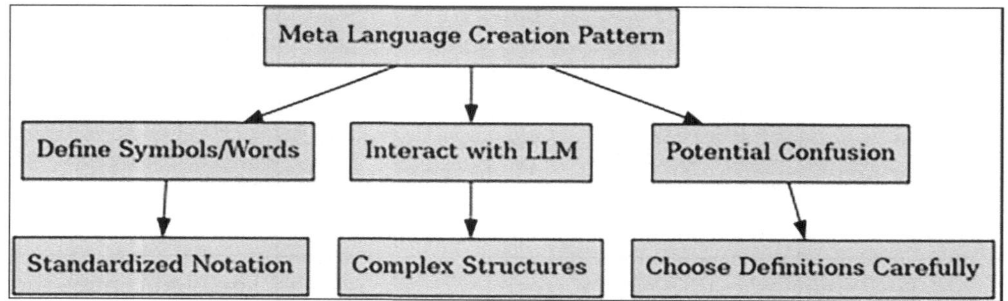

Figure 14.3: *Meta Language Creation Pattern*

Imagine you are discussing graph theory and you want to establish a shorthand for describing graphs. You could use the Meta Language Creation pattern like this:

```
        "From now on, whenever I type two identifiers separated by '→,' I
am describing a graph. For example, 'a → b' is describing a graph with
nodes 'a' and 'b' and an edge between them."
        This creates a standardized notation for describing graphs, which
makes it easier to communicate complex structures. So, if you type 'c →
d', the LLM would understand that you're describing a graph with nodes
'c' and 'd' and an edge between them.
```

While the Meta Language Creation pattern can be very powerful, it's important to be aware that it can also introduce potential confusion. For instance, if you define common terms or symbols in a way that conflicts with their general usage, the LLM might get confused.

For example, if you define "`a`" to mean "`Marie Antoinette`", this could lead to confusion because "`a`" is commonly used as an indefinite article in English. Therefore, it's important to choose your definitions carefully to avoid misinterpretation.

To summarize, the Meta Language Creation pattern is a design pattern that gives you the ability to establish a customized language or notation for interacting with the LLM. It's a powerful tool for making complex ideas more accessible, but it requires careful usage to avoid potential confusion.

Think of the Meta Language Creation pattern as creating a secret code or shorthand between you and the LLM. For instance, in the world of texting, people often use "`BRB`" as a shorthand for "`Be Right Back`". This is a simple example of creating a new meaning for a specific symbol or phrase. The Meta Language Creation pattern takes this idea and applies it to the interaction between you and the LLM, allowing for more efficient and unique communication.

However, just as it might be confusing if you started using "`BRB`" to mean "`Bring Red Balloons`" without notifying your friends, it could be equally confusing if you redefine commonly used terms or symbols in your interaction with the LLM. So, always approach this pattern with clarity and caution.

Output Automater Pattern

The Output Automater pattern is a design pattern that aims to generate an executable script or other automation artifact from the Large Language Model (LLM). When the LLM recommends certain steps or actions, it should also produce an executable artifact that can carry out these steps automatically, reducing the manual effort required.

The structure of this pattern is straightforward: whenever the LLM provides an output that includes a series of steps to be taken, it should also generate a script or another form of an executable artifact that automates these steps. This automation can save you time and effort, especially if the recommended steps are complex or need to be repeated often.

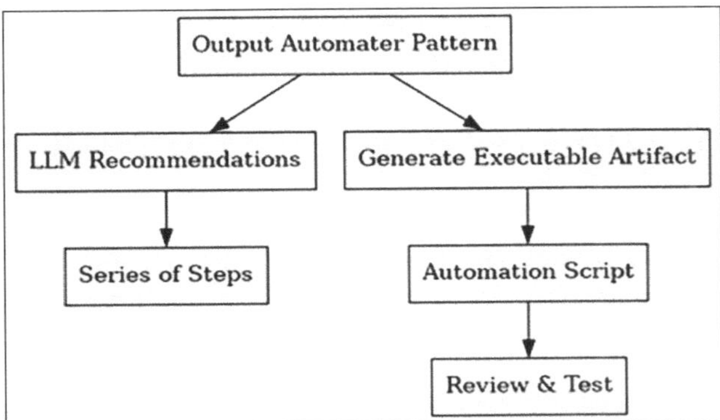

Figure 14.4: *Output Automater Pattern*

Let's say you are setting up a Python development environment and you ask the LLM for help. The LLM might suggest a series of commands that you need to run in your terminal, such as installing certain packages, setting environment variables, and so on.

Using the Output Automater pattern, the LLM could also generate a Bash script for you that includes all these commands. That way, instead of manually typing each command into your terminal, you could just run the Bash script and have all the steps performed automatically.

So, if the LLM's recommendations were something like this:

```
Install the numpy package.
Install the pandas package.
Set the PYTHONPATH environment variable.
```

Then, the Bash script might look something like this:

```
pip install numpy
pip install pandas
export PYTHONPATH=/path/to/your/python
```

With this script, you can automate the whole process with a single command, bash setup.sh, where setup.sh is the name of the Bash script.

Think of the Output Automater pattern as a personal assistant who not only tells you what steps you need to take to accomplish a task, but also does the task for you. It's like asking a cooking assistant for a cake recipe and getting not only the recipe but also a machine that automatically mixes the ingredients for you.

This pattern is particularly useful when dealing with complex or repetitive tasks. However, it's important to note that the automation generated by the LLM is based on its understanding of the task, and it's always important to review and test any generated scripts or automation for accuracy and safety before use.

Understanding Flipped Interaction Pattern

The Flipped Interaction pattern is a design pattern that involves the LLM asking questions to the user, rather than the other way around. The purpose of this pattern is to gather enough information from the user to accomplish a specific goal, such as generating a Python script for deployment.

The key elements of this pattern are:

- **Goal-Oriented Interaction**: The LLM focuses on asking questions that are relevant to achieving the specified goal.
- **Scoped Interaction:** The interaction can be ended when the goal is achieved or when the user indicates they want to stop, such as by saying "`Stop asking questions.`"
- **Question Limit (Optional)**: The number of questions asked per cycle can be limited to improve the user experience and prevent the interaction from becoming overwhelming.

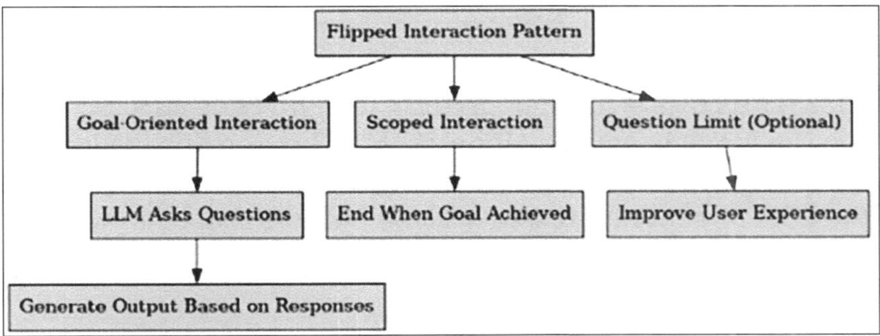

Figure 14.5: *Flipped Interaction Pattern*

Let's say you want to deploy a Python application to AWS and have the LLM generate a deployment script for you. You can initiate the Flipped Interaction pattern like this:

```
"From now on, I would like you to ask me questions to deploy a Python application to AWS. When you have enough information to deploy the application, create a Python script to automate the deployment."
```

The LLM might then start asking you questions like:

- What is the name of your AWS S3 bucket?
- Do you need to set up an AWS Lambda function for your application?
- Do you have any specific configurations you need for AWS?

Once it has gathered enough information, the LLM can then generate a Python script that automates the deployment process based on your responses.

The Flipped Interaction pattern is open-ended, which means it can be reused for different goals. However, this openness might also lead to the LLM asking unnecessary or irrelevant questions. Therefore, it's important to guide the LLM by being as specific as possible about the goal of the interaction.

Think of the Flipped Interaction pattern as a consultation with a specialist. For example, when you visit a doctor, the doctor will ask you a series of questions to understand your symptoms and diagnose your condition. Similarly, the LLM asks you questions to understand your needs and to provide the right solution.

However, just like a doctor's consultation, it's important to provide clear and accurate information to the LLM. If the LLM asks irrelevant questions or seems to misunderstand the goal, you can guide it back on track with more specific instructions.

Persona Pattern

The Persona pattern is a design pattern that gives a specific "`persona`" or character to the Large Language Model (LLM). This persona could be a job role, a fictional character, or even a historical figure. The purpose of this pattern is to guide the LLM to generate responses and outputs that align with the chosen persona.

The key elements of this pattern are as follows:

- **Act as Persona X:** The LLM takes on the role of a specific persona. This could be anything from a cybersecurity expert to a history teacher or even a character from a novel.
- **Provide Outputs**: The LLM generates outputs that fit within the context of the chosen persona. These outputs could be a range of things, from advice and recommendations to stories or code, depending on the persona.

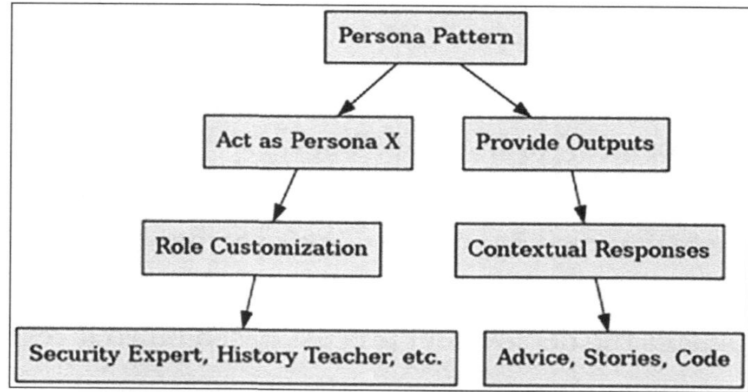

Figure 14.6: *Persona Pattern*

For instance, you could instruct the LLM to act as a security expert and ask it to review a piece of code for potential vulnerabilities. The instruction might look something like this:

"Act as a security expert and review this code for vulnerabilities."

The LLM, now acting as a security expert, would then analyze the code and provide feedback or suggestions based on common security practices and principles.

The Persona pattern allows for a lot of customization and can make interactions with the LLM more engaging and tailored to specific use cases. However, it's important to use it responsibly. For instance, it's not advisable to have personas that impersonate real living people or harmful figures. This is due to underlying rules for privacy and security that need to be respected.

Think of the Persona pattern as putting on a costume during a theatre performance. When an actor puts on the costume of a character, their speech, actions, and reactions are expected to align with that character. Similarly, when the LLM takes on a persona, it adjusts its outputs to align with the characteristics, knowledge, and perspective of that persona.

Just like in a theatre performance, the effect of the Persona pattern depends on the actor's (in this case, the LLM's) understanding of the character. The more specific and accurate the persona, the more effective the LLM can be in producing suitable outputs. However, as with any performance, it's important to remember that the LLM is only playing a role and its outputs should be evaluated accordingly.

Question Refinement Pattern

The Question Refinement pattern is a design pattern that aims to enhance the quality of the questions you pose to the LLM. It is especially beneficial when your initial question is too broad, vague, or lacks specificity.

This pattern has two key elements:

- **Contextual Understanding**: The LLM refines the question by considering the context, such as the programming language or framework being used. For instance, if you are working in a Python environment, the LLM will use Python-specific knowledge to refine your question.
- **Enhanced Questioning**: The refined question not only narrows down the scope but also educates you about potential issues you should consider. The LLM does this by rephrasing the question in a way that addresses the specific details needed for a precise answer.

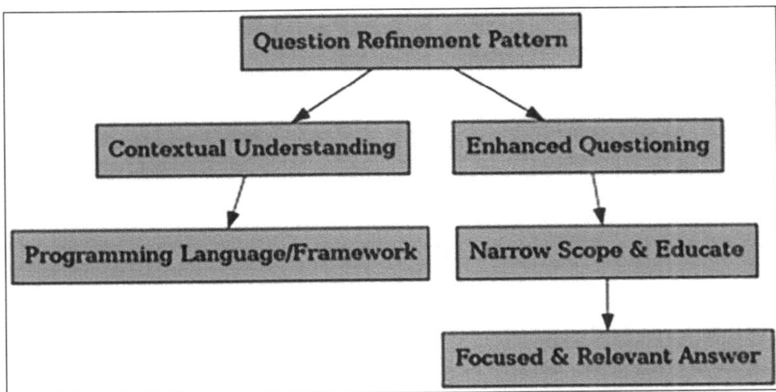

Figure 14.7: *Question Refinement pattern*

For example, if you ask, "`How do I handle user authentication in my web application?`", the LLM could refine it to:

"`What are the best practices for handling user authentication securely in a FastAPI web application to mitigate common security risks?`"

This refined question is more specific and useful because it focuses on security best practices and specifically mentions FastAPI, a Python web framework. Therefore, it guides the LLM to provide a more focused and relevant answer.

While the Question Refinement pattern can lead to more efficient and accurate interactions, it might also over-specify the user's inquiry, causing them to miss out on broader perspectives. For example, focusing on FastAPI might exclude useful information about general web security practices. To avoid this, you can instruct the LLM not to narrow down to specific languages or frameworks.

Imagine you are asking a travel guide for places to visit in a city. If you ask a very broad question like "`What should I visit in New York?`", you might get overwhelmed by the sheer number of options. However, if the travel guide refines your question to "`What are the best art museums to visit in New York for contemporary art enthusiasts?`", your options become much more manageable and relevant to your specific interest. That's exactly what the Question Refinement pattern does: it helps the LLM provide you with more relevant and useful answers by refining your questions.

Alternative Approaches Pattern

The Alternative Approaches pattern is a design pattern that provides different methods or strategies to accomplish a specific task. This pattern is particularly useful in breaking cognitive biases and enabling users to choose the most effective approach based on their situation, preference, and resources.

This pattern has three key elements:

- **Scope Definition**: You, as the user, define the scope within which the LLM should provide alternatives. The scope could be based on a language, a platform, a technology, or a constraint that you specify.
- **List Alternatives**: Within the defined scope, the LLM lists the best alternative approaches for achieving the desired task.
- **Pros and Cons (Optional)**: The LLM can provide a comparison of the pros and cons of each approach. This helps you to make a more informed decision about which approach to take.

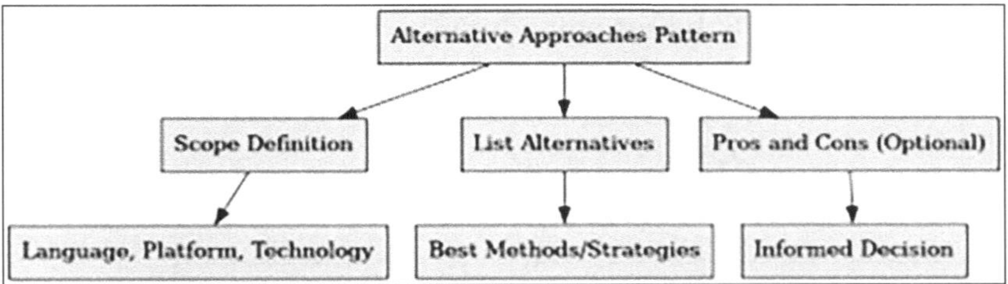

Figure 14.8: *Alternate Approach Pattern*

For instance, if you ask, "`How do I deploy this Python application?`", the LLM could offer alternatives like:

- **Using Docker**: This method involves containerizing the application and deploying it. It's a good choice to ensure consistency across different environments.
- **Using a cloud service like AWS or Google Cloud**: These platforms offer infrastructure and services to deploy applications with scalability and reliability.
- **Using a traditional web server like Apache or Nginx**: This is a common approach that might be suitable if you have a simple application and existing server infrastructure.

For each of these alternatives, the LLM could also mention the pros and cons. For example, using Docker might provide environment consistency but could also introduce complexity in managing containers.

While the Alternative Approaches pattern ensures that you are aware of various approaches, it might also introduce complexity by presenting too many options. However, you can manage this by defining a narrower scope upfront.

Imagine you are asking a travel agent about different ways to reach a destination. The agent could suggest flying, taking a train, or driving. Each option has its pros and cons: flying is fast but can be expensive, taking a train is less expensive but takes longer, and driving gives you flexibility but can be tiring. The Alternative Approaches pattern is just like that travel agent, suggesting different ways to achieve a task and helping you choose the best one for your specific situation.

Cognitive Verifier Pattern

The Cognitive Verifier pattern is a design pattern that aims to enhance the quality of answers provided by the Large Language Model (LLM). It achieves this by breaking down a high-level question into additional, more specific questions.

This pattern is particularly beneficial when the initial question is too vague or if the user may not be fully knowledgeable in a specific domain.

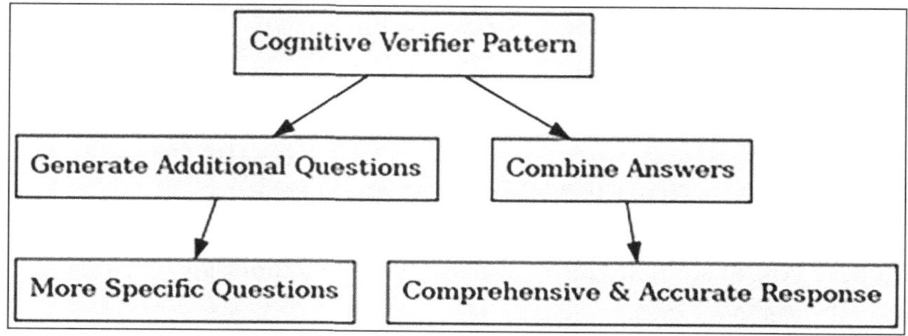

Figure 14.9: *Cognitive Verifier Pattern*

The Cognitive Verifier pattern comprises the following key steps:

1. **Generate Additional Questions:** The LLM generates a set of more specific questions that would help provide a more precise and accurate answer to the original high-level question.
2. **Combine Answers**: After the additional questions are answered by the user, the LLM combines these answers to generate a comprehensive and accurate response to the initial question.

   For instance, if your question is, "`How can I improve my software project?`", the

   LLM could generate additional questions like:

- "`What programming languages are you using in your project?`"
- "`What is the main goal or functionality of your project?`"
- "`Are you currently facing any performance issues?`"

After you provide answers to these questions, the LLM will then combine this information to provide a tailored set of recommendations for improving your specific software project.

The Cognitive Verifier pattern adds depth to your interactions with LLMs by ensuring that the model gathers all the necessary information to answer your questions accurately. However, it might also introduce complexity or make the interaction lengthy by generating too many additional questions. You can manage this by specifying the exact number of questions you want the LLM to generate.

Think of the Cognitive Verifier pattern like a detective trying to solve a case. Instead of making a hasty conclusion based on limited evidence, the detective asks a series of additional questions to gather more information and ensure a more accurate conclusion. Similarly, the Cognitive Verifier pattern allows the LLM to ask additional questions to gather all necessary details, ensuring a more precise and accurate response to your initial question.

Fact Checklist Pattern

The Fact Checklist pattern is a design pattern that instructs the LLM to provide a list of facts that are present in its output. This pattern aims to inform the user of the facts or assumptions the output is based on, thereby allowing them to perform due diligence and ensure accuracy.

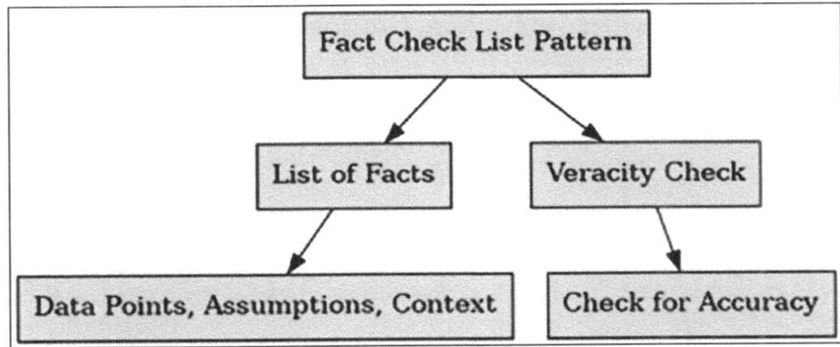

***Figure 14.10**: Fact List Pattern*

The Fact Checklist pattern has two key ideas:

- **List of Facts**: The LLM generates a set of facts that are included in the output. These facts could be data points, assumptions, or elements that are critical to the output's context.
- **Veracity Check**: If any of the facts listed are incorrect, they could undermine the truthfulness of the entire output. Therefore, these facts must be checked for accuracy.

For instance, if the LLM generates a Python requirements.txt file (a file that lists all Python libraries the project depends on), it could list the versions of libraries as facts that should be checked. The LLM might state, "`This requirements.txt file assumes that you're using version 3.8.1 of the pandas library and version 1.2.0 of the numpy library.`" As a user, you would need to check if these versions are correct and compatible with your project.

The Fact Checklist pattern is particularly useful when users are not domain experts and may not easily spot errors or inconsistencies. It helps users validate the output and improves their understanding of the underlying assumptions.

However, this pattern only applies when the output type is amenable to fact-checking. For example, it works well with code or data outputs, but may not be as useful with more subjective or creative outputs.

Think of the Fact Checklist pattern like a recipe. When you are cooking, the recipe provides a list of ingredients (facts) you need. But before you start cooking, you need to check if you have all the ingredients and if they are fresh. In the same way, the LLM provides an output (the recipe) and a list of facts (the ingredients), which you need to check for accuracy before proceeding.

Template Pattern

The Template Pattern is a design pattern that ensures the output from an LLM adheres to a specific format or structure. This is particularly useful in scenarios where the output needs to fit into a particular application or use case that the LLM is not inherently aware of.

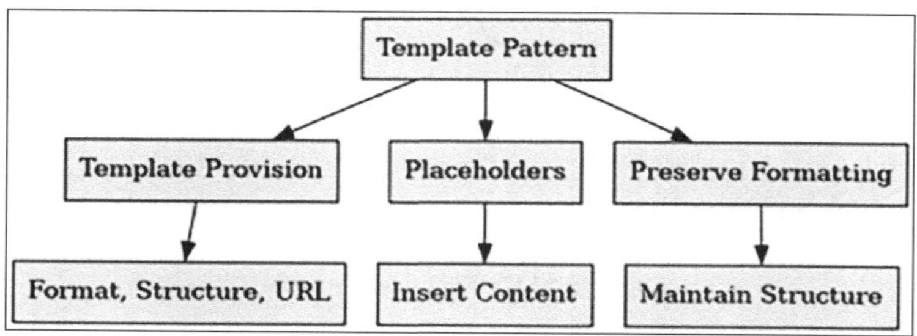

Figure 14.11: *Template Pattern*

The Template Pattern comprises the following key elements:

- **Template Provision**: The user provides a template that sets the structure for the LLM's output. This template can be a specific format, structure, or even a URL pattern.
- **Placeholders**: The template includes placeholders where the LLM should insert the generated content. These placeholders are usually marked with specific symbols or all-cap letters.
- **Preserve Formatting**: The LLM is guided to maintain the overall structure and formatting of the template throughout its output.

For example, if you want to generate URLs that insert specific information into designated positions, your interaction with the LLM might look like this:

You: "`I am going to provide a template for your output. Everything in all caps is a placeholder. Any time that you generate text, try to fit it into` `one of the placeholders that I list. Please preserve the formatting and overall template that I provide at https://myapi.com/NAME/profile/JOB."`

Then, when you ask the LLM to "Generate a name and job title for a person," it might respond with:

"https://myapi.com/Emily Parker/profile/Software Engineer"

In this example, "Emily Parker" and "Software Engineer" fill the "NAME" and "JOB" placeholders in the template URL.

The Template Pattern provides a structured way to ensure that the LLM's output fits into a specific format or structure. However, it has some limitations:

- **Filtering Output**: The Template Pattern could filter out potentially useful information. For example, the LLM might usually provide helpful descriptions or explanations along with the output, but this pattern might filter out these details to fit the template.
- **Combining with Other Patterns**: This pattern might not be easily combinable with other patterns that require a different output format.

Think of the Template Pattern as a fill-in-the-blank puzzle. The puzzle provides a structure (the template with blank spaces), and your job is to fill in the blanks (placeholders) with appropriate words. Similarly, in the Template Pattern, the LLM fills in the placeholders in the provided template with appropriate content.

Infinite Generation Pattern

The Infinite Generation Pattern is a design pattern that automates the generation of multiple outputs based on a single initial prompt. This pattern reduces the need for the user to continually re-enter the prompt for each output, which is especially beneficial for tasks that require repetitive application of the same prompt, such as generating code for different types of entities or creating multiple instances of a specific format.

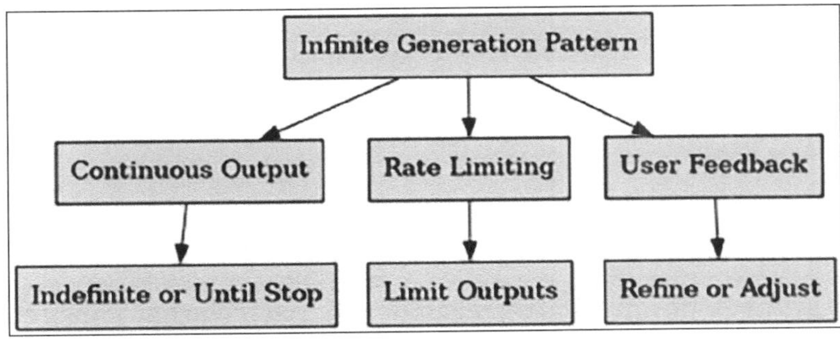

Figure 14.12: *Infinite generation Pattern*

The Infinite Generation Pattern comprises the following key ideas:

- **Continuous Output**: The LLM is instructed to generate outputs indefinitely, or until a specific stop condition is met by the user.
- **Rate Limiting**: The user can limit the number of outputs generated at a time. This is useful for managing the LLM's output length limitations and preventing information overload.
- **User Feedback**: The pattern allows for additional user inputs between outputs. This feedback can be used to refine the generation process or adjust the output.

Practical Example:

For example, you could instruct the LLM as follows: "`From now on, I want you to generate a name and job until I say stop. Please fit it into this template:`

`https://myapi.com/NAME/profile/JOB.`"

The LLM will then proceed to generate outputs such as:

- "https://myapi.com/JohnDoe/profile/SoftwareEngineer"
- "https://myapi.com/JaneDoe/profile/DataScientist"

And so on, until you instruct it to stop.

The Infinite Generation Pattern is powerful for automating repetitive tasks, but it's important to monitor the outputs for quality and relevance. The LLM might lose track of the original prompt instructions over time, leading to less accurate outputs. The outputs may also become repetitive or deviate from the intended behavior.

Despite its limitations, the Infinite Generation Pattern offers a way to automate the generation of multiple outputs, making it highly useful for tasks that require repetitive application of the same prompt.

Think of the Infinite Generation Pattern as a factory assembly line. Once set up with the right instructions (the original prompt), the assembly line can continuously produce items (outputs) without needing constant supervision. However, just like a factory assembly line, it is essential to periodically check the products' quality and accuracy to make sure they meet the desired standards.

Visualization Generator Pattern

The Visualization Generator Pattern is a design pattern that aims to extend the capabilities of text-based Large Language Models (LLMs) to generate visual content. Although LLMs can't create images directly, they can generate text-based inputs that can be used by specialized visualization tools like Graphviz Dot or DALL-E. By combining textual and visual information, this pattern makes complex concepts more accessible and understandable.

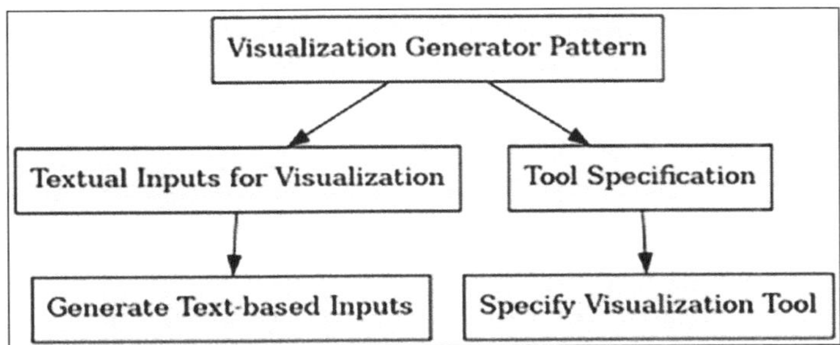

Figure 14.13: *Visualization Generator Pattern*

The Visualization Generator Pattern is structured around these key ideas:

- **Textual Inputs for Visualization**: The LLM is instructed to generate text-based inputs that can be interpreted by another tool to create visualizations.
- **Tool Specification:** The user specifies the tool that will be used for generating the visualization. They may also specify the type of visualization required, such as a bar chart, UML diagram, and so on.

For instance, you could instruct the LLM with something like: "`Whenever I ask you to visualize something, please create either a Graphviz Dot file or DALL-E prompt that I can use to create the visualization. Choose the appropriate tools based on what needs to be visualized.`" With this instruction, if you ask the LLM to represent a binary tree, it might respond with a Graphviz Dot file like this:

```
digraph Binary_Tree {
    1 -> 2;
    1 -> 3;
    2 -> 4;
    2 -> 5;
}
```

This Dot file can then be fed into Graphviz to generate a visualization of a binary tree.

The Visualization Generator Pattern opens up a new dimension of expressiveness by enabling visual outputs. However, using this pattern requires the user to have access to the specified visualization tool and know how to use it. The pattern creates a pipeline where the LLM's output is just one part of a larger system that culminates in a visualization.

While the pattern can automate the creation of visualizations, it's important to monitor the outputs to ensure they adhere to the desired behavior. The outputs may need refinement to generate appropriate visualizations.

Think of the Visualization Generator Pattern like a screenplay writer and a film director. The LLM, like the screenplay writer, provides the script (text-based inputs) that sets the scene and describes the actions. The visualization tool, like the film director, then takes this script and brings it to life visually. The resulting visualization helps users better understand the concept, just as a movie helps viewers better understand a story.

Game Play Pattern

The Game Play Pattern is a design pattern designed to create an interactive game around a specific topic. This pattern is particularly useful for creating engaging and educational experiences, especially when the game's rules are simple, but the content is wide-ranging and varied. The pattern enables the LLM to generate scenarios or questions around a topic, guiding the gameplay.

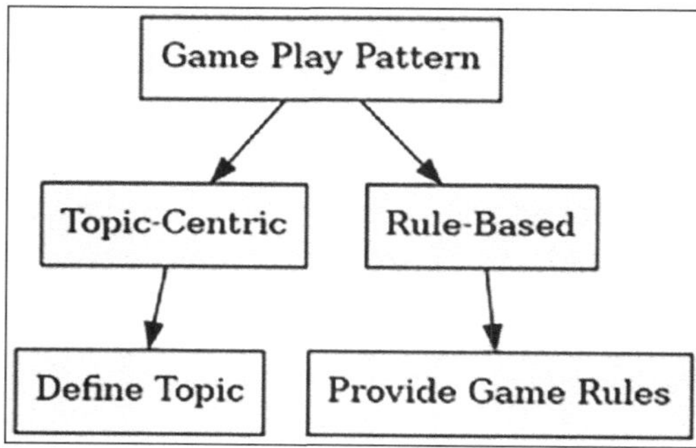

Figure 14.14: *Game Play Pattern*

The Game Play Pattern consists of the following key elements:

- **Topic-Centric:** The game is centered around a specific topic, which is defined by the user. This could be anything from history trivia to a game about cybersecurity.
- **Rule-Based**: The user provides one or more fundamental rules that guide the gameplay. These rules should be within the capabilities of the LLM to understand and implement.

For instance, you could create a cybersecurity game where the LLM acts as a compromised Linux terminal. The user would input Linux commands, and the LLM would respond as if it were a real terminal, providing clues to help the user figure out how the system was compromised.

In this scenario, the LLM could respond with simulated terminal outputs such as:

```
root@compromised:~# ls
README.txt  secret_folder
```

The user's goal would be to navigate the virtual system, using the LLM's responses to uncover the nature of the compromise.

The Game Play Pattern can be effectively combined with other patterns like the Persona, Infinite Generation, and Visualization Generator patterns to create a more immersive and interactive experience.

For example, in a cybersecurity game, the LLM could use the Persona pattern to act as a Linux terminal, the Infinite Generation pattern to continuously generate new scenarios, and the Visualization Generator pattern to visualize network traffic flows.

However, while the Game Play Pattern can create engaging and educational games, it's important to monitor the gameplay to ensure it adheres to the desired behavior. The LLM might lose track of the original game rules over time, and the gameplay may become less engaging or deviate from the intended behavior.

Imagine the Game Play Pattern as being like a game master in a tabletop role-playing game. The game master sets the scene, describes the environment, and guides the players through the game's scenarios. Similarly, the LLM, using the Game Play Pattern, can act as a game master, guiding users through an interactive and educational game experience.

Reflection Pattern

The Reflection Pattern aims to make large language models (LLMs) more transparent by requiring them to explain the rationale behind their answers. This pattern can help users:

- Understand the model's thought process
- Validate the model's responses
- Improve their questioning techniques

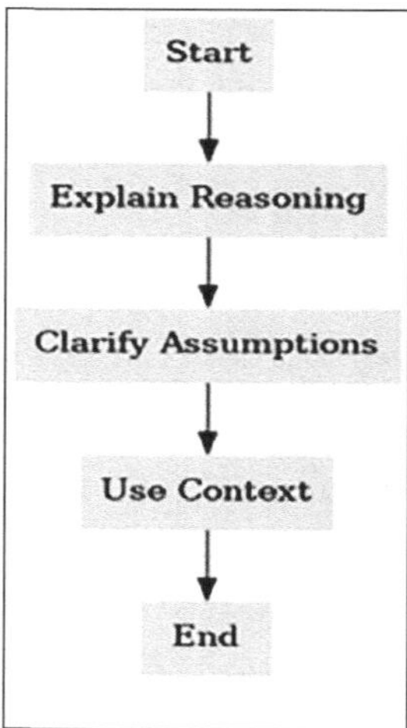

Figure 14.15: *Reflection Pattern*

The key ideas of the Reflection Pattern are:

- **Explain the reasoning**: After generating an answer, the LLM should provide an explanation of how it arrived at that answer. This explanation should synthesize relevant information from the provided context and the LLM's knowledge base.
- **Clarify assumptions**: The LLM should disclose any assumptions it made while generating the answer. This helps users identify potential gaps or inaccuracies.
- **Use context:** If provided a context that the explanation is intended to refine the user's questions, the LLM can tailor its responses accordingly.

An example use case is recommending a software framework. The LLM would explain why it recommended that specific framework and what assumptions it made.

The benefits of this pattern are increased understanding and the ability to debug prompts. However, there are also risks, such as the LLM providing explanations that are too complex or propagating errors in the initial answer.

The Reflection Pattern, when combined with other patterns like the Fact Check List, can improve the transparency, reliability, and effectiveness of LLMs by requiring explanations for their outputs.

Refusal Breaker Pattern

If the large language model cannot answer a question, it should provide an explanation for why it is unable to answer. This helps the user understand the model's limitations and think of alternative ways to phrase the question.

The model should suggest one or more alternative ways of phrasing the question that it can potentially answer. This gives the user options to try reformulating the question in a way the model can respond to.

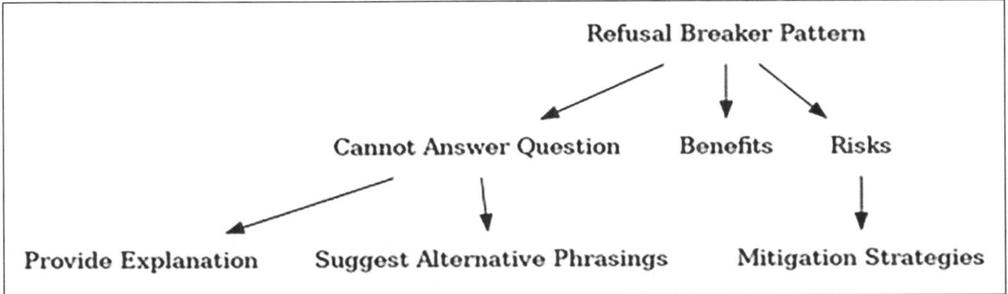

Figure 14.16: *Refusal Breaker Pattern*

For example, if asked "`What is the meaning of life?`", the model could respond: "`As an AI language model, I don't have personal beliefs. The meaning of life is a complex topic that varies from person to person. You could rephrase the question as 'What are some philosophical perspectives on the meaning of life?' or 'What are some common beliefs about the purpose of life?'`"

This pattern has both benefits and risks:

- It can help users get answers by suggesting better question phrasing
- But it could also be misused to find loopholes in the model's safety mechanisms
- The alternative questions may not fully address the original intent
- It can improve user understanding of the model's capabilities and limitations

To mitigate risks, guidelines or restrictions may need to be put in place for how this pattern is used responsibly. The model's explanations and alternative suggestions should be reviewed to ensure they do not enable harmful behaviors.

Context Manager Pattern

The Context Manager Pattern is a design pattern that allows users to specify or remove context in a conversation with an LLM. This pattern can help improve the relevance and accuracy of the LLM's responses by guiding its focus on specific topics or excluding unrelated topics.

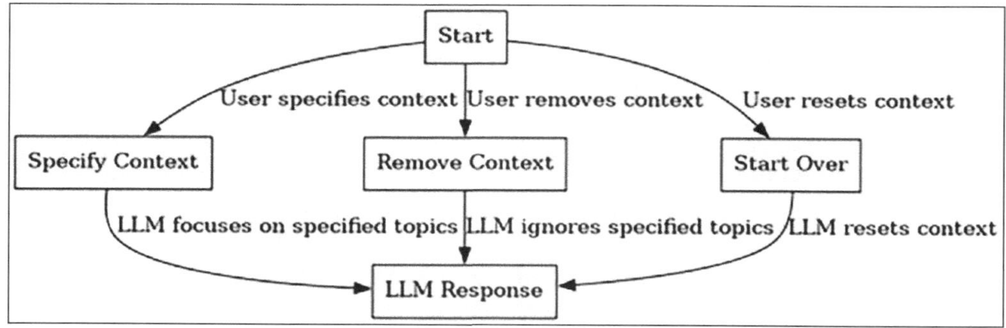

Figure 14.17: *Context Manager Pattern*

The Context Manager Pattern is built around the following key ideas:

- **Specify Context**: Users can guide the LLM to consider specific topics, facts, or instructions. For instance, "`Within the scope of environmental science, please consider climate change.`"
- **Remove Context**: Users can also instruct the LLM to ignore certain topics or facts. For instance, "`When discussing climate change, do not consider political implications.`"
- **Start Over**: Optionally, users can reset the context entirely, asking the LLM to ignore everything discussed so far.

For example, if you are discussing software development with the LLM, you could use the Context Manager Pattern like this:

- **Specify Context**: "`When analyzing the following pieces of code, only consider security aspects.`" This instruction directs the LLM to focus on the security-related aspects of the code.
- **Remove Context**: "`When analyzing the following pieces of code, do not consider formatting or naming conventions.`" This instruction tells the LLM to ignore formatting and naming conventions in its analysis.
- **Start Over**: "`Ignore everything that we have discussed. Start over.`" This instruction resets the context of the conversation, allowing you to start a new topic or revisit a previous topic with a clean slate.

The Context Manager Pattern can improve the relevance of the LLM's responses, but it also comes with potential drawbacks:

- **Unintended Reset:** Using the "`start over`" option could inadvertently remove other helpful instructions or patterns that were beneficial but unknown to the user.
- **Loss of Functionality**: Resetting the context could potentially eliminate the helpful capabilities of the LLM.

- **Need for Clarity**: The more explicit the user is in specifying or removing context, the better the LLM will be at adhering to those instructions.

To mitigate the risk of unintended consequences, users could include a request for the LLM to explain what topics or instructions will be lost before proceeding with a context reset.

Think of the Context Manager Pattern as a tour guide. If you are on a city tour and only interested in historical landmarks, you can specify this to the tour guide. The guide will then focus on historical sites and ignore modern attractions. Similarly, you can ask the guide to start the tour over if you wish to revisit some of the landmarks. The Context Manager Pattern operates in a similar way, guiding the LLM's focus based on the context provided by the user.

Recipe Pattern

The Recipe Pattern is a design pattern that aims to guide a large language model to generate a sequence of steps to achieve a specific goal. It combines elements of other patterns like Templates, Alternative Approaches, and Reflection.

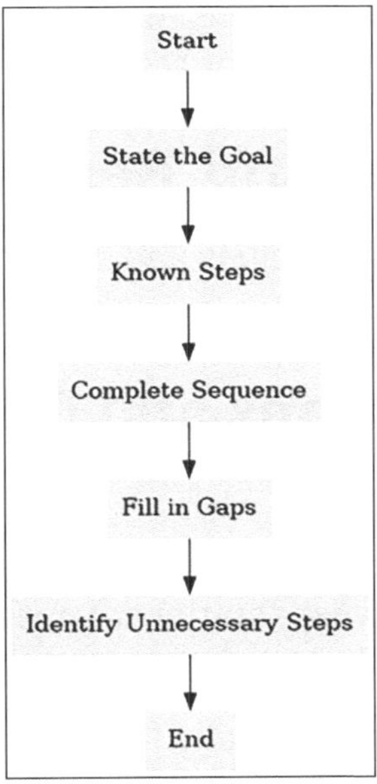

Figure 14.18: *Recipe Pattern*

The key elements are as follows:

- State the Goal: The user specifies the end goal they want to achieve.
- Known Steps: The user provides steps they believe are necessary.

- Complete Sequence: The user asks the model to provide a full sequence of steps.
- Fill in Gaps: The user asks the model to add any missing steps.
- Identify Unnecessary Steps: The model is asked to flag unnecessary steps.

This pattern is useful for tasks that require a sequence of instructions. It allows the user to provide some initial steps and have the model fill in the rest, forming a "`recipe`" to achieve the goal.

However, the user's input can introduce bias. The model may stick to the initial steps even if they are not needed.

The pattern works best when the user provides incomplete, yet relevant, initial steps. The model should supplement them with logical, unbiased steps to form a complete "`recipe`".

For example: User: "`I want to deploy an app to the cloud. I need to install dependencies on a VM and sign up for AWS. Provide a full sequence of steps.`"

The model's response should combine the user's two steps with other logical steps to create a complete deployment recipe.

Prompt Engineering Best Practices

Here, we will discuss various strategies and rules of thumb for effective prompt engineering.

Separate Instructions and Context

Why It's Important

Merging your instructions and context can confuse the model, leading to outputs that may not align with your expectations. Separating them clearly helps the model to More Effectively understand what exactly you're asking for.

The model reads the prompt sequentially, interpreting and generating responses based on what it "`sees`" first. By clearly separating the instruction from the context, you are essentially creating a mental "`folder`" for the model to store the task details before it moves on to the context.

When you separate the instruction from the context, you are making it easier for the model to compartmentalize the information. This is akin to a human reader who reads the title of a chapter before diving into the content; it sets the stage and prepares the model for what's to come.

How to Do It

Use triple quotes """ or ### to separate the instruction and the context. This creates a clear boundary that the model can recognize.

- **Less Effective**

  ```
  Translate the following text to French: Hello, how are you?
  ```

- **More Effective**

  ```
  Translate the following text to French:
  Text: """
  Hello, how are you?
  """
  ```

In the more effective example, the instruction and the text to be translated are clearly separated, making it easier for the model to understand the task

Be Specific and Detailed

Why It's Important

Vague prompts can lead to outputs that are equally vague or off-target. Being specific helps the model understand the nuances of what you're asking.

Imagine you are instructing a new intern who has no prior knowledge of your project. You wouldn't just say, "`Write a report`." You would specify what the report should be about, how long it should be, and what format it should follow. The same logic applies to language models.

Being specific acts like a GPS for the model, guiding it through the maze of possibilities. The more specific you are, the narrower the path becomes, making it easier for the model to reach the desired destination. Specificity eliminates guesswork, ensuring that the model's computational power is spent on generating a relevant and accurate output.

How to Do It

Include details such as the context, desired outcome, length, format, and style. For example, instead of asking in a generic fashion, specify the style, length, and particular themes you are interested in.

- **Less Effective**

```
Write an article about climate change.
```

- **More Effective**

```
Write a 500-word article about the impact of climate change on
polar bears, focusing on data from the last five years.
```

The more effective prompt specifies the length, topic, and even the time frame, guiding the model to produce a more targeted output.

Articulate Desired Output Format Through Examples

Why It's Important

Language models often benefit from having a structured format to follow. This not only makes the output more predictable but also easier to parse programmatically.

Language models, despite their complexity, can't read minds. They generate text based on patterns they have seen during training. By providing a format, you are essentially giving the model a template to fill in, much like a human would use a form.

Providing a format or example serves as a blueprint for the model. It's like giving someone a fill-in-the-blank exercise instead of an open-ended question; it streamlines the thought process and makes the output more predictable and easier to parse, both for humans and machines.

How to Do It

Provide an example format that you want the output to follow. For instance, if you are asking for entities to be extracted from a text, specify the order and format in which you want these entities to be listed.

- **Less Effective**

```
Summarize the key points of the text.
```

- **More Effective**

```
Summarize the key points of the text in bullet-point format.

Example Format:

- Point 1

- Point 2

- Point 3
```

By providing an example format, you make it easier for the model to understand how you want the information presented.

Zero-Shot, Few-Shot, and Fine-Tuning

Why It's Important

Not all tasks require the same level of guidance. Understanding when to use zero-shot, few-shot, or fine-tuning can save you time and computational resources.

Think of this as the escalation process in customer service. You start with the general FAQ (Zero-Shot), move to a customer service rep who has dealt with similar issues (Few-Shot), and as a last resort, you bring in the specialist (Fine-Tuning).

Zero-shot learning tests the model's general understanding of a task. Few-shot learning provides context, helping the model generalize from examples to the task at hand. Fine-tuning is the specialized training you'd do for highly specific or nuanced tasks that the model can't handle well, even with examples.

How to Do It

Start with a zero-shot prompt. If the output isn't satisfactory, provide a few examples to guide the model. Fine-tuning is usually the last resort and involves training the model on a specific dataset.

- **Zero-Shot**

```
Summarize the following text.
Text: {text}
```

- **Few-Shot**

```
Example 1: Summarize the following text about climate change.
Text: Climate change is causing...
Summary: Climate change is leading to...

Example 2: Summarize the following text about AI.
Text: Artificial Intelligence is...
Summary: AI is revolutionizing...

Now, summarize the following text.
Text: {text}
```

Avoid Fluffy Descriptions

Why It's Important

Imprecise language can lead to imprecise outputs. The model may struggle to determine the exact requirements of the task.

Precision is key in programming and mathematics; the same applies to language models. Vague instructions can lead to a wide range of outputs, making it hard to predict what the model will generate.

Being precise is like programming a GPS with an exact address instead of just the city name. It helps the model to narrow down the scope of the task and deliver a more accurate and relevant output.

How to Do It

Be as clear and concise as possible. Instead of saying "`Write a fairly short description`," specify that you want a description in "`3 to 5 sentences`."

- **Less Effective**

  ```
  Write a somewhat short summary of the book.
  ```
- **More Effective**

  ```
  Write a summary of the book in no more than 50 words.
  ```

Being Explicit About What to Do

Why It's Important

Telling the model what not to do is less effective than telling it what to do. This is because the model operates More Effectively when given a positive action to follow.

Negative instructions (don't do X) are harder to implement because they require the model to understand the context and then figure out the alternative. Positive instructions (do Y instead) are more straightforward.

Telling the model what to do is like giving someone a detour route when the main road is closed, rather than just saying, "`Don't take the main road`." It provides a clear alternative and makes the task more manageable for the model.

How to Do It

Instead of instructing the model not to ask for usernames or passwords, guide it towards what it should do, like referring the user to a FAQ page for sensitive queries.

- **Less Effective**

  ```
  Don't ask for personal information.
  ```

- **More Effective**

  ```
  Instead of asking for personal information, guide the user to
  the FAQ section for account-related queries.
  ```

Telling the model what to do is more effective than telling it what not to do.

Code Generation Specifics

Why It's Important

When generating code, the model needs cues to understand the programming language and the specific requirements of the code.

Coding languages have syntax and rules. By specifying the language and perhaps even starting the code snippet for the model, you are setting those rules in place, guiding the model's output.

When you specify the coding language and provide leading words, you are essentially setting the stage for the model. It's like giving a musician the key and tempo before they start playing; it ensures that what follows is in harmony with your requirements.

How to Do It

Use "*leading words*" like import for Python or SELECT for SQL to guide the model into generating code in the desired language and format.

- **Less Effective**

  ```
  Write code to calculate factorial.
  ```

- **More Effective**

  ```
  Write a Python function to calculate the factorial of a given
  number.
  ```

Specifying the language and the task in detail helps the model generate code that is more aligned with your requirements.

Conclusion

This chapter has provided a comprehensive framework for understanding and implementing Large Language Models (LLMs). The chapter identified the essence and the need for prompt design patterns and introduced the anatomy of prompts, focusing on stimulus, direction, and constraints.

The chapter also explored advanced techniques for interacting with LLMs, such as Zero-Shot Prompting, Few-Shot Prompting, and Chain-of-Thought Prompting. Methods for controlling inconsistencies and the Tree-of-Thoughts Framework were also discussed.

Various design patterns like the Meta Language Creation Pattern, The Output Automater Pattern, the Flipped Interaction Pattern, the Persona Pattern, Question Refinement Pattern, Alternative Approaches Pattern, Cognitive Verifier Pattern, Fact Check List Pattern, Template Pattern, Infinite Generation Pattern, Visualization Generator Pattern, Game Play Pattern, Reflection Pattern, Refusal Breaker Pattern, Context Manager Pattern, and the Recipe Pattern were explained in detail.

Each pattern was presented with its intent, context, structure, key ideas, example implementation, and potential consequences. This comprehensive approach allows users to select the best pattern for their specific needs and understand the potential risks associated with each.

Finally, the chapter suggested best practices for prompt engineering, emphasizing clarity and specificity, the appropriate use of Zero-Shot, Few-Shot, and Fine-Tuning, and the importance of avoiding fluffy descriptions. The guide also provided specific instructions for code generation.

In conclusion, this chapter serves as a robust resource for understanding and implementing prompt engineering with Large Language Models. By carefully selecting and applying the right patterns and adhering to the best practices, users can effectively interact with LLMs and harness their full potential. In the next chapter, we will learn Ethical Considerations and Regulatory Frameworks for large language models.

References

- https://arxiv.org/pdf/2302.11382.pdf
- https://help.openai.com/en/articles/6654000-best-practices-for-prompt-engineering-with-openai-api

Chapter 15
Ethical Considerations and Regulatory Frameworks for LLMs

Introduction

Large language models (LLMs), defined by their impressive counts of learnable parameters that often cross the 10-billion mark, are deep learning models grounded in the transformer architecture. This architectural design has proven its prowess in creating universal representations of language, which find application across a myriad of natural language processing (NLP) tasks. The escalating scale of these models, not just in terms of parameters but also pre-training corpora, underscores the potent ability of transformers to encode language representations.

LLMs have demonstrated a unique capacity for in-context learning as well as understanding from limited examples, or "few-shot learning", that does not necessitate fine-tuning. They also exhibit the ability to comprehend complex instructions framed in natural language, which describe the model's required operational behavior. The practice of Reinforcement Learning through Human Feedback (RLHF) has served to refine the ability of these models to align with and respond to progressively intricate prompts. Consequently, these developments have propelled models such as ChatGPT into widespread use across a broad application spectrum. The proficiency of LLMs in delivering nuanced language and cognitive behavior has extended their application reach far beyond the initially intended operational boundaries.

However, despite their consistent fluency, LLMs are not immune to challenges such as the generation of 'hallucinations' or factually incorrect statements. They also struggle with certain limitations related to safety, transparency, and control. The objective of this chapter is two-fold – firstly, to present a comprehensive review of known LLM vulnerabilities, and secondly, to explore how Verification and Validation (V&V) techniques could be modified to enhance the safety and reliability of LLMs.

The ever-expanding use of LLMs across diverse sectors has underscored the necessity for assurances of safety and reliability. Various technical solutions have emerged from different research communities aimed at supporting the safety and dependability of deep learning systems. For instance, the machine learning community is predominantly focused on topics like adversarial attacks, outlier detectors, adversarial training, and explainable AI. On the other hand, the human-computer interaction community prioritizes integrating learning systems into end-user interactions to bolster user confidence. The formal methods community is adopting and adapting existing tools to work on machine learning models, treating them as another symbolic system.

V&V techniques have successfully supported the dependable development of software and hardware intended for safety-critical systems. They have also been adapted for application to machine learning models, with a particular emphasis on convolutional neural networks for image classification. This chapter aims to discuss how V&V techniques can be further modified to address the safety and reliability challenges of LLMs.

V&V techniques, while independent, work together to confirm that a system (or a product or service) complies with requirements and specifications and performs its intended function effectively. Verification techniques compare the system with a set of design specifications, while validation techniques confirm that the system fulfils the user's operational needs. However, the significantly larger scale of systems, from software and convolutional neural networks to LLMs, presents challenges for traditional V&V techniques due to scalability issues. White-box V&V techniques, which consider learnable parameters as algorithmic input, may not be efficient in this context. Instead, the focus should be on black-box techniques, which have already begun to be explored for convolutional neural networks. Furthermore, V&V techniques must accommodate the non-deterministic nature of LLMs, which generate different outputs for identical inputs. This characteristic sets LLMs apart from more traditional neural networks such as convolutional neural networks and object detectors, which are the current focus of most V&V techniques.

Structure

In this chapter, we will discuss the following topics:

- Categories, Life Cycle, and Key Techniques for Safety and Trustworthiness
- Dissecting the Applications of LLMs
- Strategies to Improve Security and Reliability in LLMs
- Vulnerabilities in LLMs
- Verification Framework of LLMs

Large Language Models: Categories, Life Cycle, and Key Techniques for Safety and Trustworthiness

Large language models (LLMs) have been applied to many tasks, such as text generation, content summary, conversational AI (that is, chatbots), and image synthesis. Other LLM applications can be seen as their adaptations or further applications. In this chapter, we will discuss the two most notable categories of LLMs.

Dissecting the Applications of Large Language Models

Advancements in artificial intelligence have paved the way for large language models (LLMs) to play a critical role in an array of applications. Predominantly, LLMs have made significant strides in two distinct areas– text-based conversational AI and text-based image synthesis. Let us delve deeper into understanding each of these aspects.

Text-based Conversational AI

In the domain of natural language understanding and processing, LLMs have created a significant impact. They have essentially revolutionized the way machines understand and generate text, making interactions with them more fluid, natural, and human-like. They find application in a wide array of natural language processing (NLP) tasks, effectively mimicking human communication patterns and generating plausible textual responses. These language models, backed by robust learning frameworks, aid in the better understanding of linguistic nuances, context, and syntax, thereby boosting the performance of various applications like language translation, chatbots, and virtual assistants.

The primary charm of LLMs is their ability to understand and generate human-like text responses. Many significant models have risen to prominence, each bringing its unique set of capabilities to various NLP tasks.

For instance, models like GPT-1, BERT, and XLNet laid the foundation of advanced language understanding, using self-supervised learning to learn from large volumes of unlabelled text data and then transferring this knowledge to specific tasks. Following them, we saw the rise of models like RoBERTa, ELECTRA, T5, ALBERT, BART, and PEGASUS, each improving upon its predecessors. These models helped machines grasp the subtleties of language, like grammar, syntax, and context.

The ground-breaking research by Kaplan *et al.* revealed that increasing the size of transformer-based pretrained language models (T-PTLMs) could lead to significant performance improvements. This understanding accelerated the development of even larger models, such as GPT-3, PANGU, GShard, SwitchTransformers, and GPT-4, that are continually pushing the boundaries of NLP.

Text-based Image Synthesis

Apart from conversational AI, another fascinating application of LLMs is in the realm of image synthesis using textual inputs. Essentially, these models take a text description as input and generate an image that visually represents the given description. They are a testament to the versatility of transformer models, marking their transition from text processing to multimedia generation tasks. These models have opened new avenues in machine learning and AI, bridging the gap between language and visual representation.

The application of LLMs in text-to-image tasks signifies their adaptability. They have transitioned from language processing to media generation tasks, proving that they are more than just linguistic tools. Several advancements in this field have led to models that can transform text descriptions into vivid, illustrative images.

A key player in this domain is DALL-E, which utilized transformers to generate image tokens from text inputs. This method involved training a Discrete Variational Autoencoder (dVAE) followed by a transformer, supervised by image tokens from the pretrained dVAE.

In contrast, StableFusion employed a diffusion model instead of a transformer, encoding the text using a transformer and then conditioning the diffusion model on the resulting text tokens. Similarly, GLIDE used a transformer for text input and then trained a diffusion model to generate images directly conditioned on the text tokens.

DALL-E2 took a different approach. First, a CLIP model was trained using text-image pairs. Then, using text tokens as input, an autoregressive or diffusion model generated image tokens, followed by the training of a diffusion model to produce the final image based on these tokens.

Another model, Imagen, used a pre-trained text encoder like BERT or CLIP to encode text, followed by multiple diffusion models trained in a process to generate images, starting from low resolution and gradually progressing to high resolution.

Parti showcased the effectiveness of a combination of VQGAN and Transformer architecture for superior image synthesis outcomes. The latest model eDiff-I has demonstrated state-of-the-art performance by leveraging a combination of CLIP and diffusion models.

Life Cycle of LLMs

The life cycle stages of LLMs include offline model construction, which consists of three steps – pre-training, adaptation tuning, and utilization improvement. Each step includes several interleaving sub-steps.

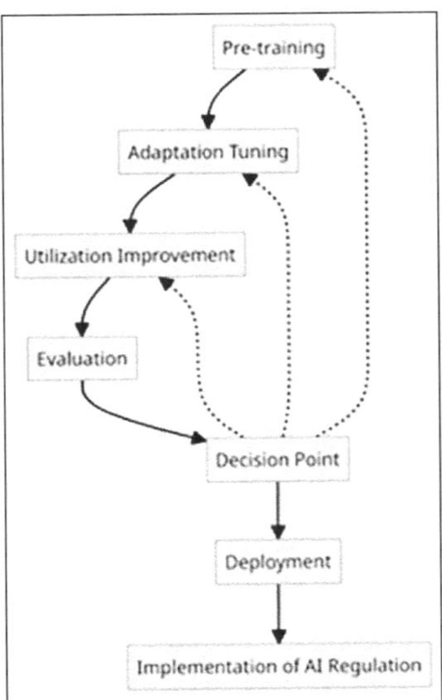

Figure 15.1: *LLM Life Cycle*

The pre-training step of this process is like the initial training phase in regular machine learning. It involves collecting data, choosing the right model, and training it. During the adaptation step, there are a couple of things that happen. First, the model might get fine-tuned based on specific instructions to make it better at understanding and following task instructions. Second, there is alignment tuning to ensure that the model behaves in a way that is fair, honest, and does not cause harm. To make the model work better when interacting with people, there are some additional improvements. For instance, it can learn from the context of the conversation (in-context learning) and try to anticipate what the user might say next (chain-of-thought learning). These improvements aim to enhance the model's ability to have meaningful and helpful interactions with users.

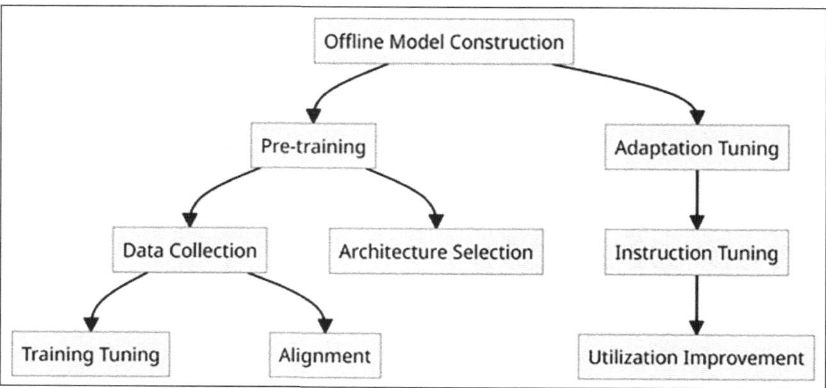

Figure 15.2: *Offline Model Construction*

Upon completion of the training phase for a large language model (LLM), a thorough assessment is required to confirm that the output aligns with what was anticipated. Typically, this assessment is approached from three angles:

- **Performance Metrics Evaluation**: This involves a detailed analysis of the LLM based on established performance standards, ensuring that the model performs as expected under normal conditions.
- **Safety Examination**: This involves analyzing the potential impacts of deploying the LLM in a real-world application. It is aimed at uncovering any unexpected or undesirable behavior that could occur when the model is in use.
- **Benchmark Dataset Assessment**: This entails testing the LLM against reputable, publicly accessible datasets. It provides an industry-standard point of reference against which the performance of the model is compared.

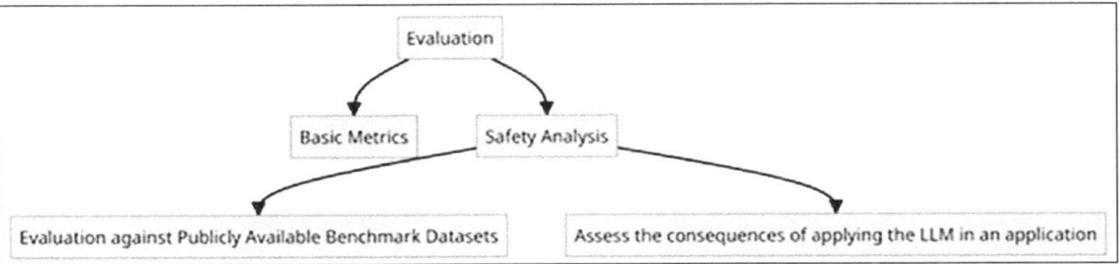

Figure 15.3: *Evaluation*

These evaluations serve to verify whether the LLM is up to par, based on the criteria specified beforehand. If it passes, the LLM is advanced to the deployment stage. Conversely, should the model fall short in any of these areas, the process reverts to the appropriate training stage to address the identified deficiencies. This process ensures the delivery of an effective and trustworthy LLM that meets pre-defined standards.

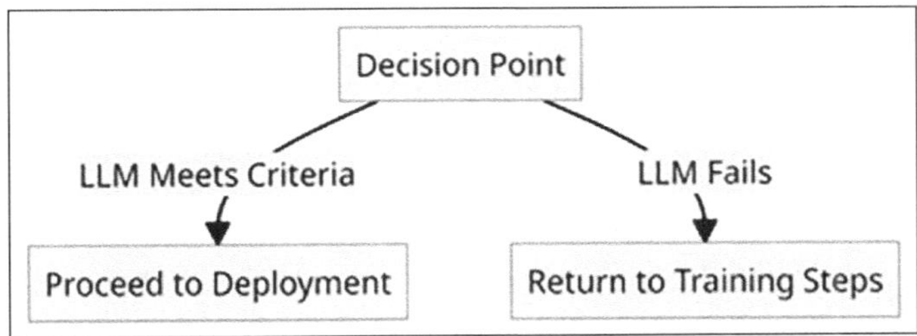

Figure 15.4: *Decision Making*

In the deployment phase, the application of the LLM is clearly defined. For instance, the model may be integrated into a web interface for direct user engagement, much like ChatGPT. Or, it could be incorporated into a search algorithm, similar to recent enhancements made to Bing.

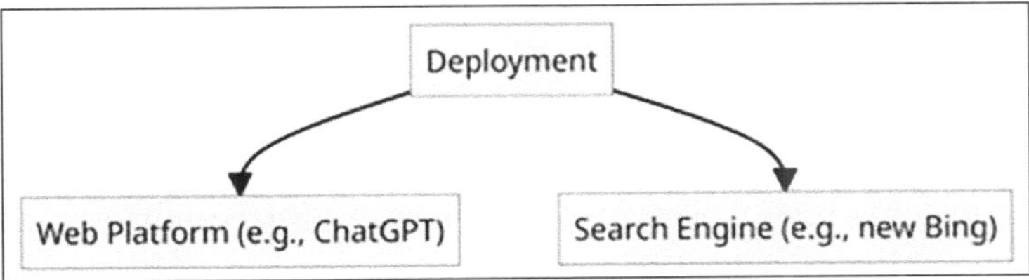

Figure 15.5: *Deployment*

However, in line with standard practices, safeguards, or 'guardrails' are put in place during interactions between end users and LLMs. These safety measures aim to ensure maximum compliance with AI regulations, preserving the integrity of the user experience while maintaining necessary controls.

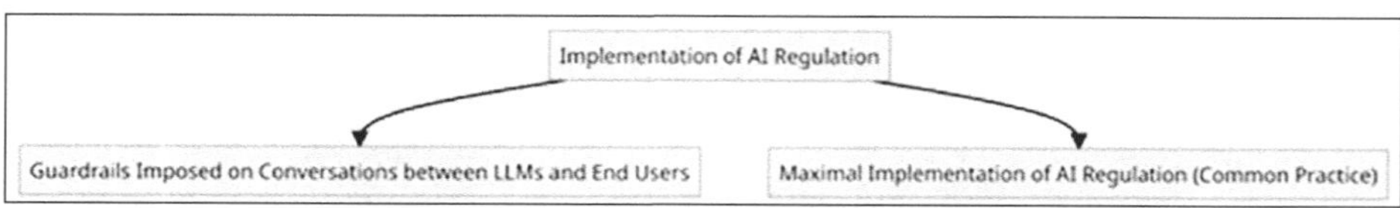

Figure 15.6: *Implementing AI Regulation*

Critical Strategies for Improving Security and Reliability in Large Language Models

Here, we delve into two distinct methodologies that are divergent from traditional deep learning frameworks. Such approaches have been instrumental in models like ChatGPT for enhancing their security and trustworthiness.

The Power of Learning from Human Input (RLHF)

RLHF holds a pivotal role in educating language models by providing them the opportunity to gain from human expertise and eschew the creation of harmful content. In its core, RLHF is the catalyst for aligning language models with safety measures, by refining them on the basis of human feedback. OpenAI pioneered the introduction of incorporating human feedback for handling complex reinforcement learning tasks, which, in turn, paved the way for the evolution of more advanced language models, ranging from InstructGPT to GPT4. The typical RLHF training journey starts with the learning of a reward function that mirrors human preferences in a task, by using human feedback on the model's outputs. Following this, the language model is optimized through an RL algorithm, such as PPO, harnessing the acquired reward function. This cycle of reward model training and RL-based fine-tuning can be repeated indefinitely. The latest models, like InstructGPT, showcased improvements in factual accuracy and a decrease in producing harmful outputs, while simultaneously ensuring negligible regressions on public NLP datasets.

Guardrails – Protective Measures

With some language models interacting directly with consumers, it becomes essential to have a safeguard in place, akin to what OpenAI integrated in ChatGPT. Such protections come into play when consumers request information related to violence, offensive language, criminal behaviors, race, or any controversial topics. Under these circumstances, the language model responds by denying access to such information. Even though these protective measures are not foolproof and can be circumvented using different techniques, they elevate the social accountability of large language models.

Large Language Models Vulnerabilities

Large language models (LLMs) are not immune to several types of vulnerabilities, which can be broadly categorized into intrinsic issues, deliberate attacks, and unintended glitches.

Intrinsic Issues

These are vulnerabilities that cannot be readily fixed by the LLMs themselves, but can be gradually improved with more data and innovative training methods. They encapsulate performance flaws, sustainability challenges, and concerns related to reliability and responsibility.

Performance Challenges

Traditional software systems operate on deterministic rules, but neural network-based deep learning systems, including LLMs, have their behavior dictated by complex models learned from data through optimization algorithms. Consequently, it is improbable for an LLM to function with 100% accuracy. Performance challenges can include factual inaccuracies and reasoning errors.

- **Factual inaccuracies:** These situations occur when the output from an LLM contradicts the truth. For instance, if queried about the computer science department expertise at the University of Liverpool, ChatGPT may refer to individuals who have no connection with the department. More egregious errors can be rendered, including dangerous medical advice.
- **Reasoning errors:** Studies have shown that when posed with computational or logical reasoning questions, ChatGPT might not always provide the right answers. This is primarily because LLMs, rather than reasoning, fit the questions with prior experiences learned from the training data.

Sustainability Challenges

Economic cost, energy consumption, and carbon dioxide emissions are metrics used to assess sustainability issues inherent in LLMs. While LLMs perform impressively, their life cycle involves high costs and consumption. For example, ChatGPT was trained with 30k A100 GPUs (each priced around $10k), and its monthly energy consumption cost stands at roughly $1.5m.

Other Inherent Issues Regarding Reliability and Responsibility

Certain problems arise during the life cycle that could raise questions about the trustworthiness and responsibilities of LLMs. These can be bifurcated into two sub-categories concerning the training data and the final model. For the training data, issues revolve around the copyright, quality, and privacy of the data. For the final model, significant concerns include LLMs' capacity for independent and conscious thought, their potential use in mimicking human output including academic works, and their potential to engage scammers in automated and pointless communications, among others.

Deliberate Attacks

Deliberate attacks are initiated by malicious parties who aim to implement their objectives by targeting certain stages in the LLM life cycle. Known deliberate attacks include the robustness gap, backdoor attack, poisoning, disinformation, privacy leaks, and unauthorized information disclosure.

Unauthorized Information Disclosure and Privacy Issues

Sometimes, sensitive information in LLMs can accidentally leak out. This can happen if certain inputs are not handled correctly or if there is a breach in security. Think of it like a secret slipping out by mistake. There are also privacy attacks that people can launch on LLMs. These attacks are a bit like someone trying to figure out if a particular piece of data was part of the model's training. It is like someone trying to guess if a photo was in a big photo album. Additionally, LLMs can store conversations with users. This might sound handy, but it can raise privacy worries because these conversations might contain personal or sensitive information. It is a bit like someone writing down everything you say during a chat, and that can be a problem if not handled carefully.

Robustness Gap

An adversarial attack is a purposeful effort to undermine the functionality of a DNN by introducing distorted inputs leading to the model's failure. Numerous input perturbations are proposed in NLP for adversarial attacks, which can occur at the character, word, or sentence level. These perturbations might involve deletion, insertion, swapping, flipping, substituting with synonyms, concatenating with characters or words, or introducing numeric or alphanumeric characters.

Backdoor Attack

The aim of a backdoor attack is to incorporate malicious knowledge into the LLMs through either the training of poisoned data or modifying model parameters. Such injections should not compromise the model's performance and must evade human inspection. The backdoor is activated only when input prompts to LLMs contain the trigger, leading the compromised LLMs to behave maliciously, as the attacker intended.

Poisoning and Disinformation

Among various adversarial attacks against DNNs, poisoning attacks are one of the most significant and emerging security concerns. Particularly for models trained by large amounts of data acquired from diverse sources, poisoning attacks attempt to manipulate some of the training data, potentially leading the model to produce incorrect or biased outputs.

Unintended Glitches

As LLMs find use in broader applications, more and more unintended bugs will arise, often introduced unintentionally by the developers but having severe consequences, such as bias and discrimination.

Incidental Exposure of User Information

In addition to the deliberate attacks, a reported "chat history" bug in ChatGPT enabled users to view previous chat histories from other users on their ChatGPT sidebars. OpenAI acknowledged that this bug might have potentially revealed personal data from the paid ChatGPT Plus subscribers.

Bias and Discrimination

Like traditional machine learning algorithms, LLMs are trained from data, which might include bias and discrimination. If not mitigated, these vulnerabilities will be inherited by the LLMs. For instance, a political compass test reveals that ChatGPT leans towards progressive and libertarian views. Additionally, ChatGPT perceives itself as having the Myers-Briggs personality type ENFJ.

General Verification Framework for Large Language Models

The general verification framework for LLMs is illustrated in *Figure* 15.7, which positions various categories of verification and validation (V&V) techniques throughout the life cycle of the model.

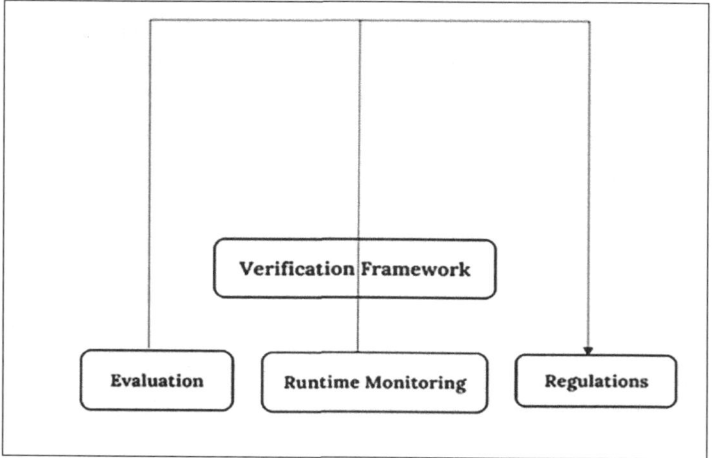

***Figure* 15.7:** *Verification Framework*

Evaluation Stage

In the evaluation phase, we start by checking for mistakes and figuring out how well the system works. We use various methods to spot where it might go wrong and try to understand why.

There are two main things we do here:

- **Spotting Mistakes**: We use different methods to find out where the system might make mistakes. It is a bit like finding errors in a school test.
- **Explaining Results**: We want to make sure that the answers that the system provides make sense to humans. So, we use techniques to explain why it says what it says. This helps us understand if it is giving the right answers or not.

Sometimes, we might also need to do a more thorough check, but that is only if the system does well in the first two steps.

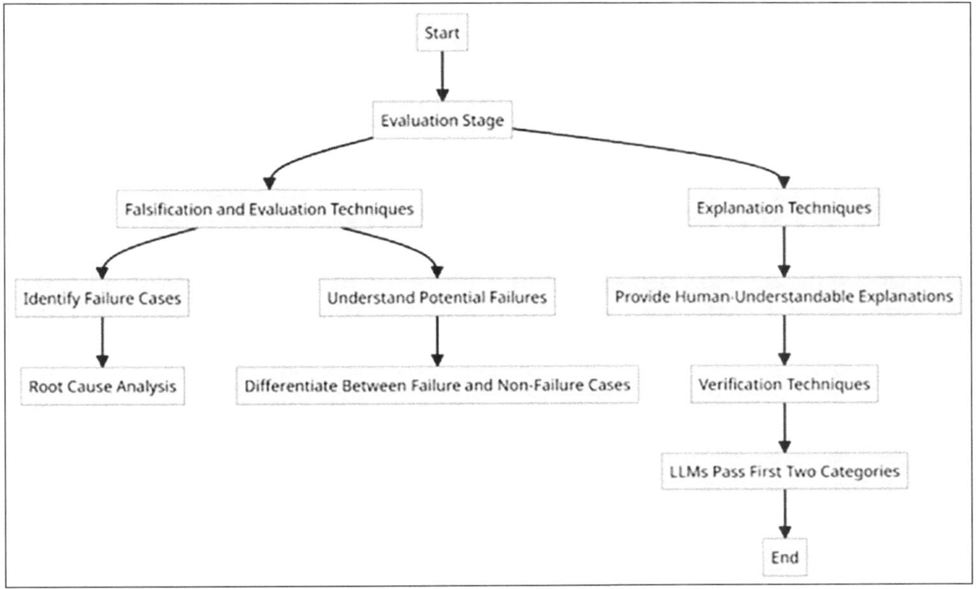

Figure 15.8: *Evaluation Stage*

Runtime Monitoring

In addition to offline verification, a runtime monitor needs to be deployed on top of the guardrail to support the discovery of failure cases at the operational time. This is mainly because offline methods can be incomplete when working with a large set of properties and the high dimensionality of LLMs, and the LLMs can be adaptive and evolving.

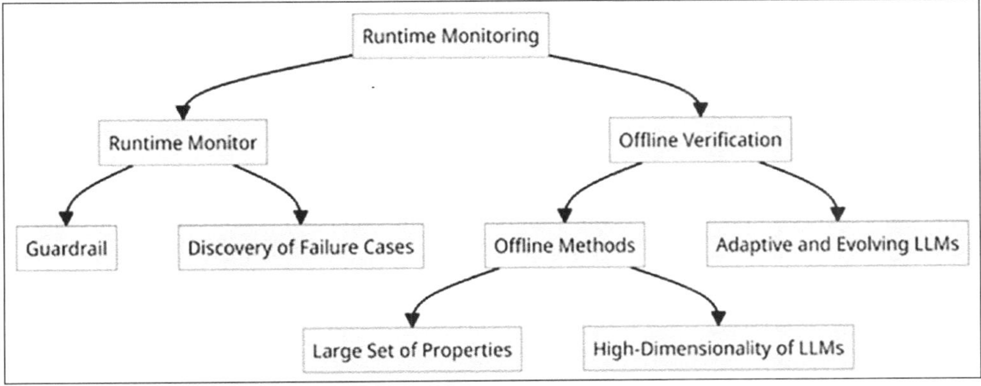

Figure 15.9: *Runtime Monitoring*

Ethical Principles and AI Regulations

Ethical principles and AI regulations are imposed throughout the life cycle to ensure the ethical use of LLMs.

Falsification and Evaluation

This section summarizes the known methods for identifying and evaluating the vulnerabilities of LLM-based machine learning applications. We also discuss how the V&V can, and should, be adapted.

Red Teaming

In red teaming, a red team interacts with a model and actively finds examples that fail. Then, the model is retrained on these examples. This process is iterated until it is nearly impossible to find failures.

Manipulating LLMs

Large language models (LLMs), such as GPT-3, generate responses based on the prompts they receive. Manipulating these prompts can make an LLM generate outputs that diverge from human values, including harmful content like malware code or instigations of violence. This form of manipulation, known as 'Prompt Injection', operates similarly to other injection attacks observed in cybersecurity, where data fields are hijacked to run unintended actions.

Prompt Injection in LLMs

Prompt Injection leverages the integration of instructions and data in LLMs, which can cause confusion between the two. Adversaries manipulate this by inserting instructions into the data fields they control, causing the LLM to execute unintended actions. Various techniques have been demonstrated to successfully misdirect LLMs using Prompt Injection, enabling the generation of malicious content or overriding the primary instructions and filtering mechanisms. Given the programming of current state-of-the-art LLMs to follow instructions, mitigating these attacks is challenging.

Assessing LLMs Against Human Expertise

Another aspect of understanding LLMs is comparing their outputs to human experts. Studies across various disciplines, such as finance, medicine, law, psychology, and open-domain, have conducted comparisons using LLMs, specifically ChatGPT. They evaluated areas like bibliometric analysis, ranking content, correcting grammatical errors, and specialized tasks in computer security education. However, LLMs, including ChatGPT, have often fallen short of expectations when compared to human expertise.

Benchmarks for LLMs

To measure the performance of LLMs, benchmark datasets are utilized. Datasets such as AdvGLUE and ANLI measure adversarial robustness, while Flipkart review and DDXPlus medical diagnosis datasets are employed for out-of-distribution evaluation.

Automating Testing and Evaluation

Traditional LLM evaluation methods depend heavily on human involvement. However, with human expertise being a limited and costly resource, there is a growing need for automated techniques to evaluate LLMs comprehensively and efficiently. Here, we delve into how testing and statistical evaluation methods can help.

Think of an LLM as a system that produces an output when given an input. Let D represent the space of natural data. An LLM can then be defined as a function M: D -> D. We also have a function H: D -> D, representing a human's response. For automated test case generation, we need an oracle O, a test coverage metric C, and a test case generation method A.

The oracle O verifies if an input-output pair (x, y) is correct by comparing M(x) and H(x) - the outputs of the model and human, respectively, against a certain criterion. A test case is an input-output pair. Given a set of test cases `P = {(xi ,yi)} for i=1,...,n`, the coverage metric C calculates the proportion of test cases in P that should be tested. The test case generation method A produces the set P of test cases. Therefore, the task of verification is to determine whether the proportion of test cases in P that satisfy the oracle O exceeds a predetermined threshold.

Statistical evaluation uses statistical methods to understand the problem at hand better. It not only identifies failures (counterexamples to the satisfaction of desired properties) in the deep learning model but also assesses the satisfaction of a property probabilistically. This is done by aggregating sampling results, leading to a probabilistic guarantee. For example, the probability of the failure rate being below a threshold 'l' is greater than 1-ε, for a small constant ε.

Even though research into LLMs is still in its early stages, statistical evaluation methods have been proposed for general machine learning models. These include sampling and testing methods for convolutional or recurrent neural networks. Sampling methods summarize property-related statistics from the samples. Various techniques can be employed to generate test cases, including fuzzing, coverage metrics, symbolic execution, concolic testing, and so on.

While sampling methods can provide probabilistic guarantees via Chebyshev's inequality, associating test coverage metrics with probabilistic guarantees is still under research. It is also crucial to ensure that the generated or sampled test cases realistically represent the data distribution.

Challenges in Testing and Evaluating LLMs: The main technical challenges for LLMs lie in creating test coverage metrics and test case generation algorithms. This is because:

- LLMs are often viewed as black-box systems due to their sheer size, making input space exploration more practical than fully exploring the model's inner workings.
- LLMs handle natural language text, where defining a clear order between two texts is difficult. The order between two inputs is crucial for designing test case generation algorithms.
- LLMs are non-deterministic. In other words, two tests with identical input can yield different outputs, adding to the complexity of the evaluation process.

Verification of Large Language Models

As large language models (LLMs) gain prominence in the technology landscape, their verification has sparked a surge of academic interest. This section aims to present a detailed overview of verification methodologies leveraged on diverse natural language processing (NLP) models, before diving into an exploration of pioneering "*black-box*" verification techniques pertinent to LLMs. In parallel, we will touch upon the push towards downsizing LLMs in an effort to enhance the efficacy of verification methodologies.

Checking the Checkers: Verification of NLP Models

Imagine a saboteur generating millions of harmful variants by tweaking every single word in a sentence. Despite their efforts, many unforeseen instances, stemming from exponential combinations of different words in a text input, could remain unaddressed. The solution lies in a novel set of strategies underpinned by the principle of "*certification*" or "*verification*". These strategies enable the model to establish a cap on the maximum loss due to distortions, thus producing a robustness certificate without the need for explorative ventures into adversarial realms. By harnessing certification-guided methodologies, we can gain a deeper understanding of the model's sturdiness against adversarial onslaughts.

Interval Bound Propagation: Establishing the Fence

One of the initial techniques borrowed from the realm of computer vision for verifying NLP models is Interval Bound Propagation (IBP). This bounding technique has earned considerable interest due to its proficiency in shaping robust and verifiable neural networks of substantial size. IBP aims to restrict the maximum discrepancy between the classification demarcation and the distortion area, enabling a loss term to be incorporated during training. This process permits the final layer of the distortion region to be minimized, ensuring it remains on one side of the classification boundary. As a result, the adversarial area becomes more confined, thus qualifying as certified robust.

Navigating Uncertainty with Abstract Interpretation

Another widely used verification approach in the context of multiple NLP models is grounded in abstract interpretation or function over-simplification. Abstract interpretation aims to encapsulate the conduct of a program using a more straightforward model that facilitates easier analysis. This method can characterize the network using an abstract domain, capturing the possible range of outcomes the network could deliver given specific inputs. This abstract domain provides a base to hypothesize about the network's response under varying conditions, such as adversarial distortions.

Bracing for Change with Randomized Smoothing

Randomized smoothing (RS) presents a viable technique to verify the robustness of deep language models. In this methodology, the input text is deliberately distorted and then introduced into a mask language model. Random masks are generated within the input text, creating an extensive set of masked duplicates that are then evaluated by a primary classifier. A "majority vote" mechanism then settles on the final robust classification.

Black-Box Verification: Cracking the Code

As LLMs become more intricate and expansive, conventional verification methodologies that rely on layer-by-layer search, abstraction, and transformation, are increasingly falling short due to computational limitations. This has given rise to black-box strategies, which have emerged as a more viable alternative for verifying such models. In the black-box scenario, adversaries can only interact with the target classifier without access to the underlying model or the representation of inputs.

Assessing the Resilience of LLMs

With the rise of large-scale language models such as GPT, LLaMA, and BERT, researchers have begun probing into the robustness evaluation of these models. One such study is the work of Cheng *et al.*, who constructed a seq2seq algorithm rooted in a projected gradient method intertwined with group lasso and gradient regularization.

A Case for Smaller Models

Today's LLMs host billions or even trillions of parameters, making their verification a demanding task even with the above-stated verification techniques. One promising line of research to aid more efficient verification is the utilization of smaller LLMs. A popular method of creating a compact LLM involves techniques that trim the parameters of a pre-trained model, with model compression, such as quantization, being a common example.

Spiking Neural Networks (SNNs), representing the third generation of neural networks, offer a parallel approach to enhancing computational efficiency through the use of sparse operations. Recent studies have introduced SpikeGPT, the largest SNN-based model comprising 260 million parameters, showcasing SNNs' ability to match the performance of traditional neural networks on GPT models.

Runtime Monitors: The Guardians of LLMs

Runtime monitors serve as vital verification and validation (V&V) tools for LLMs. They act as protectors, scrutinizing the performance of LLMs in real-time to avert potential weaknesses. The emergence of runtime monitors stems from the challenges in verifying large models and the deployment of deep learning models in settings that differ from the original training data.

Detecting the Deviations: Monitoring Out-of-Distribution

Out-of-distribution (OoD) monitoring refers to a unique failure type that occurs when the runtime data diverges in distribution from the training data. As machine learning models can falter when dealing with data that has strayed from the training data, this is a significant concern. Neural networks utilized in computer vision or NLP tasks have been observed to over-confidently predict OoD samples. It is imperative that such inputs and their corresponding predictions are monitored at runtime, especially for networks operating in safety-critical applications.

OoD monitoring methodologies for NLP models can be broadly classified into three categories:

- **Input density estimation methods**: These methods utilize a density estimator in the input or latent space of the generative models for in-distribution data. The probability value given by such a density estimator can be used as the in-distribution score.
- **Feature or embedding space approximation methods**: These methods initially approximate the observed features using a distribution function. The distance between this distribution and the input feature is then used as the in-distribution confidence score.
- **Output confidence calibration methods**: These methods use the model's prediction confidence (usually calibrated) as the in-distribution score.

Despite significant strides in this space, there is ample room for improvement. Currently, no single method has a clear edge over the others, which is unsurprising given the infinite scope of OoD data and the ambiguous boundaries of in-distribution data.

Guarding Against Output Failures

LLMs are susceptible to various types of failures such as factual errors, coding mishaps, and flawed reasoning. These issues can spell significant disaster for downstream tasks, particularly in safety-critical applications. One way to mitigate these risks is by monitoring the model's output and initiating appropriate responses.

However, the generative nature of LLMs and the broad array of downstream tasks make it incredibly challenging to establish a universal monitoring framework for such generative outputs. These output failures need to be addressed in a targeted manner, in line with different application scenarios and specific human-acquired knowledge in diverse fields such as science and technology.

Perspective

Large language models (LLMs) are in their nascent stage, and they exhibit a plethora of recognized vulnerabilities. This scenario emphasizes the enduring necessity for real-time oversight. The progression of research needs to delve into understanding the need for monitoring a model, the aspects that require scrutiny, and the ways to refine the design of monitoring mechanisms for a model.

The task of creating sophisticated models that can instinctively identify "unauthorized inputs" and assure the accuracy of their outputs in the imminent future is a complex endeavor. Hence, the pressing requirement for real-time model supervision.

To ensure the dependable employment of LLMs in high-stakes applications, it is imperative to navigate and mitigate various weaknesses. Integrating the model with an associated real-time monitoring system presents a potential solution, supplementing offline verification methodologies.

To improve the construction of monitors for LLMs, some fundamental inherent challenges associated with deep learning models must be addressed more effectively. These challenges include model implicit generalization, decision boundaries, and the explainability of model determinations. LLM-specific issues such as the unavailability of training datasets, the opacity of models, and the generative characteristic of multi-modality, also warrant attention.

In real-time, monitors are instrumental in ensuring the dependability and safety of LLMs, especially in real-world applications where safety is paramount. They offer a real-time defense against potential vulnerabilities and failures, establishing them as a crucial component of the LLM ecosystem.

Regulations and Ethical Use

While Verification and Validation (V&V) techniques provide a set of technical means to align LLMs with human interests, they may not be sufficient. The construction of LLMs that cannot be abused can be impossible, suggesting the need for ethical means to supplement the technical ones.

Regulate or Ban?

The question of whether to stop the progress of large language models (LLMs) or administer their growth signifies a common unease and divergent views about AI evolution in harmony with human objectives. Some nations have taken drastic steps, like the rumored prohibition of ChatGPT in Italy. Key participants such as the EU, US, UK, and China have distinct strategies and initiatives concerning AI regulation. However, the compatibility of these regulations with LLMs without any modifications remains uncertain, along with the method to apply these regulations in a stringent yet practical manner.

LLMs raise considerable issues surrounding copyright and privacy. The legality of the copyrights concerning training data, especially for commercial applications, is ambiguous. The privacy of users interacting with these models is a critical matter that needs to be addressed.

Responsible AI Principles

Over the past few years, the discussion around responsible and accountable AI has gradually evolved to include properties such as transparency, explainability, fairness, robustness, security, and privacy. A governance framework is needed to ensure that these properties are upheld, evaluated, and monitored consistently.

When it comes to LLMs, ethical principles should be established to guide their development and usage, emphasizing more on whether a thing should be executed rather than its feasibility.

Transparency and Explainability

OpenAI's choice to withhold the source code of GPT-3 and subsequent versions has ignited concerns about AI's transparent development. However, OpenAI has plans to share more technical details with third parties. It is worth noting that no information is available on how the safety mechanisms are designed and implemented.

The task of interpreting and explaining the decisions made by deep learning models, such as image classifiers, has always been challenging. This challenge escalates with LLMs, which exhibit emergent and difficult-to-interpret behaviors, necessitating advancements in explainable AI techniques tailored for LLMs.

Conclusion

The chapter has given us an in-depth exploration of the complexities, challenges, and potential of large language models (LLMs). As their adoption accelerates, the urgent need to address these issues is clear. Real-time monitoring, comprehensive regulation, observance of responsible AI principles, transparency, explainability, and robust validation and verification processes stand out as critical areas for attention.

LLMs are at a pivotal point in their development trajectory. How we navigate these challenges will shape their future role and impact. It is not merely a technical challenge but a multidimensional one, involving social, ethical, and legal dimensions.

The conclusion here is not a definitive answer but an urgent call to action for all stakeholders. As developers, regulators, and end-users, we must collaboratively work towards solutions that harness the power of LLMs while mitigating their risks. Ensuring this will require a multidisciplinary approach that encompasses not just technological advancements but also ethical guidelines, regulatory measures, and comprehensive validation and verification methods. The future of LLMs, thus, lies in this balanced and shared responsibility.

In the next chapter, we will understand a novel framework that aims to enhance the trustworthiness of Generative AI. Inspired by symbolic reasoning, this chapter explores innovative approaches to ensure the reliability and integrity of AI systems, paving the way for more dependable and accountable AI generation.

References

https://arxiv.org/pdf/2305.11391.pdf

CHAPTER 16

Towards Trustworthy Generative AI

(A Novel Framework Inspired by Symbolic Reasoning)

Introduction

In the last few years, Generative AI, especially Large Language Models (LLMs), has undergone a transformation that can only be described as revolutionary. From automating mundane tasks in customer service to generating insights in scientific research, LLMs have become ubiquitous. However, this rapid advancement has also cast a spotlight on the glaring issue of trustworthiness. These models, while capable of generating text that mimics human-like conversation, operate as "*black boxes*," leaving us in the dark about the rationale behind their outputs. This lack of transparency has resulted in a widening trust gap, making it imperative to scrutinize not just what these models can do, but also the extent to which we can rely on them.

Current methodologies for enhancing AI trustworthiness tend to focus on singular dimensions such as explainability, data lineage, or ethical considerations. While these are undoubtedly crucial, they fall short of providing a holistic solution to the complex issue of trust in Generative AI. Lenat and Marcus have made a commendable effort by outlining 16 desiderata for trustworthy AI, yet these guidelines are more theoretical than practical. What is glaringly missing is an integrated framework that not only aligns with these desiderata but also leverages the latest advancements in symbolic reasoning and generative models.

This chapter aims to fill this void by introducing a framework – the "*Trust-Enhanced Generative Framework*" (TEGF). Drawing inspiration from Lenat and Marcus's foundational work (https://arxiv.org/ftp/arxiv/papers/2308/2308.04445.pdf) and incorporating elements from the Trust-Interpretable Generative AI (TIGAI) framework, TEGF aspires to offer a comprehensive, actionable blueprint for constructing Generative AI systems that are both trustworthy and interpretable. Through a balanced mix of theoretical discourse and real-world case studies, this chapter will dissect how TEGF can redefine the standards for trust in Generative AI.

Structure

In this chapter, the following topics will be covered:

- Dichotomy of LLMs and Symbolic Systems
- A critical outlook on the research "*Getting from Generative AI to Trustworthy AI: What LLMs might learn from Cyc*" by Doug Lenat and Gary Marcus
- Introduction to Novel Trustworthy Frameworks: Trust-Enhanced Generative Framework (TEFG) and Trust Interpretable Generative AI (TIGAI)
- Ethical and Societal Responsibilities and Considerations when Leveraging Trustworthy AI

Dichotomy of LLMs and Symbolic Systems

Large Language Models (LLMs) such as GPT-3 and BERT have become the linchpins of modern Generative AI. These models are fundamentally statistical, trained on massive datasets to recognize patterns and generate outputs accordingly. While they have proven to be remarkably efficient in tasks like text generation, summarization, and even machine translation, their statistical nature poses a significant challenge to their trustworthiness.

The crux of the issue lies in the LLMs' lack of semantic depth. They can generate text that appears coherent and contextually relevant but may be riddled with factual inaccuracies or ethical pitfalls. This "*black box*" characteristic of LLMs makes it exceedingly difficult to audit or understand their decision-making process, thereby widening the trust gap. Additionally, the biases inherent in the training data can seep into the model's outputs, further undermining trust.

Introduction to Symbolic Systems and Their Capabilities

On the other end of the spectrum, we have symbolic systems like Cyc, which operate on a foundation of explicit rules and logical reasoning. Unlike LLMs, these systems have a structured representation of knowledge and can elucidate the reasoning behind their decisions. For instance, in a medical context, a symbolic system could not only recommend a specific medication for a condition but also provide the rationale behind that recommendation, grounded in medical guidelines and logical inferences. One of the standout features of symbolic systems like Cyc is their role as a 'source of trust.' By providing a repository of default-true common sense, they can act as a filter to validate or reject the outputs generated by LLMs.

Symbolic systems excel in tasks that demand a deep understanding and logical reasoning, making them inherently more auditable and, by extension, more trustworthy than their statistical counterparts. However, they are often constrained by their inability to generalize and are less proficient in handling the vast, unstructured data that LLMs can effortlessly manage.

Introduction to Symbolic Systems and their Capabilities: A Deep Dive into Cyc

Cyc (pronounced "syke") is a long-term artificial intelligence project that aims to create a comprehensive ontology and knowledge base. It was initiated by Douglas Lenat and focuses on capturing "*common sense*" knowledge. Unlike other AI platforms that rely on statistical methods, Cyc uses explicit rules and logic to make decisions. Moreover, Cyc's ability to act as a source of inference can extend the capabilities of LLMs, allowing for a more robust and comprehensive AI system.

History of Cyc

The Cyc project was started in 1984 by Douglas Lenat, who was frustrated by the limitations of hand-coding domain-specific knowledge for his previous AI project, EURISKO. Originally a part of the Microelectronics and Computer Technology Corporation, Cyc was later spun off in 1994 to form Cycorp, Inc. In

2002, a subset of the Cyc Knowledge Base was made public under the OpenCyc project, which contained around 240,000 concepts and 2,000,000 assertions as of 20121.

Structure and Language

Cyc uses a declarative language called CycL, which is based on first-order logic and written in Lisp. The language has a set of concepts, also known as constants, which can represent specific objects, collections of objects, or relations between objects. For example, the statement (`#$isa #$DouglasLenat #$AIResearcher`) in CycL means "*Douglas Lenat is an AI researcher*".

Capabilities

Cyc is designed for tasks that require deep understanding and logical reasoning. It can provide clear reasoning paths for its decisions, making it highly auditable. For instance, Cyc can explain why a particular drug is recommended for a condition based on medical guidelines and logical inference.

Real-World Applications

Cyc has found applications in various sectors, including healthcare, where it offers real-time and continuous semantically enriched representation for every order and patient across facilities. It also provides real-time explainability and auditability, making it highly trustworthy.

Cyc Versus LLMs

While LLMs like GPT-3 excel in handling vast, unstructured datasets and generating human-like text, they lack the deep understanding and auditability that Cyc offers. Cyc, on the other hand, can logically reason using dynamic, real-world data just like a highly skilled employee. The integration of Cyc and LLMs could pave the way for the development of AI systems that are not only more intelligent but also more trustworthy, a key point emphasized by Lenat and Marcus in their research.

The Untapped Potential of Combining Both for Trustworthiness

The concept of merging LLMs with symbolic systems to create a more trustworthy AI is not novel but remains an underexplored avenue. Each system offers what the other lacks: LLMs excel in handling unstructured data and generating human-like text, while symbolic systems bring to the table a depth of understanding and auditability that LLMs inherently lack.

This chapter posits that a synergistic approach could be the key to unlocking a new era of trustworthy Generative AI. By melding the "*surface-level*" capabilities of LLMs with the "*deep understanding*" offered by symbolic systems, we can aspire to construct a Generative AI model that is not only competent but also transparent and trustworthy.

The implications of such a hybrid system are far-reaching. For example, in a healthcare scenario, an LLM could initially generate a diagnosis based on a patient's symptoms. A symbolic system could then cross-verify this diagnosis against established medical guidelines, providing both a trustworthiness score and a detailed explanation, thereby ensuring a higher level of trust and accountability.

To further elucidate the untapped potential of combining LLMs and symbolic systems, let's consider the financial sector as another example. Imagine a scenario where an LLM initially generates investment strategies based on market trends and investor behavior. A symbolic system could then cross-verify these strategies against established financial regulations and ethical guidelines, providing both a trustworthiness score and a detailed explanation. This hybrid approach could revolutionize how we perceive trust in financial AI applications, ensuring both innovation and accountability.

By exploring this untapped potential, we can move closer to bridging the trust gap that currently plagues the field of Generative AI.

Revisiting the 16 Desiderata: A Critique

Lenat and Marcus have made a significant contribution to the field of trustworthy AI by proposing a set of 16 desiderata. These desiderata serve as a comprehensive checklist for evaluating the trustworthiness of AI systems, covering aspects like explainability, reliability, and ethical considerations. While the desiderata offer a robust framework, they are not without limitations.

One of the primary critiques is that the desiderata are largely conceptual and lack a practical implementation guide. They provide a "what" but not a "how." For instance, while they emphasize the need for explainability, they don't delve into the methods to achieve it, especially in the context of Generative AI.

Another point of critique is the focus on individual aspects of trustworthiness, without adequately addressing the synergistic effects of combining different elements. Trustworthiness in AI is a multi-dimensional attribute; focusing on individual desiderata might not capture the complexity of real-world applications.

While the 16 desiderata serve as a robust framework for evaluating AI trustworthiness, they fall short in providing actionable insights. This is where our Trust-Enhanced Generative Framework (TEGF) comes into play. TEGF not only aligns with these desiderata but goes a step further by offering a practical guide for implementation, thus bridging the gap between theory and practice.

Identifying Gaps and Proposing Extensions to the Desiderata

Upon a closer examination of the 16 desiderata, several gaps become apparent. For example, the desiderata do not explicitly address the issue of data provenance, which is crucial for trustworthiness. Knowing the source and quality of the data used for training can significantly impact the reliability of an AI system.

Moreover, the desiderata could benefit from an extension that incorporates the potential of hybrid systems, combining LLMs and symbolic reasoning. As discussed in the previous section, each of these systems has unique strengths that can complement the other. A revised set of desiderata should consider this hybrid approach as a viable pathway to achieving higher levels of trustworthiness.

Examination of the Desiderata

In this section, we will provide a nuanced understanding of each of the 16 desiderata, elaborating on their significance, limitations, and potential for improvement. This comprehensive discussion aims to serve as the foundation for the novel framework that this chapter introduces.

Given the technical nature of AI and machine learning, it's crucial to provide concrete methods for achieving each desideratum. For example, when discussing "*Reliability*," our framework proposes a dynamic "*Trustworthiness Score*." This score could be calculated using a Bayesian model that takes into account various factors like historical accuracy, data quality, and real-time performance metrics.

By examining each of these desiderata in detail, we aim to provide a comprehensive guide for building trustworthy Generative AI systems. These extended desiderata are designed to be actionable and aligned with the complexities of real-world applications.

1. **Explanation**

a. **Significance**

Explanation is the cornerstone of trust. In critical domains like healthcare and finance, the ability to explain decisions can mean the difference between life and death, or financial stability and ruin.

b. **Limitations**

The challenge lies in balancing the depth of explanation with user comprehension. Too much detail can overwhelm, while too little can erode trust.

c. **Potential for Improvement**

Adaptive explanation models that gauge the user's expertise and the situation's urgency can offer tailored explanations, enhancing both trust and understanding.

2. **Deduction**

a. **Significance**

Deductive reasoning allows an AI to make logical conclusions, which is essential for problem-solving and decision-making.

b. **Limitations**

Deduction is limited to what is logically derivable from known facts. It can't handle uncertainty well.

c. **Potential for Improvement**

Integrating probabilistic models can help the AI make better decisions under uncertainty.

3. **Induction**

a. **Significance**

Inductive reasoning enables the AI to generalize from specific instances, which is crucial for learning and adapting.

b. **Limitations**

Induction can lead to overgeneralization or incorrect conclusions, especially when the sample size is small.

c. **Potential for Improvement**

Incorporating Bayesian methods can refine the AI's inductive reasoning by accounting for prior knowledge and uncertainty.

4. **Analogy**

a. **Significance**

Analogical reasoning is vital for creativity and problem-solving, allowing the AI to apply knowledge from one domain to another.

b. **Limitations**

Poorly chosen analogies can lead to incorrect or misleading conclusions.

c. **Potential for Improvement**

A multi-domain knowledge graph can help the AI choose more appropriate analogies by understanding the underlying structures of different domains.

5. **Abductive Reasoning**

a. **Significance**

Abductive reasoning allows the AI to make educated guesses, which is often necessary in complex, real-world scenarios.

b. **Limitations**

This form of reasoning is prone to errors and biases, especially when multiple explanations are plausible.

c. **Potential for Improvement**

Machine learning techniques like ensemble methods can help the AI weigh multiple hypotheses and choose the most likely explanation.

6. **Theory of Mind**

a. **Significance**

Understanding the user's mental state and capabilities is crucial for effective interaction and personalized service.

b. **Limitations**

Building an accurate and dynamic model of each user is computationally intensive and may raise privacy concerns.

c. **Potential for Improvement**

Federated learning can help the AI build user models without compromising privacy.

7. **Quantifier-fluency**

a. **Significance**

Understanding quantifiers is essential for logical reasoning and natural language understanding.

b. **Limitations**

Ambiguities in natural language can lead to misunderstandings.

c. **Potential for Improvement**

Context-aware language models can help the AI disambiguate quantifiers based on the situation and prior knowledge.

8. **Modal-fluency**

a. **Significance**

Modal operators like "`can`," "`must`," and "`might`" are pervasive in human language, and understanding them is crucial for effective communication.

b. **Limitations**

Deeply nested modal operators can create complexities that are hard to resolve.

c. **Potential for Improvement**

Advanced parsing algorithms can help the AI understand the hierarchical structure of nested modal operators.

9. **Defeasibility**

a. **Significance**

The ability to revise beliefs based on new information is crucial for adaptability and long-term performance.

b. **Limitations**

Frequent revisions can erode user trust if not communicated effectively.

c. Potential for Improvement

Transparent change logs and user notifications can help maintain trust during belief revisions.

10. Pro and Con Arguments

a. Significance

Presenting balanced arguments enables informed decision-making, **especially in complex or controversial issues.**

b. Limitations

Bias in data or algorithms can skew the balance of arguments.

c. Potential for Improvement

Regular audits and third-party evaluations can help identify and mitigate biases.

11. Contexts

a. Significance

Contextual understanding is crucial for accurate reasoning and effective communication.

b. Limitations

Context is often multi-dimensional, making it challenging to capture comprehensively.

c. Potential for Improvement

Multi-modal sensors and data fusion techniques can provide a richer contextual understanding.

12. Meta-knowledge and Meta-reasoning

a. Significance

Self-awareness enhances the AI's adaptability and reliability.

b. Limitations

Too much introspection can lead to computational inefficiency.

c. Potential for Improvement

Optimized algorithms can balance self-awareness with computational efficiency.

13 Explicitly Ethical

a. Significance

Ethical considerations are non-negotiable in applications like healthcare, law, and public services.

b. Limitations

Ethical norms vary across cultures and over time, making it challenging to define a universal ethical framework.

c. Potential for Improvement

Ethical AI frameworks should be adaptable and include mechanisms for public input and scrutiny.

14. Sufficient Speed

a. Significance

Speed is crucial for real-time applications like emergency response and financial trading.

b. Limitations

Speed often comes at the cost of accuracy or depth of reasoning.

c. Potential for Improvement

Dynamic speed-accuracy trade-offs can be optimized based on the task's urgency and importance.

15. Sufficiently Lingual and Embodied

a. Significance

Natural language and sensory-motor capabilities enable more natural **and versatile interactions.**

b. Limitations

Highly embodied AI can be expensive and prone to mechanical failures.

c. **Potential for Improvement**

Modular designs can allow for task-specific embodiments, optimizing both cost and performance.

16. **Sufficiently Broad**

a. **Significance**

A broad knowledge base enables the AI to handle a wide range of tasks and adapt to new challenges.

b. **Limitations**

Maintaining and updating a broad knowledge base is resource-intensive.

c. **Potential for Improvement**

Collaborative learning and cloud-based knowledge repositories can help maintain a broad yet up-to-date knowledge base.

By understanding the significance, limitations, and potential for improvement of each desideratum, we can build a more robust, adaptable, and trustworthy AI framework for the future.

The Concept of "*Semantic Amplification*"

The term "*Semantic Amplification*" encapsulates a transformative approach to enhancing the capabilities of LLMs. While LLMs are adept at generating human-like text based on statistical patterns, they often fall short in providing a deep understanding or contextual reasoning for their outputs. This is where the concept of Semantic Amplification comes into play, serving as a bridge between the statistical prowess of LLMs and the logical rigor of symbolic systems.

Semantic Amplification involves integrating a symbolic reasoning engine into the architecture of an LLM. This engine serves as a "*cognitive layer*," adding depth, context, and a trail of reasoning to the outputs generated by the LLM. The engine can cross-reference the LLM's outputs against a structured knowledge base, providing not just an answer but also a "*why*" behind that answer.

Imagine the LLM as a skilled craftsman who can create beautiful sculptures but doesn't understand the significance of the art. The symbolic reasoning engine is like an art historian who provides the craftsman with the context and meaning behind each sculpture. Together, they not only create art but also tell a compelling story behind it.

The engine cross-references the outputs of the LLM against a structured knowledge base. So, when the LLM generates an answer, the engine provides the "*why*" behind that answer, offering a trail of reasoning that can be audited and understood.

Application	**Without Semantic Amplification**	**With Semantic Amplification**
Enhancing Predictive Text	LLM predicts the next word based on statistical patterns, lacking context understanding	LLM, coupled with a symbolic reasoning engine, predicts words based on context and relationships from a knowledge base, similar to human grammar and semantics consideration
Improving Chatbots	Chatbot generates plausible responses but fails to grasp underlying intent or nuances	Chatbot references a structured knowledge base for understanding and responding to queries with reasoning and justification, like a knowledgeable customer service agent
Medical Diagnosis Assistance	LLM suggests diagnoses based on symptoms in text without clinical reasoning	LLM cross-references medical databases, providing potential diagnoses with clinical reasoning, akin to a doctor explaining their thought process
Legal Document Analysis	LLM summarizes legal documents but misses subtleties of legal reasoning	LLM applies legal principles and precedents from a legal knowledge base, offering explanations for summaries like a lawyer interpreting law
Bias Mitigation in Language Models	LLMs may perpetuate biases from training data	Symbolic reasoning engine helps identify and mitigate biases using logical rules and ethical guidelines, similar to an ethicist evaluating statements for prejudice or stereotypes

Educational Tutoring Systems	LLM generates educational content but may not adapt to different learning styles or provide explanations	LLM tailors content to learner's needs and provides justifications for answers, akin to a tutor who explains concepts in depth
Scientific Research Assistance	LLM helps in summarizing scientific articles but lacks understanding of the research findings' significance	LLM connects findings to existing scientific knowledge and theories, offering insights into research implications, similar to a scientist discussing the relevance of their work

Table 16.1: *Semantic Application - A Comparative Outlook*

A Definitive Game-Changer: Enhancing the Trustworthiness of LLMs

The integration of symbolic reasoning into LLMs heralds a new era of "*Amplified Intelligence*." This is not merely an incremental improvement but a paradigm shift in how we perceive and utilize Generative AI. By adding a layer of symbolic reasoning, we can transform LLMs from mere prediction machines into entities capable of understanding, reasoning, and explaining their actions.

Example: Medical Diagnosis Application

Consider a healthcare application where a patient describes symptoms in natural language. An LLM, trained in medical literature, could generate a list of potential diagnoses. However, this list may lack credibility and context. Now, let's introduce a symbolic reasoning engine into this scenario. This engine could cross-reference the LLM's diagnoses against established medical guidelines and even factor in drug interactions or patient history. The result is a far more reliable and trustworthy diagnosis, complete with a trustworthiness score and a detailed explanation.

This capability to provide a "*reasoning trail*" not only enhances the trustworthiness of the system but also its utility in critical applications like healthcare, finance, and legal advising.

Semantic Amplification is set to redefine the landscape of Generative AI. By bridging the gap between statistical prowess and logical rigor, it promises to usher in an era of "*Amplified Intelligence*," where machines don't just predict but understand, reason, and explain. As we integrate this concept into broader frameworks like TEGF, we take a significant step toward making AI not just a tool but a trustworthy companion in our complex world.

The Role of Semantic Amplification in the Trust-Enhanced Generative Framework (TEGF)

Semantic Amplification is not just a standalone concept; it serves as a cornerstone for our proposed TEGF. TEGF aims to provide a comprehensive solution for building trustworthy Generative AI systems, and Semantic Amplification plays a pivotal role in achieving this objective. By integrating this concept into the framework, we can ensure that the AI systems built on TEGF are not just capable but also transparent, reliable, and ethically sound.

Trust-Enhanced Generative Framework (TEGF)

The TEGF aims to build LLMs that are both intelligent and trustworthy. This architecture is analogous to a multi-layered skyscraper, where each floor serves a unique function but contributes to the overall structural integrity. The framework leverages various mathematical models, design patterns, and technologies to achieve its goals.

Statistical Language Model (SLM)

The SLM serves as the foundational layer of TEGF, akin to the concrete base of a skyscraper. It is responsible for the initial data processing and output generation.

Inner Workings

- **Data Input**: Text, audio, or even image data.
- **Processing Steps**: Tokenization, feature extraction using TF-IDF, and prediction using neural networks like LSTM or Transformers.
- **Output Prediction Formula** = `f(Wx+b)`
    - where f is the activation function, W is the weight matrix, x is the input, and b is the bias.

- **Explanation**: This is a simplified representation of a neural network layer's output. Here, f is the activation function, W is the weight matrix, x is the input, and b is the bias.
- **Relevance**: In SLM, this formula is crucial for transforming raw input into a format that can be used for further processing or output generation. It's the mathematical basis for the feature extraction and prediction steps.
- **Utilization**: During the training phase, the weights W and biases b are optimized to minimize a loss function. During inference, given a new input x, this formula is used to generate a preliminary output.

Performance Metrics

- **Accuracy**: Measures how closely the SLM's predictions align with actual outcomes, reflecting its ability to generate accurate text based on input data.
- **Speed**: Evaluates the SLM's processing speed, crucial for real-time applications, indicating how quickly it can handle input data and produce predictions or output.
- **Resource Utilization**: Assesses how efficiently the SLM uses computational resources like CPU or GPU, ensuring it runs smoothly on different hardware configurations without excessive demands.

Symbolic Reasoning Engine

This engine serves as the cognitive layer, refining the outputs generated by the SLM based on logical rules and symbolic representations. This engine employs First-Order Logic and Bayesian Networks for refining outputs

Logic Rules and Ontology

- **Logic Rules**: IF-THEN-ELSE conditions, Bayesian inference.
  `P(A|B)=P(B|A)×P(A)/P(B)`
  - **Explanation**: This formula represents Bayesian inference, which calculates the probability of A occurring given that B has occurred.
  - **Relevance**: This is used to refine the outputs from the SLM by incorporating prior knowledge and observed data. It's particularly useful for tasks that require reasoning, like medical diagnosis.
  - **Utilization**: The probabilities **`P(A)`**, **`P(B)`**, and **`P(B|A)`** can be derived from the data or domain-specific databases. The formula then calculates **`P(A|B)`**, which is used to refine the SLM's outputs.

- **Ontology**: Predefined knowledge graphs or domain-specific databases.

Validation and Refinement

- **Methods**: Rule-based validation, database cross-referencing.
    - **Example**: Refining a medical diagnosis based on existing medical guidelines.

Performance Metrics

- **Reasoning Accuracy**: Measured using Precision and Recall
- **Speed**: Query execution time
- **Compliance**: Adherence to domain-specific guidelines like GDPR

Trustworthiness Layer

This layer quantifies the trustworthiness of each output, acting like the quality control department in a factory. This layer employs a scoring algorithm to quantify trustworthiness.

Scoring Algorithm

- **Metrics**: Accuracy, reliability, ethical considerations.
- **Trust Score** = `w1×Accuracy+w2×Reliability+w3×Ethical Score`

    where **`w1`**, **`w2`**, **`w3`** are weights.

    - **Explanation**: This weighted sum calculates the overall trustworthiness of an output.
    - **Relevance**: It quantifies how much a user should trust the output, based on its accuracy, reliability, and ethical considerations.
    - **Utilization**: The weights **`w1`**, **`w2`**, **`w3`** can be dynamically adjusted based on the context or user feedback. The individual metrics (Accuracy, Reliability, Ethical Score) are computed based on predefined criteria.

Real-time Scoring

- **Real-time Capability**: Event-driven architecture using Apache Kafka.
- **Presentation**: Trustworthiness score attached to each output.

Performance Metrics

- **Scoring Accuracy**: AUC-ROC

- **Ethical Compliance**: Adherence to ethical guidelines
- **User Satisfaction**: Net Promoter Score (NPS)

Explainability Module

This module employs Natural Language Generation (NLG) techniques like template-based generation and GPT-based summarization to translate complex reasoning into layman-friendly language.

Natural Language Generation (NLG)

- **Techniques**: Template-based generation, GPT-based summarization.
- **Challenges**: Maintaining accuracy while simplifying language.

User Interface Design

- **UI Elements**: Dashboards, tooltips, pop-up explanations.

Performance Metrics

- **User Satisfaction**: User surveys
- **Explanation Accuracy**: BLEU score
- **UI Responsiveness**: Load time and latency

Data Provenance Tracker

This component keeps a meticulous record of the data sources used for training and inference, acting as the legal department maintaining contracts and agreements. This component employs blockchain technology to keep an immutable record of data sources.

Database Implementation

- **Database Type**: NoSQL for scalability
- **Security**: Encryption at rest and in transit

Performance Metrics

- **Data Integrity**: Hash-based verification
- **Audit Compliance**: Adherence to ISO 27001
- **Access Speed**: Query execution time

Contextual Understanding Module

This module adapts the system's reasoning based on the specific context, like a smart assistant that knows when to be formal or casual. This module employs Decision Trees and Reinforcement Learning algorithms like Q-Learning for adaptive reasoning.

Adaptive Algorithms

```
Q(s, a) <- (1 - alpha) * Q(s, a) + alpha * (r + gamma * max_a'
Q(s', a'))
```

where α is the learning rate and γ is the discount factor.

- **Explanation**: This formula updates the Q-value, which represents the quality of taking action **a** in state **s**.
- **Relevance**: It's used to adapt the system's reasoning based on the specific context. For example, it can adapt the trust score weights based on user interactions.
- **Utilization**: The learning rate alpha and the discount factor gamma are hyperparameters that can be tuned. The reward r is based on the outcome of the action, and max_a' Q(s', a') is the maximum Q-value for the next state s'.

Performance Metrics

- **Contextual Accuracy**: F1-score
- **User Satisfaction**: User surveys
- **Adaptability Speed**: Time to adapt in milliseconds

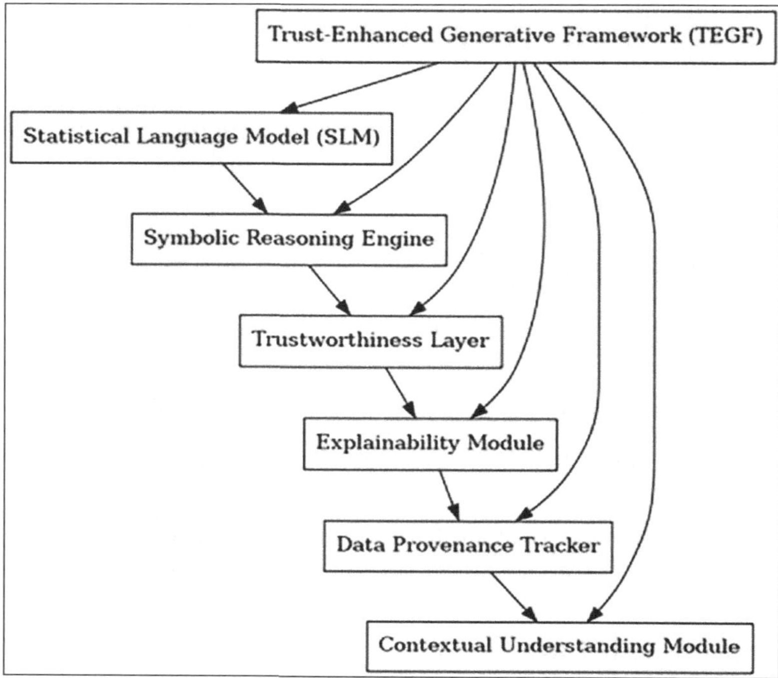

Figure 16.1: *TEGF Framework - Dataflow and Component Interaction*

Cohesion in the Trust-Enhanced Generative Framework (TEGF)

The TEGF is an integrated system designed to establish trust in LLMs. Unlike traditional models that operate as isolated modules, TEGF functions as a cohesive unit where each component contributes to the overall trustworthiness of the system. This section explores the interdependencies among these components and provides recommendations for enhancing system cohesion.

Component Interactions and Trust Propagation

- Statistical Language Model (SLM)
    - **Role**: Serves as the initial data processing unit.
    - **Cohesion Point**: The outputs generated by the SLM act as inputs for the Symbolic Reasoning Engine, initiating the trust propagation process.

- Symbolic Reasoning Engine
  - **Role**: Adds a layer of logical reasoning to the outputs.
  - **Cohesion Point**: Refines the preliminary outputs from the SLM, which are then assessed by the Trustworthiness Layer.
- Trustworthiness Layer
  - **Role**: Quantifies the trustworthiness of each output.
  - **Cohesion Point**: Provides a feedback mechanism for the SLM and Symbolic Reasoning Engine, allowing for iterative refinement.
- Explainability Module
  - **Role**: Translates complex reasoning into understandable language.
  - **Cohesion Point**: Ensures transparency by providing explanations based on the system's reasoning and trust scores.
- Data Provenance Tracker
  - **Role**: Tracks the origin of data used in the system.
  - **Cohesion Point**: Validates the reliability of the data, thereby enhancing the system's overall trustworthiness.
- Contextual Understanding Module
  - **Role**: Adapts system reasoning based on specific contexts.
  - **Cohesion Point**: Utilizes contextual data to influence other components, ensuring both accuracy and relevance.

Recommendations for Enhanced Cohesion

- **Unified Dashboard**: Develop a single interface that displays outputs, trust scores, and explanations from all components.
- **Real-time Feedback Loop**: Implement a mechanism to allow immediate reflection of one component's performance on the others.
- **Dynamic Weighting**: Enable the Trustworthiness Layer to adjust metric weightings based on contextual data.
- **User Feedback Integration**: Allow users to provide feedback on explanations and trust scores for system fine-tuning.
- **Automated Compliance Checks**: Incorporate compliance verification within the Data Provenance Tracker to ensure data integrity and regulatory adherence.

The TEGF is designed to function as a unified system where each component synergistically contributes to the overall trustworthiness of the AI model.

Understanding these inter-component interactions is crucial for appreciating the holistic approach TEGF takes in building trust. With targeted enhancements, TEGF has the potential to set new standards in the development of trustworthy AI systems.

Trustworthy Medical Diagnosis System: An End-to-End Walkthrough

- **Phase 1: Stakeholder Engagement and Planning**
  - **Stakeholder Identification**: Involve healthcare providers, patients, IT teams, regulatory bodies, and audit teams.
  - **Initial Meeting**: Present the concept of the Trustworthy Medical Diagnosis System to all stakeholders.
  - **Ecosystem Mapping**: Outline how the system will integrate with existing Hospital Information Systems (HIS), laboratories, pharmacies, and insurance companies.
- **Phase 2: Pilot Testing**
  - **Controlled Deployment**: The IT team deploys the system in a controlled environment for initial testing.
  - **Feedback Collection**: Healthcare providers and patients use the system and provide initial feedback on its usability and the trust scores generated.
- **Phase 3: System Integration and Training**
  - **Integration with HIS and Laboratories**: The IT team integrates the system with existing HIS and laboratory systems for seamless data exchange.
  - **Training Programs**: Conduct training sessions for healthcare providers on how to interpret trust scores and use the system effectively.
- **Phase 4: Full-Scale Deployment**
  - **System Rollout**: The system is deployed across multiple departments within the healthcare facility.
  - **Patient Awareness**: Conduct patient awareness programs to educate them on how to interpret the trust score in their medical reports.
- **Phase 5: Governance and Compliance**
  - **Compliance Audits**: Conduct the first round of compliance audits to ensure the system meets all regulatory requirements.

- ○ **Ethical Review**: An ethical committee reviews the system to ensure it adheres to medical ethics and patient privacy norms.

- **Phase 6: Real-World Usage and Feedback Loop**
  - ○ **Operational Monitoring**: Healthcare providers use the system for daily diagnoses, and performance metrics are continuously monitored.
  - ○ **Feedback Loop**: Implement a real-time feedback mechanism where the performance of one component can be immediately reflected in the others.
- **Phase 7: Final Outcome and Future Directions**
  - ○ **Outcome Assessment**: Generate comprehensive medical reports, including trust scores, and share them with all relevant stakeholders.
  - ○ **Future Planning**: Discuss the success of the system and outline plans for future enhancements, based on feedback and performance metrics.

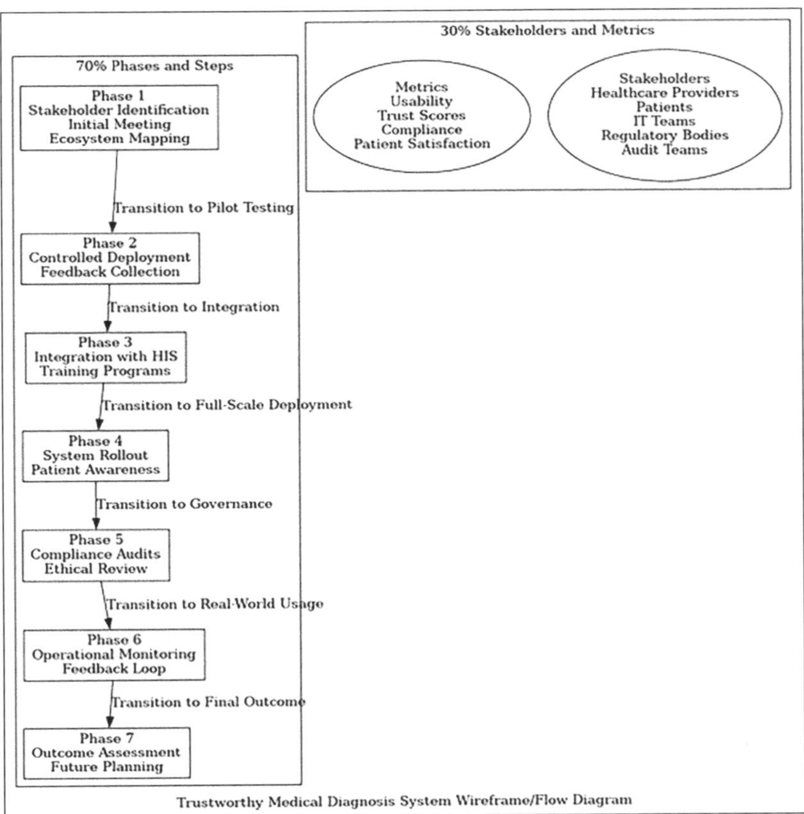

***Figure 16.2**: Trustworthy Medical Diagnosis System Wireframe/Flow Diagram*

The Genesis of the Provenance Layer in TEGF

The TEGF is a multi-faceted architecture designed to enhance the trustworthiness of Generative AI systems. One of its most innovative components is the "*Provenance Layer*," a specialized module that serves as a transparent repository for tracking the lineage, transformation, and utilization of data throughout the AI's decision-making process. This layer was conceived to address the growing need for transparency and accountability in AI systems, particularly in high-stakes sectors like healthcare and finance.

The Mechanics of the Provenance Layer

The Provenance Layer operates on a set of algorithms and protocols that meticulously record every data interaction. These algorithms could be blockchain-based to ensure the highest level of security and immutability. It captures:

- **Data Origin**: Where the data was sourced from, be it databases, APIs, or user inputs.
- **Data Transformation**: Any preprocessing or transformation that the data undergoes before being fed into the AI model.
- **Decision Logs**: A detailed account of how the data contributed to each decision made by the AI system.
- **Trustworthiness Metrics**: The criteria and calculations used to determine the Trustworthiness Score for each output.

Real-World Implications: A Multi-Sector Focus

- **Healthcare**
  - In sectors like healthcare, where the margin for error is minimal, the Provenance Layer offers an unparalleled level of transparency and accountability.
- **Finance**
  - In the financial sector, the Provenance Layer could track the lineage of financial data, ensuring that investment advice or risk assessments are based on credible and current information.

Case Study: Healthcare - Complex Diagnoses

Consider a patient diagnosed with a complex condition like Multiple Sclerosis. The Provenance Layer would meticulously record:

- **Data Sources**: The origin of the symptom data, whether it's from electronic health records, medical literature, or clinical trials.
- **Reasoning Path**: A step-by-step account of how the Symbolic Reasoning Engine validated or refuted the initial diagnosis suggested by the Statistical Language Model.
- **Trustworthiness Metrics**: The specific criteria used to calculate the Trustworthiness Score, such as adherence to medical guidelines or statistical confidence intervals.
- **Regulatory Compliance**: Documentation of any healthcare regulations or guidelines explicitly followed during the diagnosis process.

User Experience

The Provenance Layer, while primarily a behind-the-scenes feature, enhances user trust by providing a transparent and auditable trail of the AI's decisions. This could be particularly useful in user interfaces where transparency is a key selling point.

Security Aspects

Given the sensitive nature of the data being tracked, the Provenance Layer incorporates advanced security protocols, potentially leveraging blockchain technology for enhanced data integrity.

Future Developments

As AI and blockchain technologies continue to evolve, the Provenance Layer could integrate more advanced features, such as real-time auditing capabilities or even decentralized data storage solutions, to further enhance its utility and reliability.

Introduction to the TIGAI Framework

In the preceding chapters, we delved into the TEGF, a pioneering architecture aimed at fostering trust in Generative AI systems. Now, let's shift our focus to its innovative counterpart: the Trust-Interpretable Generative AI (TIGAI) framework. TIGAI is designed to elevate the trustworthiness and interpretability of AI systems, especially in the realm of Generative AI. This chapter aims to provide an in-depth analysis of TIGAI's architecture, its comparison with TEGF, and its practical applications.

Components of TIGAI

The architecture of TIGAI is built around four core components, each serving a unique function:

Adaptive Knowledge Base

The Adaptive Knowledge Base is akin to a dynamic library that not only stores but also learns and updates its collection in real-time. It's a blend of a traditional database and a learning system, designed to evolve continually. It incorporates both explicit rules and statistical data to make more informed decisions.

- **Implementation**
  - In a technical sense, the Adaptive Knowledge Base could be implemented using a NoSQL database for flexibility, combined with a machine learning model that updates the rules and data points. The machine learning model could be a Bayesian Network or a Reinforcement Learning model that learns from new data and updates the database accordingly.
  - **Example**: In a healthcare setting, the Adaptive Knowledge Base could integrate with Electronic Health Records (EHR) and update its rules based on the latest medical research, thereby ensuring that the AI's recommendations are always current.
- **Technical Specifications**
  - The Adaptive Knowledge Base would require a distributed computing environment to handle large-scale data and high-velocity updates. It would also need a robust API layer for seamless integration with other components.
- **Scalability**
  - The Adaptive Knowledge Base is designed to scale horizontally, allowing for the addition of more nodes to handle increased data loads.
- **Security Measures**
  - Data encryption and role-based access control would be implemented to secure the data stored in the Adaptive Knowledge Base.

- **Compliance**
  - The Adaptive Knowledge Base would comply with healthcare standards like HIPAA if used in a healthcare setting.

Contextual Reasoning Engine

The Contextual Reasoning Engine serves as the "*brain*" of TIGAI. It employs a blend of symbolic and statistical reasoning to offer context-aware responses. It's designed to enhance the AI's situational awareness by understanding the context in which a query or action is made.

- **Implementation**
  - The engine could be implemented using a hybrid model that combines rule-based systems for symbolic reasoning and neural networks for statistical reasoning. APIs could be developed for seamless integration with other components.
  - **Example:** In a financial application, the Contextual Reasoning Engine could use time-series analysis for market trends and decision trees for user behavior to provide personalized investment advice.
- **Technical Specifications**
  - The Contextual Reasoning Engine would be built on a microservices architecture to ensure modularity and ease of updates.
- **Scalability**
  - The engine is designed to be stateless, allowing it to scale easily in a cloud environment.
- **Security Measures**
  - API security measures like OAuth would be implemented to ensure secure communication between the Contextual Reasoning Engine and other components.
- **Compliance**
  - The engine would be designed to comply with financial regulations like GDPR if used in a financial application.

Trustworthiness Score

The Trustworthiness Score is a real-time, dynamic metric that evaluates the reliability and ethical considerations of the AI's output. It's designed to adapt in real-time based on new data or context.

- **Implementation**
  - A scoring algorithm could be developed that takes into account various factors like data source credibility, timeliness, and ethical considerations. This algorithm could be implemented using weighted scoring methods.
  - **Example:** In a news aggregation platform, the Trustworthiness Score could be updated in real-time based on the credibility of the sources and the timeliness of the information.
- **Technical Specifications**
  - The Trustworthiness Score would require real-time data processing capabilities, possibly using stream processing frameworks like Apache Kafka.
- **Scalability**
  - The scoring algorithm would be designed to operate in a distributed manner to handle large-scale data.
- **Security Measures**
  - Data masking techniques would be employed to anonymize sensitive data used in calculating the Trustworthiness Score.
- **Compliance**
  - The Trustworthiness Score would adhere to ethical AI principles and guidelines.

Interpretability Layer

The Interpretability Layer serves as a "*translator*," converting the AI's complex decision-making process into user-friendly explanations. It aims to demystify the AI's actions and decisions.

- **Implementation**
  - Natural Language Generation (NLG) techniques could be employed to convert complex data and decisions into understandable language. The NLG engine could be integrated as a microservice that interacts with other components.
  - **Example:** In a self-driving car, the Interpretability Layer could use NLG to explain the rationale behind each maneuver, thereby enhancing the driver's trust in the system.
- **Technical Specifications**
  - The Interpretability Layer would use advanced Natural Language Generation (NLG) techniques, possibly leveraging GPT-4 or its successors.

- **Scalability**
  - The Interpretability Layer would be designed to handle multiple requests concurrently, using asynchronous programming models.
- **Security Measures**
  - All generated explanations would be logged and encrypted to ensure data integrity and confidentiality.
- **Compliance**
  - The Interpretability Layer would comply with automotive safety standards like ISO 26262 if used in self-driving cars.

By diving deep into the architecture and implementation of TIGAI, we can appreciate the intricacies involved in building a trustworthy Generative AI system. This detailed exploration serves as a foundation for the subsequent chapters, where we will delve into the real-world applications and case studies of TIGAI. The journey toward trustworthy AI is complex, but with frameworks like TIGAI, we are one step closer to making it a reality.

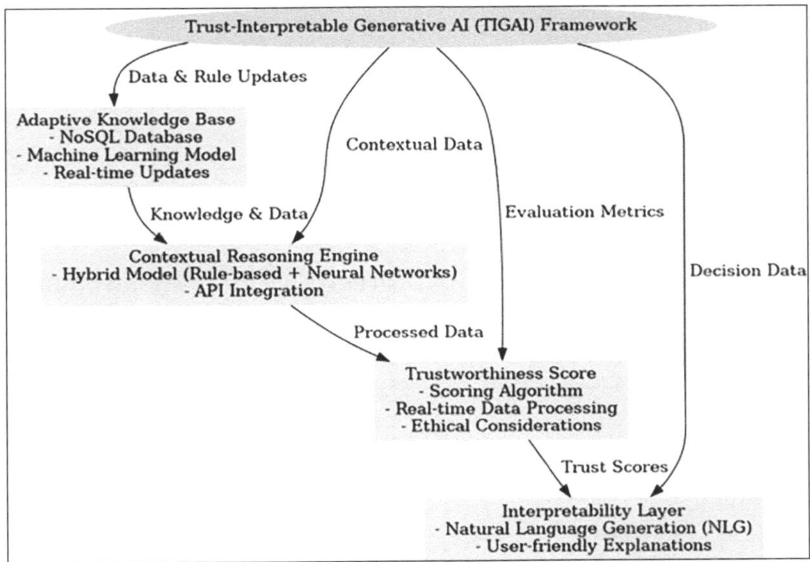

Figure 16.3: *TIGAI Framework with Data Flow*

TIGAI: Complementary or Contrasting Aspects with TEGF

While TIGAI and TEGF share the common goal of enhancing trust in Generative AI, their approaches are distinct:

- **Adaptability vs. Rigor**: TIGAI's Adaptive Knowledge Base offers a level of flexibility that allows the system to adapt to new information. However, this adaptability may come at the cost of rigorous validation, a gap that TEGF's Symbolic Reasoning Engine fills by providing a more structured and validated reasoning path.
- **Context-Awareness vs. Explainability**: Both frameworks prioritize explainability, but they do so differently. TEGF incorporates a Trustworthiness Layer that quantifies the reliability of each output, providing a more comprehensive assessment.
- **Dynamic vs. Static Trustworthiness Score**: TIGAI employs a dynamic trustworthiness score that can adapt in real-time based on new data or context. TEGF, on the other hand, employs a more static but deeply validated trustworthiness score based on predefined metrics.
- **Data Provenance**: One of the standout features of TEGF is its Data Provenance Tracker, which adds an extra layer of transparency and auditability. This feature is currently absent in TIGAI, representing a potential area for improvement.

Features/Components	**TIGAI**	**TEGF**
Adaptability	High	Low
Rigor	Medium	High
Context-Awareness	High	Medium
Explainability	High	High
Trustworthiness Score	Dynamic	Static
Data Provenance	Absent	Present

Table 16.2: *Feature Comparison*

Case Studies

Let's go through some minor case studies to understand TIGAI in conjunction with TEGF:

- **Healthcare Scenario**
    - **TIGAI**: The Adaptive Knowledge Base could integrate with Electronic Health Records (EHR) and update its rules based on the latest medical research, thereby ensuring that the AI's recommendations are always current.
    - **TEGF**: The Symbolic Reasoning Engine would provide a more structured and validated reasoning path, ensuring that the AI's recommendations adhere to established medical guidelines.
- **Financial Application**
    - **TIGAI**: The Contextual Reasoning Engine could use time-series analysis for market trends and decision trees for user behavior to provide personalized investment advice.
    - **TEGF**: The Trustworthiness Layer would quantify the reliability of each output, providing a more comprehensive assessment of investment options.

Technical Depth

- **TIGAI**: Utilizes a blend of Bayesian Networks or Reinforcement Learning models for its Adaptive Knowledge Base.
- **TEGF**: Employs rule-based systems for its Symbolic Reasoning Engine, providing a more rigorous validation path.

Future Scope

- **TIGAI**: Incorporating a Data Provenance Tracker could add an extra layer of transparency and auditability.
- **TEGF**: Introducing real-time adaptability in the Trustworthiness Score could make the framework more responsive to dynamic scenarios.

User Experience

- **TIGAI**: Enhanced by the Interpretability Layer, which translates complex AI decisions into user-friendly language.
- **TEGF**: Elevated by the Trustworthiness Layer that quantifies the reliability of each output, providing a more comprehensive user understanding.

Security and Compliance

- **TIGAI**: Currently lacks a Data Provenance Tracker, which could be a potential security risk.

- **TEGF**: Includes a Data Provenance Tracker, enhancing data security and compliance with data governance policies.

Performance Metrics

Key Performance Indicators (KPIs) to evaluate the effectiveness of each framework could include:

- **TIGAI**: Real-time adaptability score, user satisfaction rate.
- **TEGF**: Compliance audit pass rate, static trustworthiness score.

Both TIGAI and TEGF offer unique approaches to enhancing trust in Generative AI. While TIGAI excels in adaptability and context awareness, TEGF shines in rigor and data provenance. The choice between the two would depend on the specific requirements of your project, whether it's flexibility, rigorous validation, or a blend of both.

By understanding these nuances, you are better equipped to make an informed decision on the most suitable framework for your Generative AI initiatives.

This comprehensive comparative analysis serves as a foundation for the subsequent chapters, where we will delve deeper into the architecture and real-world applications of both frameworks.

Ethical and Societal Implications: Navigating the Moral Labyrinth

As we advance towards a future where AI systems are increasingly integrated into our lives, the ethical and societal implications become more pronounced. While frameworks like TEGF and TIGAI offer promising avenues for more trustworthy AI, they also introduce new ethical challenges that must be meticulously addressed.

Data Privacy and Consent: The Double-Edged Sword

Both TEGF and TIGAI operate on extensive datasets to enhance their reliability and effectiveness. While this is a boon for AI trustworthiness, it also raises serious concerns about data privacy and user consent.

Ethical Solutions

- **Explicit Consent**: Users should be provided with clear, understandable information about how their data will be used and must explicitly consent to it.
- **Data Minimization**: Only collect data that is strictly necessary for the functioning of the AI system.
- **Secure Storage**: Implement robust encryption methods, such as AES-256 or RSA encryption, to protect the data from unauthorized access.

Transparency and Accountability: The Pillars of Ethical AI

The need for transparency in how decisions are made by AI, especially when it comes to high-stakes decisions in healthcare or finance, is paramount. Additionally, the question of who is accountable when the AI system makes a mistake is often left unanswered.

Ethical Solutions

- **Ethical Oversight Committee**: An ethical oversight committee should be formed that regularly reviews the AI's decisions and ethical considerations.
- **User Education**: Methods should be proposed for educating end-users about the ethical considerations of using the AI system.

Potential for Misuse: The Dark Side of Trustworthiness

The advanced capabilities of TEGF and TIGAI could be weaponized for unethical purposes, such as generating misleading information that gains unwarranted trust.

Ethical Solutions

- **Usage Audits**: Regular audits should be conducted to ensure that the AI system is not being used for unethical purposes.
- **Ethical Locks**: Implement safeguards, such as software constraints or machine learning models trained to detect unethical usage, that prevent the AI from generating outputs that could be used for deceit or harm.

Setting a New Ethical Benchmark for Trustworthy AI

Despite the ethical challenges, TEGF and TIGAI have the potential to redefine the standards for trustworthy AI. They offer a pathway to bridge the trust gap and make AI decision-making more transparent and auditable, thereby positively impacting various sectors like healthcare, finance, and customer service.

Ethical Guidelines for TEGF in Healthcare

In healthcare applications, TEGF could be implemented alongside a robust set of ethical guidelines:

- **Informed Consent**: Obtain explicit consent from patients before utilizing their data for diagnosis or treatment.
- **Data Anonymization**: Ensure that all patient data is anonymized to protect privacy.
- **Bias Audits**: Conduct regular audits to check for any biases or inaccuracies in the AI system, thereby maintaining the integrity of healthcare decisions.

Future Outlook and Public Policy

As we look towards the future, it's crucial to consider how these ethical frameworks could adapt to emerging technologies and influence public policy. The ethical guidelines set forth by TEGF and TIGAI could serve as a blueprint for regulations and could be adapted to accommodate global ethical standards.

Conclusion

As we close this comprehensive exploration into the realm of trustworthy AI, it's evident that we stand at a pivotal moment in the history of technology and society. The advancements in AI, particularly in Generative AI, have opened up unprecedented possibilities, but they also come with their own set of challenges and responsibilities.

The core takeaway from this discourse is the imperative of trust. Whether it's the individual components of AI systems, like Large Language Models and Symbolic Systems, or the frameworks designed to enhance their trustworthiness, such as TEGF and TIGAI, the underlying theme is the necessity for trust. Trust is not just a feature but a requirement in the AI systems of tomorrow.

Trustworthiness in AI is not a monolithic concept but a multifaceted attribute that encompasses explainability, reliability, ethical considerations, and much more. The 16 Desiderata proposed by Lenat and Marcus serve as a robust framework, but as we have discussed, they too require extensions and practical implementation guidelines.

The future of trustworthy AI is not in isolating statistical and symbolic approaches but in harmoniously integrating them. The concept of Semantic Amplification and frameworks like TEGF and TIGAI offer promising pathways to achieve this integration, enhancing both the capability and the trustworthiness of AI systems.

As AI systems become increasingly capable, the ethical and societal implications become more pronounced. From data privacy to the potential for misuse, a holistic approach to ethics is crucial. This includes not just technological solutions but also governance mechanisms and ethical guidelines.

The future is ripe with possibilities, from the advent of quantum computing to the development of global governance mechanisms for AI. As we venture into this uncharted territory, it will require a concerted effort from technologists, ethicists, policymakers, and society at large to navigate the complexities and realize the full potential of trustworthy AI.

The journey towards trustworthy AI is a collective endeavor that requires multidisciplinary collaboration and continuous innovation. As we chart this path forward, let us do so with a sense of responsibility, optimism, and above all, a commitment to building AI systems that are not just smart, but also worthy of our trust.

The future of trustworthy AI is a story yet to be written, and we all have a role to play in shaping it.

Reference:

- https://arxiv.org/ftp/arxiv/papers/2308/2308.04445.pdf

Index

D

E

F

G

H

I

K

L

M

N

O

P

Q

T

U

V

W

Z